P9-DZO-178

RENNER
LEARNING RESOURCES CENTER
ELGIN COMMUNITY COLLEGE
ELGIN, ILLINOIS 60120

A CHILLING EFFECT

ALSO BY LOIS G. FORER

Money and Justice:
Who Owns the Courts?

Criminals and Victims:
A Trial Judge Reflects on Crime and Punishment

The Death of the Law

No One Will Lissen:
How Our Legal System Brutalizes the Youthful Poor

A
CHILLING
EFFECT

*The Mounting Threat
of Libel and Invasion of
Privacy Actions to the
First Amendment*

Lois G. Forer

"Whenever a man publishes, he publishes
at his peril."
—LORD MANSFIELD

RENNER LEARNING RESOURCE CENTER
ELGIN COMMUNITY COLLEGE
ELGIN, ILLINOIS 60123

W·W·Norton & Company · New York · London

Copyright © 1987 by Lois G. Forer
All rights reserved.
Published simultaneously in Canada by Penguin Books Canada Ltd., 2801 John Street,
Markham, Ontario L3R 1B4.
Printed in the United States of America.

Reprinted with permission, Grobel, *Conversations with Capote* (New York: New American
Library, 1985), p. 112.

The text of this book is composed in Times Roman, with
display type set in Perpetua. Composition and
manufacturing by The Haddon Craftsmen, Inc.
Book design by B. Klein.

First Edition

Library of Congress Cataloging-in-Publication Data
Forer, Lois G., 1914–
A chilling effect.
Bibliography: p.
Includes index.
1. Libel and slander—United States. 2. Freedom of
the press—United States. I. Title.
KF1266.F67 1987   345.73'0256   86–21660
347.305256

ISBN 0-393-02396-6

W. W. Norton & Company, Inc., 500 Fifth Avenue, New York, N. Y. 10110
W. W. Norton & Company Ltd., 37 Great Russell Street, London WC1B 3NU

1 2 3 4 5 6 7 8 9 0

*To the lawyers who have persevered in the struggle
to secure freedom of expression*

Contents

. . . the calm of the mountain signifies the care that must be used in imposing penalties; the fire moves rapidly on, burning up the grass, like lawsuits that should be settled speedily.

—K'ang-Hsi, *Book of Changes*

Acknowledgments

THIS book is based on decades of experience as a lawyer and fifteen years as a trial judge. I owe much of my understanding of the legal process to my fellow members of the bar, my clients, and the many lawyers and litigants who have appeared before me. I am grateful to them. I wish to thank the Rockefeller Foundation, which gave me a month of leisure in Bellagio, Italy, to work on the book, Professor Francis Allen who discussed some of the ideas with me, Nancy Harrold who cheerfully assisted with the tedious checking of citations, Ilene Suplee who uncomplainingly typed and retyped the manuscript, and my editor, Donald S. Lamm, for his invaluable criticisms and suggestions. As always, I am indebted to my husband, Morris L. Forer, for his unfailing encouragement.

A CHILLING EFFECT

Introduction

*To write a book is, in any proper existential sense, an
absurd undertaking, vain, risky, egotistical, problematic
in the extreme.*

—PAGE SMITH

I N 1774, the great English jurist, Lord Mansfield, declared, "Whenever a man publishes, he publishes at his peril."[1] More than two
centuries later, those who publish in the United States do so at their
peril.

The first ten amendments to the United States Constitution,
known as the Bill of Rights, were drafted by persons familiar with
the law of England and the colonies. They were well aware that those
governments had used their power to license the press in order to
stifle dissent and to protect office holders from criticism. They
wanted to ensure that their newly created government would be
unable to continue these restraints on the expression of unpopular
ideas, the words of maverick politicians, and the utterances of a
restive and independent populace.

The adoption of the First Amendment in 1791 was intended to
establish freedom of the press as an inviolable principle of the basic
law of the United States. The language is in absolute terms: "Congress shall make no law . . . abridging the freedom of speech, or of
the press. . . ." Madison viewed the provision as an essential element
of a democratic society. He declared, "The people shall not be deprived or abridged of their right to speak, to write, or to publish their
sentiments, and the freedom of the press as one of the great bulwarks
of liberty, shall be inviolable."[2] A belief that the public has a constitu-

tionally guaranteed right to speak, to read, and to know has become a part of the national ethos.

The Supreme Court, however, has never accepted this view of the First Amendment. During the past two centuries, the Court has repeatedly cautioned that the public has no express constitutional "right to know." In numerous decisions, the Court has upheld encroachments and limitations on the right of the press to publish and the electronic media to broadcast. Press criticism of the courts in pending litigation has been punished as contempt. "Fighting words" have been held to be suppressible even when they do not cause riots or disturbances. Libel, pornography, and obscenity have been ruled to be excluded from the ambit of the First Amendment.

Public perception is that the Supreme Court decisions in *New York Times* v. *Sullivan*[3] and the *Pentagon Papers*[4] case secured freedom of expression. *New York Times* v. *Sullivan** was a libel action brought by L.B. Sullivan, a commissioner of Montgomery, Alabama, based on a paid advertisement in the March 29, 1960, issue of the *New York Times* describing mistreatment of blacks and civil rights workers in Montgomery and asking for contributions. Sullivan was not mentioned. Suit was brought in the Alabama courts. A jury instructed in accordance with Alabama law awarded Sullivan $500,000. The verdict was upheld by the Alabama Supreme Court. In 1964, the Supreme Court reversed and held, contrary to all precedent, that libel actions are subject to the First Amendment protections of freedom of expression. In the *Pentagon Papers* case, the federal government sued to restrain the *New York Times* from publishing the *Pentagon Papers.* The trial court granted the injunction. The Supreme Court reversed, holding that prior restraint of publication violated the First Amendment. But in the two decades following these decisions, countless verdicts in the millions of dollars have been returned in favor of libel plaintiffs against authors, publishers, and the media. The government has continued to attempt to enjoin publications.[5] Prosecutions against authors and publishers for distributing allegedly obscene literature[6] and for fraud[7] and breach of contract[8] have been upheld by the courts.

Even when authors and publishers have won on appeal, their victories have been Pyrrhic because of the enormous expenses of litigation. Authors and publishers spend an average of some $200,000 per case to defend a libel suit. The *Progressive,* a Wisconsin

---

*This case is discussed more fully in Chapter II.

magazine, spent a third of its annual income defending an action by the government to enjoin publication of an article describing the workings of a hydrogen bomb. All the material in the article was derived from public information. Ultimately the prosecution was dropped. *Penthouse* magazine spent $8 million to defend the libel suit brought against it by La Costa and its owners. The suit concerned a story that alleged that La Costa had ties with organized crime. The case was settled in 1986 after ten years of litigation.[9]

In 1964, when the Supreme Court issued its landmark decision in *New York Times* v. *Sullivan,* it was hailed by journalists, publishers, lawyers, and academicians as a new charter of liberty. Professor Alexander Meiklejohn, a leading civil libertarian, declared: "It is an occasion for dancing in the streets." Professor Harry Kalven, Jr., of the University of Chicago Law School, wrote, "Whatever history may suggest, the Sedition Act is now unconstitutional." But joy and satisfaction were short-lived, as it soon became apparent that novel doctrines imposed by the Supreme Court in subsequent cases were unfair and unworkable. These include the distinctions among public figures, private figures, and limited public figures, the "actual malice" test of liability for public figures, the "of and concerning" doctrine to identify unnamed persons who sue for libel, and the "matter of public interest" test. In more than sixty-seven cases dealing with freedom of speech and of the press decided by the Supreme Court from 1964 to 1986, the law continually has been rewritten. Each new decision has created more unprecedented and complicated doctrines, rules, and distinctions that constitute hurdles for both plaintiffs and defendants. The Court itself is fragmented frequently issuing as many as five or six different opinions on sharply conflicting grounds in a single case. It is little wonder that lawyers and judges as well as litigants are bewildered.

All the justices, whether writing the prevailing decision or concurrences or dissents, pay lip service to the principle that freedom of expression should not be "chilled" by the actions of the courts. But this has been the inevitable result of the torrent of litigation. *Time* magazine refers to this increased caution on the part of the media as "the blanding of newspapers."[10] Even the Supreme Court noted in a case involving a multimillion dollar securities fraud that the journalist who was informed of the situation failed to report the story because "he feared that publishing such damaging hearsay might be libelous."[11]

During this same period, from 1964 to 1986, more than 1,029 lower court opinions involving freedom of speech and the press, exclusive of obscenity, have been reported. At least twenty-five times that number have undoubtedly been before the trial courts. Most trial court decisions are not reported. Until a verdict is appealed and the case is decided by an appellate court, there is usually no record of the matter in published legal reports. Verdicts against the press of millions of dollars are not reported except in the news media. Even such a significant case as that brought by the famous playwright, the late Lillian Hellman, against author Mary McCarthy, Dick Cavett, and PBS does not appear in the official legal reports. On the Dick Cavett program, McCarthy charged that Hellman was a dishonest writer, that every word she wrote, including "and" and "the" was a lie. Hellman sued for libel. The trial court upheld the action. Before trial, Hellman died.

Countless libel cases are being docketed in state and federal trial courts every day. The increase in libel litigation is extraordinary and anomalous. Although there is a popular belief that in the last quarter century in the United States there has been a so-called litigation explosion, a careful reading of statistical reports reveals that, with the exception of special problems such as bankruptcies, prisoners' petitions, and libel cases, there is no more litigation per capita now than in earlier times. In fact, from 1981 to 1984 (the latest available figures examined by researchers), there has been a reduction in the number of legal cases.[12]

Libel litigation, however, has increased enormously. This is a strikingly new phenomenon. As recently as 1947, Professor Zachariah Chafee of the Harvard Law School wrote:

> An able American has too much else to do to waste time on an expensive libel suit. Most strangers will not read the article, most of his friends will not believe it, and his enemies, who will believe it, of course, were against him before. Anyway, it is just one more blow in the rough-and-tumble of politics or business. Even if his reputation is lowered for a while, he can make a fresh start at his home or in a new region and accomplish enough to overwhelm old scandals. A libeled American prefers to vindicate himself by steadily pushing forward his career and not by hiring a lawyer to talk in a courtroom.[13]

The current penchant for libel suits has caused consternation among the legal profession, the media, and the public. There is pervasive dissatisfaction with libel law as it now stands. The general press, radio, and TV talk shows, and legal and academic symposia devote countless amounts of space and time to the subject of libel. At least 500 articles on libel and privacy have been published in scholarly journals. Litigants, their lawyers, and academics are busily engaged in a new industry: rewriting the law of libel.

This is not an irrational, monomania that has suddenly afflicted Americans like the craze for tulips that swept over Holland in the seventeenth century,* rather it reflects the fact that current libel law affords little protection to the citizen who has been smeared by a lie or to the press that publishes the news. Reporters are held in contempt and jailed with monotonous regularity. Verdicts are unpredictable and frequently astronomical. Hurt feelings are awarded millions, while those who have been truly exploited have been denied recovery. A few examples illustrate the arbitrary and irrational results of recent libel law.

The Hill family who had been held hostage by a band of escaped criminals was denied recovery for emotional harms resulting from a story about the crime and their ordeal published long after the tragic event.[14] But a notorious divorcee who had been married to a member of the wealthy Firestone family recovered $100,000 in a libel suit based on a minor error in a contemporary news account of the divorce.[15] In the case of *Bindrim* v. *Mitchell,* an award to a therapist who claimed to recognize himself in a novel in which he was not identified by name or by physical description was denied review by the Supreme Court.[16] Mayor Damron of Ocala, Florida, who was a candidate for re-election, was falsely reported to have a criminal record. After losing the election, he sued for libel. The Supreme Court set aside a verdict in his favor.[17] But the recipient of a federal grant for research who had been named for one of Senator Proxmire's satiric "Golden Fleece Awards" sued the senator for libel. A verdict in his favor was upheld by the Supreme Court.[18] An aspirant for a federal appointment sued an irate citizen who had written to the president criticizing the contemplated appointment. The aspirant won the suit, and the Supreme Court upheld the award *(McDonald* v. *Smith).*[19] The list of irrational, inconsistent, and unfair decisions in free speech cases is virtually endless. Although the Supreme Court declared that seditious libel is dead, the announcement is premature.

---

*Dumas's *The Black Tulip* recounts the story of the wild speculation in tulip bulbs known as tulipomania.

Why should a busy trial judge add to the proliferation of words about this subject? There are many other significant legal problems confronting the courts and the nation. We judges must decide many issues: the right to live and the right to die, problems of crime, pollution, and espionage. We are also kept busy by battling spouses, runaway children, landlords and tenants, buyers and sellers, and all of the problems of the 14 million parties who decide to sue each year.

The public is concerned with the outcomes of many civil lawsuits. The results of some cases affect the air we breathe, the water we drink, the food we eat, the safety of our workplaces, the products we use, and the right to control our bodies and our lives. A single case, like the antitrust action against A T & T, affects everyone who uses the telephone. Much litigation significantly affects the quality of life and the contents of the pocketbooks of most Americans. Important as these cases are, it is not hyperbole to state that the reach of the First Amendment vitally concerns all persons in a democratic society.

Litigation concerning First Amendment rights is qualitatively different from other lawsuits. Although defamation cases are treated like any other civil claims brought by a plaintiff against a defendant, they involve the interests of all of us. But the public is not represented. Even in actions brought by the government against authors and publishers for injunctions and criminal prosecutions, the government attorney does not represent the public but rather the position of the administration then in power. In such cases, the government seeks to ban publication or punish the defendants. The public interest is in having free and untrammeled access to information and entertainment. No one speaks for the people.

In defamation cases, plaintiffs demand redress—including millions of dollars in damages; defendants seek to avoid liability. Courts must weigh and decide the rights of these two parties. Although plaintiffs, defendants, and judges wave the tattered banner of the First Amendment, the readers and viewers whose access to information and entertainment is affected by these cases have no standing. While the courts give lip service to the values of free speech, what is actually decided in each libel case is whether or not the plaintiff recovers money from the defendant and, if so, how much.

The standard definition of libel, unchanged for centuries, is a statement that tends to hold a person up to hatred, contempt, or ridicule. Obviously many news reports dealing with alleged wrongdoing, discussions of public policy and policy makers, as well as countless articles, books, and media presentations that deal with activities of living persons can, under this protean definition, be deemed to be libelous.

In the late twentieth century, Americans live in an enormous, highly technological, interdependent world. No individual or group has the time or skills to investigate the many facts and opinions regarding war and peace, public safety and welfare, and competence and honesty of government officials. The government of the United States is not conducted in a New England town meeting that each of us can attend, where we can listen, speak, and be heard. We rely on our elected and appointed government officials to speak and act for us. We rely on a host of public and private experts to develop scientific, medical, and other skills for our benefit. And we rely on the press, radio, television, and a multitude of writers and speakers to inform, alert, warn, and entertain us. When the rights of authors, publishers, and the media are threatened, the rights of the public are in jeopardy.

If the law were reasonably clear, most cases would be tried quickly or settled. The vast majority of civil cases, even those involving difficult and complicated fact situations and large sums of money, never go to trial. They are settled because counsel know what the law is and advise their clients as to the likely outcome if the case were to go to trial. A survey of lawyers practicing in the field of libel reveals widespread dissatisfaction with the law.[20] The lawyers agree that a major reason for their displeasure is the fact that the law is unclear. Indeed, if the litigants and their lawyers knew what the law was, many lawsuits would not even be instituted. The parties would come to a reasonable adjustment without going to court.

Like the other critics, I am dismayed by the costs of litigation and by results that cannot be attributed to irrational juries or trial judges, but rather are due to the legal doctrines that govern these cases.

I am impelled to add another voice to the cacophonous symphony of a thousand critics of libel law because my viewpoint and, therefore, my recommendations are very different. As a trial judge, I look at the problem from the bottom. The Supreme Court and its critics see the forest. I see the trees. To me the thicket of libel law is not an undifferentiated mass of green. I see different trees: hemlocks, aspen, birch, and even crab apple trees. Each species needs a different kind of soil, different amounts of light, air, and water to survive. We would consider a veterinarian simple-minded if he treated a dik-dik, an elephant, and a tiger with the same medicine and the same dosage

for all diseases and injuries simply because all of them are quad-
rupeds. All libel suits are not the same.

The public is aware of a small number of libel cases brought by
well-known individuals that have been widely reported in the media.
Among the most notorious are the suits brought by U.S. General
William Westmoreland and General Ariel Sharon of Israel.[21] Westmoreland sued CBS, Mike Wallace, and "60 Minutes," alleging that
a documentary entitled, "The Uncounted Enemy: A Vietnam Deception," was libelous. It concerned estimates of enemy troop strength
during the Vietnam War. Westmoreland claimed that the program
charged him with a conspiracy to suppress and distort intelligence
as to the size of the enemy's forces. He asked $120,000,000 in dam-
ages. After eighteen weeks of trial, when the money to finance the
litigation was running out, Westmoreland withdrew his suit. The
defendants issued a statement declaring that Westmoreland was a
patriotic American. It is likely that at all times they had been willing
to make such a concession. The estimated costs to both sides for this
aborted trial range from $6,500,000 to $10,000,000. General Westmoreland and his backers are said to have spent about $3,250,000 to
prosecute the case. The cost to the public was at least $150,000.

Sharon's action was based on a February 21, 1983, article in *Time*
magazine entitled "The Verdict is Guilty." The only paragraph alleged to be libelous stated:

> One section of the report, known as Appendix B, was not published at
> all, mainly for security reasons. That section contains the names of
> several intelligence agents referred to elsewhere in the report. *Time* has
> learned that it also contains further details about Sharon's visit to the
> Gemayel family on the day after Bashir Gemayel's assassination. Sharon
> reportedly told the Gemayels that the Israeli army would be moving into
> West Beirut and that he expected the Christian forces to go into the
> Palestinian refugee camps. Sharon also reportedly discussed with the
> Gemayels the need for the Phalangists to take revenge for the assassina-
> tion of Bashir, but the details of the conversation are not known.

After three months of trial and eleven days of jury deliberation,
a verdict was rendered in favor of *Time*. The jury was instructed to
return three separate verdicts. (Although special verdicts are occasionally used, it is uncommon for a judge not to give all the instructions at one time and for the jury to return special verdicts one at
a time.) The jury was asked to decide three questions: (1) Was the

statement in the paragraph in question defamatory? They answered
"Yes." (2) Was the statement false? They answered "Yes." (3) Did
plaintiff prove actual malice on the part of *Time* or any of its responsible employees? The answer to that question was "No." The jury,
however, volunteered the opinion that *Time* was negligent. The legal
bills of both parties exceeded $3,000,000. The cost to the public was
more than $75,000.

Although Westmoreland has settled his claim and Sharon's case
is terminated, libel litigation arising out of these alleged libels continues. Greg Rushford, a witness for CBS in the Westmoreland trial has
filed suit against Renata Adler, the *New Yorker,* and Martin Barron,
the *New Yorker*'s fact checker based on Adler's critique of the trial
that appeared in the *New Yorker* magazine.[22] *Time* magazine wrote
to the *New Yorker* refuting the article. The prospective book publisher delayed publication for months.[23] No one knows how many
prepublication letters by counsel for aggrieved potential libel plaintiffs have stifled publication of articles and books.[24]

Countless unknown, essentially anonymous individuals, also sue
the media for libel and invasion of privacy. Under the rubric of libel,
individuals and businesses sue credit companies for false reports;
individuals sue novelists and their publishers claiming to be libeled
by fiction and fantasy; they sue cartoonists and their publishers.
Disappointed candidates for jobs and promotion sue the people who
gave them unfavorable recommendations. Academics who fail to get
their degrees or tenure sue the members of committees who failed to
vote for their advancements and the universities. Restaurant owners
sue the critics who do not like their food. Manufacturers sue publications that report less than enthusiastically about their products. All
these and many more kinds of fact situations give rise to libel suits.
Under the present state of the law, all are subject to the same legal
doctrines, the same requirements of proof, and the same laws of
damages. And all defendants are entitled to claim the protections of
the First Amendment.

Plaintiffs and defendants and their counsel want to rewrite libel
law to favor their respective interests. Academics have entered the
fray with learned critiques of appellate court opinions and conceptu-
ally tidy but impractical proposals. General Westmoreland is now
addressing bar associations urging that libel cases be removed from
the courts. This is a simple but dangerous proposal. Litigants can
always settle their differences if they wish to do so and thus avoid
litigation. But to substitute a private court system operating behind

closed doors without legal and constitutional restraints for a public court of law would deprive both plaintiffs and defendants of a judgment based on the facts and the law. It would also deprive the public of information with respect to the litigants and the operations of the courts.

Practicing lawyers and law professors, as well as litigants, have recommended a variety of changes in libel law.* Each examines the problem from the viewpoint of his or her own interests. Trial judges have a different perspective. We see cases from their inception. We must preside over trials that take weeks and months to complete. We must attempt to explain to juries arcane and confusing legal doctrines. We see plaintiffs who have suffered little, if any, harm demanding and receiving huge sums in damages. We see defendants successfully resisting payment regardless of their own carelessness and the infliction of distress. Regardless of whether the plaintiffs or defendants win, the public is the ultimate loser.

My colleagues in all fifty states and on the federal trial bench are faced with formidable problems in trying the thousands of defamation cases now on our dockets. Appellate judges face the not inconsiderable task of deciding whether the trial courts correctly anticipated Supreme Court decisions when we charged the juries in the cases before us and when we ruled on innumerable pretrial and trial motions. Trial judges are also very conscious of the fact that libel cases take a great deal of trial time, that while we are hearing these cases involving compensation for hurt feelings, other litigants who have suffered serious physical harm or have commercial claims that may involve the jobs and investments of many people, as well as those charged with crime who are in jail awaiting their day in court, are delayed while we spend weeks and often months attempting to apply murky, amorphous, evanescent legal doctrines.

Most proposals for rewriting libel law have focused on the language of Supreme Court opinions. In essence they are messages directed to the justices in the hope or blind faith that a sufficient number of them to constitute a majority will change their views and modify the law. Even assuming such an unlikely occurrence, the Supreme Court cannot rewrite the entire law of defamation in a single opinion. Courts can decide only cases and controversies. They can deal only with the rights of the plaintiffs and defendants in the particular cases that are before them. Probably another score of years

*These proposals are discussed in Chapter XIV.

would be required before at least one of each of the various kinds of libel cases would reach the Supreme Court for review. Meanwhile, probably tens of thousands more cases will be instituted, laboriously tried, and appealed. Many will undoubtedly be remanded for new trials. Some for a third trial.

The need to try these cases more expeditiously and less expensively is evident to all trial judges. United States District Court Judge H. Lee Sarokin who under the law was compelled to grant a third full-scale jury trial in a defamation case pensively remarked, ". . . the Court wonders whether the cost to the litigants in this suit, the ultimate cost to the media from all suits, and the final cost to the First Amendment may be too expensive a price to pay."[25] This is a question the Congress should consider.

The Supreme Court cannot write a textbook or a statute prescribing rules of law that must be followed in the multitude of factual situations that are not at issue before the Court. Despite its many decisions, the Court has not covered the spectrum of fact situations that give rise to the libel and privacy suits that are now being tried. Many of these problems were not contemplated by the justices. Nonetheless, trial judges must attempt to extrapolate principles from these confusing and conflicting opinions that arise out of limited and often anomalous fact situations, and to apply these principles in the cases before us. This is a chancy and undesirable predicament, costly to the litigants and the taxpayers.

This book is not a legal text. No attempt has been made to discuss or cite all the thousands of relevant cases or to engage in examination of the fine doctrinal distinctions expressed in the multitude of concurring and dissenting opinions.[26] This book is not a guide to perplexed judges, nor is it addressed to the justices of the Supreme Court. Rather it is meant for the American people and their representatives in the United States Congress.[27] In my view, a federal statute governing the law of libel is urgently needed.* A statute can address the entire law of defamation and define rights and obligations. It can provide appropriate rules for different fact situations. It can establish rules of procedure, standards of liability, and legal requirements for assessing damages. At present, although the vast majority of libel defendants are engaged in communications of a national nature, each case, whether tried in state or federal courts,

---

*The statute here proposed would not abridge freedom of speech or of the press but rather would make the exercise of First Amendment rights less fraught with the probability of libel suits.

RENNER LEARNING RESOURCE CENTER
ELGIN COMMUNITY COLLEGE
ELGIN, ILLINOIS 60123

must be decided in accordance with the common law and statutes of a particular state. The law as to rights of privacy, publicity, and defamation varies considerably from state to state. Under a federal statute, plaintiffs would not be able to "jurisdiction shop," looking for the state with the most favorable laws. Although defendants would still have to defend where they are sued, their rights would be governed by one law instead of fifty.

Litigants, lawyers, and trial judges find statutes very useful. Rights and obligations are established. Words are defined. They do not change from decision to decision. When there are lacunae and ambiguities, the judge can look to legislative history for guidance. Legislatures conduct hearings. Congress can obtain hard statistical data on numbers of cases, length of trials, amounts of verdicts, and costs of insurance. Congress can also hear from plaintiffs and defendants and their counsel. A congressional committee can question journalists to find out whether libel suits have made them more accurate or more reluctant to pursue the kind of investigative reporting the public needs. Based on such information, Congress can make findings of fact and declare public policy. Although all laws are subject to the mandates of the Constitution, a statute carries a presumption of constitutionality and is not lightly set aside.[28]

Before setting forth my views as to what such a libel statute should provide, it is only right that the reader should know my basic premises. I do not speak for either plaintiffs or defendants. I believe that laws and judicial decisions should clarify rights and obligations and thus reduce the need for litigation. I am convinced that the public has a great stake in the libel controversy. Even though the Supreme Court has held that there is no public "right to know,"[29] I believe that legislation should insure, insofar as possible, the broadest right of the public to see, hear, and read whatever the people or any segment of them want.

I believe that individuals have a right to be let alone, that people are not fair game for exploitation.

I believe that the law should require wrongdoers to pay those they have harmed. I do not believe that plaintiffs should recover unless they have proved that they were harmed. And I believe that damages should be compensatory not punitive.

I believe that the courts have a significant role in protecting the rights of all parties and in seeing that cases are decided fairly and expeditiously.[30]

A statute is not a panacea. No statute is ever drawn so precisely and so comprehensively that it covers all eventualities. If a statute were enacted, inevitably there would be litigation testing the reach and interpretation of specific provisions and the constitutional rights of the parties. The rules and doctrines, however, would be clarified and simplified.

A statute provides a practical and immediate step toward resolving a problem that is deemed to be unsatisfactory by everyone involved in libel litigation or the threat of it and by judges on all levels of courts, including the justices of the Supreme Court. A statute has the further virtue of being amendable. If a provision proves to be unsatisfactory, it can be changed without awaiting the long and aleatory process of review by the Supreme Court.

In our complicated and dangerous world, citizens of a democracy want and need information. They ought to know what is happening. They should have a right to the widest variety of opinion and discussion. Free people should also have the right to express themselves not only with respect to politics and government but in all forms of art, literature, and entertainment regardless of artistic merit or redeeming social importance. A policy based upon individual rights must protect individuals from intrusive exploitation and also recognize that there is a "right to know." Because the ad hoc judicial interpretations of libel law have failed to acknowledge and protect these fundamental interests, it is time for legislative action.

A Reasonable Approach to the Problems of Libel Law

*Reason is the life of the law; nay the common law is
nothing else but reason. . . .*

—SIR EDWARD COKE

A poignant picture shows a tiny Icarus falling from a lonely sky. On the shore below, scores of people are going about their daily tasks unaware of the tragedy occurring in their presence. They do not know about Icarus's dreams and his daring adventure. They know only what happens in their own small village.

In the late twentieth century, with the exception of a very few isolated neolithic people, the five billion inhabitants of the globe are aware and concerned about happenings on all parts of this planet and in outer space. Today more people are literate than at any time in history. Even illiterates receive news, information, and entertainment via the electronic media.

For Americans unrestricted access to the spoken and printed word is of vital importance. We consider the right to speak and to hear, to write and to read an inherent and essential aspect of our unalienable freedoms guaranteed by the Constitution. Libel suits, however, are having an insidious effect upon our access to news, information, and entertainment. This chilling effect is both dangerous and contrary to our First Amendment rights.

The dangerous effects of libel suits require examination and discussion. They cannot be sloughed off by the general public as legal issues to be relegated to lawyers and judges. Restriction of information, literature, and entertainment is incompatible with a free society.

When government imposes limitations on expression, the danger is clear and is resisted. Such actions by government officials are bitterly litigated. But when the restrictions are the result of economic coercion and self-censorship, there is little opportunity for the public to protest. No one can compel the press to publish information that is kept secret. Readers and viewers cannot require editors to publish and the electronic media to air programs they have suppressed in order to avoid litigation.*

There is no accurate measure of this growing caution. But a number of recent developments portend more than a mere "blanding" of the press. TV personality Phil Donahue devoted a program to press fears of litigation. He asked, "Is the press becoming wimpy?"[1] In response, Gene Roberts, executive editor of the *Philadelphia Inquirer,* stated: ". . . There are so many libel suits that letters to the editor, your letters to the editor, are not being run by some newspapers because you are being sued and the paper is being sued by politicians because they don't want you to make criticisms of them. . . ."

Although this book is concerned primarily with civil defamation suits, government prosecutions also constitute a serious threat to First Amendment rights. Columnist Anthony Lewis warns of "Silence by Lawsuit."[2] He compares the British Official Secrets Act with the prosecution and conviction of Samuel Loring Morrison, a U.S. Naval employee, who sent the respected British publication, *Jane's Defense Weekly,* classified photos of a Soviet aircraft carrier. His prosecution under the Espionage Act was extraordinary and unprecedented in peacetime.[3] This act also formed the basis of the unsuccessful effort to enjoin publication of the *Pentagon Papers.*

Alarming as such government prosecutions are, civil libel actions probably present more serious threats to free expression because of the mounting numbers of these cases and the extremely high monetary awards.

Although the national networks and large newspapers are extremely wealthy, many magazines, book publishers, local papers, and radio stations have modest assets.[4] For such defendants, the cost of

---

*On occasion, as with respect to the Gulf of Tonkin Resolution, the media are aware of the facts that were concealed from Congress but do not publish them. In other instances, such as the Grenada invasion, government concealed facts from the media. Note, however, the Report of the Twentieth Century Fund Task Force on the Military and the Media concluding that the press should be given the fullest possible access to military operations (*New York Times,* May 29, 1985, p. A9).

defending a libel suit, much less paying a judgment of $100,000 or more, is catastrophic. Defense of a libel suit entails more than simply retaining high-priced expert counsel. The editor and staff have to spend hours of time preparing documents, attending depositions, and obtaining both defensive and offensive evidence. For a small enterprise, this use of management and staff time is a real hardship. During the past ten years, many smaller publications and radio stations have severely curtailed investigative reporting and publication of controversial pieces.[5]

The national media and magazines will probably continue fearlessly to report international and national news and activities in metropolitan areas. But in a country as geographically large and diverse as the United States, many significant state and local activities cannot adequately be reported by the national media. The people in smaller communities must rely on local sources for information. Many periodicals like the *Nation,* the *New Republic,* the *Atlantic,* and *Dissent,* with a national but small readership, make a significant contribution by publishing stories about events and ideas that are not covered by the giant weeklies and monthlies. Diversity of opinion is a desirable end in itself. Small publications also provide an outlet for new, unknown commentators and authors of fiction and nonfiction. Any substantial diminution of the number of publications seriously restricts the opportunities for expression to the detriment of the entire public.

No defendants can ignore the costs of litigation, particularly when their insurance is cancelled or the deductible amount is so high that the media and publishers become, in effect, self-insurers. CNA Insurance Co. ceased writing insurance for the media as of December 31, 1985.[6] Other companies have also stopped writing insurance for publishers and the media. Even when the publisher has insurance coverage, the author may have to expend large sums to compel the insurance carrier to defend a libel action.*

In the 1970s, defense of a typical libel suit brought to trial cost $20,000. In 1985, the average defense of a libel suit that goes to trial is estimated at $150,000. Some lawyers give a figure of $250,000. Inevitably these facts affect editorial policy.

---

*Joe McGinniss, author of *Fatal Vision*, obtained a declaratory judgment against his publisher's insurance carrier requiring it to defend the libel suit brought by Captain Jeffrey MacDonald. The court refused to award damages for fees and expenses incurred in the suit brought to compel the carrier to defend him. Joe McGinniss v. Employers Reinsurance Corporation, U.S.D.C. SD NY, November 17, 1986.

It is now a common practice for newspapers, as well as publishers of magazines and books and the electronic media, to have their material examined by lawyers before release. This vetting may be deemed defensive journalism. It is intended to save defendants the expense of future litigation. But it is a costly and essentially nonproductive practice. Defensive journalism, like defensive medicine, is not good for either the reader or the patient. When doctors practice defensive medicine, patients are subjected to unnecessary tests and invasive procedures, all of which are costly and often painful. These procedures are followed not for the purpose of benefiting the patient but of protecting the doctor. When defensive journalism is practiced, readers and viewers are given sanitized print and electronic material, not for their benefit but to save the authors, publishers, and producers the expense of litigation and the possibility of substantial damage awards. Floyd Abrams, attorney for many media defendants, points out that, "The ultimate way to avoid the risk is not to write the story."[7]

There are no reliable statistics on the extent of this kind of defensive action by publishers and the media. Some financially strong newspapers and television networks may take a hard line, refuse to settle, and fight every lawsuit in the hope of discouraging or outlasting litigious plaintiffs. Less secure newspapers, radio and television stations, magazines, and book publishers undoubtedly find that discretion is the better part of valor and that survival is all.

Authors of unpublished manuscripts and unaired programs have no legal right to compel publication or production of their works. Readers and viewers can write letters of protest when comic strips, columns, and radio and TV programs are cancelled or withdrawn. But they have no legal right to compel publication or production of such works. To date, no one has advanced any credible legal theories that would permit them to bring such suits. When editors and media personnel decide, for any reason, to refuse or to cancel publications and programs, those decisions cannot be contested. The public will probably never know about manuscripts consigned to the wastebasket to avoid lawsuits. Such expressions of opinion or creative works that are quietly and privately stifled have no right to life. No member of the public has standing to sue on their behalf.

Editors and publishers frequently insist on changes to avoid possible litigation. The unhappy author is then faced with a Hobson's choice of acceding to the alteration of the manuscript or rejection. If such softening of comments or opinions was ordered by the government, as happens in many countries, it would be held to be unconstitutional censorship. When practiced by publishers and broadcasters, it is deemed to be editorial discretion from which there is no appeal.

These new developments may be viewed in several ways. In one scenario, it is the triumph of privatism over government. In many other situations, private parties have assumed traditional government functions and supplant government agencies. In the 1980s, it is argued that private enterprise is more efficient and economical than government and that the reduction of government is a good in itself. Under principles of privatism, schools, hospitals, prisons, mental institutions, and even alternative courts are operated by private industry for a profit.* In libel suits, private litigants supplant government agencies in curbing free expression.

Another scenario sees the media as arrogant, intrusive, and hostile to both government and the public. The media are castigated for not publishing good news and for publishing material unfavorable to the administration. Publication of views opposing the Vietnam War and the corruption of the Nixon administration undoubtedly contributed to this attitude. The Reagan administration is overtly hostile to those critical of its philosophy and policies, including lawyers and judges, as well as members of the media. There is an alarming trend to equate criticism of government with "unAmerican" attitudes harking back to the McCarthy era. Because writers and the media are in the business of expressing opinions and exposing unpleasant facts, they bear the brunt of the criticism by those in power. American authors and newspapers have a long and honorable history of "muckraking," exposing business and government wrongdoing. From Upton Sinclair and Ida Tarbell to Bob Woodward and Carl Bernstein, authors and the media have been instrumental in uncovering corruption. From the Teapot Dome scandals in the Harding administration to corruption in the New York City government under Mayor Koch

*The American Bar Association Criminal Justice Section has called for a slowdown in the nationwide move toward privatization of prison and jail operations. 54 Law Week, February 18, 1986, p. 2416. Judicate, Inc., a national private court system founded in 1983 has registered its securities offering 2.25 million units at $1 per unit. The Legal Intelligencer, April 26, 1985, p. 1. The National Institute for Dispute Resolution in Report 2 "Public Ends and Private Means: Accountability Among Private Providers of Public Social Services," 1986, pointing out that billions in public funds are funneled into the hands of private providers, warns of the need for public accountability. There can be no public accountability from publishers and the media that exercise self-censorship. At the same time privatism is lauded, government is taking intensive and paternalistic actions with respect to sexual activities and choice of reading matter of individuals. The action of the Attorney General's Commission on Pornography in sending letters to periodical sellers threatening to list them as distributors of pornography is a signal example of paternalism. See 55 U.S. Law Week 2045, 1986 (hereinafter cited as LW).

and the corruption in the Chicago courts, it has been the media who have been instrumental in forcing the prosecution of wrongdoers for the public benefit.

The attempts to discredit the press, however, have been particularly shrill and persistent in the 1980s. Some criticisms are probably justified. Andrew Kull, an American lawyer living in Paris, charges that the *London Sunday Times* deliberately quoted Prime Minister Margaret Thatcher out of context in stating that she was angry at the BBC for scheduling a program featuring an interview with Martin McGuinness of the Provisional Irish Republican Army. As a result of the *Times* report, the program was cancelled.[8]

The failure of *Stern,* a German magazine, to investigate the authenticity of the Hitler diaries is another shocking example of irresponsibility. The purchase for $8,000 by *Life* magazine of an exclusive interview of Bernard C. Welch, the killer of Dr. Michael Halberstein, who was brutally slain in a holdup, reveals gross insensitivity and an extraordinary moral myopia.

Another instance of alleged arrogance and refusal to consider the feelings of the libeled subject has been charged by William Tavoulareas, former president of Mobil Corporation. He sued the *Washington Post* for libel based on an article alleging that Tavoulareas had helped his son, a former clerk, set up a shipping business using Mobil resources. He won a verdict of $2 million. As of this writing, the case is on appeal. Tavoulareas has written a book, *Fighting Back,*[9] charging *Washington Post* editor, Benjamin C. Bradlee, with "tweedier than thou arrogance."[10] Tom Goldstein, a former *New York Times* reporter, has written a book, *The News at Any Cost: How Journalists Compromise Their Ethics to Shape the News,* detailing scores of examples of unscrupulous, arrogant, and tactless behavior by the media.[11]

Typical of the criticisms of the press is that of the Twentieth Century Fund Task Force Report "For a National News Council, a Free and Responsive Press." It states, "This concentration of nationwide news organizations—like other large institutions—has grown increasingly remote from and unresponsive to the popular constituencies on which they depend and which depend on them."[12]

A Harris poll found that of fourteen institutions included in its survey of popular confidence, universities, the military, and the medical professions were trusted most.[13] The press ranked eighth. Such criticism and resultant distrust may explain in part the extraordinarily high verdicts returned against the media. The function of the courts has become one of disciplining or taming the recalcitrant print and electronic media in the guise of protecting the rights of the subject.

A third scenario treats the media as purely commercial enterprises. In disputes arising out of the publication of news, information, and literature, and the airing of entertainment and electronic programs, all too often the courts apply the law appropriate to those engaged in the purveying of goods without considering the impact of the First Amendment on the rights of the defendants or the public.* Under all these concepts, the public interest is, if not ignored, subjugated to the economic interests of the litigants.

The public has little, if any, interest in most civil litigation. These lawsuits involve the resolution of purely private disputes. Does A owe B money? Has A injured B, and should A be required to pay damages? Judges decide these cases in accordance with well-established legal principles governing commercial rights and obligations, unfair competition, the rights and duties of manufacturers of dangerous goods, and the obligations of the average citizen to act with reasonable care not to injure others.

The application of such doctrines to cases involving publication of printed matter and the dissemination of information, entertainment, and news by the electronic media has subtly displaced the First Amendment from its preferred status. Freedom of expression has become simply another legal argument to be considered in balancing the rights of plaintiffs and defendants.

During the winter of 1984–1985, the American public read the day by day accounts in the press of the trials of General Westmoreland and General Sharon that were being conducted at the same time in the courthouse in New York City. One had a sense of the theater of the absurd. The media, whose rights were under attack, reported the cases as if they were a happening, a public spectacle without antecedents or consequences. There was little indication that these cases marked a drastic departure in the direction of the path of the common law that might have profound consequences not only to the parties but also and more seriously to the public. At the conclusions of the trials, both plaintiffs and all defendants claimed victory, which was logically impossible and contrary to fact. Public commentators, lawyers, and judges concluded that the American legal system had worked fairly and properly. Even counsel for the defendants in the *Westmoreland* case declared that public officials would be deterred

---

*The Supreme Court has also granted First Amendment protections to what are only commercial or political transactions (see Chapter XI).

from bringing libel suits. The inference of many editorials and commentaries was that henceforth the public could forget the implicit threats to freedom of the press and that the news would be reported responsibly and vigorously. Such assurances are, I believe, ill founded and premature.

If the *Westmoreland* case had gone to verdict, the jury would have had to decide whether the charge that he had falsified the body count was, in fact, true. To make such a determination, the jury would have had to decide what the actual body count was and whether Westmoreland had known that fact when he presented his body count. These are not the kinds of facts that any jury could determine on the basis of evidence admissible in court. Any verdict, at best, would have been an informed surmise; at worst, mere speculation. It is a fundamental principle of law that juries cannot reach verdicts on the basis of surmise or speculation, but that the conclusions must be based on factual evidence.

The confidence that freedom of the press had been safeguarded is premature because thousands of other defamation actions have already been filed in American courts throughout the country, and the likelihood is that many more raising other difficult questions of fact and law will be brought.

Generals are not the only persons who have gone to court to demand enormous sums from the media. Politicians, lawyers, doctors, criminals, crime victims, beauty queens, therapists, socialites, professors, and ordinary citizens have joined the unseemly rush to the courthouse to claim substantial amounts of money for hurt feelings. Although neither Westmoreland nor Sharon recovered money damages, other plaintiffs have won enormous verdicts against the media. TV star Carol Burnett won a verdict of $300,000 in compensatory damages and $1,300,000 in punitive damages against the *National Enquirer,* reduced by the appellate court to $50,000 in compensatory damages and $150,000 in punitive damages.[14] The four-sentence item in a gossip column on which the action was based stated:

In a Washington restaurant, a boisterous Carol Burnett had a loud argument with another diner, Henry Kissinger. Then she traipsed around the place offering everyone a bite of her dessert. But Carol really raised eyebrows when she accidentally knocked a glass of wine over one diner and started giggling instead of apologizing. The guy wasn't amused and "accidentally" spilled a glass of water over Carol's dress.

A month later the following retraction and apology was published:

> An item in this column on March 2 erroneously reported that Carol
> Burnett had an argument with Henry Kissinger at a Washington restau-
> rant and became boisterous, disturbing other guests. We understand
> these events did not occur and we are sorry for any embarrassment our
> report may have caused Miss Burnett.

The California Supreme Court wrote a learned seventeen-page opinion. Three justices dissented.[15]

Richard Sprague, a lawyer, won a $4,500,000 verdict against the
Philadelphia Inquirer.[16] A businessman won a $7,500,000 verdict
against a magazine. Irving MacLeder of Englewood, N.J., was
awarded $1,250,000 in a suit against WCBS TV. The jury found that
he had not been libeled by a report on the dumping of toxic wastes,
but that his privacy had been invaded by the camera cover. Plaintiff's
counsel contended that the crew had "chased [him] virtually like a
hunted animal."[17] These cases and hundreds of others are being
appealed. The largest sum actually paid in a libel suit as of early 1985
was $495,000 paid by the *New York Post* to Greenleigh, Associates,
Inc., a contracting company that had been charged in the press with
submitting bloated and fraudulent invoices to the New York City
Board of Education.[18]

The list of well-known people who have brought suits against the
media is virtually endless—Jacqueline Kennedy Onassis, Ralph
Nader, Norman Mailer, Jack Anderson, Elizabeth Taylor, Governor
Edward J. King of Massachusetts, Mayor William J. Green of
Philadelphia, and Governor William Janklow of South Dakota, to
name only a few.

The media have also countersued. The *Sacramento Bee* sued Senator Paul Laxalt after it was sued by the senator in a $250 million libel
suit based on an article stating that Laxalt's enterprises in Nevada
had been financed by organized crime. The publisher of the *Cincin-
nati Post* countersued an ambulance driver who had sued it for libel.
The *Charleston Gazette* of West Virginia has countersued two plaintiffs who have brought libel suits against it and is reported to be filing
more countersuits.* A Libel Defense Resource Center has been established to keep track of this torrent of litigation.†

---

*The publisher of the *Charleston Gazette* sued attorney Stanley E. Presser who had brought
some nine libel related suits against the paper for malicious prosecution. Five suits were settled
and one was dropped (*National Law Journal,* July 21, 1986), p. 1.
†In 1981, The Libel Defense Resource Center was established in New York. It grew out of a

In most civil lawsuits, plaintiffs sue for money damages. When the defendants are not wealthy, recoveries are limited to the amount of the defendant's insurance. Even individuals who have suffered serious physical injuries and/or severe financial losses as the result of another's wrongdoing, rarely sue when advised by counsel that the recovery will probably not be sufficient to compensate for actual losses plus the expenses of litigation. Most people are sensibly governed by a cost/benefit calculation. Because the print and electronic media are big business, however, there is usually a deep pocket defendant (a party who can pay a six- or seven-figure verdict) to sue in defamation cases. A single book, article, or TV show can bring authors and producers enormous financial returns. This is undoubtedly a factor in the increased amount of litigation by subjects against authors. Because awards in these cases are so greatly in excess of the verdicts in other comparable actions, the incentive to sue is proportionately greater.

Often the lawyers are blamed. One is reminded of Cervantes's pithy comment about doctors in the *Dialogue of the Dogs.*

One dog remarks: "Of the five thousand students enrolled in the University, two thousand are studying medicine."

"And what do you infer from that?"

"Either those two thousand doctors will have patients to cure (which would be a great calamity and misfortune) or they themselves will die of hunger."

There were more than 650,000 lawyers in the United States in 1985 and more than 60,000 law students. To date, none of them has died of hunger. But it is the clients who are looking for enormous recoveries. Successful libel suits mean big money for plaintiffs although, perhaps, not always equal to their hopes.

Reports of verdicts of hundreds of thousands of dollars and some in the millions naturally fuel the expectations of those who believe they have been unfairly criticized or commented upon. Although many libel plaintiffs are genuinely outraged, others welcome such attacks with glee in the hope of a successful libel suit that will apply the balm of money to their hurt feelings. One of my fellow judges who had been scathingly attacked in the press gleefully remarked

lawyers' ad hoc group. Sponsoring organizations for the LDRC include the *Washington Post,* the *Times Mirror Co., Time* magazine, The American Newspaper Publishers Association, the Radio-Television News Directors Association, the Reporters Committee for Freedom of the Press, and the major libel insurance companies. Their stated goal is "to make their special expertise and resources available to all libel defendants, for the protection of small and large alike." It monitors libel cases in the fifty states. *Congressional Quarterly,* October 23, 1981, p. 771 et seq.

that he was suing the newspaper and expected to recover a substantial verdict and then retire.

Before attempting to consider appropriate legal doctrines, it is helpful to understand why suits for defamation have become so popular in the 1970s and 1980s. It is common to blame a litigious society, rapacious plaintiffs, and greedy lawyers. Although greed on the part of lawyers and litigants is undoubtedly a factor in many civil lawsuits, this explanation is simplistic. It ignores the positive benefits of litigation and the general principle that those who have been wronged should obtain legal redress through the courts. During the social and economic unrest commencing in the 1960s Americans were urged to look to the courts for redress for deprivations of rights rather than take to the streets to protest. When legislatures and executives, both state and federal, failed to act, those who were deprived and discriminated against turned to the courts. And the courts did act. They defused hostility. They resolved centuries' old inequities peacefully and in accordance with the law. Rights of the poor, minorities, women, children, and the handicapped were enunciated and enforced by the courts. During the past half century, the law materially expanded the ambit of rights entitled to legal protection. Not only physical harms but also emotional harms were recognized as compensable. Property rights were enlarged to include such intangibles as sunlight, quiet, and lack of pollution. Relational interests of parents and grandparents were accorded protection.

These developments in the law have been salutary and long overdue. But what began as a movement to help the oppressed and to implement the democratic promises of American life has developed into a popular belief that the courts should provide money damages for every wrong, no matter how slight. Many plaintiffs are now claiming protection for a wide variety of new and old rights. Among these new classes of plaintiffs are subjects who sue authors demanding enormous sums in damages.

The insatiable demand of the print and electronic media for material has increased the number of references to living persons, thus giving rise to many more potential libel suits. With recent technological developments that enable news to be transmitted almost instantaneously and the rapid growth of the electronic media, the public demand for information and entertainment has risen exponentially. Before transatlantic cables, governments and the public had to wait weeks and months to learn the outcome of battles. Today, the entire world watches the bombs falling. News is reported both in the press and on the air while events are occurring. Radio stations air "all news all the time."

The legal equating of oral and written expression with property is of very recent origin. But it, too, is an essential component in the analysis of the conflict between damage claims and First Amendment rights. The concept of property underlies much of Anglo-American law. Right to property was also a significant element of Locke's philosophy that strongly influenced the American founding fathers. An early draft of the Declaration of Independence proclaimed that among the unalienable rights with which all men are endowed are "life, liberty, and property." The Fifth and Fourteenth Amendments to the Constitution provide that "no one shall be deprived of life, liberty or property without due process of law."

For centuries, British and American civil courts were concerned primarily with property rights. Loss of real and personal property and damage to property was compensated with money, the fair value of what was taken or damaged. Gradually it was recognized that loss of bodily parts and functions resulted not only in pain but also in economic loss, the ability to work. Such injuries became compensable in money damages. In the twentieth century, pain, suffering, and loss of life's pleasures were also recognized as compensable losses. Damage to reputation has for centuries under English law been awarded compensation. In the past few decades, seclusion, peace of mind, and privacy have been accorded limited recognition as legal rights. The remedy for infringement of all these rights is monetary damages.

A large element of news involves individuals and their activities. People want to know which government officials made a particular decision and which individuals opposed it. People are interested in the identity of generals, civilian officials, captains of industry, and movers and shakers in all fields of human endeavor. They also want to know more than the names and positions of newsmakers. They are interested in learning about the lives and characters of the persons making decisions that affect society. Publications like *People* magazine and the *National Enquirer* cater to this natural interest in the lives of people in the news. As more news is reported and presented more fully, inevitably more individuals are mentioned by name, described, and commented upon in all publications.

Moreover, people are not satisfied with the bare bones of facts. They want "in depth" reporting that is more informative. Books, news magazines, and weekly and special documentaries on the air attempt to meet this demand for more information and explanations about a world that is increasingly complex and bewildering to the average person.

Anything more than a summary account of facts ineluctably involves judgment and opinion. Decisions as to items included and excluded, what is to be stressed and what is to be mentioned only briefly are made by the author. The subject may well disagree. Such differences of opinion as to fairness and accuracy lead to litigation.

News is not the only source of conflict between subject and author. Today there is a far greater demand for entertainment in print, on the stage, and on radio and TV. Again authors turn to real-life stories to fill this demand. Such books, articles, fiction, and drama frequently give rise to litigation by subjects against authors.

Many of these situations are strikingly similar to the use of material about living people and comments about them by writers of earlier times. A suit was brought recently by a man against his wife for using him as the prototype of a character in her novel.* His name was not mentioned; his identity was not disclosed. Leo Tolstoy admittedly used his wife and her actual experiences in childbirth as the subject of graphic scenes in his novels.

A widow whose husband was killed in an accident sued the author and publisher of an article describing the accident and the adjustment of the widow and the family to his death. The widow was pictured as a cold woman whose house was dirty and shabby. Plato's dialogues not only purport to repeat Socrates's conversations with his pupils but also depict Socrates's wife, Xantippe, as a shrew. Unfavorable portrayal of real people by their contemporaries is probably as old as written language. But suing for defamation is a distinctly contemporary American phenomenon.

Until very recently, money and speech were not considered comparable or interchangeable. Freedom of speech was deemed to be a right entitled to judicial protection from government restraint and from criminal prosecution. It was considered part of the penumbra of individual political liberties beyond which government may not intrude. But in late twentieth-century American society, free speech cannot easily be exercised beyond one's drawing room without the expenditure of money. Flyers and broadsides are expensive. With the demise of the penny postcard, even the simplest communication to the public is costly. Election campaigns for almost every public office

*For a discussion of libel suits arising out of fiction see Chapter X.

cost hundreds of thousands of dollars, and in many campaigns, millions of dollars. It is not unreasonable to recognize the nexus between money and access to the media in order to exercise one's First Amendment rights. Whether limitations on the right of an individual to spend his own money in his election campaign should be viewed as an unconstitutional restriction on freedom of speech as the United States Supreme Court has held[19] is certainly an issue on which there are substantial arguments pro and con. Acknowledging that the law now protects the expenditure of money for political speech does not, however, require that speech and expression be equated with money or property.

It cannot be doubted that publishing, movies, and the electronic media are profit-making enterprises. Even public radio and TV are subject to budgetary restrictions and compulsions and the need to raise money in addition to public subsidies. University presses and scholarly journals are also bound by economic constraints at least not to lose too much money. It is difficult to imagine any oral, written, or visual communication to the public or any limited segment of it that does not in some way depend upon financial support.

Nonetheless, the courts have endeavored to draw a bright line between commercial speech and noncommercial speech, between profit motives of authors and publishers and other presumably more elevated motives. These novel tests of the applicability of First Amendment rights have resulted in subordinating the free expression of authors to the property claims of subjects. There is an easily discernible difference between advertising and all other types of expression. But courts have gone beyond the simple dichotomy of advertisements and other written and oral speech. They have probed the motives of the author, the significance of the speech, and whether it panders to prurient curiosity or exceeds common decency.

This test of "commercialism" requires courts to examine the minds of the authors as to purpose and intent and to evaluate the merits of the speech. These are vague and subjective standards permitting restrictions on expression that have little, if any, relationship to the allegedly offensive language or the rights of the subject.

These changing, confusing, and novel legal doctrines are also a significant factor in the increasing number of libel suits. The results of such lawsuits are so conflicting and confusing that litigation may be likened to a lottery. Every plaintiff hopes to strike it rich. The number of gamblers appears to be unlimited. Success or failure appears to be more a matter of chance than of law.

This confusion in the law can be attributed, at least in part, to the common law training and traditions of American courts. We lawyers and judges in attempting to resolve disputes rely on precedent. We look to what our predecessors have done. We pore over the language they have used. We adopt their words in order to justify our decisions. Because all these cases involve the interpretation of the First Amendment, judges turn indiscriminately to the language used in earlier cases involving freedom of speech and of the press.* Many of these cases were decided long before the invention of the cable, telephone, radio, and television. The conditions of life and the expectations of individuals were radically different. The context in which these earlier defamation suits were brought bear little resemblance to contemporary life. But under the rubric of the First Amendment, these cases constitute binding precedent. It is obvious that rules and doctrines that yield a fair decision in one set of facts when applied to different situations frequently result in irrational and unfair decisions.

The vast majority of First Amendment cases prior to *New York Times* v. *Sullivan* involved attempts by government—often successful—to prevent the publication of writings and the showing of films, as well as to punish with criminal sanctions authors, publishers, and film makers and distributors. From time to time, the federal courts set aside some of the most egregious decisions authorizing these restraints. Consequently, they were perceived as the protectors of the press and the public. Careful analysis of these landmark cases involving freedom of the press, however, reveals the often limited and deceptive nature of those decisions. Government censorship has not been wholly eliminated, nor have other governmental actions punishing writers and publishers.

Libel actions differ substantially from the earlier prosecutions and suits for injunction brought by government. The facts are different; the parties are different; the relief requested is different. The policy considerations that guide the courts should, I believe, reflect these differences. But the courts generally have relied upon language from earlier and totally dissimilar cases.

---

*In deciding each of these libel cases against the media, courts, as they must, have focused on the particular speech or writing that was the subject of the controversy and decided the rights of those parties in that context. The attempt to apply the rules and the language developed in these discrete situations to other cases is known by the Latin phrase *stare decisis*, "let the decision stand." In judicial parlance, it is used as a shorthand expression for the application of precedent. The process has been fraught with injustice and dissatisfaction in cases involving all kinds of written and oral communications.

I do not subscribe to Justice Holmes's oft-quoted statement that "The life of the law has not been logic but experience." Sometimes experience is simply a pretentious mask for a blundering process of trial and error. The experience of American courts in dealing with the conflicts between subject and author during the past few decades has been characterized by one ad hoc decision followed by another. Trial courts muddle through, attempting to apply confusing and conflicting precedents. Experience in this field of the law has failed to provide either certainty or justice.

There is another approach to the process of developing legal doctrine. Law can be created by courts or legislatures as a logical and reasonable response to social, economic, and political realities. It can be an instrument to establish norms of human behavior. It can provide appropriate criminal penalties for those who transgress these standards and suitable monetary damages for those harmed by wrongful deviations from the rules. Law can also provide a carefully structured and orderly system of resolving conflicts.

If one follows Sir Edward Coke's view of the law as an application of reason to human problems, it should be possible to rationalize the protean problems arising out of the conflict between First Amendment rights and individual claims for defamation and invasion of privacy. This can be accomplished by a process of legal taxonomy or classification based on the character of the writings or electronic programs. As Thomas Mann observed, "Order and simplification are the first steps in the mastery of a subject . . . ."

Despite the wide variety of factual situations giving rise to lawsuits against writers, publishers, and the media, and the many claims and defenses asserted, all these cases involve a conflict between two parties who will be here denominated the "plaintiff" and the "defendant." The plaintiff is the subject, the person or entity about whom the defendant or defendants have written or aired programs over the electronic media. The defendants are the author—the actual writer or reporter—and also the editors, publishers, producers, radio and TV stations, and networks responsible for the allegedly libelous statement. Among themselves these defendants often have conflicting claims and interests.[20] In the context of suits brought by subjects, however, they can be considered as a unit because their defenses are essentially the same.

Blaming victims for their misfortunes is a common phenomenon. Many suggest that the media have invited litigation by their obtrusive and irresponsible behavior. Although there are instances of such conduct by publishers of books and magazines, as well as the news media, this is only a partial and limited cause of libel litigation. Defamation suits have been brought against many other types of defendants. Employees and former employees have brought libel suits against their employers because of unfavorable references or failure to give references. Libel actions have also been brought against credit organizations like Dun & Bradstreet for giving customers erroneous information about the plaintiff. Students have sued teachers and teachers have sued students for defamation. All such lawsuits are an inevitable response to the uncertainty and confused state of the law of defamation.

The justices of the Supreme Court are well aware of the results engendered by the Court's opinions. Supreme Court Justice Hugo Black wrote in 1967, "No one, including this Court can know what is and what is not constitutionally obscene or libelous under this Court's rulings."[21] Since that time, there have been many more conflicting decisions. Each obscures, limits, and casts doubt on previous decisions. A federal judge in Kansas, attempting to follow the law as enunciated in high court opinions, wrote in frustration that trying to decide [libel cases] was "like nailing a jellyfish to the wall."[22]

Courts need guidance. Lawyers and litigants must have some reasonable assurance of the legal principles that will govern their claims and defenses and the factual and procedural burdens they will have to meet in order to prevail. In the present state of the law, no one can speak with reasonable certainty. This very uncertainty is provocative of litigation. When no one can safely advise a client as to the likelihood of success, there is little incentive for plaintiffs to refrain from suit or defendants to settle claims against them.

Disagreement among the justices should not be attributed simply to personality or philosophical or political differences. Such divisions have not been limited to the Supreme Court under Chief Justice Warren Burger, rather they have characterized the Court in the past, notably in the early part of the twentieth century when Justices Holmes and Brandeis frequently dissented. Any group of nine persons is bound to have widely differing views on many subjects. This has always been true of the Supreme Court. In a large proportion of cases, however, the justices are able to arrive at a majority consensus. Frequently the Court is unanimous. Despite the deep divisions in the Court and the differences in attitudes, the justices are able to reach agreement when either there is a well-understood public policy or there is a clear precedential history on which to build a sound jurisprudence. For example, the decision outlawing public school segregation was unanimous.[23] There were only two dissents to the decision establishing "one man, one vote."[24]

The inability of the Court to provide an acceptable rationale for decisions in libel cases leaves lawyers, litigants, and trial courts on uncharted seas without a rudder or compass. Lower court judges must attempt to pick and choose among a multitude of conflicting and confusing rules, reasons, and policies.

Justice Powell, writing for a majority of the Court in *Gertz* v. *Robert Welch, Inc.,*[25] stated that although deciding each case involving subject against author on an ad hoc basis might be the most utilitarian method, ". . . this approach would lead to impracticable results and uncertain expectations. . . . We must lay down broad rules of general application." Significantly, in that case only four justices agreed. There were four dissents and one concurrence.

In attempting to establish broad general rules applicable to all defamation cases, the Supreme Court has promulgated novel tests and standards. These new doctrines are not limited to the context in which the allegedly defamatory statement was made. Each prior rule appears to result in an unsatisfactory decision when applied in another context. The Court has then added new refinements and distinctions, again without reference to the factual matrices giving rise to the statements. These refinements have added to the confusion rather than simplifying or clarifying the law.

In almost all cases involving the rights of subjects and authors, the courts quote from prior decisions ringing statements proclaiming the sanctity of freedom of the press. Then various newly created standards are examined. The courts must now decide whether the plaintiff is a public figure, a limited public figure, or a wholly private person. The public or private character of the subject is not simply a novel, unprecedented legal standard. In practice it has proved to be extraordinarily difficult to apply. Almost every subject of written or electronic media reports is, of necessity, a person who by his or her voluntary or involuntary action is of some public interest. Unless housewives are mad, authors do not write about them. All subjects of allegedly libelous statements are to some extent public persons, whether voluntary or involuntary. The public versus private figure test makes little sense when the courts do not distinguish between the rights of crime victims and the rights of public officials or between news stories purporting to be factual and satire or fiction.

The test of commercialism is also unrealistic and difficult to apply.

Any court and jury can readily distinguish between paid advertisements and other writings or programs. Beyond that sharp dichotomy, distinctions blur. In the United States, the vast majority of writers expect or hope to earn royalties. Publishers and the media likewise expect to have monetary or other economic returns from publications and programs. There are few samizdats or privately circulated manuscripts. Vanity press publications, paid for by the author, rarely have wide distribution. To date they have not been involved in this type of litigation.

The concept of fault recently imported into the law of defamation is wise and sensible. But fault has not been defined. It has been left to the vagaries of the laws of the fifty states. Reckless disregard for truth or falsity has been the standard applied to all cases involving public figures regardless of the type of communication or the context in which it occurred. The right of privacy also depends upon the very different laws of the states. The same legal principles have been applied regardless of the nature of the context in which allegedly offensive words occurred. News, commentary, docudrama, fiction, biography, credit reports, and letters of reference are all subjected to the same legal tests. Quotable language taken from an opinion involving the use of a photograph in an advertisement should not bind a court in deciding a case involving a news report. Nor should a statement of principle enunciated in a case arising out of political speech be deemed to control a case involving the rights of a crime victim.

Reason dictates that the rules of law applicable to these different types of cases should not necessarily be the same but should reflect the factual differences, even though First Amendment rights are involved. In other areas of the law when rights of litigants are in conflict, courts weigh the respective interests of the parties in the light of all the circumstances, as well as considerations of public policy. Such analyses do not occur in First Amendment cases because courts are bemused by language employed in prior cases, no matter how dissimilar the parties, the statements, and the contexts in which the statements were made.

Rationalization of the law governing rights of subjects and authors is designed to promote several important societal goals. It should provide rules that lead to more just and sensible decisions. Subjects who have been harmed by the carelessness of authors should receive redress. Authors should not be compelled to pay enormous sums to subjects who have not suffered any provable harm. Rationalization should clarify the law and thus reduce the amount of litigation. Subjects who know they are unlikely to prevail will probably not sue. Authors who know they are probably liable will usually settle. Clarity of the law would also protect the public interest. If authors were not influenced by the fear of litigation and the inability to predict their liability, they would undoubtedly be less timid in their publications and broadcasts.

Ultimately, the law of defamation, like all law, must be perceived as rational and just. As Austin observed, the body of the people are in a habit of obedience to the law. This is true of the American people. Despite crime waves and periods of civil disobedience, the legal system functions. Rarely does anyone resort to self-help or adamantly refuse to obey the orders of a court, no matter how distasteful they may be to the losing party. Once the habit of obedience is broken there is no authority but brute force or fear to compel obedience to law. Neither is acceptable in a democratic society.

·II·

A Backward Glance

The old way of dealing with the law as a body of
empirical rules has definitely broken down. Stare decisis
["let the decision stand"] means little in a changing
society when for every new case the number of
precedents is practically unwieldy.

—MORRIS RAPHAEL COHEN

WINSTON CHURCHILL characterized the Middle Ages as a
thousand years without a bath, a myopic and limited but probably
accurate description. Similarly one could simplistically characterize
the history of Anglo-American libel law as a thousand years without
free speech. Both in England and in the United States, criticism of
government officials and policies and uncomplimentary statements
about individuals have been punished severely under criminal law
and by substantial damage awards in civil libel cases. Although in
New York Times v. *Sullivan,* the United States Supreme Court
boldly declared that it was "writing on a clean slate," it was, in fact,
reinterpreting centuries of English and American law. In common
law countries, no court ever has the opportunity of writing on a clean
slate. Judicial opinions may more properly be likened to a palimpsest
on which each succeeding generation of judges writes over the opinions of a long line of predecessors.

The singular and unsatisfactory nature of libel law has been recognized by countless scholars. Thomas M. Cooley, writing at the turn
of the century, observed that "Unfortunately the English law of
defamation is not the deliberate product of any period. It is a mass
of verbiage that has grown by aggregation with very little intervention from legislation, and special and peculiar circumstances have
from time to time shaped its varying course. The result is that

perhaps no other branch of the law is as open to criticism from its doubts and difficulties, its meaningless and grotesque anomalies. It is, as a whole, absurd in theory, and very often mischievous in its practical operation."[1]

Professor Prosser, the author of the standard text on the law of torts in the United States, frankly declared:

> It must be confessed at the beginning that there is a great deal of the law of defamation which makes no sense. It contains anomalies and absurdities for which no legal writer ever has had a kind word, and it is a curious compound of a strict liability imposed upon innocent defendants, as rigid and extreme as anything found in the law, with a blind and almost perverse refusal to compensate the plaintiff for real and very serious harm. The explanation is in part one of historical accident and survival, in part one of the conflict of opposing ideas of policy in which our traditional notions of freedom of expression have collided violently with sympathy for the victim traduced and indignation at the maligning tongue.[2]

Sir William Pollock noted in 1894 that the law of defamation "went wrong from the beginning."[3] Many knowledgeable people in 1987 believe that libel law is still wrong.*

Among the remedies proposed in subsequent chapters is disclosure by authors of the purport and character of their writings. It is, therefore, appropriate that I explain my reading of legal history. All branches of history are subject to changing fashions. The past is, of necessity, viewed from the vantage of the historian's own era. In every generation, historians examine not only verifiable facts such as names, dates, and battles, they also look at customs and mores; they infer intentions and motivations. They bring to their tasks the learning and the prejudices and limitations of their own times. Within this framework, history is written from many viewpoints. Contemporary historians forthrightly label their works as social history, economic history, psycho-history, black history, feminist history, and many other subspecialties. Even the history of science has undergone considerable revision. Ptolemaic astronomy was replaced by Copernican astronomy; Newtonian physics by the theory of relativity and the

---

*Author Renata Adler has been a libel plaintiff and a potential libel defendant. Her book, *Reckless Disregard,* reporting on the *Sharon-Time* and *Westmoreland-CBS* trials provoked allegations that she was motivated to write the book by a desire for revenge. These charges delayed publication of the book. Adler describes libel law as "one of the slums of Anglo-Saxon law." (*Insight,* January 12, 1987, p. 61.)

numerous refinements and corrections of Einstein's theory; eugenics has been completely rewritten since the turn of the century when racial differences in intelligence were accepted as undisputed fact.

Legal history has also been subject to fashions, fads, and prejudices. But the basic source materials of Anglo-American law remain unchanged. They are the decisions and opinions of countless judges and courts for the past millennium. Adherents of natural law read these cases seeking to extract immutable principles. Legal realists read the same cases as presenting a practical accommodation to what Justice Holmes described as "the felt necessities of the times." The proponents of the new "critical legal studies" read the cases as an account of the power struggle by contending forces in society.

Legal historians of all persuasions give great weight to the language in opinions. All too often opinions contain noble sentiments, statements to which few people could take exception, but which are belied by the actual results of the case. This is particularly true of cases in which claims of freedom of speech and press are asserted. As Professor Rabban points out

> ... these First Amendment cases typically invoked formal pieties at the expense of rigorous analysis, thus precluding the interchange and criticism necessary to the evolution of doctrine. At the same time that they issued platitudes about the importance of First Amendment values, judges failed to recognize free speech claims. Even when the courts addressed the free speech issues presented, they generally resolved them on an ad hoc basis.[4]

This practice prevails in the opinions involving rights of subjects and authors. Professor Gilmore aptly states:

> The judges, like the professors, rarely, if ever, bothered with the facts of the cases they cited or with the reasons why the cases had been decided as they had been. Nor did the judges make any attempt to explain the reasons for their decisions. It was enough to say: The rule which we apply has long been settled in this state.[5]

I read legal opinions, not as a statement of eternal principles, or a practical accommodation, or a power struggle, but as an anthology of stories. Each case is a story about real people involved in a real conflict so important to them that it could be resolved only by the courts. The decision . . . which party won and which party lost

... is at least as significant as the language used by the judge to justify his conclusion.[6] The emphasis on language has often obscured the real import of the case. Judges, like the devil, can quote scripture. The sacred writings of the law are the opinions of the high courts. In reading these opinions, it is necessary to look behind the patina of appealing phrases to the actuality of the holding.

Unless there is a statute or a clear and precise decision in a prior case involving the same factual situation, judges must reason by analogy, extrapolate from prior decisions, and find a legal doctrine that appears to yield a just result within the constraints of the Constitution and the Bill of Rights. Whether one believes that the meaning of the Constitution was fixed for all time by the founding fathers or that it must be interpreted in the light of contemporary problems, it is evident that many of the disputes now before the courts involve factual situations that were never contemplated and, indeed, were unimaginable two centuries ago. In vitro fertilization of a human egg, nuclear energy, toxic chemicals, motor vehicles, airplanes, and telecommunications are the factual matrices giving rise to much litigation. In the conflicts between subject and author involving First Amendment rights, instant reporting of news over the air, television docudramas, national publications, and video programs raise novel problems for which there are no clear and precise precedents.

Wise judges, like Janus, look both backwards and forwards. They look back for guidance and they look ahead attempting to foresee the likely effects of their rulings. If one reads early defamation cases carefully, examining the facts, not merely the language of the opinions, it is apparent that the law consists of a curious meld of two dissimilar factual situations. One, known as seditious libel, is based on a criticism of government or public officials. The other involves an uncomplimentary statement about a nongovernmental individual that can best be described as name calling. Both actions, however, are treated as defamation and subject to the same rules of law, standards of proof, and damages.

Seditious libel was derived from Roman law. It was known as *Libella Famosa*. In contrast, the libel suit for vindication of reputation was alien to early British law. It developed as a less lethal alternative to the duel fought by gentlemen in defense of their "honor." Dueling was a French importation that, like the use of the fork, was deemed somewhat effete but fashionable. It was never popular among the mass of Englishmen. Aristocrats and gentlemen of fashion sued for libel. Judicial combat, in which a duel was used in lieu of a criminal prosecution, was abolished in 1818. The duel of honor persisted in England in several celebrated combats until about 1840. Although duels were fought in the American colonies, they were not a popular or widely used means of settling disputes. Judicial combat was not imported into the American colonies. But both seditious libel and libel for vindication of honor did take root in the colonies and have persisted in American law.

The lineage of libel as a slur on a gentleman's honor is clearly evident in the nature of the statements deemed to be libelous. The classic definition of a defamatory statement is one that tends to hold a person up to hatred, contempt, or ridicule. Thus, as late as 1971, a leading American textbook declared that statements defamatory on their face are allegations that the plaintiff has committed a crime, is insane, is poor, has attempted suicide, has made improper advances, has wife troubles, is about to be divorced, is an unchaste woman, or has been raped.[7]

That a charge of poverty is defamatory on its face attests to the upper-class bias of this peculiar tort. Obviously the average man or woman would have little use for such a legal action. An analysis of recent libel cases points out that more than 70 percent of the plaintiffs are males engaged in corporate or public life.[8] There is no breakdown by race or socioeconomic status. But it is evident from their occupations that most libel plaintiffs are persons of relatively elite standing in their communities. A libel suit, unlike other tort actions, is usually brought by wealthy and powerful people who can afford the expense, time, and emotional stress of protecting their "honor." The contingent fee agreement under which the lawyer is paid a percentage of the plaintiff's award if the plaintiff wins and nothing if the plaintiff loses has opened the courts to many poor litigants who have suffered physical injuries. But not many lawyers are likely to invest the time and money needed to win a libel suit brought by an impoverished woman or a delinquent child who has been defamed.

The other types of statements legally held to be actionable are plainly anachronistic, if not unconstitutional. Today it is unthinkable that a statement that a woman is unchaste would lead to a libel suit. Bar associations, university alumni groups, and foundation think tanks send invitations to the addressee and his or her "companion." The Census Bureau has a category known as "POSSLQ," persons of opposite sex sharing living quarters. A statement that is defamatory to one sex without being defamatory to the other might run afoul of laws prohibiting discrimination based on sex and the constitutional right of equal protection of the law.

Public attitudes toward rape victims have changed markedly. The complainant in a rape case is no longer treated as a seductress. Most states have, by statute, prohibited cross-examination of the complainant as to her prior sexual experience. Similarly, society's attitude toward insanity has altered drastically. Insane people are no longer exhibited for the amusement of the public. They have rights to dignity and treatment in the least restrictive environment.

On its face, a charge of criminality would appear to hold up to hatred or contempt one so charged. Recent experience, however, indicates the contrary. Although President Nixon was an unindicted defendant in the Watergate break-in, a few years thereafter he is in demand as an elder statesman, has published several widely read books, and makes many public appearances. Other Watergate felons, after serving brief prison sentences and paying minimal fines, are invited to speak on university campuses and are paid substantial honoraria. Convicted white-collar felons serve on the boards of charities and civic organizations and are elected to public office. It is difficult to find anyone who is held up to contempt or obloquy in contemporary society for criminal conduct. As Diderot declared in *Rameau's Nephew,* "It's impossible to disgrace yourself, no matter what you do if you are rich." Only in prison does one find remnants of old-fashioned morality. There child abusers are subject to abuse at the hands of other inmates convicted of such unstigmatizing crimes as robbery and murder. In an age when the concepts of honor and shame are elastic, to say the least, one must question the premises of this type of libel action. What is a good reputation? Is it worth millions of dollars? A statute should revise the definition of libel to make it consonant with contemporary mores.

Until the current spate of libel suits seditious libel was by far the more popular type of defamation action in both England and the United States. Until the mid-twentieth century, most of the cases involving seditious libel were criminal prosecutions brought by the government, not civil tort actions brought by the offended public official. This is another legacy from medieval English law, in which the distinction between tort and crime was not clearly defined. Maitland, the historian of English law, points out that prior to the Norman conquest there was no differentiation between a crime in which harm is willfully inflicted and a civil tort in which harm is negligently done. In either event, the victim was entitled to monetary damages. The notion of "malice" which so bemuses the courts in libel suits today can be traced to this melding of willfulness and negligence.

Although the law distinguished between oral defamation, known as slander, and written defamation, known as libel, that distinction is of no significance today in cases involving subjects and authors. Any defamatory statement broadcast over radio or television is sensibly treated as libel because it can accurately be reproduced and offered in evidence in open court in the same manner as a written document.

Under both criminal and civil libel, the wrong is the defamatory statement. It is unnecessary to prove harm. Both the evil consequences of the act and the damages are presumed. The standard explanation recites the basis of liability as if it were a self-evident fact. Pollock states:

> Reputation and honour are no less precious to good men than bodily safety and freedom. In some cases they may be dearer than life itself. Thus it is needful for the peace and well-being of a civilized commonwealth that the law should protect the reputation as well as the person of the citizen. In our law some kinds of defamation are the subject of criminal proceedings, as endangering public order, or being offensive to public decency or morality.[9]

Having justified civil actions and criminal prosecutions of defamation as essential to the well-being of a civilized community and necessary to protect the security of the state, it followed that severe consequences would befall one who defamed either an individual or the state.

It is not then astonishing that the penalties for defamation in English law were Draconian. Under the laws of Alfred the Great, a slanderer's tongue was cut out. As late as the sixteenth century, John Stubbs's hand was amputated for writing an attack on the prospective marriage of Queen Elizabeth I.[10] In the case of *Rex* v. *Barmondiston* in 1684, the hapless but wealthy defendant was fined £10,000, an enormous sum at that time, for expressing adverse political opinions in a letter addressed to a friend.[11] The crime was the "scandal," not the harm done or the intent of the writer to harm the state. Nonetheless, the conviction was justified by the court on the grounds that libelous statements stirred up the people and endangered the stability of the government. Significantly, there was no evidence that the people were stirred up or that the stability of the government was endangered by this letter.

The only check on government prosecution of its critics under English libel law was the intransigence of juries that refused to convict. In 1581, Lord Henry Cromwell was prosecuted for "scandalum magnatum."[12] But the jury held that the statement, "you like not of me since you like those that maintain sedition against the Queen's proceedings" was not defamatory.

A century later, the members of the jury that refused to convict William Penn and William Meade were prosecuted. This extraordinary proceeding is known as "Bushell's case."[13] It is usually cited for the proposition that in libel cases the only issues of fact to be decided by the jury are: (1) the intentional publication of the document, and (2) whether it can be read as having a defamatory meaning. The ultimate question of whether the statement constitutes a libel is to be reserved for decision by the judge because it is deemed to be an issue of law and not of fact.

Penn and Meade were prosecuted for "assembling unlawfully and tumultuously." The jury rendered a general verdict of not guilty. Thereafter, the jurors were charged with contempt of court and obstruction of justice. They were incarcerated. Bushell, one of the jurors, filed a writ of habeas corpus to obtain his freedom. The court ordered all the jurors discharged. In the course of the opinion, the court noted that the jury was not asked to give a special verdict and observed that *if* a jury is asked to return a *special* verdict on the facts only, in such circumstances the judge may rule on the law. Needless to say, Bushell's case did not involve libel. But this comment on the division of what is to be designated a question of law for the judge and what is designated a question of fact for the jury permitted the courts to take firm control of libel cases. It is interesting that the careful delineation of issues by Judge Sofaer in posing a series of special verdicts to the jury in the *Sharon* case accomplished the same result. The questions put to the jury by the device of special verdicts effectively guided the result. The jury found that the statement in *Time* magazine was defamatory. But under the actual malice test promulgated by the Supreme Court, they were unable to conclude that the defamatory statement was published knowingly and with reckless disregard of its falsity.

In the sixteenth century, seditious libel cases were heard by the Star Chamber. After this arbitrary and high-handed tribunal which sat without a jury was abolished, the English government used licensing acts to punish printers who published and sold books scandalous to the government. When the licensing law expired in 1694, it was not reenacted. This did not bring to an end the prosecution of printers either in England or in the colonies.[14]

Although there was no licensing law* in the American colonies similar to the British statute, John Peter Zenger was prosecuted in New York in 1735 for publishing a newspaper, the *Journal,* that was a rival to the official newspaper approved by the governor. The *Journal* was openly opposed to Governor Cosby and was critical of his corrupt administration. In an effort to shut down the paper, the authorities jailed Zenger. His attorney, James Alexander, was disbarred. Alexander had probably written most of the allegedly offensive material in the *Journal.* At this point, the famous Philadelphia lawyer, Andrew Hamilton, came to New York to defend Zenger. Under the law, it was clear that Zenger was guilty. The articles were defamatory. The popular and accurate adage, "The greater the truth, the greater the libel," was the law of England and the colonies. Nonetheless, Hamilton argued eloquently to the jury that the statements were true. The jury acquitted. Significantly, the trial judge did not ask the jury for special verdicts.

Exactly 250 years after the Zenger trial, a strikingly similar trial took place in England. Clive Ponting, a government employee, was accused of violating the English Official Secrets Act by giving unclassified information to a member of Parliament. The Thatcher government had, in response to a series of requests from Parliament, given false and misleading information with respect to the sinking of the Argentine ship, the *General Belgrano,* during the Falkland Islands war. This misinformation is remarkably similar to that given Congress at the time of the Gulf of Tonkin Resolution. The section of the act under which Ponting was prosecuted provides that it is a misdemeanor for anyone to use information in his possession "in any manner . . . prejudicial to the safety or interests of the State." The trial judge charged the jury: "Interest of the State, I direct you, means the policies laid down for it by the recognized organs of Government and authority. . . ." In other words, the interest of the state was identical with the interest of the party in power and the Prime Minister. Since those officials had determined that the information should not be disclosed, doing so was in the words of the statute "prejudicial to the . . . interests of the State." This was an instruction to the jury to return a verdict of guilty.

In his closing address to the jury, counsel for Ponting argued that turning over information to a member of Parliament was in the

---

*A printer who published court decisions without the imprimatur of the judges was held in contempt, (a non-jury proceeding) imprisoned, and fined. The stated grounds were that the publication had the tendency of prejudicing the public (Respublica v. Oswald, 1 Dall 319 [Pa. 1788]).

interest of the state. He closed by saying, "If what he did was a crime in English law, you say so. But if it is, God help us . . . because no Government will."[15] The jury returned a verdict of not guilty.

The *Zenger* case brought into the language the phrase "Philadelphia lawyer" as a term of perhaps grudging respect. Only a Philadelphia lawyer could have gotten an acquittal for Zenger under the then existing law. It also brought into the law a curious reverse burden of proof. The defendant, who raised the defense of truth, was required to prove truth rather than the prosecution being required to prove falsity. In all other criminal cases, the prosecution is required to prove all the elements of the crime. This reverse burden of proof, like all the other rules developed in seditious libel cases, was carried over into civil suits for libel for many years. The *Zenger* case, despite its prominence in American history books, made no significant change in the law of libel. Prosecution under state libel laws and federal statutes continued for criticism of the government and unpopular opinions expressed by unpopular individuals and published in the press and leaflets. With rare exceptions, these convictions were sustained by the highest courts of the state and by the United States Supreme Court.[16]

Civil suits for libel against the media were not involved in these criminal prosecutions. The United States Supreme Court, however, gratuitously stated time after time that although the First Amendment prohibited *prior* restraints on the press by way of injunction, libel and obscenity were outside the ambit of the First Amendment. For example, in *Patterson* v. *Colorado,*[17] the Supreme Court upheld a contempt conviction against an editor for articles and a cartoon criticizing the Colorado Supreme Court. Writing for a majority that held that the Fourteenth Amendment was inapplicable, Justice Holmes stated:

> But even if we were to assume that freedom of speech and freedom of the press were protected from abridgments on the part not only of the United States but also of the states . . . the main purpose of such constitutional provisions is to prevent all such *previous restraints* [Court's emphasis] upon publications. . . .

Justices Harlan and Brewer dissented.

A few years later, the Supreme Court upheld an injunction against the president of the American Federation of Labor prohibiting the publication of an article declaring that an employer was unfair to labor.[18] This case arose out of a labor dispute over working hours.

The trial court issued a sweeping injunction prohibiting the union from publishing statements that the employer was unfair and urging a boycott. The union officials who were imprisoned for contempt claimed that the order abridged freedom of speech and of the press. The Court held that the question was moot. But writing for the Court, Justice Lamar stated: "The Court's protective and restraining powers extend to every device whereby property is irreparably damaged or commerce is illegally restrained." In *Lewis Publishing Co.* v. *Morgan,* [19] a case involving second-class postal rates and the requirement that the publisher furnish the post office with information in order to obtain the reduced rate, the Supreme Court declared that the First Amendment prohibits all restrictions on the press except common law libel and material that offends recognized morality. Significantly, despite its generous reading of the First Amendment, the Court upheld the statute.

Schenck v. *U.S.* [20] has been cited for more than half a century as a landmark decision protecting freedom of speech because in the opinion Justice Holmes enunciated the clear and present danger test. He wrote, "No one has a right to shout fire in a crowded theater." Schenck was convicted of conspiracy to violate the espionage law and for unlawful use of the mails. The Supreme Court affirmed. In that opinion, Holmes imported into the law the notion that speech is the equivalent of action. This was a new concept. Under the common law of libel, defamatory speech was actionable simply because it was defamatory. In *Schenck,* the Court held that a leaflet opposing World War I "masks a primary intent to incite to forbidden action." There was no evidence that Schenck's little leaflet made recruitment for the military more difficult or that it had any effect whatsoever on the war effort. The Court noted that Schenck was secretary of the Socialist Party, although the fact was irrelevant to the legal issues involved. There was no theater; no one had shouted fire. If that test had actually been applied to Schenck's conviction, the decision would have been reversed.

The leading American cases arising out of the First World War involved in the main prosecutions under state criminal syndicalism laws. Most defendants were members of small, unpopular dissident political groups who posed no threat to the nation. Despite brave language in the opinions, their convictions were upheld. Although these cases bear little resemblance to the civil actions for libel brought in the 1970s and 1980s, language from those cases resonates in contemporary defamation opinions.

After this series of cases, the next major subject of First Amendment cases was obscenity. In these decisions, the Court was involved in a continuing effort to define and redefine tests for prohibiting writings deemed to be offensive. Most of these cases arose under state statutes. They, too, would seem to have little relevance to civil libel suits. Language in these opinions, however, brackets libel and obscenity as being outside the protection of the First Amendment.

In *Fox* v. *Washington,*[21] Justice Holmes, again writing for the Court, upheld a conviction under a state statute prohibiting publication of written matter "which shall tend to encourage or advocate disrespect for law or for any court or courts of justice." The defendant had edited an article entitled "The Nudes and the Prudes" discussing nude bathing. The Court sustained the conviction on the wholly unproved assumption that the article "encourages and incites" breach of state laws prohibiting indecent exposure. Similar conclusions without any evidentiary basis are characteristic of First Amendment decisions.

As the courts upheld convictions of booksellers and dealers for distributing the works of Tolstoy, Mark Twain, D.H. Lawrence, and countless other masters of prose, First Amendment lawyers and scholars focused on obscenity. Civil libel was largely ignored. Name calling cases rarely had the potential for large recoveries. In England, even so famous a person as Harold Laski was denied recovery when he sued for having been charged with advocating revolution.[22] In most cases, the substantive charges were trivial. Without a deep pocket defendant, litigation is an expensive luxury for the litigant. For the lawyer who takes such a case on a contingent fee basis, it can be a disaster. To recover a substantial victory against a judgment-proof defendant is a Pyrrhic victory. Consequently, wise counsel usually prevailed on their clients not to sue or to settle for nominal damages.

After World War II, there were a few notorious cases like Alger Hiss's suit against Whittaker Chambers, undertaken against the advice of his attorneys. Chambers accused Hiss, a well-known New Deal attorney of impeccable reputation and president of the Carnegie Foundation, of having been a Communist and of having associated with Communists, including Chambers himself. Hiss indignantly denied the charges. Several Supreme Court justices testified as character witnesses for Hiss. Hiss withdrew his libel suit after he was convicted of perjury.[23] The law of libel appeared to have been relegated to a well-deserved status as a harmless anachronism that survived principally in textbooks. There was little incentive for lawyers, academics, or legislators to engage in the reform of the law of defamation.

Libel law received an unintended revitalization when the Supreme Court issued its decision in *New York Times* v. *Sullivan.* Although this decision has been widely praised and the opinions of the Court have been subjected to intensive analyses, it is helpful to look at the facts and see what the Court actually decided and what the Court's options were. The case arose out of the civil rights movement led by Dr. Martin Luther King. A decade before, the Supreme Court had issued its seminal opinion in *Brown* v. *Board of Education,* [24] striking down segregated public schools. Almost a century after the Civil War, the Court was engaged in implementing the promise of equal rights for black Americans. Despite pockets of resistance in Little Rock and Boston, public reaction to the Court was generally favorable. *Brown* was widely perceived as being morally right and legally in the mainstream of the continuing process of adapting legal and constitutional principles to changed conditions.

As in most libel cases, the allegedly defamatory statement in the *Sullivan* case was not in dispute. On March 29, 1960, the *New York Times* published an advertisement by the Committee to Defend Martin Luther King and the Struggle for Freedom in the South. The ad listed the names of the officers of the committee and its address, and asked for financial contributions. L.B. Sullivan was a commissioner of the City of Montgomery, Alabama, whose duties included supervision of the police department. He was not mentioned by name in the advertisement, but he claimed that mention of the police referred to him. Moreover, out of the ten paragraphs in the advertisement, only the third and a part of the sixth paragraphs were the basis of Sullivan's claim of libel. The *Times* appealed the verdict of the Alabama Court. These paragraphs read as follows:

Third Paragraph: In Montgomery, Alabama, after students sang "My Country, Tis of Three" on the State Capitol Steps, their leaders were expelled from school, and truckloads of police armed with shotguns and teargas ringed the Alabama State College Campus. When the entire student body protested to state authorities by refusing to re-register, their dining hall was padlocked in an attempt to starve them into submission.

Sixth Paragraph: Again and again the Southern violators have answered Dr. King's peaceful protests with intimidation and violence. They have bombed his home almost killing his wife and child. They have assaulted his person. They have arrested him seven times—for "speeding," "loitering" and similar "offenses." And now they have charged him with "perjury"—a felony under which they could imprison him for ten years . . . .

As the Court related in its opinion, Sullivan claimed that he was being accused of "ringing" the campus with police.

He further claimed that the paragraph would be read as imputing to the police, and hence to him, the padlocking of the dining hall in order to starve the students into submission. As to the sixth paragraph, he contended that since arrests are ordinarily made by the police, the statement: "They have arrested [Dr. King] seven times" would be read as referring to him; he further contended that the "They" who did the arresting would be equated with the "they" who committed the other described acts and with the "Southern violators." Thus, he argued, the paragraph would be read as accusing the Montgomery police, and hence him, of answering Dr. King's protests with "intimidation and violence," bombing his home, assaulting his person, and charging him with perjury. Respondent and six other Montgomery residents testified that they read some or all of the statements as referring to him in his capacity as Commissioner.

As the Court stated, "some of the statements contained in the two paragraphs were not accurate descriptions of events which occurred in Montgomery." These inaccuracies did not substantially alter the facts or change the gravamen of the complaint. If the ad had correctly reported that Dr. King had been arrested four times instead of seven, as the ad stated, Sullivan would still have had the same legal claims. The Court also pointed out that the committee paid $1,800 for the ad and that approximately 394 copies of the edition of the *Times* containing the advertisement were circulated in Alabama. Of these, about 34 copies were distributed in Montgomery County. The total circulation of the *Times* for that day was approximately 650,000 copies.

Sullivan did not claim that he had suffered any pecuniary damage. Under the common law, that was not necessary. There were many legal grounds on which the verdict could have been reversed without raising the constitutional issue of First Amendment rights. But, this was a particularly appealing vehicle for a bold statement. Dr. King was a national folk hero. The lawsuit was preposterous, and the verdict outrageous. The Court might have held that the press is not responsible for the content of a paid advertisement that is not scandalous or libelous on its face. The printing of an advertisement or the reporting of a statement by another as a news item, even though libelous, could have been held to be privileged. The contrary view would require the press to censor ads and refrain from reporting newsworthy comments. The tortured identification of Sullivan with the actions of the police was unnecessary. The Court could have held that the ad was not "of and concerning" him. Under such a reading Sullivan would have had no standing to complain. The Court might also have held that, given the temper of the times in Montgomery, Alabama, the statement did not hold Sullivan up to contumely and ridicule in his community. He might also have been held to be libel-proof with respect to this statement.

Two other well-established principles of general law also militated against the verdict. The award was clearly excessive and could have been reduced to nominal damages. The Court might well have held that because of the minute fraction of a percent of papers distributed in Montgomery that the *Times* was not doing business in Alabama and, therefore, could not be sued in that state. The action should have been brought in New York.

The Court, however, chose this occasion to enunciate new law. For more than a century, the Supreme Court had repeatedly declared that libel was *not* protected by the First Amendment. The Court did not forthrightly declare that all libel was protected. Instead it created two new exceptions to the law of defamation: first, the law as applied to public officials—later expanded to include public figures—is different from the law applicable to all others; and second, with respect to public figures the plaintiff must prove that a defamatory statement, even if untrue, was made with "actual malice." Thus the old law of defamation, as rewritten by the United States Supreme Court in *New York Times* v. *Sullivan,* was as follows:

> The constitutional guarantees require, we think, a federal rule that prohibits a public official from recovering damages for a defamatory falsehood relating to his official conduct unless he proves that the statement was made with "actual malice"—that is, with knowledge that it was false or with reckless disregard of whether it was false or not.

The most striking doctrinal change wrought by the *New York Times* case was the statement for the first time in any opinion that libel is not outside the ambit of the First Amendment. The Court declared, "We hold today that the Constitution delimits a State's power to award damages for libel in actions brought by public officials against critics of their official conduct. . . . We consider that the proof presented to show actual malice lacks the convincing clarity which the constitutional standard demands . . . ." For this declaration, the opinion has received fulsome encomia from those who subscribe to the belief that freedom of the press is a significant and valuable right. It must be noted, however, that Justices Black and Douglas in their concurring opinion stated that in their view, ". . . the *Times* had an absolute, unconditional constitutional right to publish" the advertisement. Justice Goldberg, with whom Justice Douglas joined, objected to the "actual malice" standard established by the Court, declaring:

> The Court thus rules that the Constitution gives citizens and newspapers a "conditional privilege," immunizing nonmalicious misstatements of fact regarding the official conduct of a government officer . . . in my view, the First and Fourteenth Amendments to the Constitution afford to the citizen and to the press an absolute, unconditional privilege to criticize official conduct. . . .

Sullivan was unquestionably a public official. The limitation of the holding to criticisms of public officials imported a new concept into the law of libel. Under the common law, there was no differentiation between defamation of public officials and other persons. As stated by Blackstone, the common law position was that: [Libels] . . . are malicious defamations of any person . . . made public by either printing, writing, signs, or pictures, in order to provoke him to wrath, or expose him to public hatred, contempt and ridicule . . . it is immaterial with respect to the essence of libel whether the matter of it be true or false. . . .[25]

Under American law, truth was a defense to libel. But the "actual malice" test created another new and troublesome doctrine. Liability under this rule no longer depend upon whether the statement is true or false but on the state of mind of the author. This is a far more elusive standard than truth and has led to probing the minds of writers, editors, and producers. It has permitted plaintiffs to examine editorial decisions and review the files of defendants. The privacy of writers and editorial boards has been legally invaded by plaintiffs seeking to prove the recklessness of the defendants.[26]

After reading all the subsequent decisions of the Supreme Court in First Amendment cases, including the dissenting and concurring opinions, the only conclusion one can draw with certainty is that the

Court is hopelessly fragmented. The members of the Court have rarely been able to agree and, on occasion, have been unable to command a majority to adhere to a single opinion. Criticisms by the several justices in dissenting and concurring opinions have been scathing. For example, Justices Brennan, Marshall, Blackmun and Stevens, in a dissenting opinion in *Dun & Bradstreet* v. *Greenmoss* noted: "Without explaining what is a 'matter of public concern,' the plurality opinion proceeds to serve up a smorgasbord of reasons why the speech at issue here is not . . . ."[27]

Justice White protested in a dissenting opinion in *Gertz* v. *Robert Welch,* "With a flourish of the pen, the Court also discards the prevailing rule in libel and slander actions that punitive damages may be awarded on the classic grounds of common law malice . . . ."[28] Justice Brennan, dissenting in *Time, Inc.* v. *Firestone,* declared that the majority opinion "savages the cherished values of the First Amendment."[29]

Regardless of their disagreements as to the law and irrespective of the factual differences in the cases before the Court, in every subsequent decision, all members of the Court have turned to *New York Times* v. *Sullivan* as the seminal and binding declaration of the law.

A few striking developments in the law must be noted. Sullivan was a public official and the actual malice doctrine as enunciated applied only to public officials. In a pair of cases, *Curtis Publishing Co.* v. *Butts* and *Walker* v. *Associated Press,*[30] the Court promulgated the vague category of public figure holding that such plaintiffs must also prove actual malice. Retired General Edwin A. Walker was a well-known individual strongly opposed to federal intervention in racial disputes. He had been in command of the federal troops during the school desegregation confrontation in Little Rock, Arkansas, in 1957. He sued the Associated Press in the Texas courts seeking $2,000,000 in compensatory and punitive damages based on a news dispatch giving an eyewitness account of the riot at the University of Mississippi in 1962, arising out of federal efforts to enforce a court decree ordering the enrollment of a Negro student, James Meredith. The report stated that Walker had taken command of the crowd and led a charge against federal marshals. The jury returned a verdict of $500,000 in compensatory damages and $300,-000 in punitive damages. The Supreme Court reversed, holding that the AP correspondent was trustworthy and competent. The trial court had found that the AP was not negligent. The Supreme Court declared that Walker was a "private citizen" at that time. Although the decision was desirable, one must question whether the holding, without discussion, that Walker was a private figure was appropriate in view of his past history and the Court's finding that he "could fairly be deemed a man of some political prominence." If there had been substantial inaccuracies in the dispatch, the Court's failure to treat Walker as a public figure would have resulted in a different outcome.

Butts was the athletic director at the University of Georgia and head football coach. An article in the *Saturday Evening Post* stated that Butts gave the secret plays of the Georgia team to a rival, the University of Alabama. Georgia lost the game. The jury returned a verdict of $60,000 in general damages and $3,000,000 in punitive damages. Although the University of Georgia was admittedly a public, tax-supported institution and Butts was the coach, his salary was paid by funds raised by the alumni. The Court, therefore, concluded that he was not a public official. Many "employees" of public educational institutions are paid in whole or in part from grants by foundations. Nonetheless, they are considered to be members of the faculty. Butts certainly worked for the university and as a "borrowed employee" could have been deemed to be a public official. But as a result of this hair-splitting analysis of who is a "public official," the Court created a new category: "public figure," and ruled:

> We consider and would hold that a "public figure" who is not a public official may also recover damages for a defamatory falsehood whose substance makes substantial danger to reputation apparent, on a showing of highly unreasonable conduct constituting an extreme departure from the standards of investigation and reporting ordinarily adhered to by responsible publishers.

"Public figure" was defined as occurring either by status, as was the case with Butts, or with respect to Walker "by his purposeful activity amounting to a thrusting of his personality into the 'vortex' of an important public controversy." Both the category and the definitions created more confusion in succeeding litigation. The Court found for Butts and against Walker.

Although there was no evidence of the kind of outrageous behavior the common law ordinarily requires in order to justify an award of punitive damages, the Court did not strike the damages awarded to Butts. Punitive damages in enormous amounts continue to be demanded and awarded in libel cases without proof of spite, ill will, or outrageous conduct. There was little proof of damage to Butts as a result of the article. But the Court affirmed the law of "presumed damages." Both these doctrines fueled the impetus to sue for libel.

The Court soon found the public figure test too limiting and established still another standard. In *Rosenbloom* v. *Metromedia*, [31] the plaintiff was a magazine dealer. A spot newscast announced his arrest for selling allegedly pornographic materials. He and his business associates were described as "smut distributors" and "girlie book peddlers." Rosenbloom was subsequently acquitted of the charges and sued the radio station. The jury returned a verdict for the plaintiff and awarded $25,000 in general damages and $725,000 in punitive damages, which was reduced by the trial court to $250,000. The Supreme Court reversed, creating another legal category of protected comment, i.e., "all discussion and communication involving matters of public or general concern, without regard to whether the persons involved are famous or anonymous." Three justices concurred and three dissented.

Despite the much discussed demise of the public figure/private figure test, it has surfaced again in several cases with amazing results. In 1974, just ten years after *New York Times* v. *Sullivan,* the Supreme Court decided *Gertz* v. *Welch.* [32] This case involved a clearly libelous, intentionally harmful and demonstrably false statement, with no legal or factual justification. The plaintiff, a lawyer in private practice, represented the family of a murder victim in a civil suit against a policeman, Richard Nuccio, who had been convicted of murder. An article entitled "FRAME-Up: Richard Nuccio and the War on Police" was published in *American Opinion,* a monthly described by the Supreme Court as being an "outlet for the views of the John Birch Society." Robert Welch was the head of the organization that published *American Opinion.* The article contained numerous inaccuracies. It labeled Gertz a "Leninist" and a "Communist fronter." It charged that the National Lawyers Guild, of which Gertz had been an officer, was a Communist organization that "probably did more than any other outfit to plan the Communist attack on the Chicago police during the 1968 Democratic Convention." Gertz sued Welch. The jury awarded $50,000 to Gertz. The District Court set aside the verdict and the Court of Appeals affirmed on the ground that the plaintiff had failed to show by clear and convincing evidence that the defendant had acted with "actual malice" as defined in *New York Times* v. *Sullivan.*

The Supreme Court held that there was no evidence that the publisher had cause to be aware of the probable falsity of these statements. The majority opinion declared, "The principal issue in this case is whether a newspaper or broadcaster that publishes defamatory falsehoods about an individual who is neither a public official nor a public figure may claim a constitutional privilege against liability for the injury inflicted by those statements." Of course, the issue could have been framed differently. The Court might well have asked whether one who publishes a statement defamatory on its face acts negligently in failing to investigate the truth of the charges. Instead the Court declared apodictically ". . . there is no constitutional value in false statements of fact." The Court then weighed the competing interests of First Amendment freedoms and redressing wrongful injury. Because Gertz was not a public figure and "did not thrust himself into the vortex of this public issue," the Court held that the *New York Times* standard was inapplicable. It reversed and remanded the case for a new trial to determine whether "a jury was allowed to impose liability without fault and was permitted to presume damages without proof of injury." There were four dissenting opinions and one concurrence. The second jury also found in favor of Gertz.

Two years later in *Time, Inc.* v. *Firestone,* [33] the Supreme Court again reexamined the public/private figure rule and its implications. The divorced wife of the heir to the wealthy Firestone family sued *Time* magazine for publishing an account of the divorce and recovered a judgment of $100,000. The case had been widely reported in the Florida press while the litigation was proceeding, and seamy charges were aired. The brief item read as follows:

DIVORCED. By Russell A. Firestone, Jr., 41, heir to the tire fortune: Mary Alice Sullivan Firestone, 32, his third wife; a one-time Palm Beach schoolteacher; on grounds of extreme cruelty and adultery; after six years of marriage, one son; in West Palm Beach, Florida. The 17-month intermittent trial produced enough testimony of extramarital adventures on both sides, said the judge, "to make Dr. Freud's hair curl."

The alleged falsehood was the statement that a divorce was granted on the grounds of "adultery." The Court held that the plaintiff was not a public figure, that her resort to legal process was not "voluntary." Truthful accounts of litigation contained in official court records are privileged, the Court held. The Court narrowed the privilege of reporting judicial proceedings, declaring that the details "would add almost nothing toward advancing the uninhibited debate on public issues thought to provide principal support for the decision in *New York Times.*"

The Supreme Court then made pivotal the issue of absolute accuracy of the report. Mr. Firestone alleged adultery as one of the grounds for divorce in his counterclaim. The judgment read: "counterclaim for divorce be and the same is hereby granted." Admitting that the decree was unclear, the Court held that this "does not license [*Time*] to choose from among several conceivable interpretations the one most damaging to [Mrs. Firestone]." The Supreme Court found no difficulty with an award of $100,000 in presumed damages although there was no evidence that the plaintiff was damaged in any way. The matter was remanded to the Florida courts to determine whether there was "fault" on the part of *Time* under Florida law even though the error in the report, according to the Supreme Court was "clear and convincing evidence of the negligence" of *Time.* The Supreme Court did not establish a standard of fault but left that issue to the state court. The public versus private figure test that was the critical issue in the *Firestone* case was still the subject of dissension among the justices in 1985 and 1986.[34]

The remnants of the *New York Times* holding have been further shredded by new concepts of the "commercial motives" of the publisher. Gerald Ford's book, *A Time to Heal,* was to be published by Harper & Row, which contracted with *Time* for an exclusive prepublication excerpt of 7,500 words from the book for a $25,000 fee. Prior to publication, the *Nation* published an article discussing the Ford book and, in particular, the Nixon pardon. Three hundred words were quoted from the 200,000-word book. Harper & Row sued the *Nation*[35] for copyright infringement. Here there could be no question that Ford was a public figure and that the matter in question involved a serious public issue and that publication would further the promotion of "uninhibited debate," one of the criteria in *New York Times* v. *Sullivan.* Instead of deciding the case on First Amendment issues, the majority held that this was not a "fair use" of copyrighted material. The Court admitted that under the law, facts and news are not copyrightable. Even if the copyright act compelled such a conclusion, such interpretation might well have been found to violate the First Amendment rights of the *Nation.* The public interest in Ford's discussion of the Nixon pardon was totally ignored.

Irrelevant facts and pejorative language color the majority opinion of Justice O'Connor. The Court pointed out that *Time* had cancelled the contract after publication by the *Nation* and refused to pay the balance of $12,500. This was not a suit by Harper & Row or Gerald Ford for breach of contract, a remedy that was available to them. The Court declared that the *Nation*'s possession of the material was "not authorized," although in the *Pentagon Papers* case, it had refused to consider the means by which the papers were obtained. The Court also noted that two years were spent "producing and marketing the [Ford's] book." Whether Ford wrote the book himself in a week or whether a staff of researchers spent a decade working on it was also immaterial. The *Nation* article was described as "piracy of verbatim quotation for the purpose of 'scooping' the authorized first serialization." Piracy is a harsh word to use with respect to a legitimate periodical. "Scooping" is not illegal. All news media and periodicals attempt to present stories before their rivals do. The Court then declared: "Fair use distinguishes between a true scholar and a chiseler who infringes a work for personal profit." The standing of an author either as a writer of potboilers or a Pulitzer Prize winner is irrelevant to First Amendment rights. Should the rights of the *Nation* be different depending upon whether the article was written by a scholar or a journalist? Courts will be faced with extraordinary problems if they must decide who is a true scholar entitled to protection and who is not. The profit motive of the *Nation* stressed by the majority opinion also raises difficult questions for the courts. Many books and periodicals are written with some expectation or at least some hope of profit. Should they be excluded from the protections of the First Amendment? Ford and Harper & Row certainly expected to make a profit on the book. One is reminded of Justice Holmes's irrelevant and pejorative remarks about Schenk.

The implicit intermingling of money and speech permeates this decision and raises new hurdles for authors and publishers to overcome in asserting First Amendment rights. In several decisions of the United States Supreme Court, the equation of speech and money was made explicit in cases having nothing to do with the rights of subjects and authors. But these decisions significantly contributed to the peculiar and unprecedented use of the First Amendment to protect property rights in the guise of free speech. Conversely, in other contexts, commercial interests of subject and author have been used to limit free speech.

The Supreme Court has held that statutory limitations on the expenditure of campaign funds by individuals and independent polit-

ical committees to further a candidate's election violate the First
Amendment, declaring "A restriction on the amount of money a
person or group can spend on political communication during a
campaign necessarily reduces the quantity of expression by restricting the number of issues discussed, the depth of their exploration,
and the size of the audience reached."[36] In another case, without any
discussion of facts or the long history of political corruption leading
to the enactment of the Federal Election Campaign Act, the Court
concluded that there is insufficient "compelling governmental interest in preventing corruption" to support a finding in favor of the
constitutionality of the act under the "rigorous" standard of review
required when the First Amendment is involved.[37] Justice White, in
a dissenting opinion joined by Brennan and Marshall, declared, "I
cannot accept the cynic's 'money talks' as a proposition of constitutional law."

The relationship of money and speech and the commercial or
profit motives of subject and author is a recurring theme in the
contemporary struggle between subjects and authors. Subjects claim
property rights in themselves, their life stories, and their performances. They assert protected property rights to exploit themselves
to the exclusion of authors. Some subjects assert a right to be let
alone as a protected property right. Authors claim a property interest
in their own works to the exclusion of the claims of subjects.

In subsequent chapters, recently developed rights of publicity,
privacy, and biography that have been grafted on to the law of libel
are discussed. They have no counterpart in the history of libel prior
to the twentieth century. Nor does the notion of money as an attribute of speech have legal antecedents. These new concepts have been
commingled with all the old doctrines and subjected case by case to
refinements of definition of public and private figure, actual malice,
public interest, and fault that the courts have frantically been import-
ing into the law of libel.

The common law of libel was a hybrid, unsatisfactory doctrine for
centuries in English law. In the United States, the failure of the
courts to recognize the supremacy of the First Amendment led to
legally sanctioned censorship and punishment for seditious libel. In
the late twentieth century, confusion has been compounded. Old
doctrines of malice and presumed damages prevail even though they
were obsolete centuries ago. Despite the many judicial innovations,
libel remains an anachronism that is ill adapted to American mores
and the needs of contemporary life.

·III·

Against the Grain

It is agayns the process of nature.

—GEOFFREY CHAUCER

MOST complaints about civil litigation focus on delays and expenses of trial. Criticisms of libel law, by contrast, are focused on substance, the legal doctrines that govern who wins and who loses these cases. Diane Daniels, counsel for *Newsweek,* perceptively commented that the law of libel is counter-intuitive. It goes against the grain of the common law and common sense. The law violates those rules and procedures that prevail in most other cases, rules and procedures that American lawyers and the public at large believe are fair and reasonable.*

To understand why libel law creates so many problems, it is helpful to compare the progress of an ordinary tort case with that of a libel suit—from pleadings through verdict—under American law as it was in the first half of the twentieth century and as it is believed to be in 1986. The term "believed to be" is used advisedly because from day to day and state to state there is no certainty as to what the latest statement of the law is. The significant differences explain

---

*A Report of a Special Committee of the American Bar Association notes ". . . the continuing role of tort law as an epicenter of jurisprudence, not simply as a set of guides and standards for the decisions of many thousands of private lawsuits, but as a reflection of how American society feels about justice at dozens of focal points of social tension" (ABA, "Towards a Jurisprudence of Injury: The Continuing Creation of Substantive Justice in American Tort Law" 1984). The signal problem of libel law today is its failure to reflect American attitudes toward justice.

to a large extent the general dissatisfaction on the part of the legal profession and the public with the law of libel.

Libel is generally agreed to be a tort. A tort is a wrong done by one party to another. It covers a multitude of noncriminal harms occurring to individuals, corporations, associations, animals, and real and personal property. Tort differs from crime in several ways. Under American law, crimes are defined by statute. Torts are based on common law as well as a few state statutes. A crime, except for minor offenses, requires proof of an intent to do harm or an intent to violate the law. The same act may be both a crime and a tort; for example, striking a pedestrian with an automobile. If the driver violates a statute by going faster than the speed limit or going through a red light, that constitutes a violation of law and the state may prosecute the driver. The standard of guilt in a criminal case is proof beyond a reasonable doubt. The penalties may be suspension of the driver's license, a fine and/or imprisonment or probation, and in some states limited compensation to the victim of the accident. The driver's action may also constitute a tort for which the victim can recover damages in a civil lawsuit for all harm suffered. Similarly, if a blow is struck with the intent of harming the person it is a crime. But if the blow is struck unintentionally but negligently, it is a tort.

An essential element of all crimes is the evil intent of the wrong-doer. The intent may be real or it may be an implication supplied by law. If Jones willfully and intentionally shoots Smith, Jones is guilty of a crime. If Jones fires the gun intending to hit Clark but by mistake hits Smith, the law will supply the intent with the presumption that malice, or ill will, follows the bullet. Jones is still guilty of a crime. The essential difference between a crime and a tort is that the criminal has an evil intent and the tort-feasor does not. A tort is committed negligently.

Authors who write libelous statements do intend to write what they have, in fact, written. There are some few instances, as in fiction, when the author had no intent to refer to the subject but inadvertently used the actual name of a real individual. But the vast majority of libel cases involve intentional and knowing statements by the author. In almost all other torts, the harm was done unintentionally. The driver did not intend to hit the pedestrian. He may have been watching the traffic light and inadvertently knocked down a pedestrian. If he was careless and failed to see a person in his path, he is held responsible in tort. Similarly in product liability cases, drug manufacturers do not intend to cause death or illness to the purchasers of their products. Except for the most extraordinary situations, they are not guilty of crimes but they are responsible in civil damages if the product was defective.

The most common tort action is for personal injuries negligently inflicted. Such cases provide a simple, well-understood example of general principles of tort law. Following an accident, the injured party files a complaint against the alleged wrongdoer asserting the following: the facts giving rise to the injury, the allegedly wrongful conduct of the defendant, the injury to the plaintiff, the causal relation between the wrongdoing and the harm done, and the extent of the damages. A typical complaint states that on a specified day and time at a specific place the plaintiff was struck by the defendant's automobile, that the defendant was operating the vehicle in a negligent manner, that the plaintiff suffered certain injuries, that these injuries were caused by the defendant's negligent conduct, and that as a result the plaintiff incurred certain damages, including out-of-pocket expenses, past and future earnings, pain, suffering and loss of life's pleasures.

The defendant must then file an answer or other pleading admitting or denying each and every one of the plaintiff's averments. The defendant, for example, may admit that there was a collision but deny that he or she was negligent. The defendant may deny that the plaintiff's injuries were the result (in legal language, "were not proximately caused by") the actions of the defendant. The defendant may also deny that the plaintiff suffered any injuries or that the damages, if any, were not so severe as claimed.

The plaintiff must establish by the preponderance of the evidence all these elements in order to win the lawsuit and recover damages. If the plaintiff fails to prove any of the essential facts that form the basis of the complaint, a verdict will be entered in favor of the defendant.

The gravamen of every complaint in a tort action is that the defendant was at fault and that as a result the plaintiff suffered damages. Fault in most civil cases is measured by the time-tested "reasonable man" standard. The jury or the judge is required to decide whether the defendant acted as a reasonable person would have acted under the circumstances. Juries and judges have little difficulty in applying this standard. They themselves are reasonable people. They put themselves in the shoes of the defendant and decide how they would have acted in such a situation. If the defendant was

driving on a narrow street in a densely populated residential neigh-
borhood on a sunny afternoon, a reasonable person would exercise
extreme caution and look carefully for children who might be play-
ing in the street. Failure to proceed very cautiously is unreasonable.
On the other hand, if the defendant was driving on a four-lane
highway in the country, it is unreasonable to expect children to run
across the road, and the defendant would not be held to such a high
standard of care. The plaintiff must prove that his or her injuries
were caused or aggravated by the defendant's wrongful conduct.

The plaintiff must also prove the damages that he or she claims
to have suffered as a result of the accident. This is usually done by
presenting the testimony of a doctor who describes the nature and
extent of the plaintiff's injuries. Each item of damages for which
recovery is allowed must be proved. These items include medical
expenses, loss of earnings, future loss of earnings, pain, suffering,
impairment of activities, disfigurement, and loss of life's pleasures.
Underlying these rules is the common sense principle that one who
hales another into court should have to prove all the elements of the
claim, including the amount of damages suffered.

In a libel action, prior to *New York Times* v. *Sullivan* and its
progeny, the plaintiff's complaint had to contain only these averments: (1) that the defendant published a defamatory statement, (2)
that the statement was of and concerning the plaintiff, and (3) that
the plaintiff's reputation was injured thereby.

In most cases, the statement and its publication were proved by
submitting a copy of the newspaper, a magazine, or a transcript of
the broadcast. With respect to an article in the press or a statement
broadcast on radio or television, publication was obvious and admitted. Usually the defamatory statement mentioned the plaintiff by
name. If it did not, the plaintiff had only to produce a witness who
would testify that he or she had read the statement and understood
it to refer to the plaintiff. It was presumed that reputation was
harmed. Damages were awarded without any proof of harm or loss.

A complaint in libel usually contained language alleging that the
statement was false, malicious, scandalous, and libelous. But, the
plaintiff did not have to prove malice, falsity, or the scandalous
nature of the statement. Rather the defendant, in some jurisdictions,
had the burden of proving either that the statement was true or that
it was privileged. The defendant could also rebut the presumption of
culpability for making a defamatory statement by proving that he or
she acted without knowledge that the statement was, in fact, defama-

tory. For example, to state that the plaintiff was a Negro was considered to be defamatory. The defendant could prove that he or she believed that the plaintiff really was a Negro and, hence, had no knowledge that the statement was defamatory even though the plaintiff was, in fact, a Caucasian. Such instances of lack of knowledge were rare.

The most common and difficult defense was truth. In some jurisdictions, the real burden of proof was thus shifted from the plaintiff to the defendant, contrary to the rule in all other civil actions. If a defamatory statement asserted that the plaintiff had bribed a public official, the burden was not on the plaintiff to prove that it was false. The defendant had to prove that it was true.

It was and is the rule in all jurisdictions that the plaintiff does not have to prove that the defamatory statement caused any harm.* Nor does the plaintiff have to prove that he or she suffered any economic loss or any emotional trauma. These rules are contrary to the principles of law applicable in all other tort cases. They inevitably lead to results contrary to those in other lawsuits, results that often strike the average person as well as lawyers and judges as being wrong.

A hypothetical case based on a real incident illustrates the difficulties with the old law of libel and the law as recently revised by the Supreme Court.

A recent item in the press reported that movie actor Rock Hudson was suffering from AIDS.[1] There has been no report that Hudson brought a libel suit on the basis of this news story before his death. Let us assume that a similar report was published about another well-known actor, whom we shall call Simpson Stone. Stone sued the newspapers that printed the articles, the national and international news agencies, and the radio and TV stations that broadcast the report.

Under Anglo-American libel law as it was for centuries, that statement would be actionable whether it was true or false and regardless of whether the actor was injured in any way by the story. A statement that a person has a loathsome disease or has committed a crime was and still is defamatory on its face. The law assumes that

---

*Some language in recent Supreme Court opinions indicates that damages must be proved. But there has been little proof of harm in damages of hundreds of thousands of dollars that have been upheld by the Court. But see the decision of federal district judge Sarokin in Schiavone Construction Co. v. Time, Inc., 55 LW 2281 (1986) holding that a public figure may not recover damages against a media defendant absent a showing of compensable injury to reputation. The Supreme Court has not adopted this sensible rule.

such an accusation would lower the person in the estimation of the public. There is no indication in any of the cases that this definition of libel or the reasons that the statement is actionable have changed. Today compassion rather than contempt characterizes public response to the leper, those suffering from cancer, mental illness, venereal disease, and AIDS. One must ask why such statements should be actionable.

Prior to *New York Times* v. *Sullivan,* it would have been been sufficient for Stone simply to prove the publication of the statement. The defendants in some states would have had to prove the truth of the statement in order to avoid liability. Even though the defendants may have relied on information from the hospital where Stone was being treated or his doctor, that would be insufficient to relieve them of liability if, in fact, the statement was erroneous. In other jurisdictions, Stone would have had to prove that the statement was false in order to recover. If the news story had been published in a national publication or aired over national radio or TV, the rights of the parties would have depended upon the state in which the suit was filed.

Whether the plaintiff or the defendant had the burden of proof was the decisive factor in many cases. If, for example, one doctor testified that Stone did have AIDS and an equally eminent physician testified that he did not, the jury would have been instructed that they must decide whether the party who has the burden of proof has established the truth or falsity of the statement. Thus, if Stone had to prove falsity, he would probably not recover. If the defendants had to prove truth, Stone probably would recover. Juries, on the whole, are composed of sensible people. Hearing diametrically opposite testimony from two eminent doctors, their decision would turn on whether the plaintiff or the defendant had the burden of proof. Until 1986, it was unclear whether as a constitutional principle the plaintiff or the defendant had the burden of proof. But in 1986, the Supreme Court held that, contrary to precedent and the law of several states, a private plaintiff does have the burden of proof of falsity in libel cases.* This is another example of the slow, case by case decisions of the Supreme Court bringing the law of libel into closer conformity to general common law principles.

If an action were brought on the basis of this news story in 1986,

---

*The Supreme Court held in Philadelphia Newspapers, Inc. v. Hepps, 54 LW 4373 (1986), that the plaintiff has the burden of proving falsity although the law of Pennsylvania in which the action arose and where it was tried, placed the burden on the defendant.

there would be a multitude of questions the court or jury would have to decide other than truth or falsity. The statement that Stone had AIDS would still be considered defamatory even though it is highly questionable that the story would lower Stone's reputation in the esteem of anyone.

Recovery might well turn on whether Stone was a public or a private figure.* This is not an easy question. The defendants, claiming First Amendment rights, would try to show that Stone was a public figure. The mere fact that he was well known to millions of people would be insufficient. It might be necessary, or at least advisable, for the defendants to show that Stone had given many interviews, that his life and activities had been written up in magazines and other publications in order to prove that he had thrust himself into the public eye. Stone would assert that he was not a public figure simply because he was a well-known actor. Stone would also argue that even if he was a public figure, the state of his health should not be held to be a matter "of public concern." To date there is no reliable legal standard under which this question of public concern can be decided. Stone might also claim that his privacy had been invaded. Whether a public figure has any right to privacy is another issue that has not been definitively decided.

Assuming that the plaintiff was found to be a public figure, the issue of truth or falsity would fade in significance. The issue would be the defendants' reckless disregard for truth or falsity. The judge or jury would have to decide, not whether the reporter was negligent, but whether he or she believed the statement to be true.

Let us assume that all doctors agreed that Stone did not have AIDS, but that at the time the report was issued, a resident had misdiagnosed Stone's illness and erroneously called it AIDS. Let us assume further that the reporter had checked with the hospital and learned from a spokesperson that Stone had indeed been diagnosed as having AIDS, but that later that day Stone's own doctor, a specialist, had examined him and decided that Stone did not have AIDS but was suffering from a different illness. Assume also that the editor of the city desk knew Stone personally and doubted the diagnosis. He questioned the reporter who said that the diagnosis had been confirmed by the hospital.

Assume that prior to the trial, Stone's lawyers subpoenaed the

---

*See the tortured reasoning of the New Jersey Supreme Court in Sisler v. Gannett Co. Inc., 55 LW 2241 (1986), in avoiding the results of the public/private figure test established by the Supreme Court.

reporter's notes and the editor's notes. Both were deposed. The editor testified truthfully as to his doubts about the story. The judge or jury would then have to decide whether the editor acted with "actual malice," that is reckless disregard for truth or falsity.

No matter how these arcane issues were decided, it is reasonably certain that the following questions would not be put to the court or jury and that they would be irrelevant: (1) Was the newspaper negligent in reporting the story? (2) If so, did the negligence cause the plaintiff harm? (3) If it did cause harm, what, if any, damages did the plaintiff suffer as a result of the report?

As of this writing, it is clear that the plaintiff must prove some "fault" on the part of the defendant under the appropriate state law. What constitutes fault and the degree of proof necessary to establish fault depend upon the vagaries of state law.

A public figure must prove, "actual malice," that is the defendants' mental state of recklessness. It is a peculiarly onerous burden. In other tort actions, a plaintiff is required to prove objective facts: the occurrence of an incident and the defendant's negligence. The quantum of proof is the preponderance of the evidence or clear and convincing evidence. A plaintiff seeking monetary damages for a wrong that is not willfully committed is not held to the standard of proof "beyond a reasonable doubt" that prevails in criminal cases. This difference in proof between civil and criminal cases is sensible. It has stood the test of time. A person accused of crime who, if convicted, may lose his liberty or even his life should be protected against unfounded accusations and should not be subjected to such severe consequences unless the finder of fact, either the judge or jury, is really convinced of the defendant's guilt. Moreover, when punitive damages are claimed in tort cases, other than libel, the plaintiff is required to prove outrageous conduct, an objective standard based on what the defendant did, not the defendant's state of mind.

The most dramatic difference between libel law and all other civil law is the question of damages. If the jury found that the editor acted with "actual malice," even though the reporter was not negligent, a verdict would be returned in favor of Stone. Assume also that the following day all the defendants published a correction and that the news that Stone did not have AIDS was as widely disseminated as the earlier report. This would not relieve the defendants of liability. Although sensible juries might conclude that Stone had not been harmed, he would still be entitled to recover damages. Stone would not have to prove that his reputation had been harmed in any way, or that he had suffered any economic losses. A jury would not be instructed as to the measure of damages or how they should be computed. Stone might win a verdict of $1 or $1,000,000. The trial judge would equally be without standards or rules in deciding whether to reduce the verdict. A jury might also give Stone a few million more in punitive damages.

Compare Stone with Martha Loring* who was struck by a drunken driver as she was crossing the street. She suffered a broken leg, face lacerations, and bruises. She was out of work for three weeks and returned to her job on crutches because she needed the money. The jury was instructed that she could recover for only three weeks' lost wages, medical expenses, and pain and suffering. The doctors agreed that her facial scars would heal and be imperceptible. No recovery was allowed for disfigurement.

Let us compare Loring's case with two typical libel cases. Willingboro* is a well-known, wealthy contractor who is the successful bidder on many public projects. He is a heavy contributor to the political party in power. The press reported that according to a "reliable source," Willingboro had ties with organized crime. Watkins,* is a city employee whose job is to inspect maintenance of city property. He earns $35,000 a year. His name has never appeared in the papers. To the people of his community he is anonymous. The same source reported that Watkins also had ties with organized crime.

Both Willingboro and Watkins sue for libel. It is reasonably clear that Willingboro will win unless the press can show real involvement with criminal activities. Again Willingboro will not have to prove damages, even though most of his friends and acquaintances are well-known crime figures. He may recover a verdict of at least six figures. Watkins who was not a civil service employee has lost his job. Watkins will lose unless he can prove "actual malice" on the part of the press. In both instances, the reporter simply repeated a rumor without verifying it. He was clearly negligent as was the editor in failing to require some corroboration. But neither negligence on the part of the defendant nor actual losses suffered by the plaintiff will be issues submitted to the jury. The test of public versus private figure will control the standards by which the press will be judged.

Damage awards in many libel cases shock the public, terrify the media, and cause the courts great difficulty. In every other branch of American civil law, a plaintiff must prove some dereliction on the part of the defendant and that the plaintiff was harmed as a result

*These are fictional names of real plaintiffs.

of the act or failure to act on the part of the defendant, and the extent of the injuries suffered, both economic and emotional.

A simple everyday example illustrates the operation of these basic rules. A common fact situation giving rise to a tort claim is a rear-end automobile collision. Obviously, if one driver runs into the rear of another car, the driver of the striking vehicle is at fault unless the struck vehicle stopped suddenly without warning. If the striking vehicle simply hits the bumper of the other car and no damage occurs to the vehicle or the driver and passengers, there will be no recovery against the driver of the striking vehicle. Clearly the driver is at fault. No one should run into another car. But the law of damages is sensibly designed not to punish the negligent wrongdoer, but to require the wrongdoer to pay for the harm he or she has done. As the language of the law aptly puts it, damages are to replace the losses of the injured person, not to give a windfall or a bonus and not to penalize the unintentional wrongdoer. The plaintiff must prove by credible evidence the extent of his or her losses.

This is also true in the law of contracts. A vendor agrees to sell the buyer certain goods on a certain day for a set price. If the seller fails to deliver the goods, the contract is breached. But if the same goods could have been purchased at the same price on the open market on that day the buyer did not suffer any loss. Even though the seller was wrong in breaching the contract, the seller is not punished by being forced to pay money to the buyer, and the buyer is not given a windfall for nonexistent losses.

In libel actions, both harm to the person defamed and damages are presumed. The plaintiff is not required to prove either harm or damages. In libel suits, juries do occasionally return verdicts that accord with common sense and fairness, despite the law. John R. Lakian, an unsuccessful candidate for Governor of Massachusetts, brought a libel action against the *Boston Globe* for publishing an article stating that the *Globe* "found what appears to be a pattern of discrepancies between what he [Lakian] says and what the records show about his upbringing, schooling, military service and business career." The jury found that Lakian had been libeled by five paragraphs of the article, and that with respect to three paragraphs the *Globe* had "knowledge of its falsity." The jury refused to award damages.[2]

Jury deliberations are secret. But one can infer that the jury probably found that Lakian was untruthful and enlarged on his past history and concluded that such a person was simply not entitled to recover for relatively minor misstatements of fact. The jury perhaps unconsciously relied on the tried and true equitable doctrine of "clean hands" that prohibits recovery against a defendant who is a wrongdoer if the plaintiff is also a wrongdoer.

In countless other suits, however, juries have awarded substantial verdicts to plaintiffs who failed to prove any damages. What harm did Mrs. Firestone suffer from a small item in *Time* magazine stating that her husband had been awarded a divorce on the grounds of adultery? Far more intimate and scandalous information about her had been published in the local papers with respect to the charges and countercharges made by the battling spouses. But the jury awarded her $100,000.

The fear of substantial verdicts often induces media defendants to pay large sums in settlement of libel suits even when it was reasonably clear that the plaintiff had not suffered any provable damages. A typical settlement involved the former mayor of Philadelphia, William J. Green, who sued a radio station because it falsely announced in several flash newscasts that he was under investigation by the United States Department of Justice for alleged wrongdoing. This was a serious charge. It was defamatory on its face. If untrue, it was actionable. Had he been seeking a second term of office, it might have affected the outcome of the election. At the time the charges were made, however, Green had already decided not to run for a second term. He immediately brought suit. The press and all the electronic media carried the news of his suit and the fact that the charges were untrue. The denial was more widely publicized than the false charge. The case was settled for a reported $250,000. What damage did he suffer? Had he been required to prove some loss of reputation, the defendant probably would not have settled so quickly and for so large a sum.

A verdict of $4.5 million in favor of Richard Sprague, a highly successful Philadelphia lawyer, against the *Philadelphia Inquirer* would probably not have been awarded if he had been required to prove the extent of his damages. Sprague sued over a series of articles that he claims suggest that, as first assistant district attorney ten years earlier, he had taken part in a cover-up to keep a friend's son from being accused of a man's death. In fact, his law practice boomed after all the publicity surrounding the defamation charges. His income increased, not the reverse. What damages did he suffer? The inequity of the rule of presumed damages has not been discussed by any of the justices of the Supreme Court, although there are many indications that punitive damages will soon be abolished. It appears that it would be salutary to require proof of loss for compensatory damages in libel cases in the same manner that damages must be proved in all other civil cases.

Whether punitive damages even for outrageous conduct are desirable in contemporary life in any type of action is a policy issue that might more appropriately be addressed by the legislature than by the courts.[3] It is obvious that in most cases the wrongdoer, the negligent reporter, or corporate or public employee, the person who actually was at fault and caused harm to the plaintiff, does not pay the punitive damages, no matter how grossly careless or willfully wrong his or her actions were. The burden of paying an award of punitive damages is placed on the shareholders of a corporate defendant or the taxpayers when the defendant is a public agency.

Another troubling difference between libel cases and all other tort cases is the nature of the gravamen of the complaint. In most tort cases, the basic issue in dispute is one of fact that can be proved by objective evidence. Was there an accident? Was the defendant negligent? Was the product defective?

In most cases of defamation, the allegedly false and defamatory statement is not an allegation of a single fact that can be proved by objective evidence. A statement that the plaintiff had been convicted of crime, that he had AIDS, or that he had bribed a named official at a certain time or place are facts that can be proved or disproved by objective evidence. More frequently, the plaintiff's claim is based on a statement that is a composite of fact, inference, and opinion.

The statements upon which General Westmoreland's suit was based, for example, involved complex reasons for the escalation of American military action in Vietnam. Historians will debate the underlying facts for generations and probably never reach a consensus. Forty years after President Truman ordered the dropping of atomic bombs on Hiroshima and Nagasaki, responsible, knowledgeable people in both countries are divided in their opinions as to whether Japan would have surrendered promptly if the bombs had not been dropped and whether more lives were saved than lost by the explosion of the bomb. Statements about such controversial questions are really expressions of opinion rather than statements of fact. For generations, ever since the law of libel recognized truth as a defense, it was clear that one could not be libeled by an opinion. The Supreme Court has repeatedly stated that there is no such thing as a "false opinion." Nonetheless, libel suits continue to be brought on the basis of statements that are a mixture of fact and opinion.

During the twentieth century, most aspects of the law have been gradually modernized, except the law of libel. The process of change has occurred slowly and steadily from generation to generation. Both legislatures and courts have been extraordinarily successful in adjusting the scales of justice when they were weighted too heavily in favor of one segment of society against another without destroying basic legal concepts and procedures. For example, the principle of freedom of contract, wise in itself, proved disastrous when applied to employer-employee contracts in a drastically changed labor market. When employer and employee ceased to be on an equal plane of bargaining, the notion of a willing seller of labor and a willing buyer of services striking a fair bargain in the marketplace failed abysmally. Employers, on the whole, had enormous resources, whereas individual employees who desperately needed jobs had no bargaining power. A legal fiction no longer corresponded to reality. Laws were enacted to legalize unions, establish minimum wages, and prohibit the exploitation of women and children in the workplace.

Workers' compensation laws were enacted to overcome judicially created doctrines that effectively prevented injured employees from recovering for work-related injuries. When the workplace or the machinery causing the injury was dangerous, courts had held that the employee assumed the risk of the dangerous conditions. If the injuries occurred as a result of the negligence of another employee, the injured worker was barred by the doctrine that prevented recovery for harms caused by a fellow servant, i.e., another employee. For the most part courts lagged behind public sentiment and the legislatures in overcoming anachronistic common law rules and acknowledging the constitutionality of protective legislation.

Similarly, the common law relating to the family—marriage, divorce, custody of children, and ownership of property—failed to meet the needs of the vast majority of people when the family unit ceased to be an economic enterprise, when women demanded control of their property and their earnings, and men demanded equal parental rights. Updating of the law both through legislation and litigation continues as women assert the right to control their bodies and both spouses demand the right to terminate their marriages and to obtain custody of their children.

Although the judiciary has often thwarted the will of the legislature* by interpretation and by declaring protective legislation uncon-

---

*On occasion the legislature acts to reverse rulings of the Supreme Court.

stitutional, the courts themselves initiated many necessary reforms to update the law and bring it into conformity with the needs of contemporary society. Notable judicial innovations occurred with respect to sales of goods, injuries arising from malfunction of products, and contracts and leases between parties of obviously unequal bargaining power. A number of cases recognize this inequality in the positions of the parties and interpret the rules in light of the obvious facts. A telling decision is *Fuentes* v. *Shevin.*[4] This concerned the right of vendors under installment sales contracts to repossess the goods on an alleged default in payment without a hearing. The printed contracts supplied by the vendor contained a waiver of hearing. The Supreme Court dismissed the vendors' reliance on the contract with the following comment:

> The purported waiver provision [allowing seller to repossess goods] was a printed part of a form sales contract and a necessary condition of the sale. The appellees [vendors] made no showing that even the appellants [buyers] were actually aware or made aware of the significance of the fine print now relied upon as a waiver of constitutional rights.

The law of contracts was not impaired. Instead, the long-standing principle that there must be a knowing and voluntary relinquishment of rights was applied to test the validity of this particular provision of the contract.

Other aspects of contract law, appropriate and reasonable in the eighteenth and nineteenth centuries, were clearly anachronistic by mid-twentieth century. One was the doctrine of privity of contract, limiting liability to the parties who had actually entered into the agreement. At a time when most goods were sold by the maker to the purchaser, the rule made sense. Today most products are not sold directly by the manufacturer or producer to the consumer. They are distributed through a chain of intermediaries—wholesalers, agents, and retailers. The principle of *caveat emptor,* let the buyer beware, worked admirably when goods could be easily inspected and intelligently appraised by the buyer before the purchase was made. The buyer of a horse was in as good a position as the seller to evaluate the soundness and worth of the animal. The doctrine is obviously grossly unfair when applied to the sale of automobiles, computers, other complicated pieces of machinery, pharmaceuticals, and the vast majority of packaged goods. Even buyers who have degrees in engineering are unable to make meaningful inspections and evaluations of the products they purchase. By mid-twentieth century, it was abundantly clear that both privity of contract and caveat emptor had outlived their usefulness for many of the ordinary transactions of life.

Relying upon another time-honored doctrine, *cessate rationem, cessate lex,* when the reason ceases the rule ceases, the courts abandoned both privity of contract and caveat emptor without the command of legislation. After a number of tortured cases in which the doctrine of causation was twisted and stretched to place responsibility on the producer who was in the best position to be responsible for the defects in his products, the doctrine of products liability came into the law by way of the Restatement of Torts.

In 1963, this scholarly treatise quietly promulgated a new legal concept:

1. One who sells any product in a defective condition unreasonably dangerous to the user or consumer or to his property is subject to liability for physical harm thereby caused to the ultimate user or consumer, or to his property, if
    a. the seller is engaged in the business of selling such a product, and
    b. it is expected to and does reach the user or consumer without substantial change in the condition in which it is sold.
2. The rule stated in Subsection (1) applies although
    a. the seller has exercised all possible care in the preparation and sale of his product, and
    b. the user or consumer has not bought the product from or entered into any contractual relation with the seller.[5]

Within a few years, the doctrine of products liability was accepted by many courts seeking a legal doctrine suitable to contemporary needs. It is now the law of most American jurisdictions, without statutory mandate, that the manufacturer of a defective product is liable to the reasonably foreseeable user for harms resulting from the use of the product. The injured plaintiff is not required to prove the impossible: namely, that the manufacturer was negligent. If the manufacturer fails to meet the standards of the state of the art and, as a result, harm occurs, the plaintiff can recover his or her provable damages.

Despite all these changes wrought by products liability law, certain fundamental principles remain. Liability is predicated on fault. The plaintiff must prove that the manufacturer was at fault by failing to meet the state of the art and that the harm suffered occurred as a result of the defendant's fault. And the plaintiff must prove the extent of the damages incurred.

But while all these modernizations of tort law proceeded, libel law remained the anachronism that it had been for centuries. As recently as 1951, in *Beauharnais* v. *Illinois*, [6] the United States Supreme Court declared:

> Libelous utterances, not being within the area of constitutionally protected speech, it is unnecessary either for us or for the State Courts to consider the issues behind the phrase "clear and present danger." Certainly no one would contend that obscene speech, for example, may be punished only upon a showing of such circumstances. Libel, as we have seen, is in the same class.

That case involved a prosecution under a state criminal libel statute of a white supremacist who distributed "anti-Negro" literature. At the trial, the defendant was not permitted to raise the defenses of truth, fair comment, or privilege. No clear and present danger arising out of the distribution of the leaflets was shown.

The most significant recent changes in libel law are recognition that defamation is not excluded from the reach of the First Amendment and the requirement that the plaintiff must prove some fault on the part of the defendant in order to recover. With these exceptions, the law of libel remains out of harmony with general principles of law. The distillation of countless decisions is found in the Restatement of Law, an authoritative series of legal texts published by the prestigious American Law Institute. The most recent promulgation of American libel law was issued by the Institute in 1984. The elements of contemporary libel are briefly stated as follows:

> a. a false and defamatory statement concerning another;
> b. an unprivileged publication to a third party;
> c. fault amounting at least to negligence on the part of the publisher;
> d. . . . actionability of the statement irrespective of special harm or the existence of special harm caused by the publication.

This relatively simple statement of the law is, in fact, complicated and rife with anomalies. The definition of defamation has not been updated for centuries. The Restatement repeats this ancient formula:

> A communication is defamatory if it tends so to harm the reputation of another as to lower him in the estimation of the community or to deter third persons from associating or dealing with him.

As has been pointed out, it is questionable whether even convictions for crime lower persons in the estimation of the community. Certainly imputations of unchastity, poverty, and illness do not. Few, if any, opinions discuss this issue which, I submit, should be a question of fact to be decided by the jury, not a question of law.

A few cases have held that the plaintiff's reputation was so tarnished before the alleged libel was published that he is libel-proof. In *Wynberg* v. *National Enquirer,*[7] Elizabeth Taylor's former boyfriend, who had behaved in a most ungentlemanly fashion, sued for libel. When these incidents were reported, the court held as a matter of law that he was libel-proof. This is a harsh all-or-nothing rule. Even a criminal or a cad may have a vestige of honor that has been besmirched. It would be consonant with general tort law to let the jury decide what, if any, harm was done to that sullied reputation.

Privilege also has no counterpart in general tort law. People are not privileged to do harm. Even parents who, under the common law and many state statutes, are permitted to use corporal punishment to discipline their children, are liable in tort if they negligently inflict harm on a child in the course of such "discipline" and guilty of crime if they willfully injure the child. Statements made in the legislature or as part of court proceedings are absolutely privileged, whether true or false. When repeated outside the legislature or the courtroom, however, they are actionable. This has been the law for centuries. It still prevails. These two absolute privileges are a necessity. Legislative debate would be stifled if legislators had to fear possible libel suits. Similarly, it would be extremely difficult to compel witnesses to testify at trials if they were subject to libel suits on the basis of their testimony. Most witnesses are not volunteers. They testify pursuant to subpoena and under threat of contempt of court if they fail to appear or refuse to testify. Obviously no one should be put to such a Hobson's choice.

Difficult questions arise under the doctrine of "conditional privilege." Defamatory statements may be conditionally privileged under certain rather vague conditions. The law is stated as follows:

1. An occasion makes a publication conditionally privileged if the circumstances induce a correct or reasonable belief that there is information that affects a sufficiently important interest of the recipient or a third person, and the recipient is one to whom the publisher is under a legal duty to publish the defamatory matter or is a person to whom its publication is otherwise within the generally accepted standards of decent conduct.

2. In determining whether a publication is within generally accepted

standards of decent conduct it is an important factor that the publication is made in response to a request rather than volunteered by the publisher or a family or other relationship exists between the parties. A publication is also conditionally privileged if the circumstances induce a correct or reasonable belief that there is information that affects a sufficiently important public interest, and the public interest requires the communication of the defamatory matter to a public officer or a private citizen who is authorized or privileged to take action if the defamatory matter is true.[8]

Who can know for certain whether information "affects a sufficiently important public interest"? What are "generally accepted standards of decent conduct"? The courts have wrestled with concepts of decency and obscenity for generations. Each new definition creates more problems than it solves. Standards differ from community to community. But most publications and radio and television programs are distributed nationwide. Does decency depend upon a few words or the statement taken as a whole? Must there be redeeming social importance? If these standards were contained in a criminal statute rather than in civil case law, the legislation might well be held unconstitutionally void for vagueness. When liability for damages of more than a million dollars depends upon such standards, questions of due process are implicit. But this is another issue that has not been addressed by the Supreme Court.

Most Americans have a fundamental belief in the validity of the rule of law. Juries, like judges, are sworn to follow the law whether they agree with it or not. In libel cases, juries and trial judges follow the dictates of the appellate courts because it is their duty to do so.

The *Sharon* jury clearly indicated its disapproval of the "actual malice" standard it was compelled to apply. Juries in libel cases before me have also followed my instructions as to the law. But they have done so reluctantly. After rendering their verdicts, many thoughtful jurors have expressed to me their belief that the law is wrong. Jurors have never done so in other types of cases. When jurors in criminal cases have acquitted persons accused of serious crimes, they have admitted their misgivings. But they did not doubt the fairness of the law that required proof beyond a reasonable doubt. They did not disagree with the principles of law they were sworn to apply. It is only in libel that the law goes against the grain of justice and common sense.

·IV·

A View from the Bench

*Yet Justice is a universal of all cultures. It is a tightrope
that man walks, between his desire to fulfill his wishes,
and his acknowledgment of social responsibility.*

—JACOB BRONOWSKI

BETWEEN reader and author, two strangers, there is an extraordinarily intimate interchange. The author presents characters who
are a distillation of his or her deepest emotions. The reader identifies
with them. Whether the reader is a young girl who sees herself as
Scarlett O'Hara or Elizabeth Bennett, a teen-aged boy who glories
in the deeds of Lancelot or Rambo, or a middle-aged reader who
understands the world-weary angst of Mr. Sammler, it is this en-
largement of self that makes reading a uniquely satisfying experience.

Readers have similar relationships with authors of judicial opinions. Practicing lawyers identify with counsel for the litigants involved in the case. They delight in the successful ploys of the winning
lawyer and conjure up more appealing arguments for losing counsel.
Law professors and students read Supreme Court opinions as if they
were members of an even higher court, criticizing the logic and
scholarship of the justices. When I read appellate court opinions, I
identify with the usually anonymous trial court judge and wonder
how I would have dealt with the issues if it had been my lot to preside
over that trial.

A learned opinion by the distinguished United States Court of
Appeals for the Second Circuit in the libel case of *Lerman* v. *Flynt*[1]
caused me considerable anguish. The facts in this case were simple.
It was admitted that plaintiff's picture in a topless pose was published

by the defendant without plaintiff's consent. It was identified as being that of a "starlet." Plaintiff sued for libel and other associated claims. The opinion identified more than twenty legal issues that had to be resolved by the jury. The trial judge would have to give clear, precise, comprehensible instructions on the law as to each and every one of those questions. I realized that I would be incapable of meeting the requirements demanded by that court. I doubt that many trial judges could do so, and I am sure that few juries could follow such a multitude of complex instructions.

In my fifteen years on the bench, I have presided over countless jury trials. Many involved complicated facts, multiple parties with conflicting interests, and difficult legal issues. But I managed to give the juries clear and comprehensible instructions as to the law and, with few exceptions, they returned sensible verdicts. None of these cases was reversed because of errors in the charge. The juries in my court, like those in any other metropolitan area, are composed of a broad, representative mix of the population. They include men and women of all ages, races, educational backgrounds, and socioeconomic strata. On an average jury, there are usually one or perhaps two retired persons or employees of the post office or some other government agency. Such people like jury duty. It causes them no economic hardship, and it is a welcome break in the monotony of their daily routine. They make good jurors. Juries often include persons who have been laid off from their jobs or are temporarily unemployed. The permanently unemployed rarely serve on juries. Occasionally, professionals, corporate executives, and high-income individuals are chosen for jury duty. The average Americans who comprise most juries are reasonably intelligent and very conscientious individuals. They listen attentively to the evidence no matter how boring and repetitious it is. They are able to understand the intricacies of aerodynamics, nuclear fission and fusion, banking practices, leveraged buyouts, pulmonary diseases, mental illness, and other esoteric subjects when carefully explained by expert witnesses. They follow legal instructions as to liability, burden of proof, defenses, and assessment of damages. And they return fair and sensible verdicts that are seldom reversed. But even if properly instructed, I seriously question whether the best of these juries could understand and apply the instructions as to the law required by the court in *Lerman* v. *Flynt.*

It is, I believe, helpful to analyze the issues in this unremarkable case in order to understand why libel cases cause so much more difficulty than other kinds of litigation. The case received little notice in the press. Neither the plaintiff, a wealthy author of books on nudity, nor the defendant, Larry Flynt, well known as the publisher of *Hustler,* was a particularly sympathetic litigant. Few lawyers or journalists saw this suit as a great First Amendment case. The public's alleged right to know was not seriously infringed by a verdict against the defendant, nor were individual rights abrogated by the reversal of that verdict. But the legal principles so carefully enunciated by one of the nation's most respected courts will be applied in other cases that do involve dissemination of material in which the public has a vital interest and persons whose privacy has been unjustifiably invaded. The learned opinion reveals the problems encountered in applying constitutional doctrines to state statutes when the intersection of the two was never contemplated. It discusses a multitude of substantive and procedural problems implicit in many libel cases.

When appellate courts* write opinions, they are not simply deciding the case that is before them. That can be done by a simple one-word order: "affirmed" or "reversed." An enormous number of appeals are decided in this fashion. Other appeals are decided in unpublished opinions, read only by the litigants and their counsel. A published opinion is a message to the trial bench, a textbook that judges are supposed to study and follow when presiding over similar cases. In this way, the law develops by accretion. Each trial judge does not have to stumble through the thickets of the law without a road map repeating the errors of predecessors. The trial bench relies on the appellate courts for guidance.

When I was a young lawyer, I served as a law clerk to John Biggs, Jr., the distinguished chief judge of the United States Court of Appeals for the Third Circuit. With the self-confidence of inexperience, I assumed that appellate opinions were addressed to the Supreme Court. To that end, I was concerned with fine-honed, fine-spun logic and erudition. Every judicial opinion, other than the opinions of the

*The nomenclature of courts is confusing. In some jurisdictions, trial courts are called supreme courts, in others, district courts or superior courts. The final court is usually called the supreme court, but in some jurisdictions, the court of appeals. In general, in both the federal and state systems there are three tiers of courts: the trial courts, intermediate appellate courts, and a final appellate court. From the decision of the highest state court, a litigant can seek discretionary review, known as certiorari, from the United States Supreme Court. In this book the term "Supreme Court" is used to refer to the United States Supreme Court. The terms "trial court" and "appellate court" are used to designate all other courts. The minor state judiciaries, which try small claims, traffic violations, and misdemeanors, are rarely involved in defamation and privacy actions.

Supreme Court, is of course an effort to persuade those who may consider an appeal that the decision was correct. Since fewer than 150 cases a year are decided by the Supreme Court with opinions, it is extremely unlikely that most opinions of trial and appellate courts will be read by that august body. The vast readership of judicial opinions consists of lawyers and trial judges. The lawyers advise their clients on the basis of these opinions. And the trial judges attempt to follow the legal doctrines set forth.

The facts in *Lerman* v. *Flynt,* as in many libel actions against the media, were not seriously in dispute. A copy of the May 1980 issue of the magazine *Adelina* contained a topless photograph of the plaintiff. The picture was identified in the magazine as the photo of a "starlet" appearing in a film written by the plaintiff and produced by her husband. Plaintiff had not consented to the use of her photo. Defendant is a successor to the original publisher of the magazine. The offending picture was reissued in advertising solicitations and in a subsequent issue of the magazine.

The trial judge issued a preliminary injunction restraining distribution of the May issue of the magazine and granted plaintiff's motion for summary judgment for violation of her rights under a New York statute prohibiting the use of a photograph without consent of the subject. Plaintiff also alleged that she had been libeled. In a learned thirteen-page opinion, the appellate court reversed the trial judge's decision. The opinion commences with a ringing defense of freedom of the press. The court declared:

> Freedom of expression preserves all other liberties so inseparably that freedom of the press and a free society either prosper together or perish together. Yet, because of its enormous power, the contemporary press is under heavy attack because of a widely held perception that it uses its special First Amendment status as a license to invade individual privacy.

The opinion then stated:

> This case illustrates the *complexity of the concerns* when these interests clash [Emphasis supplied].

It does indeed indicate what I believe are unnecessary complexities that leave trial courts and the public bewildered. Despite the unambiguous language of the New York statute at issue that made the unauthorized use of a person's name or picture for advertising purposes actionable, the appellate court found it necessary to consider the following questions: Did the publisher know that the plaintiff's photo was used without her consent? Was she an all-purpose public figure or a limited public figure or a wholly private person? Was malice, defined as reckless disregard of truth, proved? Was the use informational or "completely exploitive and commercial"? Was the use for the purpose of informing the public about a newsworthy event? Was the use merely incidental to a privileged use? Was the use in connection with a newsworthy event? Did the use of the photo have any real relationship to matters under discussion, or was it merely an advertisement in disguise? Even if newsworthy, was the use infected with "severe falsity"?

It was undisputed that the picture was that of the plaintiff and not of an unnamed "starlet," as the caption indicated. The distinction between falsity and "severe falsity" may be likened to the concept of being a little bit pregnant. While in many libel cases the alleged defamation involves what is essentially an opinion, a statement not susceptible to proof or disproof, this case involved a discrete, readily ascertainable fact. Was the nude picture a photograph of the plaintiff? Either the caption was false or it was true. The concept of degrees of falsity adds further complexity to what could have been a simple, easily resolved case.

The court also found it necessary to discuss the issues of the "public's right to be informed," whether the context in which the photo occurred was "fictionalization," whether the misidentification of a nude photo was defamatory, whether a book about nudity is a matter of "public controversy," and whether it is obscene or contains any redeeming values.

Because First Amendment issues are now assumed to be involved in every libel case arising out of printed matter or the electronic media, whether verbal or not, the court found it necessary to consider whether the defendant in using the plaintiff's picture "acted with the requisite fault," still undefined by the Supreme Court.

The plaintiff asserted that her right of privacy had been invaded and her right of publicity infringed. These common law rights, claimed with increasing frequency, are really twentieth-century concepts unknown to earlier law. In order to claim a right of publicity, it has been held that the plaintiff must have developed the use of his or her person for commercial purposes.*

*See Chapter V for further discussion.

A judge and jury spent several weeks in the trial of this case. A learned appellate court composed of three judges devoted considerable time and attention to the review of the trial. Had that case been decided under general principles of law applicable to all other tort actions, the jury would have been asked to decide only a few simple questions. Because the printing of plaintiff's picture without her permission was an admitted fact, the jury would have had to decide only whether the defendant was negligent, and if so, the amount of the harm actually suffered by the plaintiff.

The test of negligence is "what a reasonable publisher would have done under the circumstances." Plaintiff would probably have presented the testimony of an expert, a respected editor, or a professor of journalism. This expert would have testified that it is good journalism to obtain the written consent of the subject of a photograph before publishing it unless the picture is an on-the-spot photograph of a news event such as the raising of the flag at Iwo Jima or the grief-stricken girl kneeling over the body of a fellow student shot at Kent State, or the onlookers at an accident scene.

The defendant would then probably have presented testimony accounting for its possession of the picture and the reasons for its belief that it was the photo of a "starlet." The jury would undoubtedly have been interested in learning why the plaintiff had her nude photo taken and how it found its way to the defendant.

Assuming that the jury found that there were no exigent circumstances requiring publication of the picture before obtaining a release, it would have found that the defendant was negligent. The court would also have asked the jury to decide whether the photograph was used for advertising purposes and, if so, it would have instructed them to return a verdict for the plaintiff. But in *Lerman* v. *Flynt,* the trial court enjoined the release of the entire magazine, not simply the picture. That was clearly a violation of the First Amendment. Restraint of publication has been prohibited in a long line of cases.*

The real question under the statute or general principles of tort law would have been the amount of damages, if any, the plaintiff had suffered. Damages would not be presumed. The plaintiff would have to have proved some actual harm resulting from the publication of the picture. Had the plaintiff been a schoolteacher, a public official,

*But see the restraint of publication of the biography of J.D. Salinger discussed in Chapter IX.

or a social worker, she most likely could have proved some economic loss and emotional distress. If she had been a housewife who was a member of the PTA, the garden club, or active in church work, she would probably have been able to demonstrate emotional distress, as well as loss of good name. But this plaintiff was an outspoken advocate of nudity. There was no provable reduction of her very substantial income earned from writing about nudity. What harm did she suffer from the publication of her photograph, even assuming that she was recognized by her friends and acquaintances? The jury under instructions applicable to general tort law would probably have returned a nominal verdict. There would have been no practical reason for the defendant to appeal.

If general principles of tort law applied to libel actions, it is highly unlikely that Mrs. Lerman would have sued. Certainly no sensible lawyer would have undertaken that case on a contingent fee basis with little prospect of a substantial verdict. Most potential plaintiffs, even if very wealthy, are loath to risk their own funds on a lawsuit that lawyers find unpromising unless they have some political or ideological motive. In such instances, the expenses of litigation are often defrayed by contributions from like-minded individuals and organizations. Except for such committed ideologues, most individuals and organizations do not file suit or defend actions unless they reasonably believe that there is a good prospect of succeeding. Plaintiffs who have little likelihood of winning rarely sue. Similarly, when defendants' chances of success are poor, they will usually settle. In fact, the vast majority of all civil cases are not litigated to verdict. Instead they are settled or withdrawn when the parties have had the opportunity to examine their opponent's evidence prior to trial. Not many lawyers undertake hopeless cases even for adequate compensation.

This sensible practice obtains in libel suits that are based on a verifiable misstatement of fact. *Poisoning for Profit: The Mafia and Toxic Waste in America* by Alan A. Block and Frank R. Scarpitti stated that Waste Management, Inc., the nation's largest waste disposal company, had borrowed money through an organized crime loan-shark operation. The company filed a libel suit. During pretrial discovery, it was learned that the authors had confused the plaintiff with an unrelated company having a similar name. The publisher and the authors admitted their error, apologized, and the publisher agreed to destroy any copies of the book in its inventory as well as any subsequently returned.[2] Such a result was probably possible for the following reasons: (1) there was an admitted misstatement of fact, not an expression of opinion or inference; (2) the plaintiff was a corporation not an individual and probably more interested in conserving the time of its staff and avoiding legal expenses rather than achieving some moral vindication and possible enormous verdict several years in the future; (3) the book was not a best seller. It is unlikely that the limited circulation caused the plaintiff any financial harm. Unfortunately, such a combination of circumstances rarely occurs in libel litigation.

The likelihood of appeal in libel cases is greater than in other kinds of cases because: (1) the probability of a successful appeal is greater when there are so many legal issues that the possibilities of error in the jury charge are multiplied, and (2) when the plaintiff is successful the verdicts are so large as to compel a prudent defendant to seek a reversal.

Jury duty is usually the jurors' first (and only) experience with the American legal system other than a ticket for traffic violation. Aside from what they remember from a high school civics course, the jurors must rely on the judge's instruction for every phase of their deliberations. A jury much listen to the judge explain each of these complicated, unfamiliar legal doctrines, as well as general principles of law such as burden of proof, quantum of proof, and general conduct of jury deliberations. They must try to comprehend and remember all of these rules and apply them to the facts of the case. It would take a careful, very terse judge at least two or three hours to explain the law governing all the issues adumbrated by the court in *Lerman* v. *Flynt*. In addition, the judge must instruct the jurors as to their general duties with respect to credibility of witnesses, expert witnesses, unanimity or plurality of decisions, and damages. The instructions are given orally. Although Judge Sofaer in the *Sharon* case permitted the jurors to take notes, this practice is generally disapproved, and for good reasons. Jurors are not professional court stenographers. Their notes will certainly be incomplete and may be inaccurate. It is likely that those jurors who did not take notes or whose notes do not mention a particular bit of evidence will be guided by the notes of other jurors rather than their own recollections. I believe it would be preferable for the trial judge to distribute to the jury copies of written instructions in complicated cases rather than permitting them to rely on their own notes.

During the televised debates between President Reagan and Senator Mondale, the media concluded that the attention span of the average American is twenty minutes. I find that most juries become restive after twenty-five minutes. For television viewers, this is the interval for the commercial, the time to get up and get something to eat or drink before settling down for the second half of the program. If the charge to the jury takes less than a half hour, a judge can usually be confident that the jury will understand and follow the instructions. There are relatively few cases in which jurors are unable to agree on a verdict.

In the usual civil case, a jury rarely has to decide more than four or five legal issues. Often a jury will ask me to repeat the instructions on a particular point of law after they have been deliberating for an hour or two. Obviously there is a disagreement as to what they have heard and remembered. After they have heard the instruction repeated, they usually return a verdict within ten or fifteen minutes.

In most civil and criminal cases, the law is reasonably clear; it is the facts that must be developed in both pretrial and trial procedures. Was the defendant negligent? Was the plaintiff also negligent? These are questions that must be decided on the basis of testimony and other evidence adduced at the trial. Was the defendant's product dangerous? Did it conform to the state of the art at the time? Reasonable minds can differ as to all these facts. The result will depend in large part on how convincing the testimony and physical evidence are.

In most homicide cases, the death of the victim is an admitted fact. What must be developed at trial by evidence is whether it was the defendant who killed the deceased. If so, did the defendant act in self-defense? Was he insane or mentally impaired? Was there sufficient provocation to reduce the crime from murder to manslaughter? Was there criminal intent or was the killing accidental? These are facts that lay people who sit on juries are competent to decide. The legal principles are sufficiently clear that they can be adequately explained to the jury in less than a half hour.

In contrast, in a libel case, the trial judge must guess correctly on many legal issues in which there are no definitive rulings from a majority of the Supreme Court justices. In an ordinary libel case against a newspaper, the transcript of the charge of the trial judge to the jury was ninety-three pages.[3] Reading very fast it would take approximately two hours to deliver the charge. Reading at a normal pace and stopping, as I do, to look at the jurors to see if they appear to understand or are perplexed and then repeat the difficult passage, it would probably take three hours to deliver. The court in that case charged the jury on seventy-five issues of law. The correctness of the charge on many of these questions is not free from doubt. For example, is the standard of proof of defamation: (1) the preponderance of the evidence, (2) clear and convincing evidence, (3) so clear, direct, weighty, and convincing as to enable the jury to come to a clear conviction without hesitancy of the truth of the precise facts in issue, or (4) strong, positive evidence free from doubt"? Does the plaintiff or the defendant have the burden of proving truth? Is the test of falsity literal truth, substantial truth, mere falsity, or severe falsity? What is the requisite state of mind of the defendant that is necessary in order to find liability? Reckless disregard for truth or subjective awareness of probable falsity, or mere negligence or gross negligence or actual knowledge of falsity? The court also had to charge the jury on the definition of public figure, private figure, and limited public figure. An error in any one of the seventy-five points could result in a new trial.

It is unreasonable to expect juries to remember and understand a charge of such length and complexity. Steven Brill reports that after interviewing jurors in the *Tavoulareas* case, he finds that they misunderstood the charge.[4] They returned a verdict of $2.05 million. This case is also on appeal. Tavoulareas is reported as saying that his legal bill was about $1.8 million before the petition to the Supreme Court.

Many classes of defendants maintain that the claims against them are so complicated that they should be tried by separate, special tribunals and that juries are unable to cope with the complexity of the cases. Such arguments are frequently made not only by subjects and authors, but also by doctors, the automobile industry, the asbestos industry, the pharmaceutical industry, and many banking and commercial interests. Significantly, those who assert that juries are unable to understand complicated factual problems usually insistently demand a jury trial.

A complicated products liability case* assigned to me illustrates that when the law is reasonably clear and accords with accepted notions of fairness, the legal system does function adequately and without undue delay. The case arose out of the crash of a helicopter.

---

*This case was also settled. The facts have been slightly disguised, but the substance of the controversy and the conclusion are accurately stated.

The pilot and the estates of the two deceased passengers were plaintiffs. The seven defendants were corporations that manufactured some critical part of the helicopter or were engaged in its assembly. There was no question that something had malfunctioned. A plane does not fall from the sky unless something is wrong. The pilot miraculously survived. He testified as to what he had done when the plane suddenly failed. It was, therefore, impossible to place the blame on him. Had the case gone to trial, a jury would have had to decide which part or parts of the plane were defective and which defendant or defendants were responsible. The plaintiffs were willing to have the case heard by a judge sitting alone. All defendants demanded a jury trial. The same pattern of jury demand prevails in most products liability and malpractice cases.

In the helicopter case, extensive discovery was undertaken. All the essential parts of the machine were examined. The pilot, eyewitnesses, and experts were deposed. Counsel for all parties met with me and asked how I would rule on certain questions of law and evidence. I responded. At the request of all counsel, I was also asked to give my opinion as to the total sum the plaintiffs should recover and the percentage of responsibility of each defendant. Within a few weeks, the case was settled at approximately the figures proposed. All parties were saved costs of trial, which would have been at least $100,000 for the defendants for a two-week trial. It would have cost the taxpayers more than $20,000. If the verdict had been unreasonable, an appeal would have been taken. And possibly three or four years later the case might have been remanded for a new trial. Most civil cases are settled in this sensible fashion. Such settlements are based upon a sophisticated appraisal of the facts by able counsel and the court and an understanding of the legal principles involved.

The facts in many libel cases are very simple. The jury does not have to delve into difficult scientific evidence or confusing testimony tracing funds through laundering of accounts. It is not the facts but the law that causes the problems. Justice Prager of the Kansas Supreme Court in a defamation case aptly declared, "This case well illustrates the confusion that has arisen as a result of the decision [*Gertz* v. *Robert Welch, Inc.*] of the United States Supreme Court. . . ."[5]

Libel cases can be settled fairly and sensibly when the parties are litigating about real economic losses not immeasurable imponderables like reputation and honor. In another case before me, a general contractor sued thirty-three businesses, a trade association of which

all the businesses were members, and an officer of the association.*
Plaintiff charged the defendants with libel for false and defamatory
statements and demanded punitive damages. The suit was based on
several communications sent by the association to its members stating that plaintiff owed his creditors more than $400,000 and urging
them to bring pressure on plaintiff to make him pay these debts. The
clear inference was that plaintiff was a poor credit risk. As a result
of these communications, the bonding company revoked all existing
construction bonds and suspended the issuance of future bonds.
Without this protection, plaintiff was forced out of business.

All defendants filed motions for summary judgment. They
claimed: (1) freedom of the press, (2) truth, (3) fair comment, (4) that
plaintiff was a public figure, and (5) that the allegedly defamatory
statements involved public issues. In denying defendants' motions,
I held that the distribution of the statements to members of the
association did not involve freedom of the press, that plaintiff was not
a public figure, and that whether or not plaintiff paid his debts was
not a public issue. This case was settled in 1980. It is doubtful that,
given the state of libel law in 1986, this sensible disposition could have
been reached. It was clear that charging plaintiff with being a dead-
beat was defamatory if false and that the statements were not privileged. In essence, the only issues for a jury to decide were whether
plaintiff owed his creditors $400,000, and if he didn't, the amount of
the damages he should be awarded. Whether plaintiff owed $400,000
was not a matter of opinion but a fact that could be verified by
examining his books and records. In pretrial discovery it was revealed, as defendants admitted, that plaintiff owed at most $200,000
and that a fair percentage of this sum consisted of 10 percent of the
bills of the subcontractors, which plaintiff was entitled to retain until
the work was approved by the customers as being satisfactory.

Since the facts were admitted and my statement of the law was
clear and simple, the parties made a fair settlement based on the
plaintiff's projected loss of profits for a reasonable period of time. The
settlement probably cost the defendants less than the expenses of
litigation. Plaintiff decided to forgo the possibility of punitive damages of $10 million that he claimed and accept compensation for his
actual losses rather than litigate and risk the possibility of not recovering at all or at best recovering five years or more later.

---

*This case was also settled. The facts have been slightly disguised, but the substance of the
controversy and the conclusion are accurately stated.

The then troublesome legal question as to which party had the burden of proof of truth was not reached because the facts were admitted. Having ruled that First Amendment rights were not involved, the standard of fault was negligence not "actual malice" (defined by the Supreme Court as reckless disregard for truth). It was clear that at the time the statements were made the defendants honestly believed that they were true. It would have been difficult to show willful or reckless disregard of truth. Under the *New York Times* v. *Sullivan* standard, this plaintiff, who suffered real losses as a result of a false statement, would have been denied recovery. Under the negligence standard, a reasonable person would certainly have investigated before making these charges and risking catastrophic losses to plaintiff. Under this standard, the plaintiff would have recovered.

By contrast, another case, which involved an alleged libel printed in the daily press, went to trial. The jury awarded the plaintiff, an attorney, $4.5 million.* The alleged defamatory article contained only minor, insignificant inaccuracies with respect to a case plaintiff had tried. These inaccuracies did not in any way change the substance of the complaint. The plaintiff had not suffered any loss of reputation as a result of the story. In fact, his practice had increased and was even more profitable, probably as a result of all the media publicity.

The trial lasted several weeks. The jury was required to decide whether the plaintiff was a public or a private figure, whether the news story involved a matter of public concern, whether the defendant acted with "actual malice." The jury was instructed that harm to reputation was presumed and that damages were presumed. Because the plaintiff demanded punitive damages, the assets of the defendant were disclosed to the jury. The disparity between the economic status of the plaintiff and that of the defendant was so great as inevitably to prejudice the jury.

Under the law, trial courts are obliged to permit this evidence to be received, even though we know that it will undoubtedly unfairly affect the verdict. Trial courts are also obliged to follow other rules and doctrines that most judges believe are confusing, unfair, and fail to protect the rights of either plaintiffs or defendants. We trial judges are obliged to instruct our juries in accordance with the law as we dimly perceive it to be from our reading of Supreme Court decisions.

---

*This case has been appealed.

Despite all the safeguards with which the Supreme Court has attempted to surround the press in protecting First Amendment rights, those very rules faithfully repeated by trial judges result again and again in crushing verdicts against the media and windfalls to plaintiffs, as in the case of the lawyer. The defendant's insurance did not cover much of the award. Counsel fees and other expenses are estimated to be about $300,000. The expenses on appeal will be substantial. Probably the case will be remanded for a new trial and the next trial judge will be equally perplexed in trying to follow the law. Countless similar cases are being litigated in courts across the nation with equally unsatisfactory results.

The Supreme Court's multiple opinions in *Rosenblatt* v. *Baer*[6] reveal the problems that face trial courts, lawyers, and litigants when attempting to follow the rules laid down by the Court. This case has been cited and relied on by almost every judge hearing a libel case for two decades. This enormous tempest was brewed in a very small teapot.

A small New Hampshire newspaper published a column obliquely criticizing the management of a publicly owned ski resort. This was obviously a matter of public interest. It did not invade the privacy of any public official. The case should have been dismissed summarily as being based on seditious libel. Instead, the newspaper and the reporter not only had to defend the action in the trial court but also through a series of appeals and a remand for a new trial. A jury verdict was rendered in favor of the plaintiff. On appeal, the Supreme Court of New Hampshire affirmed the award of damages. On certiorari, the United States Supreme Court reversed and remanded the case for a new trial. The Court found it necessary to file five opinions. Justice Clark concurred in the result. A modest verdict of $31,500 provoked this tremendous amount of judicial effort.

These are relevant portions of the column:

Been doing a little listening and checking at Belknap Recreation Area and am thunderstruck by what am learning. . . .

This year, a year without snow till very late, a year with actually few very major changes in procedure; the difference in cash income simply fantastic, almost unbelievable. . . .

On any sort of comparative basis, the Area this year is doing literally hundreds of percent BETTER than last year. . . .

When consider that last year was excellent snow year, that season started because of more snow, months earlier last year, one can only ponder following question: "What happened to all the money last year?

and every other year? What magic has Dana Beane [Chairman of the new commission] and rest of commission, and Mr. Warner [respondent's replacement as Supervisor] wrought to make such tremendous difference in net cash results?"

Plaintiff was a former employee of the public commission managing the resort. Because the article did not mention anyone by name, the Court engaged in a lengthy discussion as to whether the article could reasonably be construed to be "of and concerning" the plaintiff. The next question was whether under state law he was a public official. Certainly an employee of a public body should be deemed to be a public official, regardless of the scope of his duties. Moreover, plaintiff claimed that the article must be read as referring to him because he had some responsibility for managing the recreation area. The matter was remanded for the trial court to decide whether he was a public official and whether he could meet the malice standard of *Sullivan,* i.e., knowledge of falsity or reckless disregard for truth or falsity. The judge was ordered to decide plaintiff's status as a public official. This removed from the province of the jury a significant factual question.

Justice Stewart in his concurring opinion pointed out that "State defamation laws . . . whether civil or criminal, cannot constitutionally be converted into laws against seditious libel." But this is precisely the effect of the Court's ruling. Justices Douglas and Black would have reversed but not granted a new trial. They objected to the Court's ruling that the decision as to whether plaintiff was a public or private figure should be made by the judge rather than the jury. This would, of course, be the critical issue. If plaintiff was a public figure, he could recover only by proving actual malice. If he was a private figure, he would recover because a charge of embezzlement is unquestionably defamatory. Justice Fortas believed that the writ of certiorari was improvidently granted, that is, that the Court should not have heard the case.

From where I sit, either the Douglas-Black view or the Fortas view should have been adopted. It erodes the First Amendment when we require an unpaid columnist to defend in court his comments about a matter of public interest that did not name the plaintiff or unequivocally charge him with a crime. The facts were anomalous. It is unlikely that any other case will present the same factual pattern. None of the reported cases that have attempted to follow the rules laid down here has been closely similar. The verdict was not outrageous. The multiple and conflicting opinions make it difficult for trial courts to choose among the various doctrines announced. It is virtually impossible for courts to anticipate the fluctuating positions of the justices and to tailor their charges to the jury in cases involving dissimilar facts according to such evanescent and confusing precedents.

Plaintiff maintained that the vague statements must be read as accusing him of financial peculations. One wonders how the reporter and publisher could possibly prove the truth of such a vague statement if the burden of establishing truth had been placed on the author. Even assuming that there was a difference in revenue in the years mentioned, what more could be done to prove the truth of an accusation that was never made? Most importantly, criticism of public operation of a public recreation area is precisely the kind of discussion necessary to an informed citizenry. To require a reporter and publisher to pay the not inconsiderable expenses of trial and all the subsequent appeals and for a new trial indeed places an unreasonable burden on the press.

This case turned in some measure on New Hampshire law. The jury was instructed that under state law, "an imputation of impropriety or a crime to one or some of a small group that casts suspicion on all is actionable. . . ." If the New Hampshire law were construed to permit recovery for this statement, it should have been held unconstitutional as applied for violating the defendant's First Amendment rights.

The problems of trial judges in libel cases have been compounded by the decision of the Supreme Court in *Anderson* v. *Liberty Lobby, Inc. et al.,*[7] requiring the trial judge to determine *before* hearing the evidence "whether the evidence in the record could support a reasonable jury finding either that the plaintiff had shown actual malice by clear and convincing evidence or that the plaintiff has not." In essence, this removes from the province of the jury what is often the only real factual dispute in the case. The judge must decide whether the plaintiff is a public or a private figure or a limited public figure. Then on the basis of pretrial documents, without hearing the testimony or having the opportunity to assess the credibility of the witnesses, the judge must decide whether the plaintiff has presented sufficient evidence for a jury to find actual malice, which depends upon the state of mind of the defendant. Although members of the media have hailed this decision as a victory, I foresee enormous problems and vastly increased expense in the preparation of libel cases.

The case arose out of three articles published in the *Investigator* magazine portraying plaintiffs as "neo-Nazi, anti-Semitic, racist and fascist." At the outset, one must note that ugly as these charges are, they might best be characterized as name calling. They do not allege specific acts that can be proved or disproved. Many people have on occasion made anti-Semitic or racist remarks, told "ethnic" jokes, and expressed approbation of various regimes that others consider to be fascist. Does approval of the Sandinistas or the Contras make one a Communist or a fascist? Does disapproval of affirmative action make one a racist? While there may be a general consensus among Americans that anti-Semitism and racism are unworthy attitudes, holding and expressing such views is not criminal. Nor is the imputation to another, true or false, of such views a crime.

The researcher of the articles filed an affidavit declaring that he believed the facts to be truthful, and he filed a compilation of the evidence on which he based his views. The defendant then moved for summary judgment. The trial judge held that plaintiffs were "limited public figures" and that the actual malice standard enunciated in *New York Times* v. *Sullivan* applied. The court granted summary judgment. The court of appeals reversed, holding that at the pretrial stage the plaintiff did not have to show that a jury could find actual malice with "convincing clarity." The quantum and quality of testimony required to prove actual malice with convincing clarity is far from clear. A divided Supreme Court reversed and remanded the case to the court of appeals to reconsider whether the trial judge's decision under this standard was correct.

Justice Rehnquist, Chief Justice Burger, and Justice Brennan dissented. The Rehnquist-Burger opinion declared, "The primary effect of the Court's opinion today will likely be to cause the decisions of trial judges to be more erratic and inconsistent than before." Justice Brennan in a separate opinion trenchantly observed, ". . . I am unable to divine from the Court's opinion *how* [his emphasis] these evidentiary standards are to be considered, or what a trial judge is actually supposed to do in ruling on a motion for summary judgment." Nor am I able to find guidance as to the standards I am now required to apply when, as will be inevitable, libel defendants move for summary judgment. All the time-tested rules by which juries and judge decide whether the plaintiff has proved the allegations of the complaint are put to naught. Juries are instructed to observe the manner and demeanor of the witnesses in deciding credibility. On a motion for summary judgment, the judge has not seen or heard the witnesses. Juries are instructed that it is the quality not the quantity of the evidence or the number of witnesses that is determinative. The trial judge will make this critical decision terminating the case on the basis of piles of paper.

Those who fear the antimajoritarian power of judges have reason for concern when the Supreme Court removes from the province of the jury these critical decisions.

In most civil cases if the plaintiff wins, the amount of the recovery is reasonably related to the fault of the defendant and the harm suffered by the plaintiff. In libel cases, however, the amounts awarded are frequently unreasonable. Verdicts of several million dollars are not uncommon. Some plaintiffs have demanded more than a hundred million dollars. It is difficult to conceive of a noneconomic, nonphysical harm for which such an award would be appropriate.

In *Lerman* v. *Flynt,* the jury awarded plaintiff $7,000,000 which the trial court refused to reduce. The appellate court, I believe correctly, observed:

> No doubt such an enormous verdict chills media First Amendment rights. But a verdict of this size does more than chill an individual defendant's rights, it deep-freezes that particular media defendant permanently.

That the appellate court was shocked at the amount of the verdict is understandable. Not many people would accept with equanimity the notion that having one's picture published, even in a topless state, caused emotional damages of $7,000,000. The court took great pains to point out that plaintiff was a highly successful author of books about nudity whose books sold in thirty-two languages in millions of copies and that she had already settled part of her claim with a predecessor to this defendant for $100,000. Clearly, in the minds of the court and of most people, this plaintiff had not been harmed. An author whose stock in trade is nudity could scarcely have been emotionally disturbed by seeing her own topless picture or having it displayed with or without her consent and without her name. The opinion does not reveal when the plaintiff's topless picture was taken or by whom or how it got into the possession of the magazine. Common sense would lead to the conclusion that the wealthy plaintiff who had already recovered $100,000 had received far more than she deserved for an error that did not and could not have caused her any provable harm. The appellate court reversed.

The size of the verdicts in many libel cases is shocking. The *Washington Post* compiled a list of the ten largest damage verdicts in recent suits against the media as of January 15, 1984. These are:

1. *Guccione* v. *Hustler,* 1981—$37 million. Trial judge reduced damages to $2.85 million. Appeals court remanded the case back to trial court because damage amount was excessive. Retrial pending on amount of damages only.
2. *Pring* v. *Penthouse,* 1981—$25.025 million. Appeals court overturned judgment. Pring appealed to Supreme Court, which refused to hear case.
3. *Edgehill* v. *Philadelphia Magazine,* 1983—$5 million. *Philadelphia* magazine claims judge should disqualify himself.
4. *Cramlet* v. *Multimedia Program Productions, Inc.,* 1983— $4.2 million. Multimedia Program Productions, Inc., appealing damages.
5. *Sprague* v. *Philadelphia Inquirer,* 1983—$3 million. *Philadelphia Inquirer* plans to file to set aside the verdict or for a new trial.
6. *Rodgers* v. *Doubleday,* 1982—$2.5 million. Doubleday appealed and lost and is appealing now before the Texas Supreme Court.
7. *Green* v. *Alton Telegraph,* 1980—$2.5 million. Settled for $1.4 million total out of $9.2 million total punitive and compensatory damages.
8. *Tavoulareas* v. *Washington Post,* 1982—$1.8 million. Trial judge reversed jury, which had ruled against the *Post.* Tavoulareas is appealing.
9. *Douglass* v. *Hustler,* 1983—$1.5 million. *Hustler* is appealing the entire judgment.
10. *Burnett* v. *National Enquirer,* 1983—$1.3 million. Trial judge reduced damages to $750,000. *National Enquirer* appealed, and appeals court reduced damages to $150,000. *National Enquirer* and Burnett appealed to California Supreme Court, which refused to hear the case. *Enquirer* has appealed to the U.S. Supreme Court.

    (Source: The Reporters Committee for Freedom of the Press.)

A comparison of libel verdicts with verdicts in other tort cases reveals that these awards are unparalleled. A recent study[8] reveals

that the average awards in tort cases, exclusive of libel, doubled from
1960 to 1980. This undoubtedly reflects inflation, the rising cost of
living, and the sharply increased cost of medical services. In medical
malpractice cases, the average awards in San Francisco increased
from $89,000 in the 1960s to $457,000 in 1979. These cases involved
serious injuries. With respect to jury verdicts in cases involving
injured plaintiffs, the study reports that "jurors increased awards in
the 1970s to plaintiffs who suffered high lost income and severe
injuries. Awards for wrongful death more than doubled during
the 1970s. But the vast majority of plaintiffs received the same level
of compensation in the 1970s as they would have in the previous
decade."

Juries in libel suits are chosen from the same pool of citizens as
juries in all other civil cases. The grossly excessive amounts of awards
in libel cases as compared with awards in cases for serious injuries
and death, I believe, are attributable to the law itself. The fact that
a verdict of several billion dollars was returned in the *Pennzoil* case
does not militate against this conclusion. A battle between two billion dollar corporations is substantially different from a lawsuit by
an individual against corporate defendants alleging damage to reputation. Since 1984, there have been many more very large verdicts.
In the *Brown Williamson Tobacco* case against CBS, the jury returned a $5.05 million verdict.[9] A $2.8 million verdict was returned
against the former owner of TV station WLKY.[10] A $47.5 million
verdict in *Huan* v. *NEC Microcomputer, Inc.,* was set aside by the
trial judge and a new trial ordered.[11] Miss Wyoming sued *Penthouse*
and was awarded $26.5 million. This award was reduced to $14
million and reversed on appeal. The Supreme Court refused to hear
the case.[12] The other cases will be appealed. Many will be remanded
for new trials.

The costs to the public as well as the litigants in libel suits are not
inconsiderable. Tort cases that are settled in state courts cost the
public from $311 to $393, depending upon the jurisdiction. Federal
court expenditures range from $2,193 to $5,213. The average tort jury
trial in state courts costs the taxpayers from approximately $3,000
to $9,000; in federal courts from $8,422 to $15,028.[13] The cost of a
trial is based on the number of trial days. Average trial costs are
derived by dividing the total number of trial days by the number of
cases. Most jury trials are concluded within three days. There are
notable exceptions that materially raise the average. The trial of John
Hinckley who shot President Reagan lasted thirty-nine days. Some
product liability cases and medical malpractice cases are lengthy,

consuming weeks of trial. The asbestos litigation is costing the public and the litigants enormous sums. But with the exception of such unusual trials, it is fair to conclude that libel cases are significantly longer than other types of tort cases. The *Westmoreland* case, for example, had been in court for five months before it was settled. Uncelebrated libel cases routinely take weeks and weeks of trial time.

In all tort cases except defamation, jurors must assess damages on the basis of evidence of the plaintiff's losses resulting from the defendant's wrongdoing. Damages are not presumed. They must be proved. If the usual rule prevailed, both Mrs. Lerman and the lawyer would have had to prove either economic losses or emotional harms in order to recover more than nominal damages. Was Mrs. Lerman's income reduced? Had she lost any readership because her fans had seen her topless photograph and found it offensive? If she had claimed economic losses, the defendant could have subpoenaed her tax returns and financial records to disprove any loss of income. As for emotional harms, perhaps she could have testified that she had been humiliated or embarrassed. A friend might have testified that he or she had thought less of Mrs. Lerman after seeing the picture. The defendant could probably have countered with evidence that appearing topless was customary and admired among her acquaintances. On the basis of such evidence, the jury would probably have returned a very modest verdict. The lawyer, if subject to usual standards of proof of damages, would have had great difficulty in proving any economic losses. The defendant could undoubtedly have presented evidence of numerous articles discussing him in less than flattering terms. The emotional harm, if any, would have been minimal.

The issue of punitive damages, in my opinion, causes enormous verdicts in libel cases. Punitive damages are for the purpose of punishing the defendant's outrageous behavior in order to deter him or her from acting in a similar manner in the future. In order for the judge or jury to decide the amount of damages that will likely have a deterrent effect, the plaintiff is entitled to present evidence of the defendant's wealth and earnings.

Two ordinary cases arising out of fires illustrate how juries assess punitive damages in most cases. One defendant, Clark,* was a careless man, a bad neighbor. He rarely cleaned his front porch or back yard. The people on his street frequently complained about the state of his property. Clark's cellar was filled with oily rags, debris, and half-filled cans of paint. Somehow the trash in the basement caught

*These are fictitious names but real cases.

fire. There was a high wind and the fire spread to Mrs. Smith's house. Her out-of-pocket expenses for repairs, cleaning, and replacement of destroyed household goods was $20,000. Clark's only asset was his house that had been badly damaged. He earned $30,000 a year. The jury awarded Mrs. Smith $20,000 in compensatory damages and $10,000 in punitive damages.

In the other case, a fire broke out in a property owned by a wealthy slumlord. The neighbor who also suffered property damages of about $20,000 was awarded $200,000 in punitive damages. The jury sensibly concluded that in order to punish and deter the slumlord, the amount of punitive damages would have to be large enough to cause him real concern. In product liability cases, when juries are informed that the defendants have assets of billions, they frequently award punitive damages of a million dollars or more.

The usefulness of punitive damages in deterring dangerous or outrageous behavior on the part of a defendant is questionable. In a case before me arising out of a fire on property owned by the city, it was clear that city employees and inspectors had been grossly negligent. The jury awarded the plaintiff whose property had been damaged by the fire $500,000 in punitive damages. I set aside that award because it would have had no deterrent effect whatsoever. The negligent employees had not been fired; they had been promoted. The verdict would simply have penalized the innocent taxpayers. My decision was not appealed.

When juries learn of the wealth of CBS, the *New York Times, Time* magazine, and other target defendants, they naturally award enormous punitive damages. But it is the innocent stockholders, not the negligent reporters and editors, who pay these awards. And it is the public that suffers from increased media caution. Many thoughtful jurists question whether in any cases against corporate and public defendants punitive damages are appropriate.

The requirement of proof of damages and the abolition of punitive damages except in cases of personal spite or ill will (the common law definition of malice) would probably result in the reasonable verdicts returned by juries in other kinds of cases. Personal spitefulness on the part of authors is extremely rare. One thinks of the case of Quentin Reynolds against Westbrook Pegler. Pegler's columns falsely, venomously, and vituperatively attacked this famous reporter. None of the reported libel cases in the past quarter century have arisen out of this kind of ill will.

Requirement of proof of damages would undoubtedly reduce the stakes in libel cases. Even plaintiffs with a propensity to gamble and their counsel would exercise the usual cost benefit calculus that prevails in deciding whether or not to sue. If the provable damages were not substantially more than the costs of litigation, even if successful, not many suits would be brought for bruised feelings.

One important question that has not been addressed in articles about libel cases is the size of the jury. In the *Tavoulareas* case, the jury was composed of six persons. The few studies of behavior of actual juries, not simulated models, indicate that a jury of twelve that must return a unanimous verdict is more likely to result in a fair verdict than a small jury or one that requires only a five-sixths vote. Such juries are more easily influenced by one member.[14]

A judge is dismayed and discouraged after presiding over libel trials in which plaintiffs who have been seriously damaged by false reports or invasion of privacy are denied recovery and trials in which plaintiffs who have suffered no proven harm recover enormous verdicts. No experienced lawyer expects perfect justice, but we do look for what has been aptly called "a rough sense of justice."[15] Regardless of the outcome of a case, the lawyers usually have some sense of satisfaction. The winning lawyer has the joy of victory as well as a fee. The losing lawyer, unless the case was taken on a contingent fee basis, has at least been paid for time and labor expended. Besides, in a case in which the judge had to charge on seventy-five points of law, there is a good probability that the case will be reversed on appeal. So all is not lost.

The judge's only satisfaction at the end of a case is the feeling that justice has been done. In defamation and privacy cases, the trial judge rarely has any satisfaction. Usually I am not only dismayed by the result, I also believe that the time of the court and the money of the taxpayers has been wasted. Because almost every case is appealed, nothing is accomplished by these long and acrimonious trials.

In every trial, the presiding judge tries to uphold the law and weight the scales of justice fairly.[16] But in these cases, the law prevents the judge from protecting the privacy of subjects. The law also prevents the judge from protecting the First Amendment rights of authors. There is no way a judge can protect the interests of the public when they are not represented and they have no legal right to know. These are but a few of the problems a trial judge worries about when reading appellate opinions in defamation cases.

·V·

The Rights of Subjects

I'm NOBODY, Who are you?
Are you—NOBODY—Too?

—EMILY DICKINSON

AMERICANS in the late twentieth century have been educated to believe that every man, woman, and child is a unique person who has inherent rights entitled to respect. We also believe that it is the function of courts of law to grant redress when rights are violated. In the United States, lawsuits are brought by children and the elderly, the rich and the poor, religious believers and nonbelievers, and persons of every racial and ethnic group. All look to some phrase in the Constitution on which to predicate their claims to fair treatment by others. Many lawsuits by subjects against authors are predicated on the tacit assumption that the law should protect those attributes of personal dignity and decency that are valued in our society.

Authors rely on the First Amendment for protection of their rights of free expression. Subjects have no special constitutional language on which they can rely. They must try to fit their claims into some recognized legal right. The most available theory is that of property. Both the Fifth and Fourteenth Amendments grant protection to property rights. Legal redress for infringement of property rights and interests has been awarded for so many centuries that there is no necessity to find philosophical justification for recognition of these claims. When subjects assert rights that cannot be subsumed under the rubric of property, courts have great difficulty in finding authority or precedent for granting them protection.

The principal claims asserted by subjects against authors are defamation, right of publicity, right of biography, false light tort, and invasion of privacy. The first three have been held to be based on property interests. The other two have not. The lack of juridical foundation for those last two claims puts courts in the unenviable position of having to choose between denying redress to those who have unquestionably been harmed or creating law. It is fashionable among court critics to condemn activist judges and result-oriented decisions. But in deciding the nonproperty claims of subjects, courts have in most cases refused to move beyond precedent.

In most lawsuits, courts attempt to balance the rights of plaintiffs and defendants, giving due weight to societal interests involved. The balance struck may at times be wrong, but the process is fair and reasonable. In actions by subjects against authors based on nonproperty interests, that weighing process does not occur.

This chapter reviews both categories of claims by subjects. It suggests that property interests may be receiving more redress than is warranted by the harms suffered. It also proposes both a theory for recognizing nonproperty interests of subjects and a practical remedy.

The most common claim by subjects against authors is for defamation. The law treats reputation as a property right that is balanced against the First Amendment claims of the author. The basis for treating good name as a property asset is historical. It has rarely been questioned by contemporary courts. The law presumes without requiring proof that a good name or reputation is a financial asset. Whether such an assumption is justified in contemporary life is open to question. To date, no defendants have raised this issue. Some few subjects have been denied recovery because their reputation is so bad that they are deemed to be libel-proof. But even in such cases, the underlying proposition that good name is property has not been questioned.

Logically, injury or harm to reputation might more appropriately be deemed to be an emotional injury like pain, suffering, and loss of companionship of spouse or child. All these harms are now recognized as compensable injuries. Long before the law granted monetary recovery for such harms, however, reputation was accorded legal protection. In order to grant legal protection to this valued right, good name was treated as property. The remedy for damage to reputation, like the remedy for damage to any other property interest, was an award of money.

Although a number of verdicts awarding large sums to subjects who were defamed have been reversed, there is little indication in any of the Supreme Court opinions that a subject's right to sue for defamation will be curtailed or that the assumption that name calling causes compensable harm will be abolished. It is, therefore, unnecessary to discuss the juridical theories and precedents for granting recovery to subjects who sue for defamation.

The assumption that good name is an income-producing asset and the obverse, that loss of good name or reputation affects the property rights of the defamed person, cannot withstand scrutiny, however. Many persons convicted of white-collar crime have continued to earn huge sums. Some have been elected to political and public office. I do not suggest that a false and defamatory statement is not a tortious act entitling the person defamed to recover from the wrongdoer. Probably denial of such a claim based on a property interest would be unconstitutional. But there is no reason other than precedent to "presume" damages rather than requiring proof of actual losses both as to economic interest and emotional harm.

Under the state of defamation law in 1986, the subject's likelihood of recovery will depend not upon the falsity of the statement but upon whether the subject is deemed to be a public or a private figure. The case of *Ocala Star-Banner Co.* v. *Damron*[1] illustrates dramatically the unfairness of the "actual malice" test when applied to subjects who are public figures. Damron, a mayor who was a candidate for public office, was falsely charged with having had a criminal record. He lost the election and sued for libel. The defendant newspaper admitted the falsehood. It was the mayor's brother who had committed a crime. The editor testified that he must have had a temporary "aberration" in confusing the two brothers. The Supreme Court held that because Damron was a public figure and failed to prove that the press had acted with "actual malice" he could not recover.* But private figures who have suffered little or any provable harm do recover large verdicts.

Proposed appropriate standards of fault in defamation suits will be discussed in the chapters dealing with the various contexts in

---

*When a falsely defamed public figure sues in a jurisdiction where there is a shield law protecting the reporter from disclosing confidential sources, it is extremely difficult to prove "actual malice." In a case before me the reporter claimed reliance on a protected source; the editor claimed honest belief in the reporter's integrity despite the bizarre, unreasonable, and defamatory nature of the story. The plaintiff proved economic loss as a result of the story. Because it was unclear whether plaintiff was a limited public figure or a private figure, the case was settled after five days of trial.

which these cases arise: news, reports and docudramas based on actual crimes, fiction, biography, and commercial speech. Subjects who are held to be public figures are seriously disadvantaged in defamation cases because their recovery for false and defamatory statements is based not on any objective standard of fault but on the subjective mental processes of the defendant. This is a novel standard of liability peculiar to libel law.

Rights of publicity and biography are also predicated on the subject's property interests. These claims are not based on the assumption that plaintiff's life story or personality are property interests or that an individual has personal rights unrelated to economic assets. Rather these actions are based on the theory that individuals have the right to exploit their own lives, persons, achievements, and notoriety for their own profit to the exclusion of others. Subjects assert that their personalities and achievements are assets capable of producing income and profits.

The right of publicity is a recent innovation. It is predicated on the proposition that the subject has a salable asset. In determining whether subjects have a right of publicity, courts ask whether they have, in fact, used themselves and their prominence as income-producing property.

The burgeoning right of publicity was promulgated in order to permit individuals to reap the profits of their own fame and ability. This is a plausible and appealing argument. Why should someone else, the defendant, profit from the subject's efforts to create a name or a skill that commands public interest? Why should the defendant get a free ride at the expense of the subject? The majority of the Supreme Court has accepted this theory.

In the leading case of *Zacchini* v. *Scripps-Howard Broadcasting Co.,*[2] the Supreme Court sustained the plaintiff's right of publicity. The majority opinion states that the defendant had used without charge "that for which the performer usually gets paid." With little discussion, the Court concluded that for this reason plaintiff was entitled to recover damages. Plaintiff was a professional stunt entertainer who performed his act between the halves of a football game. The game was televised, and the plaintiff's entire performance was shown. He did not consent to the telecast; he was not paid. He sued the television station. The Ohio Supreme Court ruled in favor of the broadcaster. The United States Supreme Court reversed.

This appears to be a clear-cut case of a broadcaster getting a "free ride" at the expense of a professional entertainer, and it does not seem to involve First Amendment rights. Three justices of the Supreme Court, however, dissented on the ground that the defendant had a right to report a newsworthy event. It is far from clear whether the plaintiff would have recovered if only a portion of his performance, no matter how substantial, had been telecast without his consent and without compensation.

On the peculiar facts of the case, the decision does not appear to infringe rights of authors or to limit the reach of the First Amendment. It can scarcely be argued that the public was being deprived of entertainment. Radio and television programs normally pay performers. If the fee is too high, the performance is not broadcast.

The extension of the right of publicity to require compensation for reports of verbal communications, whether written or oral, however, would raise serious First Amendment problems. Many speakers are paid substantial fees for lectures. These talks are often later published in journals for which the speakers are paid another fee. If the speaker is a well-known person who discusses a matter of public interest, the speech will be reported in the media. If the entire speech is reprinted, does the speaker have a right of publicity that should override the rights of the media? If it were reprinted, the speaker undoubtedly would lose the fees and royalties for publication of the speech. In the language of the court, the media would be using "without charge that for which the performer [or speaker] usually gets paid."* Yet, to extend the right of publicity to such a situation would, I believe, abridge freedom of the press and would seriously cut off public access to information and opinion. Reporting of news, speeches, discussions, and ideas is qualitatively different from broadcasting musical, dramatic, athletic, and other types of performances. To date, there has been no judicial delineation of rights based on the obvious differences between performances and verbal communications.

The right of biography is also based on the subject's alleged property interest in exploiting his or her own life for profit to the exclusion of others. This claim is discussed in Chapter IX.

False light tort and invasion of privacy when asserted in the context of conflicts between subject and author, however, are predicated on the theory that individuals have rights unrelated to property. Subjects asserting such claims have difficulty in finding common law doctrine recognizing as legal rights those aspects of the subject's personality that are infringed or violated by authors. In these cases,

---

*Copyright laws would, of course, protect authors of plays and composers of music.

subjects seek to establish perimeters of a zone of exclusivity beyond which all who enter without permission must be deemed trespassers. Yet, common law trespass is limited to land. Therefore, subjects must instead make two claims: One, that if authors are going to write about the subject they must do so truthfully. The other is that the subject is not fair game for exploitation and may not be used by authors without consent. To date, neither claim has received adequate protection despite the fact that the Supreme Court has proclaimed that constitutional rights transcend property rights.[3]

In other contexts, courts have recognized that individuals do have certain rights of dignity, privacy, and conscience that may not be violated by employers, schools, and other institutions and individuals. Children attending public schools may not be required to take an oath of allegiance if that offends their religious beliefs. Persons may not be asked intimate questions on employment applications. They may not be subjected to psychological testing without consent. Employment may not be conditioned on terms that violate one's religious beliefs, such as working on the particular Sabbath that the employee observes. It could be argued that because people are free agents who can choose to accept or refuse to accept job offers, they may be said to waive all conditions by applying for or accepting employment. But courts have not expanded the concept of freedom of contract indefinitely. Whether the proposed requirement of lie detector tests and drug tests for federal employees will be enforced and, if so, whether it will be upheld by the courts cannot be predicted. Moreover, the results of polygraph tests and truth serum are inadmissible in court. The reason for exclusion is their unreliability not the privacy rights of the testees.

Both the right to be presented truthfully and the right of privacy are premised on the theory that the law should protect aspects of personality unrelated to property. But Kant's tenet that every individual is a free and rational agent whose existence is an end in itself is not a common law doctrine. On the contrary, under traditional Anglo-American legal concepts, the law protects only property rights. This view was expressed as recently as 1930. A judge declared, "The law cannot undertake to remedy sentimental injury, and it is not concerned with the feelings of a person except as discomfort and suffering are connected with the possession and enjoyment of property."[4]

During the twentieth century, the law has gradually recognized that nonphysical, nonproperty harms are entitled to compensation.

In accident cases, frequently the emotional harms—pain, suffering, and loss of life's pleasures—receive more in dollars and cents than physical injuries and property damages. The old rule prohibiting recovery for emotional harms unless there was also some physical injury, no matter how slight, has been abrogated. A parent who sees his or her child being injured or killed may recover for emotional harm even though the parent was not physically hurt. A business corporation can recover for economic losses unaccompanied by property damage, provided that the corporation can prove the defendant's negligence, the foreseeability of harm, and the causal relationship between the fault and the losses suffered.[5]

The extension of legal rights to purely emotional harms does not require a radical unprecedented leap into the unknown. It is a logical development of the continually expanding law of torts. Some states do recognize as a compensable claim the willful infliction of emotional harm. This doctrine has been applied, incorrectly I believe, to satirical comments about well-known personalities.[6] Yet, it does not protect those who suffer emotional harm from publications that falsely portray them in a nondefamatory way. Nor does it afford redress to persons whose privacy has been violated by authors who had no intent to cause harm.

More appropriate and consonant with general principles of law would be a formulation of legally cognizable rights to truth, dignity, and privacy. These are attributes of every individual that a democratic society should value. I suggest that this cluster of attributes be known as a "right of persona."[7] Jung used the term "persona" to describe the masks individuals present to the public to hide their nakedness. In a society predicated on individual rights, each person should be entitled to choose the face he or she wishes to present to the public unless that right is waived or some other right is paramount.

Infringement of a right of truth under general principles of tort law should be compensable. Instead of proving willfulness or actual malice, the subject would have to prove negligence. The document or electronic program would be examined as a whole to see whether the subject was presented accurately. In order to recover, the subject would have to prove that the author was at fault by negligently misstating the facts. Damages would be proved in the same manner as in any other action for personal injuries. Similar rules would prevail with respect to actions for invasion of privacy.

The concept of right to privacy is less than a hundred years old, a mere upstart in the common law. By contrast, property rights have been recognized for centuries. Although the right to privacy has been accorded only very limited recognition in the conflicts between subjects and authors, it has formed the juridical basis for many Supreme Court decisions. The ruling holding unconstitutional state statutes prohibiting abortion was predicated, at least in part, on a woman's right of privacy, as well as the physicians' rights.[8] The notion of privacy as a constitutional right has also been used to invalidate zoning laws restricting occupancy of single-family dwellings to persons related by blood or marriage[9] and a host of other statutes and ordinances enacted to protect and further the general welfare of the community. When such restrictions impinge on the privacy of the individual, courts have held that the right of privacy is paramount.

The genesis of the idea that in a democratic society the individual has a legal right to be let alone and not be exploited is an article by Louis D. Brandeis, later a Supreme Court justice, and Samuel Warren in the *Harvard Law Review* in 1890.[10] The phrase, "right of privacy," was first given currency in this article. It was a seminal concept advancing individual liberty even though its premise exhibits a curious insensitivity to freedom of the press. The authors state apodictically:

> The press is overstepping in every direction the obvious bonds of propriety and of decency. [M]odern enterprise and innovation have, through invasions upon privacy, subjected [the individual] . . . to mental pain and distress, far greater than could be inflicted by mere bodily injury.

No convincing evidence of articles that went beyond the bounds of decency was presented, nor did the authors attempt to define those bounds. They did not consider that this right might infringe First Amendment rights. The language and underlying principle of curbing the press strike modern readers as an expression of hostility to significant freedoms. It must be remembered, however, that generally held legal doctrine at that time excluded libel from the ambit of the First Amendment.

In the mid-1980s, courts have given increasing attention to freedom of expression. But they have sadly neglected rights of privacy. It is a thesis of this book that both are fundamental aspects of individual rights and that both must be protected. Lacking are philosophical and juridical theories on which courts can predicate legal recognition of privacy rights.

Privacy is a peculiarly modern idea. It has no analogue prior to the twentieth century. If one examines the conditions of life under which it is possible to have a measure of seclusion and freedom from the prying eyes and ears of neighbors, government officials, and church authorities, it is evident that privacy is a luxury available only to those who can afford adequate living space and who live in a state in which there are restrictions upon what government may demand of the individual and where the church is not permitted to control individual choices. Such conditions did not prevail throughout most of history. They do not prevail in most parts of the world today. Even in the United States, many people cannot afford the material requirements for privacy.

In tribal life, there was little opportunity for an individual ever to be alone. People banded together for protection and safety. Their lives were lived in full public view. In many societies, such as China, the dwelling unit houses the extended family, even though there may be individual homes within the family or communal compound. There is little opportunity for privacy and solitude under such living arrangements. In contemporary Russia, shortage of housing is a critical problem. Probably the vast majority of the Russian population has never been able to afford privacy. Language scholars state that there is no word in the Russian language for "privacy." There is an equivalent word for "private" used as an adjective. But the concept of privacy has apparently not been so widely accepted as to require a word to convey this precise meaning.

In medieval times in Western Europe, life centered around the castle or manor house. Life was essentially communal. There were no private rooms in medieval inns. Even the wealthy and powerful lived their lives in public view. As late as the seventeenth century, the queens of France gave birth in public, and kings performed their bodily functions in the presence of courtiers. The idea that one had a right not to be observed had not arrived.

Among the poor today in many parts of the world, the entire family consisting of children, parents, grandparents, others, and even animals sleep in the same room. There is little opportunity for the luxury of solitude. While it is popular for sociologists to decry the anomie of urban life and to deplore the lonely crowd, the disadvantages and detriments of a completely communal life without privacy are rarely considered.

The notion of individual living space free from the prying eyes of neighbors, the concierge, and public officials is ingrained in the contemporary American ethos. It may perhaps be traced to the pioneer tradition of self-reliance and freedom from social constraints. Communal living has had little appeal for Americans. In the nineteenth century, a few unsuccessful efforts to found idealistic communities of group living failed abysmally. More common has been the disparagement of small-town life in novels in the late nineteenth and early twentieth centuries. They depict life in such communities as characterized by snooping, gossip, and lack of privacy.

It is not astonishing that the concept of privacy as a legally enforceable right did not exist anywhere prior to its enunciation in the United States in 1890. For the past few generations, the American ideal has been a private home, whether a house or a part of a multiple dwelling, for each family. Within that home, it is considered not only appropriate but also necessary that each child have his or her own room. In deciding custody of children, courts give great weight to these living arrangements. The need for privacy within the home, a room of one's own, was apotheosized by Virginia Woolf in 1929. Today it is a truism.

Freedom from intrusion in one's private life and the right to seclusion may be viewed in two ways: as a basic attribute of the individual and as an extension of the sanctity of the home. Brandeis declared that ". . . the right to be let alone [is] . . . the most comprehensive and the right most valued by civilized men." This instinctive belief in the value of autonomy and privacy probably furnishes the only basis for the entire structure of the law of privacy developed during the past century although some reliance might be placed on the Ninth and Tenth Amendments. The Ninth Amendment provides that the rights enumerated in the Constitution "shall not be construed to deny or disparage others retained by the people." The Tenth Amendment provides that "The powers not delegated to the United States by the Constitution, nor prohibited by it to the States, are reserved to the States respectively, or to the people." Whether privacy is such a right has not been adequately explored. If any juridical authority is required to acknowledge a right of privacy or the proposed right of persona, however, these provisions should suffice.

Sanctity of the home is an old English doctrine capsulized in the phrase, "A man's home is his castle." With little discussion or philosophical justification it forms the basis for much substantive American law.* For example, the state cannot intrude into the privacy of

---

*The Fourth Amendment does provide for the right of the people to be secure in their houses, papers, and effects.

one's home even on a well-founded suspicion of wrongdoing. The police must get a warrant based on reasonable grounds that they believe a crime has been committed and that the defendant is involved unless there are exigent circumstances. Yet, to open one's house to a police officer is a far less disturbing intrusion to most people than to have one's private life spread across the pages of the daily press or a book or revealed on the electronic media. Little thought has been devoted to protecting the individual from this kind of invasion of privacy.

Although the public showing of pornographic films may be prohibited, the showing of the very same films in the privacy of the home is exempt from governmental interference.[11] The right of the state to protect children from immoral or pornographic material is always given as a sound reason for restricting the distribution of such printed matter and films. It is assumed without much discussion that such protection is a legitimate function of government. Nonetheless, the courts have not extended the laws on pornography to such materials viewed in the home.

Not all persons cherish privacy. Many seek out publicity. A cursory review of television programs discloses that hundreds, if not thousands, of people voluntarily expose themselves to embarrassing interviews. They unblushingly reveal the most intimate facts regarding their past history, their sexual behavior, their hopes and aspirations, and even their criminal conduct. The "Phil Donahue Show" is one of many that presents criminals and crime victims who willingly describe their experiences. Other shows, such as "This is Your Life," reveal private experiences of individuals whose lives have no public or news interest. These people willingly consent to appear. Such individuals, of course, could not legitimately claim that their right of privacy has been invaded.

The fact that the desire for publicity, even for its own sake, is so prevalent should not militate against the rights of those who prefer privacy, shun such publicity and exposure, and find them distasteful and painful. A contrary view would, under the rubric of First Amendment rights, permit Big Brother into the homes and lives of any subject at the will of the author. If a right of persona were recognized, new doctrines and tests would have to be employed in balancing such a right against First Amendment claims. The factors that should be considered in deciding between these rights and the rules of proof, procedure, and damages will be discussed in the chapters dealing with the different contexts in which such claims are asserted.

Those who desire seclusion and privacy in the midst of society have difficulty in satisfying these needs. Not many persons can retreat to the desert or the wilderness and live a primitive life as a hermit. Whatever freedom from intrusion an individual demands must be obtained at the expense of interests of others, the most common of which is curiosity. The desire to know about other people appears to be endemic to the human species. Authors, including the daily press, magazines, book publishers, and the electronic media, cater to this desire. They publish intimate details of the physical condition of the president and the lives and loves of an enormous number of famous and notorious people. They air these tidbits whether they are fit to print or not. Hence, there is a collision between subjects who claim rights of privacy, and authors who, finding a large audience avid for such material, assert First Amendment rights.

Although Brandeis and Warren aimed their attack at the press rather than private industry, one of the first cases[12] that attempted to rely on the doctrine arose out of commercial exploitation through advertising, not invasion of privacy by the media. A manufacturer used the photograph of a young lady without her permission on 25,000 posters advertising its flour. She sued, claiming invasion of privacy. The New York court held that there is no common law right of privacy. In response to the demand from an outraged public, the legislature enacted a new provision of the New York Civil Rights Law,[13] providing that:

> Any person whose name, portrait or picture is used within this state for advertising purposes or for the purpose of trade without [his] written consent . . . may sue for an injunction and monetary damages for any injuries.

If the defendant acted knowingly and willfully, the act provided that the plaintiff was entitled to exemplary [punitive] damages.

Legislators, both federal and state, have been more sensitive than the courts to the public's desire for privacy. Judges are limited by precedent and the facts of the particular cases before them. In contrast, legislators can respond to the wishes of the electorate. They can enact laws prohibiting conduct and prescribing remedies without engaging in juridical or philosophical discussions and justifications.

As recently as 1980, however, in *Arrington* v. *N.Y. Times,*[14] New York courts, despite the statute, continued to hold that there is no common law right to privacy. In that case, an individual's picture was published without his consent, but it was not used for advertising. He was denied recovery. The notion that one's image is peculiarly private has a long lineage. Among preliterate peoples, there is a tradition of keeping one's real name secret and guarding against the use of one's image lest they be misused. Most tourists who visit primitive areas are aware that these people resent having their pictures taken as do most people in so-called developed countries.

Shortly after the New York statute was enacted, ten states adopted similar legislation.[15] These laws, like the New York statute are aimed at prohibiting exploitation of individuals through advertising. Whether these statutes can protect individuals from advertisers is far from clear because the Supreme Court has held that commercial speech is also entitled to First Amendment protections.[16] Violations of privacy by use of pictures and words occur in a wide variety of commercial and noncommercial contexts. In such conflicts between subjects and authors, whether commercial or not, the courts under the rubric of the First Amendment have given short shrift to the claims of subjects. But Congress, with little extended juridical or philosophical discussion, has accepted the concept that privacy is a value entitled to legal protection. The Federal Privacy Act was passed in 1974.[17]

The Privacy Protection Study Commission created pursuant to that act reported its findings to President Carter in 1977. Although the focus of the commission's work was confidentiality of computerized information collected and maintained by government health agencies and credit organizations and banks, the underlying premise was that individuals have rights of privacy that should be granted enforceable legal protection. The mandate of the commission was to "report on such other legislative recommendations as it may determine to be necessary to protect the privacy of individuals while meeting the legitimate needs of government and society for information."[18]

Despite state and federal statutes establishing rights of privacy, courts have been slow to give effect to such rights. In the absence of statute, it is clear that there is no common law right of privacy. Nonetheless, legal textbooks declare that the right of privacy prohibits the following actions by authors: (1) appropriation of another's name or likeness; (2) publicity that unreasonably places another in a false light; (3) unreasonable publicity given to another's private life; (4) unreasonable intrusion on the seclusion of another.[19] These four actions are dissimilar and are predicated on very different concepts and claims. Yet all are indiscriminately lumped together under the rubric of privacy.

The first two actions—appropriation of another's name or likeness and publicity that unreasonably places another in a false light—appear to be directed at advertising and public relations. When plaintiffs have made such claims, defendants have asserted First Amendment freedoms. In an interesting and unusual case, Jacqueline Kennedy Onassis sued the Christian Dior Company to enjoin the use of a "look-alike" model in advertising its products. The New York trial court granted an injunction prohibiting the use of a model who masqueraded as Mrs. Onassis and declared, "there is no free ride."[20] The model unsuccessfully claimed that she was engaged in a work of art. Dior asserted that its rights of free speech were infringed. The defendants did not appeal. Because of the unique factual situation, this case gives little comfort to subjects or authors and not much guidance to other courts. The court did not apply the public versus private figure test. Mrs. Onassis is undoubtedly a public figure. Should she have had to prove "actual malice" in the use of the look-alike model? To date, the rules developed in libel cases have not been applied to false light tort.

The rules are also unclear as to the other two torts for which the law is supposed to grant redress: unreasonable publicity given to another's private life and unreasonable intrusion on the seclusion of another. Congress recognized privacy as a legitimate right applicable to many phases of life. But when confronted with claims of privacy, the courts phrase the issue differently. They ask whether the individual had a legitimate "expectation of privacy" under the particular circumstances of the case.

Several Supreme Court decisions indicate the very limited scope the Court grants to such expectations. It held that an individual has no "expectation of privacy" with respect to bank records[21] and public assistance reports.[22] Nor can an individual expect privacy in a motor home with the shades drawn.[23] Most recently the Court held that an individual has no expectation of privacy in his own fenced backyard and that an observation by a police officer flying over the yard in a helicopter at 1,000 feet was not an unauthorized intrusion into the sanctity of the home.[24] The Court upheld the seizure of marijuana plants growing in the yard whose existence was discovered by the low-flying police officer. The Court's conclusion that it is unreasonable to expect privacy in a high double-fenced backyard is astonishing. As the hapless defendant pointed out, his only option in order to maintain privacy would be to cover his backyard, a choice that would defeat its purpose as an outdoor living area. Obviously passengers on regular commercial flights could not observe defendant's activities in his backyard. To have to guard against police in low-flying helicopters appears to strain the concept of expectation of privacy.

The decision of the Supreme Court in *Bowers* v. *Hardwick*, [25] June 30, 1986, upholding the prosecution of consenting adults for sodomy committed in the bedroom is another example of the restrictive view of privacy adopted by the majority of the Court. The issue, as I see it in its application to rights of subjects, is not the power of the state to criminalize acts committed by consenting adults, although there are many arguments for that position, but the expectation of privacy in the home. As Justice Blackmun in his dissenting opinion observed, "We protect those rights [associated with the individual, the family, and parenthood] not because they contribute, in some direct and material way, to the general public welfare, but because they form so central a part of an individual life."

In my opinion, this decision underscores the need for a federal statute making explicit the right of privacy. Writing for the majority, Justice White observed, "The Court is most vulnerable and comes nearest to illegitimacy when it deals with judge-made constitutional law having little or no cognizable roots in the language or design of the Constitution." Privacy has little cognizable roots in either Anglo-American law or the Constitution. But it is clearly an aspect of life valued by the vast majority of Americans.

A recent case in which the jury awarded a plaintiff, Irving MacLeder, who was pursued by a camera crew, $1.25 million for invasion of privacy by a CBS station indicates that the public does feel strongly that people should not be exploited, even though the subject of industrial pollution was clearly newsworthy.[26] Whether this verdict will be sustained is, of course, questionable. CBS maintains that the First Amendment protects its right to inform the public about the dangers of dumping toxic waste and that the pictures of the plaintiff disclosed a serious threat to public safety. How the appellate courts will balance these claims is unpredictable.

Individuals who lead quiet, reclusive lives, whose achievements or misconduct do not bring them to public attention are not likely to be the subjects chosen by authors. What usually brings such people to the attention of authors is a misfortune, catastrophe, or some anomalous situation. These subjects are the victims of crime or disaster or they are in some way involved in such incidents. One must ask whether by reason of such unplanned and undesired circumstances they then become fair game, as it were, for authors to utilize as source material for extended articles, books, and TV shows. Do they lose forever any expectation of privacy?

Two cases illustrate what Edward J. Blaustein poetically and accurately describes as "the soul . . . [being] . . . bruised by exposure to the world."[27] Sidis, a prodigy whose extraordinary gifts were widely reported when he was a young child, had a singularly unhappy life attempting to escape the publicity attendant on his intelligence. He left the teaching positions for which he was well fitted and took menial employment. Years later, the *New Yorker* magazine, without his consent, wrote a long, intimate profile describing the details of his life. In denying him recovery, the Court blandly assumed that once a person is the subject of a news story he has forever lost his right of privacy.[28] Sidis was undeniably caused suffering by the publication. It was not false; it was not defamatory. But it certainly gave unreasonable publicity to his life and shattered his seclusion.

In a California case,[29] the subject's seclusion and comfort were also shattered. A movie was based on the life of a former prostitute using her real name. Years had passed since she had engaged in that occupation. She had married and led a quiet middle-class life. She sued and was denied recovery.

In another case alleging invasion of privacy, the plaintiff lost but, I believe, for the wrong reason. Sydney Biddle Barrows, known as the "Mayflower Madam" because she was a member of a very old family and allegedly ran a call-girl ring, sued her former boyfriend for selling nude photographs of her. Barrows claimed invasion of privacy. Her suit was dismissed on the grounds of the defendant's First Amendment rights.[30] This appears to be a bizarre ruling. The court might well have found that the plaintiff by her own actions had forfeited any right to privacy. But one must question whether the sale of photographs, in contrast to the sale of any other objects, involves more than a property right.

The cases decided by the Supreme Court subsequent to *New York Times* v. *Sullivan* also give short shrift to claims of privacy. These cases turn on the public/private figure test and proof of actual malice. In two strikingly similar cases, the Court reached different results: *Time, Inc.* v. *Hill*[31] and *Cantrell* v. *Forrest City Publishing Co.*[32] In both cases, the plaintiffs were victims of misfortune through no

fault of their own. Prior to the times tragedy had struck, both families were unquestionably private figures, quietly leading private lives.
They were not public officials. They had not thrust themselves into
public notice. No author had ever found either family to be a subject
of any interest whatsoever.

The Hills were victims of a crime. They were held hostage by a
band of escaped convicts. The crime was widely reported. Thereafter,
the Hills moved to another state to avoid any connection with the
incident. The episode was the basis of a play, *The Desperate Hours,*
that was a fictionalized treatment of the crime and its aftermath. The
Hills did not sue the dramatist. After the play was produced, *Time*
magazine carried a story stating that the play was a factual reenact-
ment of the ordeal of the Hill family. This was clearly and admittedly
false.

Mr. Cantrell was one of forty-four persons who were killed in the
collapse of a bridge. At the time, this incident was also widely
reported. Eight months after the accident in which Mr. Cantrell
died, the Sunday Magazine of the *Cleveland Plain Dealer* published
a feature story with photographs describing the poverty and hard-
ships the family suffered as a result of Mr. Cantrell's death.

Both the Hills and the Cantrells sued, claiming invasion of privacy
and false light tort. In both cases, juries found for the plaintiffs. Mrs.
Cantrell contended that the facts in the story about her and her
family were false. Neither story was a matter of news. Both were
published months after the incidents. There were no time constraints
on the reporters or the editors. They could have investigated the true
facts. But truth was not the principal issue in either case. Both
families objected to being wrenched out of their seclusion and being
forced to relive tragic and painful episodes that must have caused
them emotional harm. Did they have a right to resume their private
lives after tragedy struck? Were they forever at the mercy of any
reporter who chose to write about the incidents? The Supreme Court
did not address these issues.

In the *Hill* case, the Court held that the plaintiffs were public
figures. Obviously they had not asked to be held hostage. They had
not voluntarily "thrust themselves in the vortex of public" notice, the
test of public figure created by the Supreme Court. The *Hill* case was
remanded by the United States Supreme Court for a new trial on the
"actual malice" question. A trial court, with or without a jury, had
to determine whether *Time* magazine knew that the play was a
fictionalized version of the crime or whether it acted in reckless
disregard of truth or falsity.

In the *Cantrell* case, the trial judge had struck the plaintiff's claim for punitive damages, holding that common law malice, defined as evil intent or willful disregard for others, had not been proved. This is a different standard from the "actual malice" requirement imported into the First Amendment cases by the decision in *New York Times* v. *Sullivan*. I submit that a proper charge to the jury on these differing standards would result in hopeless confusion. The court of appeals was of the opinion that "actual malice" had not been proved by the Cantrells. The Supreme Court, however, searched the record for evidence. The majority opinion stated: "There was no dispute during the trial that Esterhaz [the reporter] who did not testify, must have known that a number of statements in the feature story were untrue." This is an astonishing legal doctrine. Although a negative inference may be drawn from failure to call a witness, that scarcely supplies necessary evidence. Moreover, the plaintiff could have cross-examined him as an adverse witness but did not choose to do so.

It is interesting that the distinguished civil libertarian, Professor Thomas I. Emerson of the Yale Law School, concluded that the decision in the *Hill* case was right. He declared, "An individual caught up in a public event, even through no fault of his own, cannot expect to keep it private at the time or later.[33] Emerson gave no reasons for this conclusion. He did not compare or balance the right of the author with the right of the subject or the public interest in being informed. Nor did he consider the obvious negligence of *Time* in failing to check the facts.

If one examines the right of privacy in a slightly different context, the inappropriateness of the standards employed by the Supreme Court is apparent. Instead of Mrs. Cantrell, whose husband was killed in a notorious accident, let us look at the right of Mrs. Doe, whose husband died of natural causes. Assume that eight months after his death, a reporter went to her home. Without her permission, he entered the house, took pictures, talked to her minor children, and then wrote a story describing the poverty of the Doe family and the difficulties of widows and fatherless children. Whether the story was true or false, shouldn't Mrs. Doe be entitled to privacy? Under the laws of most jurisdictions, Mrs. Doe could file a private criminal complaint against the reporter and photographer for criminal trespass. Even if they were admitted to the premises by minor children, it is clear that those children had no authority to permit strangers into their home. But it is far from clear whether Mrs. Doe could recover civil damages for invasion of privacy absent a very broad statute, or whether such a statute would prevail over the reporter's First Amendment claims.

Mrs. Doe would undoubtedly be considered a private figure. Nothing had brought her to the attention of the public. Therefore, she would not have to prove actual malice. But if the article was factually accurate, she would probably not prevail against the First Amendment claims of the author.

A later case[34] may be read as signaling a retreat from the harsh requirements of the *Hill* case. But the Supreme Court did not take that opportunity to recognize a right of privacy or to overrule the public/private figure test that was critical in the *Hill* case. Plaintiff sued *Reader's Digest* for defamation claiming that an article listing him among a number of persons identified as Soviet agents was false and defamatory. Some fifteen years before the article appeared, plaintiff had been interviewed by the FBI in connection with Soviet espionage. He had failed to respond to a subpoena ordering him to testify and had been held in contempt. He received a one-year suspended sentence. The lower court granted defendant's motion for summary judgment on the ground that the plaintiff was a public figure and had failed to prove actual malice on the part of the defendant. The issue of privacy was not raised. The Supreme Court reversed, declaring that a "private figure is not automatically transformed into a public figure just by becoming involved in or associated with a matter that attracts public attention." The Court found that the story was newsworthy, but it also pointed out that in the intervening years plaintiff had led a law-abiding life and that he did not thrust himself into public attention. Therefore, he was held to be a private figure.

This analysis should have allowed the Hills to recover. In the *Hill* case, the story was false and probably not newsworthy. But in neither case did the Court recognize a right of privacy based on the lapse of time. Rather, while still using the public/private figure analysis, in *Wolston* the Supreme Court declared that "it would be a crass legal fiction to assert that a matter once public never becomes private again." In a California case,[35] plaintiff had been convicted of a crime in 1956. He had served his sentence and led a law-abiding life ever since. Eleven years later, *Reader's Digest* published an article mentioning his crime but not indicating that it had occurred in 1956. The trial court sustained the defendant's demurrer. The California Supreme Court reversed, holding that the plaintiff had stated a cause of action for false light tort and invasion of privacy. California law, unlike federal law and the law of many states, does recognize a right of privacy. It is not clear whether if the article had given the date of plaintiff's crime he would have prevailed.

In these cases, the allegedly defamatory statements were published in national magazines. Plaintiffs' rights depended upon the peculiarities of state laws as did defendant's liability. They underscore the need for a federal statute that specifically creates a right of privacy.

The public/private figure test establishes an ill-defined distinction. In the context of claims of privacy, one must ask whether all persons held to be public figures, either voluntarily or involuntarily, have forfeited all rights to privacy. Should their sex lives, mental and physical health, family problems, finances and life styles be forever in the public domain, as it were, available to any author or publisher?

It may reasonably be argued that public officials and candidates for public office waive their rights to privacy. Certainly their moral and financial behavior are subjects of legitimate public interest. It has been aptly said that public officials should have "glass pockets." Like Caesar's wife, they should also be above suspicion in all their personal dealings. Jefferson declared, "When a man assumes a public trust, he should consider himself as public property." There can be little question that the mental problems, whatever they may have been, of Senator Thomas F. Eagleton, were reasonably relevant to his candidacy for vice-president. (Eagleton was dropped as a vice presidential running mate by Senator George McGovern, the 1972 presidential candidate, after reports that Eagleton had received psychiatric treatment were made public. He had been hospitalized for depression.) No matter how painful the disclosures may have been, it was Eagleton who made the choice to run for public office. If he valued privacy more than public life, he could have protected that interest by declining to run for office.

Henry Kissinger has asserted that he has a right to privacy and has protested certain material in a biography of him. Kissinger is undeniably a public figure. Certainly he did not cease being a public figure when he left office. He has continued to thrust himself in the limelight. But even if he had not done so, his extraordinary position of power would make him and his life and opinions a matter of public concern. But those who have not occupied such positions of power and who are involuntarily thrust into the limelight for a brief period should, I believe, after a reasonable lapse of time, be considered the private figures they were before the incident.

When issues of privacy are raised not in the context of libel suits, the courts ask, "What was the party's reasonable expectation of privacy?" Did the Hills and the Cantrells, months after the incidents, have a reasonable expectation that they would be allowed to resume their private lives? I believe the answer should be "yes." Although the answers of the Supreme Court to this question may at times have been unreasonable, the question is sensible. Drivers and passengers in motor vehicles have little expectation of privacy. Any car may be stopped on the highway for a variety of reasons—an accident, a minor traffic violation, a road check. People know these facts and, therefore, have no reasonable expectation of privacy in a vehicle. Persons in their homes do have an expectation of privacy.

Victims of crime have little expectation of privacy immediately after the incident. They must submit to questioning by the police, detectives, and prosecuting attorneys. They must testify in court. If the crime occurred in the home, police and detectives will search the premises. But after the trial is over, when the incident has ceased to be news, should they not have the same expectation of privacy as anyone else?

Justice Douglas, who dissented in the *Cantrell* case on the grounds that the First Amendment rights of the press were abridged, wisely observed that to make rights turn on the subtle distinction between common law malice and the "actual malice" standard created by the Court is to "stand the First Amendment on its head." To make the rights of subjects and authors depend on such subtle and unpredictable distinctions is to destroy those rights.

The Supreme Court refused to recognize the rights of privacy of another victimized family. In this case, it was the family of a young rape victim.[36] At the time of the incident, the press had reported the crime but not the name of the victim. Most responsible newspapers do not publish the names of rape victims even though they are a matter of public record and readily available. Some time later, a radio station broadcast the facts, including the name of the victim who was then deceased. This victim was also held to be a public figure. Her parents who sued claiming invasion of privacy were denied recovery. One must ask what First Amendment rights were advanced by the release of the victim's name and why the parents should have had to suffer the agonies of having the crime against their daughter brought to public attention.

When the crime victim is alive, the harm done by publication of the victim's name may be devastating. I presided over two rape trials in which both victims were high school girls. Dawn* was shopping

---

*These are fictious names, and the facts have been disguised slightly to protect the victims.

in a discount store when the guard ordered her into an office where she was held and raped. April* was dragged off a sidewalk and raped in a vacant lot. The police managed to apprehend both rapists. Each case came to trial about four months after the incident. By the times of the trials, both girls had recovered from the physical trauma but were having emotional problems. But both were in school and managing to cope. Both crimes and both trials were reported in the press, but the names of the victims were not disclosed.

After the conviction of Dawn's assailant, her family retained a lawyer who filed suit against the discount store. The case was promptly settled for a substantial sum because the law was perfectly clear; the store was liable.

Because April's attack occurred on the street, there was no one to sue. She did receive a small sum from the Crime Victims' Compensation Fund, which paid for some psychotherapy. Some seven or eight months after the trial, an article on crime in the streets was published. Among the cases described was the attack on April. Her name was given and a picture of her that had appeared in a local paper some time before when she was in a school play was also published. This article was the first notice that April's friends, classmates, and neighbors had of the crime. After the article appeared, April dropped out of school. She refused to leave her home. Months later the mental health therapist reported that her prognosis was not good. April's family retained a lawyer who attempted to negotiate a settlement with the magazine. On the advice of counsel the publisher adamantly refused to pay. There was no liability. The story was accurate. April was a public figure. There was no malice.

One cannot fault counsel for the publisher. Under the state of the law as enunciated by the Supreme Court, there is no liability for a truthful report of a crime even after a lapse of time. But I believe that if the Congress or any state legislature were asked whether April should have a right of privacy, the members would overwhelmingly vote that she should. This question has not been presented to them. Most responsible journalists voluntarily refrain from mentioning names of crime victims even though they are not prohibited from doing so. Neither the right of the press to publish nor the right of the people to know would be unreasonably abridged by recognizing a right of privacy in these circumstances.

Those who seek publicity have many ways to profit by public exposure. For many years, it has been a common practice for persons involved in the news and those who are famous to sell the rights to their life stories. They also advertise and endorse products. This is a legitimate means for individuals to capitalize on their abilities and fame or notoriety. Geraldine Ferraro reportedly was paid $1 million for the use of her name, likeness, and person by Pepsi Cola to advertise their product. Pepsi Cola could not have used her name or likeness without permission. Should not the Hills, the Cantrells, Sidis, April, and others who prefer seclusion to publicity have the right to give or withhold permission for the use of their life stories when they have ceased to be news?

Those who do not seek publicity or notoriety often find that their privacy has been brutally invaded. Such persons include not only victims of crimes and accidents but individuals who have suffered other misfortunes. They have rare illnesses; they are in institutions for the mentally ill, the aged, or the homeless. Many are wards of the state. They have lost their rights to liberty, mobility, control of their property, if any, and often control of their persons. They may, with limited exceptions, be subjected to psychotherapy and drug therapy against their wills and without their consent. Their access to friends and family and other medical treatment is severely restricted. Have they also lost all rights to privacy? Few legal scholars or courts have considered these questions. A Massachusetts case[37] raises the issue of the right of privacy of institutionalized persons but fails to provide definitive answers. The Massachusetts state authorities had entered into a contract with a film producer authorizing him to make a film of severely mentally disabled patients. It was to be noncommercial and nonsensational and was to illustrate the custodial, punitive, rehabilitative, and medical services performed at the institution. The contract specified that the film show an adult inmate, a youthful offender, and a correctional officer. Only persons legally competent to sign releases were to be photographed. After the film was made and shown in commercial movie theaters, the state brought an action to restrain further exhibition of the film. The trial judge who viewed the film found that it depicted nude, mentally ill patients who were ranting and also grossly deformed brain-damaged patients. The trial judge granted an injunction finding that the film was "an unwarranted . . . intrusion . . . into the right to privacy of each inmate" pictured. He further found that the "right of the public to know"* did not justify the showing of identifiable persons in such manner as to cause humiliation.

*The judge assumed that the public had such a right although the Supreme Court has cast grave doubt on the validity of that assumption.

Expert witnesses testified on behalf of the film maker and the state. As usual, the experts disagreed. Several found that the film was a work of art and that it forced society to confront the true conditions in the institution and thus promoted reform. Other experts were highly critical. It was their professional opinion that the inmates pictured were incompetent to give releases.

The appellate court modified the sweeping injunction to permit the showing of the film to limited audiences. The state sought to impose a constructive trust upon the proceeds for the benefit of inmates whose privacy was violated, but this request was denied. Both courts, in large part, based their decisions on the fact that the producer had not complied with the terms of the oral agreement under which he was given permission to make the film. They also pointed out that, following the showing of the film, conditions had been somewhat improved to the benefit of all the inmates.

Although this case may be viewed as a practical adjustment to an unfortunate situation, it failed to decide whether these inmates have a legally cognizable right to privacy. Had the court attempted to follow the doctrines set forth in *New York Times* v. *Sullivan* and its progeny, it would have had to consider whether the inmates were public or private figures. They were wards of the state. Many were undoubtedly supported by public funds.[38] In my view, however, the source of support of institutionalized persons should have no bearing on their rights to privacy. Most persons who are involuntarily institutionalized have been placed pursuant to a court order. In the Massachusetts case, there had probably been legal proceedings pursuant to which many of these inmates were committed. Court records are public. If, like the Hill family, the inmates were held to be public figures, then the court would have had to apply the "actual malice" standard of proof. The rationale given for placing this excessively difficult burden on public figures is that they have greater access to the media to rebut false and defamatory statements. These inmates had no access to the media.

The court would also have looked at the motives of the film maker. Like most authors, publishers, and members of the media, his motives were mixed. He wanted to make money, and he wanted to expose the conditions in mental institutions to bring about reforms. Which predominated? And how is a court or jury to decide such a question?

None of the considerations that figure so prominently in libel cases meets the real concerns of subjects whose seclusion is invaded. Access to the media, even if available, is the last thing the Hills, the

Cantrells, Sidis, the family of the rape victim, and the mentally impaired inmates wanted. It is doubtful that they could have received "equal billing" even if they had wanted it.

The Massachusetts court was influenced by the fact that the film, even though flagrantly violating the rights of the inmates, had accomplished some good. This balancing of harm against good, although reasonable, is predicated on the assumption that human beings are not ends in themselves, that their rights may be violated to promote good ends. This assumption does not prevail when other rights are at issue.

There can be no doubt that the managers of the institution were ill advised in granting permission for the film to be made without specifying more carefully defined restrictions and limitations. But exclusion of reporters, whether in the print or visual media, from examining conditions in a public institution also raises serious questions. The light of publicity is a corrective. The taxpayers who support state institutions should be informed of conditions. Significantly, those who saw the film likened conditions to those at Dachau.[39]

The restrictions placed on showing the film were apparently based on the unarticulated distinction between commercial and other purposes. Perhaps the rights of all parties could have been better protected by the device of blurring the faces of the inmates so that they were unidentifiable even though some of the emotional impact of the film was derived from facial expressions of despair, helplessness, and humiliation.

Wisely, the court did not order the destruction of the film. Such an order would have involved, not only the property rights of the producer, but even more serious First Amendment rights. Destruction of a film is akin to book burning. Most books destroyed in such orgies are not forever lost. Copies survive. Books can be reissued. A film once destroyed cannot be recreated. The destruction of works, even those characterized as having no redeeming social importance, is a decision fraught with difficulties of personal judgment. In my view, such power should probably never be exercised by any court.

Without more definite law, either by statute or from clear and precise judicial opinions, vulnerable people will continue to be exploited by those to whom they turn for help. At present, inmates of institutions are, as it were, fair game for those the institution chooses to admit. And the inmates have little access to those who are refused admission.

Many who are not institutionalized are also subject to exploitation by those with whom they have some professional, business, or other relationship. It could scarcely be held that individuals waive their rights to privacy by consulting persons whose services they need. Doctors, lawyers, psychiatrists, and therapists of all kinds have written about their clients and patients. As the practice becomes more widespread and lucrative, there is a danger that people will refuse to seek help for fear of exploitation. Another danger is that professionals may refuse to furnish services to notorious persons lest the professionals themselves lose their rights to privacy.

Exploitation of the professional and exploitation by the professional are revealed in two recent books. *Fatal Vision* by Joe McGinniss describes the life and trial of Captain Jeffrey MacDonald who was convicted of killing his pregnant wife and two children. His attorney is mercilessly depicted. Although lawyers who represent notorious clients must expect a measure of publicity from reports of the trial, they probably do not anticipate being portrayed in best sellers. Even though the Supreme Court has held that an attorney who represents a notorious client is still a private figure, some lawyers and doctors may well hesitate before representing or treating persons who are likely to be the subjects of books in which the professional will inevitably be pictured.

Dr. David Abrahamsen, a forensic psychiatrist, was appointed by the court to examine David Berkowitz, known as "Son of Sam." Berkowitz was an involuntary patient. After Abrahamsen found that Berkowitz was not insane, he pled guilty. Abrahamsen later wrote a book *Confessions of Son of Sam* about Berkowitz. Any criminal is a public figure at least for a limited period of time. When the book appeared, the crime was no longer news. Putting aside questions of professional ethics* of a doctor revealing information about a patient, the question of Berkowitz's right of privacy cannot be ignored.

A distressing example of the use of a person as a means not an end and the legal difficulties involved is the exploitation of a young woman known as Lisa H., who is afflicted by Elephant Man's disease. Richard Severo who was assigned by the *New York Times* to cover her story has written a book about her afflictions and the multiple surgical procedures she has undergone. The use of this unfortunate woman by the author and by her physicians, who have received

---

*I believe that doctors, teachers, lawyers, and judges have no right to exploit the persons whom they see in a professional capacity. In this book, the identities of all persons who appeared before me in my capacity as a judge have been carefully disguised.

much acclaim and publicity, raises ethical and financial questions. Did she give informed consent for the publication of her story? Did she consent to the release of information by her physicians? A timely report on a successful series of operations in this most unusual case is certainly news. But is it the kind of newsworthy event that should subject the unfortunate woman and her family to the subsequent publicity and notoriety that a best-selling book will bring? The fact that her full name is not used shows a decent sensitivity on the part of the author and medical personnel not always encountered.

Perhaps the young woman wants a book to be written about her. If she does, there should be no difficulty in obtaining her consent. If the author is to profit from her misfortunes, should she not at least be entitled to a fair share of those profits?* If she does not want a book to be written, and she decides to sue, the courts will be faced with difficult legal and moral issues. Most important, will other individuals faced with grave and unusual medical problems be reluctant to seek professional help lest they be subjected to unwanted publicity?

At this writing, no reported suits have been brought by lawyers, doctors, or patients against authors for invasion of privacy. But a father and child did sue the Department of Health and Social Services of the state of Delaware for releasing confidential material about them to a seminar on child protective services. These materials were disclosed to a reporter who published the information. The court denied recovery to the plaintiffs even though the contract between the state and federal government that provided funds prescribed that confidentiality be maintained.[40] Had the father and child sued the magazine, it is doubtful whether they could have recovered for invasion of privacy. Recognition of a right of persona would protect all such people from exploitation by those to whom they turn for help.

The number of cases in which these issues are implicit are legion. The few referred to in this chapter give only a sketchy outline of the nature of the claims asserted by subjects against authors and the legal doctrines on which these claims are based. There are no reliable conclusions that can be drawn as to whether subjects or defendants will prevail or under what circumstances. The law of defamation is in flux. The right of publicity has been upheld only in rare and

*Informed consent and requirements of a share of the profits are discussed in Chapter VIII dealing with the rights of crime victims. The same considerations should prevail with respect to other victims of misfortune who are exploited by authors.

extraordinary instances. There are few appellate decisions on false light tort. The right of privacy has barely been limned by the courts.

When interpreting First Amendment rights asserted by authors, courts can look back to almost two centuries of history and jurisprudence. No comparable body of law or philosophy exists with respect to the nonproperty, nonliberty rights of subjects. Those who are most vulnerable to unwanted exposure and most likely to suffer from invasion of privacy are least likely to be able to use the legal process for protection and redress. To date, neither courts nor scholars have adequately addressed their problems.

·VI·

Authors under Fire

*. . . freedom of speech may be taken away, and dumb
and silent we may be led, like sheep to the slaughter.*

—GEORGE WASHINGTON

BELEAGUERED authors find themselves under attack not only
from subjects who sue for defamation but also from government and
from a multitude of private groups and organizations. Although this
book is concerned only with the conflicts between subjects and authors, the problem must be viewed in perspective.

Prior to mid-twentieth century, the major threats to free expression by authors in the United States came from government.
Whether it was prosecution of unpopular political writings or censorship of books and movies, the limiting action was taken by governmental agencies. Since then, boards of censors have been abolished
by judicial decision or simply been permitted to expire. Their place
has been taken to a large extent by ad hoc citizen groups and organizations, another ominous example of privatism. These groups censor
books in school libraries. They seek to dictate the choice of textbooks. They promote boycotts of films and dramas. Organizations
like "Accuracy in Academia" surreptitiously invade classrooms to
monitor teachers. Efforts to control the press and the electronic
media are made by groups such as "Accuracy in Media" that seek
to dictate content, and by idealogues who seek to take over and
purchase newspapers, radio and television stations and networks.

Other private groups seek to control all forms of art. The effort to
have a work of sculpture by the highly acclaimed artist Richard
Serra removed is but one example. James Watt, Secretary of Interior,

opposed a concert by the extremely popular band "The Beach Boys." Showing of the movie *Hail Mary* was protested in Baltimore. Some of the cartoon strips by Garry Trudeau have been removed from newspapers. Whether this has been in response to perceived or overt pressure is not known. Episodes in popular TV programs such as "Cagney and Lacey" have been protested. *Playboy* and *Penthouse* magazines have been removed from 7-Eleven and other stores, depriving the magazines of 8,000 and 15,000 outlets respectively and depriving countless readers of ready access to these periodicals.

Unpopular views are increasingly under attack. Groups of every political and ideological persuasion exert pressure on those who write, publish, teach, and perform. Some teachers are protected by tenure. Some performers are protected by contract or union rules. But the vast majority of creative people, including authors, have no legal remedies against private interference and censorship.

Such repressive violations of freedom of expression cannot readily be tested in court. It is difficult to frame the issues in the usual adversary format of plaintiff and defendant disputing over a specific action that allegedly infringes either a property or constitutional right. All citizens acting as individuals or in groups have rights of free expression. They are free to denounce books, movies, television programs, the "liberal press," or any public or private group or action not to their liking.[1] Individuals and organizations also have the right to finance lawsuits by subjects against authors for any reason.* Both the backers of Westmoreland and the American Civil Liberties Union have the right to provide support and counsel to litigants.[2]

In all lawsuits against authors, whether brought by private groups, government, or subjects, the principal defense is the First Amendment. To understand why authors find the First Amendment a very fragile shield, it is necessary to review briefly two centuries of judicial interpretation. When compared with the history of other significant constitutional provisions, it is apparent that the treatment of the First Amendment by the courts has been exceptional. No other phrase or clause of the Constitution has been subjected to such severe limitations. Nor have those who sought to claim protection under other provisions been required to justify the very language and import of those provisions.

The First Amendment is expressed in absolute terms: "Congress

---

*The legality of the use of tax-exempt funds for such purposes is beyond the purview of this discussion.

shall make no law . . . abridging the freedom of speech or of the press." This unambiguous language has never been given literal effect. Courts might logically have held that the First Amendment guarantees to all speakers and authors the right to say and to publish whatever they choose. A great deal of difficulty would have been avoided had this position been adopted. Justices Douglas and Black have argued eloquently for this view in many dissenting opinions. But they have been unable to command a majority of the Supreme Court.

Most phrases and clauses of the Constitution have been subjected to learned judicial glosses, but the provisions themselves have not required justification. It is assumed that due process of law is a fundamental right and that it needs no philosophical or theoretical justification. The procedures needed to meet the requirement of due process are, of course, subject to extensive interpretation and many differences of opinion. Similarly, the privilege against self-incrimination is accepted as an unquestioned right. The kind of notice and warnings that must be given to an accused, the times and circumstances when suspects must be informed of their rights, and the very nature of those rights, including the right to counsel, have been subjects of much litigation. No reported decisions, however, have excluded any classes of persons or any types of activities from the protection of the due process clauses of the Fifth and Fourteenth Amendments. Courts have simply held that the mandate of due process was satisfied despite the arbitrary, high-handed, or summary nature of the procedures in question.

The Eighth Amendment's prohibition against cruel and unusual punishment has been subject to widely disparate and occasionally diametrically opposite judicial interpretations. These variations depend upon the times and the moral and social perceptions of the public and the courts. In 1910, the Supreme Court held that the use of chains and shackles on prisoners offended the Eighth Amendment.[3] Justices Holmes and White dissented stating that the ". . . mere fact that a chain is to be carried by the prisoner . . ." does not offend the Constitution. The Supreme Court held that the death penalty violated this amendment because it was offensive to evolving moral standards of society.[4] Four years later, the holding was reversed.[5] Despite many brutal conditions condoned by the Court, no opinion ever intimated that the Eighth Amendment needed to be justified philosophically, nor did the Court ever hold that certain categories of persons were beyond its protection.

The history of judicial interpretation of the First Amendment presents a startling contrast. At the outset, it was declared apodictically that libel and obscenity were excluded from the area of protected speech. Thomas Jefferson stated in 1798, ". . . libels, falsehood, and defamation . . . are withheld from the cognizance of federal tribunals."[6] For two centuries, the courts assumed that no justification was needed for denying libel and obscenity the protections of the First Amendment.

Although the definition of libel has changed very little from its enunciation in early English law, definitions of obscenity have been rewritten again and again. Many books now conceded to be literary masterpieces were held to be obscene. To name only a few: *Ulysses, Lady Chatterley's Lover,* the works of Mark Twain and Tolstoy. The publishers and distributors of these books were prosecuted and convicted. Many who sold works held to be "obscene" were imprisoned. In the twentieth century in a series of cases, each testing the obscenity of a single book, many convictions were appealed. Some, but not all, were reversed. Based on these cases, there was a popular perception that the courts were the guardians of free expression. But these decisions merely removed a particular book from the category of obscenity and, therefore, punishable expression. American courts have never taken the position that under the First Amendment all expression is protected from censorship and criminal penalties. In each case, expression has had to be justified in the opinions of the courts either by truth or "redeeming social importance." Nor have the courts taken the position that all restrictions on expression are prohibited or that there can be no civil or criminal liability for expression.

Even staunch defenders of the First Amendment have assumed that free expression must be justified by those who seek to exercise that right. Professor Alexander Meiklejohn, an authority on free speech, writes, "No one can doubt that in any well-governed society, the legislature has both the right and the duty to prohibit certain forms of speech. Libelous assertions may be, and must be forbidden and punished."[7] Professor Thomas I. Emerson posits four reasons justifying the First Amendment; namely that free expression is essential for (1) self-fulfillment, (2) advancing knowledge, (3) participating in decision making, and (4) achieving a more adaptable and stable community.[8] Only a minute, albeit important, fraction of speech, entertainment, and literature are comprehended in these categories. Much of literature and art would, under these criteria for free expression, be excluded from protection. A cursory perusal of the daily press, popular magazines, and the card catalogue of any library reveals that the overwhelming majority of publications do not advance knowledge, assist in participating in self-government, or further debate on public issues. The electronic media, with the exception of the all news stations, devote far more time to entertainment and sports than to programs informing the public for the purposes of self-governance. It would be difficult to justify many docudramas, books, and articles on notorious crimes, and much fiction, aptly described as being potboilers, as being essential to self-expression, or to claim redeeming social importance for these works. Many of the conflicts between subject and author arise out of just such docudramas, fiction, and other types of entertainment. A purely instrumental or utilitarian approach to the First Amendment as enunciated by Professor Emerson would exclude from its protection most authors not engaged in presenting news, commentary, or what is currently recognized as scholarship or literary art. To date, there has been little effort to provide a philosophical base for a more generous reading of the First Amendment that would protect all expression regardless of social importance, truth, or instrumental purposes.

Judge Robert H. Bork proposes that "Constitutional protection should be accorded only to speech that is explicitly political."[9] This is a logical extension of Professor Emerson's justification for First Amendment rights. To date, the courts have not adopted such a restrictive reading. But Bork's position is merely an extrapolation from the views that justify freedom of expression because it aids in the process of self-governance.

Redeeming social importance, like beauty, is in the eye of the beholder or reader. Juries and judges, including Supreme Court justices, do not have unclouded crystal balls. Their perceptions of literary, musical, and artistic merit as well as the validity of scientific, economic, and political theory are subject to the same prejudices, ignorance, and passions that afflict the general population. The power to ban expression, even when sensibly or sparingly applied, still constitutes censorship. Although prior restraint by government agencies censoring books and movies has largely been abolished, the power to punish still remains. In my opinion, it also constitutes censorship.

The distinction between prior restraint and subsequent punishment,[10] developed in criminal libel cases, has persisted in all First Amendment litigation. Under this curious doctrine, the courts have held that the First Amendment prohibits government from restraining distribution of material alleged to be obscene, libelous, or dangerous to the welfare and safety of the nation. But, once the material has been released, authors, publishers, distributors, and sellers can be punished. Because of the prohibition against prior restraint, the publication of the *Pentagon Papers* was permitted, despite government efforts to prevent it.

History records that some individuals are willing to sacrifice themselves and their families on the altar of principle, but their number is limited. The average person (including writers, publishers, and directors of the electronic media) finds little security in the doctrine of prior restraint if it is followed by punishment for exercising that freedom. Saints and martyrs will express themselves despite Draconian penalties. The rest of the population is likely to be silenced. Even though courts do not restrain but merely punish, the result is a serious limitation of free expression.

Although many civil libertarians and scholars have protested particular decisions resulting in censorship of literary works or political speech and writings, few have taken the absolutist position that argues that all expression should be free not just from prior restraint but from all penalties and civil damages.

Penalties imposed on famous titans of history indicate the importance of granting freedom and breathing space for political debate and for all kinds of expression. The lives and deaths of Socrates and Galileo provide eloquent testimony to the brutality with which power is exercised in repressing unpopular or heretical ideas. I do not suggest that authors against whom substantial verdicts are now being returned in actions brought by subjects have revealed eternal truths or created great literature. But the suppression of worthless and frivolous literature and commentary lays the legal foundation for the suppression of valuable contributions whose worth may not be appreciated for several generations. One will not know how many authors have been silenced by their publishers' fears of costly litigation and punishing verdicts. The authority to suppress error and works of no redeeming social importance inevitably includes the power to suppress the truth and works of great value and social importance.

This argument harks back to utilitarian theories of free speech; namely, that worthless writings should not be suppressed because there is always the danger that worthwhile literature, scientific discoveries, and social commentary will also be suppressed. That un-

happy possibility and, indeed, probability exists. But, it is my contention that freedom of expression, like privacy, is an essential attribute
of every individual in a free society and that it is worthy of legal
protection regardless of the value of what the individual expresses.
Authors have a right to create junk literature. Readers have a right
to read it. Any legal theory predicated on the value of the contents
of speech inevitably puts the courts in the position of acting as censor
and critic, and making literary, moral, political, and scientific evaluations.

The history of obscenity law provides telling evidence that judges
are ill equipped to decide the values of literature, science, and the
arts. It is extremely dubious that any other public officials or any
private groups should be entrusted with such powers. A review of
thirty or forty years of literary prizes reveals that the judgment of
those who granted these awards was extremely fallible. Unless one
opts for a system of Platonic guardians to censor books, art, and
music, the only rational choice is unfettered free expression.

The contrary view inevitably puts the courts, which are the final
arbiters under the American system of constitutional law, in the
business of determining whether individuals in a free society have the
right to read whatever they wish. The test of social value inevitably
runs afoul of the fact that many readers have low tastes. They enjoy
the bloody, the sordid, and the salacious. Authors and publishers
supply their wants. It is a common parlor occupation of self-styled
intellectuals to deplore the "wasteland of television." But it is also
indisputable that more people watch "Dallas" than high-minded
intellectual television discussions such as "The Constitution: That
Delicate Balance." Any justification of First Amendment freedoms
predicated on the social value of the contents of the speech logically
and inevitably removes from the ambit of that constitutional protection a great proportion of the material now printed or aired by the
media.

Any notion that restricting constitutional protections to political
speech would ease the burdens of the courts or remove content
evaluation is fallacious. Courts would have to decide whether political satires such as *The Good Soldier Schweik* and novels like *One Day
in the Life of Ivan Denisovich* are explicitly political. Is Orwell's *1984*
explicitly political or only inferentially so? The humorous columns
of Art Buchwald and the cartoon strips of Gary Trudeau are undoubtedly political. Are they explicitly so?

The First Amendment was adopted in order to free the people of the nation from government control of speech and press. The drafters of the Constitution and the Bill of Rights were familiar with English law. They knew that the press had been licensed in England, and they were aware of the many libel suits and prosecutions brought against critics of government policies and government officials. Instead, in the United States, criticism of government in political writings and speech has been punished under a variety of statutes. Some prohibited criminal syndicalism; others barred advocating disrespect for law or for any courts of justice. Conspiracy, an inchoate crime, has been a convenient legal device for prosecuting and punishing those who have not committed any substantive crime. It has been used to convict those who were charged with advocating or encouraging by speech or writings violation of law, even when it was clearly evident that no law was, in fact, violated.

These cases of seditious libel would appear to have little bearing on the conflicts between subjects and authors. But because language from these opinions is used precedentially to justify decisions dealing with First Amendment rights of authors in libel suits, it is helpful to examine a few of the most frequently cited cases to see precisely what the courts decided and their reasons for reaching those conclusions. All these opinions have posited reasons either justifying or limiting freedom of expression. None accepts the language of the First Amendment as a given.

Suppression of criticism of the government is particularly harsh and widespread in times of trouble and confusion. During the Civil War, President Lincoln suspended the writ of habeas corpus. Hundreds of people were arrested for unpopular speech on the premise that expression hostile to or critical of the war should be suppressed.

World War I brought about another time of widespread prosecutions for seditious libel. Eugene V. Debs, the Socialist Party candidate for president of the United States, was prosecuted and convicted.[11] Schenck, the secretary of the Socialist Party, was also convicted for printing and mailing pamphlets opposing the war.[12] His conviction was upheld by the Supreme Court in a decision by Justice Holmes that, curiously, has been cited repeatedly as expanding freedom of expression. The Supreme Court found, without any supporting evidence, that Schenck's pamphlets made recruiting of soldiers more difficult. The Court then went on to carve out a new exemption from the First Amendment, namely speech that creates a "clear and present danger." Holmes enunciated his famous aphorism that "No one has a right to shout fire in a crowded theater." Obviously there was no fire. Schenck was not in a theater. The metaphor of flaming danger masked the reality of the suppression of simple, nonthreatening pamphlets.

The following term in the *Abrams* case, the Supreme Court made the astonishing declaration that "seditious libel is dead."[13] One might have thought that it should have expired with the expiration of the Alien and Sedition laws in 1800.* But the fabulous invalid has had astonishing vitality for almost two centuries. Abrams was convicted of conspiring to violate the espionage act by printing "disloyal, scurrilous and abusive language" about the United States and its war efforts. He was convicted and sentenced to twenty years imprisonment for publishing two pamphlets. The conviction was sustained. The Court noted that Abrams was an "alien anarchist" and that the pamphlets were in Yiddish. All three facts were irrelevant. He was not an illegal alien. Being an anarchist was not a crime. Nor was the use of the Yiddish language. The inclusion of immaterial and pejorative information and language in stating the facts of cases in which speech is punished is a persistent practice of the courts.† Significantly, Abrams's two pamphlets could not have been found to create any danger, much less a "clear and present danger," the standard that had been enunciated the previous year.

In the early 1940s, the internment of Japanese-Americans was upheld by the Supreme Court, not because of any allegedly seditious speech on their part, but because of the fear that, nonetheless, these Americans were disloyal.[14] Significantly, there was not a scintilla of evidence that the Japanese-Americans constituted a clear and present danger. Four decades later, a federal court restored the good name of one of the internees.[15] The following decade saw the era of anti-Communist hysteria known as McCarthyism. It spawned a series of cases, most notably *Dennis v. United States,*[16] in which the Court declared that "freedom of speech is not absolute."

In 1984, the CIA brought a complaint against ABC before the Federal Communications Commission charging that it "falsely and without foundation alleged that the CIA conspired to assassinate

---

*In 1798, when United States relations with France were strained, a radical group espoused the French cause. The opposition claimed that French refugees in the United States were engaged in espionage. In response to public ferment, Congress enacted laws making it a crime to publish any "false, scandalous, and malicious" writing against the government, the Congress, and the President "with intent to defame" or "to stir up sedition." Some twenty-five people were arrested, eleven were tried, and ten were found guilty. Two years later, the law was allowed to expire.

†Compare the opinion of the Supreme Court in Harper & Row v. Nation discussed in Chapter II.

American citizens and committed other unauthorized and illegal acts.[17] The report involved the alleged shipments of arms to Taiwan and an attempt to destabilize the economies of several countries. The long history of governmental efforts to silence critics has by no means ended.

A trilogy of cases in the 1980s reveals the use of other legal doctrines and devices to accomplish the suppression of criticism of the American government and/or its agencies. Snepp, a former CIA employee, was accused of breaching his contract with the CIA under which he had agreed to submit all writings for prior approval. This legal vehicle was used to silence his criticisms of the CIA and government policies. In an action brought by the government, Snepp was enjoined from speaking or writing without prior approval of the CIA, and the proceeds of his book were confiscated. In addition, a fine of $140,000 was imposed.[18] This case is of special interest because of three extraordinary actions taken by the Court. It imposed a restraint on sales of the book; it adopted the novel penalty of confiscating royalties; it predicated its decision, at least in part, on the assumed commercial motives of the author. There was no evidence, other than the obvious fact that writers hope to receive profits from their work, that Snepp's sole or dominant motivation was profit. Moreover, there is nothing illegal, immoral, or against public policy for anyone to be motivated to work in the hope of receiving monetary compensation. Restraint of distribution of a book or other printed material that is not obscene and does not threaten national security is unprecedented. The use of criminal penalties is also unusual. If any legal principle is clear and undeviatingly followed it is that crimes and penalties must be clearly defined so that all persons may know in advance what conduct is prohibited and the penalties for violation of the law. There is no statute authorizing confiscation of royalties.

The reliance on motives is also unusual. In both libel and obscenity cases, the courts examine the language actually used. Good motives will not exculpate a libeler nor will evil motives make language that is not libelous wrongful. The only obscenity case in which the inferred obscene motives of the publisher prevailed over the lack of obscenity of the document was *United States* v. *Ginzburg.* [19]

In that case, the allegedly offensive writing was clearly not obscene within the meaning of the prior cases. By inferring a salacious intent from the fact that the publisher attempted to mail the document from post offices named "Blue Ball" and "Intercourse," the Court concluded that the defendant had a pornographic intent.

If Snepp had violated a binding contract that did not infringe his constitutional rights, his motives should have been irrelevant. Even if he did so out of idealistic beliefs in world unity and peace, those beliefs would not justify a breach of a valid, binding, and constitutional contract. If the contract was not valid, binding, and constitutional, then it should be unenforceable irrespective of the author's motives.

Several time-honored legal doctrines might have been employed to invalidate the contract. The most significant is the fact that it violates Snepp's First Amendment rights. Second, the restrictions are not reasonably necessary to the legitimate purposes of an employment contract, and even if some limitations on the employee's speech were appropriate, these were not the least restrictive limitations. Third, the contract was one of adhesion. This concept is used to invalidate agreements between parties of unequal bargaining power in which one party has no practical alternative to accepting the unfair conditions imposed by the other party. The doctrine is frequently employed in landlord and tenant cases when the tenant has no real option to accepting the onerous terms set by the landlord. It is also used to relieve employees of unfairly burdensome conditions imposed by employers. Here, Snepp had no practical alternative. If he had refused to sign the agreement, he would undoubtedly have lost his job and many of his accumulated benefits. The assumed commercial motivations of the author as a reason for limiting First Amendment rights is, unfortunately, not anomalous. It appears in many cases to the detriment of authors.

In the second case involving criticism of government policy, *Haig* v. *Agee*, [20] the government took the unusual legal route of lifting the critic's passport. Agee, a former CIA employee who had publicly identified certain individuals and organizations in foreign countries as undercover agents of the United States, unsuccessfully challenged the revocation of his passport without a hearing. The Supreme Court held that this action did not violate either the First Amendment or the due process clause of the Fifth Amendment.

The third case involved restraint of publication of *The Progressive* [21] in order to silence a critic of the government's Vietnam War policy. That magazine had published an article, derived wholly from information in the public domain such as encyclopedias and government publications, to describe the technique of making a hydrogen bomb. The prosecution was ultimately abandoned when similar information appeared in other publications. If this information had really been secret, a fact falsely claimed by the government, even a judge most ardently in favor of absolute unlimited First Amendment rights would have been sorely torn between constitutional principles and the national welfare. This is the only instance of which I am aware in all the cases involving the "clear and present danger test" when it might appropriately have been applied. But the evidence clearly disclosed that all the information contained in the article was readily accessible from other sources. Significantly, no reported harm of any sort resulted from the publication. Again, there was no clear and present danger. Indeed, there was no danger at all.

Many defamation cases arise out of criticism of government and government officials relating to their conduct of public business. These are matters in which the public has a legitimate interest—what has been loosely described as a "right to know." Indeed, the most common justification for free expression is the need of the public for information for the purpose of self-governance. Although the Supreme Court has never specifically enunciated such a "right to know," it has been argued in many cases. The Court has often acknowledged that the First Amendment protects not only speakers and writers, but that it was designed to protect the right of the public to see, hear, and read what they choose. This philosophy was given emphatic approval by the Supreme Court in the *Red Lion* case.[22] The Court there declared:

> It is the right of the viewers and listeners, not the right of the broadcasters, which is paramount. . . . It is the right of the public to receive suitable access to social, political, esthetic, moral, and other ideas and experiences which is crucial here.

This was probably only dictum—eloquent, quotable language not necessary to the decision. In fact, the Court held that under the fairness doctrine, a candidate did not have a right to reply to his opponents.

This so-called right to know was drastically diminished if not abolished by a subsequent decision in which the Court stated:

> The reference to a public entitlement to information meant no more than that the government cannot restrain communication of whatever information the media acquires . . . and which they elect to reveal.[23]

In that case, a radio station had obtained a court order compelling prison authorities to admit the press to observe conditions following the death of a prisoner. Obviously, this was a matter of great and legitimate public interest. It concerned alleged mistreatment by public officials of inmates in a public institution. A prison is a public, tax-supported institution. It is difficult to conjure up a more compelling fact situation in which the public needs information that the media are uniquely equipped to provide. To expect individual citizens to go to a prison and make their own investigations is absurd. The minimal access to the prison allowed the public was clearly insufficient to permit examination of the facts by anyone, even assuming that some competent trained members of the public would take the time and trouble to visit the institution. Nonetheless, the decision of the lower court granting access to the prison was set aside. The long and honorable history of journalistic muckraking and its obvious benefits to the public was ignored.[24] To foreclose access by the media to public institutions constitutes a dangerous precedent. Even more disquieting is the ruling that the First Amendment does not protect the public's access to information directly involved in self-governance. Even under Bork's restrictive proposal of protection for explicitly political speech, this information would be included as protected speech.

The Court has disregarded the public's interest in matters of public concern in several other cases. For example, it held in *CIA* v. *Sims*[25] that the government can refuse to release information under the Freedom of Information Act without any showing that the requested information was classified or obtained under a promise of confidentiality. Restricting the flow of information seriously prejudices the rights of authors and the public to whom they provide information. The character of the individual claiming constitutional rights again became a critical issue in a case involving access to a naval base at a time when the base was open to the public.[26] In this case, the persons denied admission were protesters who had previously engaged in disruptive tactics. There was no evidence that they would do so again or that government personnel would not be able to control the situation.

The most famous and notorious cases of libel involving criticism by authors of government policy or public officials have been brought against the media. The press, magazines, radio and television, and book publishers are deep pocket defendants. So are many writers. Columnist William Safire points out that former government personnel obtain seven-figure book contracts. For example, David Stockman received more than $2 million; Jeane Kirkpatrick and Tip O'-

Neill $1 million each.* Best-selling novelists like James Michener and Judith Krantz are also in the seven-figure bracket. Even an unknown author of a juicy novel in the hands of a good agent can command a six-figure contract. These writers, however, are rarely defendants in defamation suits. Reporters and most writers of nonfiction books who are defendants in libel suits are far from wealthy. Unless their defense is undertaken by their publishers, these lawsuits can be devastating. Joe McGinniss, author of the best seller *Fatal Vision,* has reportedly incurred very substantial legal expenses in defending the lawsuit that was brought against him by his subject, Jeffrey MacDonald. These costs equal or exceed his substantial earnings from the book.

A number of leading Supreme Court libel cases were brought against defendants who are far from wealthy. The effect of these decisions has often been disastrous for the author. Many defendants are not professional writers, reporters, or members of the media. For example, the defendant in *Rosenblatt* v. *Baer*[27] was an unpaid columnist for a small local paper.

Many other defendants in libel suits, although classified as authors as opposed to subjects, are not authors at all. They are simply individuals who believed that under the First Amendment they had a right to speak or write critically about government officials and government policies. Even when they win, after a series of costly appeals and a second trial, they find that the cost of liberty is excessive.

A particularly shocking case is *McDonald* v. *Smith.*[28] McDonald was under consideration for appointment to the position of United States attorney. This is a powerful and sensitive office. A United States attorney has considerable discretion in deciding which suspects to prosecute, when to accept a plea bargain, and what charges to prefer. This charging function may mean the difference between a sentence of a few months or one of many years. Defendant wrote two letters to President Reagan that were highly critical of McDonald, accusing him of "fraud," "conspiracy to commit fraud," "extortion or blackmail," and violations of professional ethics. Copies of these letters were mailed to three high government officials. McDonald did not receive the appointment. He sued Smith, seeking $1 million damages. Defendant contended that under the First Amendment he had the right to petition the government and that he was

---

*The ethics of profiting from government service is beyond the purview of this book.

immune to suit. The Supreme Court held that this clause does not grant immunity for libel. There were no dissents.

The appointment of a public official is without question a matter of public concern. Regardless of the right to petition the government, certainly all citizens should have the right to express their opinions as to the character and qualifications of persons under consideration for public office. Although the letters were artlessly worded and technically charged McDonald with crimes, they were really expressions of opinion. Smith did not say that McDonald had been convicted of these crimes. Such a charge could be proved or disproved. Either it would be true or false. But to say that a person's conduct is fraudulent or unethical is clearly a matter of opinion. In order to establish the truth or falsity of such charges, it would be necessary to have a full-scale criminal trial. McDonald had not been prosecuted or convicted. It would be impossible for anyone to prove or disprove the charges in this libel suit. Any common-sense reading of such an angry letter by a layperson would conclude that it was an expression of opinion and entitled to "breathing space." If the previous definitions of public figure were followed, McDonald should be held to be a public figure. By seeking public office, he voluntarily thrust himself into public view. Whether McDonald could prove actual malice or not, this kind of expression of opinion with respect to candidates for public office should, I believe, be privileged.

When lawyers are being considered for appointment to the federal bench, the American Bar Association solicits comments and opinions from members of the bench and bar. Often these opinions are devastating. Lawyers and judges have said that in their opinions certain candidates were unethical, that they failed to represent their clients responsibly, or that they concealed information from the courts. Such opinions can be read as charging the individual with criminal conduct. When asked for opinions with respect to judicial aspirants, most lawyers and judges give their candid views because they believe that the quality and character of members of the bench is important. If they feared that such expressions of opinion might result in defamation suits, they would be extremely hesitant to speak frankly. Martindale-Hubbell publishes a roster of lawyers and rates them as to their standing at the bar. I am frequently asked to give my opinions with respect to lawyers who appear before me. To date, there are no reported cases against Martindale-Hubbell or those who have supplied information.

Although these evaluations cannot be scientifically accurate, they do provide a public service to potential clients who want to check on the standing and reputation of members of the bar. To cut off this source of information because of fear of libel suits would be most unfortunate.*

Many private citizens have been sued for libel for expression of opinion with respect to public officials and government policies.[29] The Los Angeles Chief of Police has brought suit against a citizen who accused him of consorting with prostitutes. This is a nasty charge. But even if true, it is not a crime. Again it is the kind of statement that is practically impossible to prove or disprove. "Consorting with" is not easy to define. In another case, a woman who complained that her son was stopped by the police and subjected to a body search was sued for defamation.

A real estate developer on Long Island sued eight civic associations and sixteen residents for "injurious falsehood" because they opposed his proposed building project by saying it would increase sewage and noise. Common sense indicates that this also is an expression of opinion. Even with exact information as to the numbers of people who would be added to the population, no one can prove the amount of increased noise that would or would not result.

A toxic dump operating company filed a $1 million suit against a farmer who said there was a fishkill near the dump and that his animals had suffered mysterious ailments. Proof of truth in such a case would be almost impossible. Courts have spent months in trying to decide whether Agent Orange caused illness and birth defects. The government had scientific information and unlimited resources and scores of experts to defend against these charges. How can either the farmer or the dump owner possibly prove truth? Should not the farmer have a right to air his concerns and suspicions? He did not present the information as a fact but as a suspicious coincidence. The harmful effects of toxic wastes at Love Canal and Three Mile Island may never be proved in a court of law. But countless people honestly believe there is a connection between these emissions and illnesses and deaths. Should they not have a right to express these opinions?

In an instance strikingly similar to *McDonald* v. *Smith,* another citizen named Smith questioned a Montgomery County, Pennsylvania, township solicitor, Frank Jenkins, at a public meeting with respect to building permits that resulted in excessive sewage prob-

---

*The subject of opinions as to qualifications of professionals and employees and defamation is discussed in Chapter XI.

lems. Jenkins brought suit against Smith.[30] Even a letter to the editor published in a newspaper can provoke a lawsuit.[31] Such cases call to mind the prosecution of Emile Zola on the basis of his famous letter, "J'Accuse," published in the French newspaper, *L'Aurore.* Zola was found guilty of libel, fined, and sentenced to a year in prison.

The ever-mounting number of such lawsuits represents new and serious threats to free expression whether by ordinary citizens or by professional writers and the media. Unless summary judgment is granted in favor of these defendants, the costs and difficulties of defending against such lawsuits will not merely chill rights of free expression but permanently freeze them.

The assumed commercial motivation of authors as a limiting factor in the extent of protection offered by the First Amendment has been expressed in several Supreme Court decisions issued in the 1980s. In most instances, this plumbing of the author's intent was based on inference without any evidence. In the American economy, almost every occupation is conducted for financial gain. Unless an author is subsidized by a foundation or nonprofit organization, books and plays are written for money. Even those subsidies do not eliminate economic motives. One grant leads to another. Publication is a recognized means of academic preferment. Except for a handful of independently wealthy individuals, everyone engages in a profession or occupation with some hope of economic gain. To limit free expression to those who do not need money would be an extraordinary doctrine. Doctors, lawyers, teachers, preachers, farmers, and manufacturers are all engaged in earning money. Most of them also have other motivations. Except for the most crass, doctors want to heal; lawyers want to protect their clients' rights; teachers want to educate; and preachers want to minister to their parishioners. Samuel Johnson aptly observed that only a fool doesn't write for money. All authors at least hope to realize some financial gain, even those whose manuscripts languish in the desk drawer. So do publishers and the electronic media. On occasion all are disappointed. I believe that neither the motives of the author nor the lack of social or other value or merit should militate against full protection of free expression. For courts to draw a distinction as to the author's right of free expression based upon whether or not the writing or production was profitable would plunge the law down another slippery slope. Would a charge against General Westmoreland on public TV be privileged and the same statement made on commercial TV not be privileged? Similarly, would the author of a best-selling book be liable for defamation, but the author of an article that appeared in a scholarly journal for which there was no monetary compensation be privileged when making the identical statements?[32]

I believe the attempt to draw a bright line between commercial motivation and other, presumably more worthy intentions, is doomed to failure and inconsistency. It is provocative of more litigation and more complicated rules, distinctions, and definitions. There is no sound policy reason for preferring one motive to another. When pacifists, ecologists, animal lovers, pro-life demonstrators, and others break the law, even for what they believe are good motives, they are, nonetheless, guilty. Their good intentions may serve to mitigate the penalty but not to excuse the crime. Similarly, there is no legal precedent for denying constitutional protections to criminals or to crass and selfish money grubbers. In the cases in which the Court considered the commercial motives of the authors to be critical, there was not a scintilla of evidence that these defendants were anything but honorable men and women pursuing their occupations as writers, journalists, and publishers.

At the same time the Supreme Court has been denigrating the commercial motives of authors, it has extended the protection of the First Amendment to election campaign expenditures and to frankly commercial enterprises. This is a perplexing inconsistency. It ignores two centuries of history in which the First Amendment was interpreted as covering communication of ideas, literature, news, and entertainment.

In the so-called information society of today, the number of commercial institutions and government organizations that disseminate information is legion. To treat the purveying of credit information as the kind of speech entitled to First Amendment protection is unprecedented. In an action for libel against Dun & Bradstreet,[33] the facts were simple and uncontested. The defendant furnished incorrect credit information with respect to the plaintiff's business. The Court held that the defendant was protected by the First Amendment but then established still another qualification, that the matter be "of public concern." Justices Brennan, Marshall, Blackmun, and Stevens dissented, acidly commenting, "Without explaining what is a 'matter of public concern,' the plurality opinion proceeds to serve up a smorgasbord of reasons why the speech at issue here is not. . . ." In this state of the law, authors may well conclude that they are in the position of their counterparts in eighteenth-century England who published at their peril.

One of the most serious limitations on authors arising out of *New York Times* v. *Sullivan* and its progeny is the invasion of their privacy. The "actual malice" test turns on the actual knowledge of the author at the time of the allegedly defamatory statement. The only ways that state of mind can be ascertained by the subject are through extensive cross-examination of authors and editors and discovery of their papers. The use of the subpoena power to compel authors, especially reporters, to disclose their editorial decision-making processes and to reveal their sources is another recent, dangerous innovation.[34] Decisions overriding state shield laws in criminal cases are beyond the purview of this discussion. But if it were not for the "actual malice" test, the motives, information, and mindset of authors would be irrelevant in libel cases. If the test of liability were not whether the author acted in reckless disregard of truth or falsity, but the objective test of what a reasonable person would have done under the circumstances, there would be no need to compel the production of this information.

Another formidable barrier to authors seeking to claim the protections of the First Amendment is the requirement of truth. The principle as stated seems reasonable. The Constitution protects truthful speech. But the corollary is that falsehood is not protected. The Supreme Court has declared that there is no social value to a lie. The tacit assumption in many of these cases is that truth is a discrete, irrefragable, objectively verifiable fact much like the old concept of an atom as an infinitesimal billiard ball, an irreducible piece of matter. Some statements can be objectively proved or disproved. Whether a person has been convicted of a crime is clearly such a fact. Far more frequently the truth of the allegedly false and libelous statement is not susceptible of the quality of proof that is required by law in other cases.

Eyewitnesses must testify to the facts that they actually saw. Did the defendant fire the gun or was it another person? Expert witnesses testify as to the results of their examination of physical evidence. Was the bullet that was found in the body of the deceased fired from the weapon in the possession of the defendant? Expert witnesses can also give their opinions based on the facts that have been introduced into evidence. A doctor can testify with reasonable medical certainty that the plaintiff's physical condition did or did not result from the injury received in the accident. But how can one prove by any credible evidence the accuracy of the body count in Vietnam or whether a person is portrayed fairly? Nor can an author prove that an individual has a bad character. These are matters of judgment. To require courts to determine the truth of such statements is folly. Again, courts are put in the unenviable position of having to make decisions in the absence of reliable evidence.

Should the courts be mired in deciding questions that are simply not answerable? The short answer to all such cases should be a summary judgment in favor of the author on the ground that the allegedly defamatory statement is an expression of opinion. The Supreme Court has unequivocally declared that there is no such thing as a false opinion.

Almost all reporting involves some judgment and opinion on the part of the reporter. Despite Christopher Isherwood's claim, *I Am a Camera,* human beings are not cameras. They report what they see through the lenses of their own eyes. Even the supposedly neutral camera must be focused. This involves judgment. When TV news presented an excerpt from a committee hearing on crime in the 1950s, the camera focused on the fat hands of a reputed crime figure. His twisting, nervous movements certainly indicated unease. To many viewers, it may have connoted guilt. Defamation actions against the media were not common then. One can only speculate as to the consequences of such a sequence on the evening TV news in the 1980s.

Reporters are the first to recognize the difficulties of "neutral" reporting. In a provocative article in *Harper's* entitled, "Can the Press Tell the Truth?,"[35] Tom Wicker points out, "No matter how a journalist reports news stories, no matter how much he tries to be neutral, what he writes tends to influence policy." The facile distinctions between "deliberate distortion" and "objective" news stories is, I believe, an unworkable standard for the courts. As Wicker explains, a reporter has to make choices in reporting a story. Constraints of time and space, the limited attention span of the average reader, and the reporter's perception of what is newsworthy inevitably shape what goes into a story and what is omitted.

Nowhere is this process of selection more telling than in the reporting of trials. The vast majority of testimony is dull and boring, as jurors and judges well know. The reporter must select from a mass of verbiage what appears to him or her to be the salient evidence. Verbatim reporting of a transcript would be extraordinarily expensive and intolerably unreadable.

The use of TV cameras in the courtroom highlights the essentially selective process of any reporter. Only a small percent of trials are

reported in the press. A bare handful are televised. The decision to
report fully, briefly, mention, or ignore is usually based on the significance of the legal issues, the prominence of the litigants and witnesses, and that indefinable quality—viewer interest. The second
decision is what portions of the testimony to quote, mention, or
televise. Again the reporter must juggle the three factors of interest
and balance them against the constraints of time or space. These are
all matters of judgment on which equally qualified and neutral reporters can differ.

A trial judge who instructs juries is well aware of the perils involved in presenting even the most scrupulously fair and unbiased
summary of the evidence. Especially in a long trial, it is impossible
to condense days of testimony into fifteen or twenty minutes. Only
the highlights can be mentioned. The jury may improperly conclude
that testimony not referred to is irrelevant or of no significance. A
conscientious judge who extensively reviewed the testimony in a long
trial concluded his charge by telling the jurors, "I think I have said
enough." The appellate court reversed and remanded the case for a
new trial, holding that the judge had said too much.

Because every report involves selection and judgment, there are
bound to be differences of opinion. Those who disagree with the
reporter will call it slanting the news. A typical criticism was expressed by Herbert Schmertz, vice president of Mobil Oil. He stated,
". . . the press tends to represent American leaders and institutions
as far more corrupt and self-serving than they are. Public figures,
government officials, and especially business men are too often presented as villains . . . we think that a person who has suffered damage,
financial or otherwise, because of untrue statements in the press
should have some right to redress."

Such ex cathedra pronouncements are becoming increasingly
prevalent. They ignore the important societal and personal values of
freedom of expression. In my opinion, the public should have the
broadest access to facts, opinions, and entertainment. Authors,
whether reporters, writers of fiction, drama, satire or junk literature,
should have the right to express themselves without fear of government penalties or private actions for damages.

One is reminded of the Kaiser's cavalier pronouncement just prior
to World War I, when he stated that a treaty is only a scrap of paper.
When individuals and the media are subjected to costly libel suits and
huge damage verdicts for expressing their opinions, the First
Amendment is relegated to the status of a scrap of parchment.

·VII·

Libel Suits and the News

Mails from the North—the East—the West—the South
—whence according to some curious etymologists comes
the magical words NEWS.

—THOMAS DE QUINCY

T HE greatest difference between the second half of the twentieth
century and all the preceding millennia of human existence may well
be the transmission of news to the general population—not the atom
bomb, the conquest of space, or any of the technological marvels and
terrors of our time. This is a very recent development. Historians
report that less than two centuries ago the procession taking Marie
Antionette to the guillotine passed fishermen on the banks of the
Seine. They did not turn their heads to look because they were
unaware of what was happening. Today even the most illiterate,
deprived individual has better access to news than the monarchs of
the nineteenth century who had to rely on slow and chancy private
couriers.

People have always communicated and transmitted news by whatever means they had, whether it was drums in the jungle, smoke
signals on the plains, or space satellites. The desire to know what is
happening, whether for protection from danger or for satisfying
natural curiosity, has apparently persisted throughout human existence. The ability to transmit news immediately from and to all parts
of the planet has transformed five billion diverse, hostile, fearful,
warring groups of strangers into a global village composed of diverse,
hostile, fearful, warring groups of people who are aware of each
other. They know, if only dimly and incompletely, the problems,

strengths, weaknesses, and characteristics of their fellow inhabitants of the earth.

The demand of the American people for news is insatiable. Radio stations broadcast all news all the time. There is not a moment of the day or night when an American cannot get the latest news from the most remote part of the globe and outer space at the turn of a switch. These brief accounts are flashes, hot off the wire, beamed off a satellite. Commentators give what is billed as "in-depth coverage" in thirty minutes or an hour. The day begins for most Americans with the morning news on radio and television.

The importance of news in the late twentieth century cannot be overestimated. In dictatorships, news is a tool to control and manipulate the populace. Reports of governmental activities have been and are being suppressed all over the world. Significantly, the Inter-American Court of Human Rights ruled in 1985 that compulsory licensing of journalists is not compatible with the American Convention on Human Rights.[1] Licensing of the press ceased in England and has never been imposed in the United States. But other measures, both governmental and private, limit public access to news. For example, in the United States for many years, injunctions, prosecutions for seditious libel, and economic pressures have been the principal means of governmental suppression of news. Yet, in a free society, reporting of news is the safeguard of the people against tyranny. Those who purvey the news act as the eyes and ears of each of us, extending our vision and our hearing around the globe. They may enlighten and inform our minds or feed our prejudices, but they are indispensable.

Television as a news medium has affected the public in ways that are not completely understood. It not only transmits images of events as they occur. It also, to some extent, shapes these events as individuals and groups recognize that the all-seeing eye of the camera provides them with an extraordinary global forum to transmit their messages. Significantly, in late 1985, South Africa banned television coverage of black demonstrations. The United States government has also, on occasion, banned news coverage of important events such as the invasion of Grenada, euphemistically called the "intervention." When government has restricted media access to military posts[2] and prisons,[3] the Supreme Court has upheld these limitations with little discussion of the essential role that the media perform in enlightening and informing the public. Indeed, the Court has held that the media have no special rights even though it is obvious that the media act as the surrogates of members of the public who cannot personally attend events and make investigations.[4]

Most Americans take the news media for granted. It is only when access is cut off that we become aware of our intellectual and emotional dependence upon the continuous availability of news. When a local paper goes on strike, members of the community feel bereft despite the availability of news over radio and television. Important as these sources are, they do not replace the more leisurely, lengthy, and detailed accounts available in print. In a power blackout, the transistor radio becomes the lifeline of news for people trapped in darkened isolation in the midst of crowded cities. All these media and the information they provide are essential to contemporary life.

Under any reading of the First Amendment—utilitarian, instrumental, or absolutist—the unrestricted dissemination of news is of paramount importance to the public. This chapter examines the significance of libel suits against the media and their effect on the mandate of the First Amendment.

Government control over the news media can be challenged in the courts, although not always successfully. It is more difficult to discover and assess limitations on news reporting brought about by the multitude of defamation suits against the media. Although these cases are tried under the adversary system of Anglo-American litigation, pitting two private parties against each other, the public is the significant, silent non-party whose rights are in jeopardy. As the Supreme Court eloquently declared in *Dombrowski* v. *Pfister*, "for free expression—of transcendent value to all society, and not merely to those exercising their rights—might be the loser."[5] In that case, arising out of threatened criminal prosecution under the Louisiana Subversive Activities and Communist Control Law, the Court held that even though defendants might ultimately be acquitted, the threat of prosecution had an inhibiting effect on free speech. The Court gave currency to the phrase, the "chilling effect upon the exercise of First Amendment rights." In no other area of expression is the public's interest more directly involved than in the reporting of news.

The morning paper, once the essential of every home, delivered by the paperboy for two cents a copy, has taken second place to the electronic media. In the past quarter century, the number of newspapers has sharply dropped. I do not mean to suggest that the daily press is an endangered species. But like all other enterprises, newspapers are subject to economic constraints and the necessity for survival. Punishing verdicts against the press and other news media inevitably have an effect on policy as to what will be published or aired.

Some notion of the economic pressures on the press as a result of libel suits is revealed by this alarming fact. During a forty-six day period, eight defamation suits were filed against the *Philadelphia Inquirer*.[6] Most of these cases arose out of reporting news. The *Inquirer* is not the *National Enquirer*. It does not engage in sensationalism or irresponsible charges. There is no reason to believe that the *Philadelphia Inquirer* is exceptional or that other daily papers are not sued with the same frequency. The cost of defending a libel suit is estimated at $200,000. If the case is appealed all the way to the U.S. Supreme Court, the cost may be doubled. If the case is remanded, the second trial is almost as costly as the first one. In addition to legal fees and out-of-pocket expenses, the preparation of the defense takes the time and energies of reporters, editors, and managing personnel. To defend against such charges at the rate of fifty a year is a not inconsiderable burden even for a very wealthy paper or radio or television station.

The contents of news can be considered in three rough classifications: (1) activities and policies of governments and government officials and employees at home and abroad, (2) activities of nongovernmental persons and agencies, (3) reports of natural events— appearance of a comet, eclipses of the sun and the moon, volcanic eruptions, floods, fires, droughts, and other disasters and happenings. The third category is seldom the subject of libel litigation.

The first two categories of news are essentially about people. Readers and listeners are interested in more than a bare recitation of events. They want to know not only the names of the individuals involved but what sort of people they are, what they have done in the past and, if possible, why and how they have become caught up in the event that is being reported. In the legal climate of the 1980s when subjects disagree with the authors' interpretations of facts, when subjects believe reports are inaccurate in any detail, when subjects resent having their seclusion disturbed by being mentioned in a news story, they may well sue the authors. Because the rewards of a successful libel suit are so enormous—in the millions of dollars —and the risks are comparatively less, subjects have every incentive to sue.

First Amendment rights in reporting of news and newsworthy events in the context of litigation between subjects and authors is not a simple subject. The first question is "What is news?" Although most people have a general notion of what constitutes news, the law requires definitions. When rights depend upon terminology, it is important to be precise. The degree of precision required depends upon the rights affected. Crimes must be defined narrowly. Unless the exact conduct of the accused falls within the definition of the crime, he or she cannot be convicted. In civil statutes there is more room for interpretation, but definition is important. When liability for several million dollars depends upon a word, that word should be clearly defined. But, if the definition is too precise, inevitably it will exclude situations the draftsman had not anticipated and neglected to include. If the definition is too broad, it risks being considered void for vagueness. Sensibly the law requires that people know with a fair degree of certainty the rules and standards of conduct to which they are expected to conform. Uncertainty provokes litigation. In defining categories or classifications, one must move cautiously between the Scylla of restrictiveness and the Charybdis of overbreadth.

Commonly used words and phrases are frequently the most difficult to put in clear legal terminology.* The courts have been grappling with definitions of obscenity for more than half a century. One can understand Justice Stewart's frustrated comment about obscenity, "I can't define it, but I know it when I see it."[7] Unfortunately not all judges have the same perceptions. More precise definition is required to give guidance to the courts, counsel, and the litigants.

In seeking to define the terms "news" and "newsworthy," Webster is of little help. Instead of meanings one finds tautology. "Newsworthy" is defined as "sufficiently interesting to the general public to warrant reporting (as in a newspaper)." To follow Webster would be to permit authors unlimited scope in defining the category. Anything appearing in the press would ipso facto be newsworthy. A glance at any daily paper reveals that a large proportion of the printed matter is of no general concern—social events, club meetings, routine crimes, accidents, recipes, sports, and the like. A story may be about the habits of a remote primitive tribe in the Pacific or the state of the president's intestines. These are subjects that many people find extremely interesting, but they have little bearing on matters relevant to self-governance, the public welfare, or national security. Nonetheless, they are newsworthy.

*During an hour of argument before the Supreme Court the justices probed for a definition of the term "handicapped" (55 LW 3403 [1986]).

"News" is defined as "a report of recent events—matter that is newsworthy." But the two terms are not synonymous. News is time related. Newsworthiness is not. This is a distinction that should have a bearing on questions of truth, fault, and privacy. But no reported judicial opinion has examined these issues in the context of time. I suggest that any report of recent events be deemed news regardless of its trivial nature or limited interest. The motto of the media might well be *nihil humanum alienum est*. Nothing that affects people is beyond media coverage. Under the definition here proposed, any item that is published or broadcast with respect to recent events would be deemed news, regardless of whether it is a matter of public concern and regardless of the number of people who read, hear, or see the report.

The word "recent" is admittedly vague. The dictionary defines it as "a time not long past." Within the range of "recent" there are many variations. An outer limit of perhaps six months after the time of the event or the awareness of it should give a generous interpretation of the word. This definition making the critical date "awareness of the event," not the actual time of the event is adapted from tort law dealing with disease. The statute of limitations in such a claim begins to run not from the onset of the disease but from the date when the plaintiff becomes aware that he or she has the disease. Obviously, plaintiffs cannot take legal action until they know of their illnesses. Similarly, authors cannot report an event until they are aware of it. A crime may not be discovered for months or years after it was committed. Actions occurring during military conflicts, such as the events in My Lai, may not become known for a considerable time.

Six months from the date of knowledge of the event or incident should allow ample time for news reporting of the occurrence. Legislators who draft statutes and courts that promulgate rules and regulations might reasonably choose another limit—three months or possibly one year. The exact time is of little significance, but the concept of recent in reporting news is critical. If an incident or event is more long lasting in interest it should be deemed to be "newsworthy." Both these terms, "news" and "newsworthy," have been used in countless Supreme Court opinions, but they have never been defined nor has the distinction between them been deemed to be important.

News reporting is far from homogeneous. Some news is reported almost instantaneously. Some live TV and radio reports are simultaneous with the event. The entire nation saw Jack Ruby kill Lee Harvey Oswald. The world watched as the first human being set foot on the moon and while the space shuttle exploded. Other events are reported within minutes after they occur. These are usually "hot" news flashes on the air. Much news is reported on the electronic media within hours of the event on regularly scheduled broadcasts. Some news stories appear in the daily press, others in weekly magazines, and others in monthly journals. In-depth commentaries are presented some weeks or months after the event. Many news stories are the basis of books, dramas, movies, and docudramas published and presented years after the events they discuss or portray. These significant differences in the amount of time available to check and verify the story have not been held to be relevant to the question of fault in the reported Supreme Court decisions. But if fault is predicated on negligence, time is a crucial factor.

Before discussing the latitude of permissible error that should be accorded these many different types of news reports, one must grapple with the elusive concepts of truth and falsity. These are decisions that courts have to make in almost every defamation suit. The initial issue is whether the statement is defamatory. This is frequently said to be a question of law. The second issue—whether it is false—is clearly a question of fact. But not all facts are susceptible to the same certitude and the same degree of proof. It depends upon the nature of the news story. It may be a simple statement that an accident occurred at a certain time and place and that the subject was injured. Those are easily verified facts. A report of a crime and the apprehension of a suspect is also easily verified. But a report of the crimes of which he is accused may not be so simple. There is a significant difference between allegations and facts. Other news stories involve complex matters of policy, economics, and science. Experts differ on the truth of many theories. Should authors be expected to determine such facts with absolute certainty?

Some news stories are demonstrably false. The wrong person is mentioned. A pianist is misidentified as a violinist. A person's job is incorrectly stated. Many daily papers print a list of corrections of such errors. For example, the *New York Times* printed the following item under the headline "Correction":

A television review on Tuesday of "No Greater Gift," on ABC, misidentified the actor who played the father of a boy with a brain tumor. He was Reni Santoni.[8]

Many responsible papers regularly print corrections of errors. The practice should be encouraged by the law rather than discouraged.*

Under English law, truth was not a defense to libel. Under American law, libel plaintiffs did not have to prove that the defendant was "at fault" in publishing a false and defamatory statement until 1974.[9] The definition of fault and the standards of proof of fault are left to the vagaries of the laws of the fifty states. In other tort actions (defamation, privacy, right of publicity, and false light claims are classified as torts), fault is equated with negligence. Like most legal concepts, negligence is not monolithic.

Negligence is defined as the absence of care, failure to do what a reasonable person would have done under the circumstances, or doing what a reasonable person would not have done. The duty of care is subdivided into classifications based on the status of the defendant and the risk involved. The degree of care diminishes as the risk decreases. Those who deal with dangerous objects like explosives, electricity, gas, and wild animals are held to the utmost caution. Common carriers—railroads, airplanes, buses, and other public transportation—are held to the highest duty of care. This exacting standard is imposed by law in part because carriers have a licensed monopoly and in part because they serve the public. People have little choice in selecting the carrier. They must use what is available. In most cases, they cannot compare which bus line has better equipment, better training of personnel, and a better safety record. Essentially users of public transportation are captive customers. Even where there is a choice, the rider is rarely in a position to obtain the information and make an informed decision.

Innkeepers have always been held to a high degree of care because they serve the public. It is logical and reasonable to hold hotels to a higher standard of care to their guests than individual hosts and hostesses who invite guests into their homes.

Manufacturers of dangerous goods are held to the standard of "the state of the art." Even though the manufacturer is not negligent, if it fails to use what is known and available in the industry to make the product safe, it is responsible for harms that occur because the product does not conform to the state of the art.

Similarly, doctors are required to provide care that conforms with the state of medical technology and skill established in the commu-

---

*See Chapter XII, Preventive Law, discussing the use of corrections, retractions, and apologies.

nity where the doctor practices. A doctor in a rural area that does not have sophisticated equipment like a CT scan may err in his diagnosis. But he will not be held to the same standard of care that is required of a doctor practicing in a large metropolitan area where all the latest technology and expert consultants are available. A reasonable standard of care is used as the measure of the doctor's negligence or fault.

What should be the standard of accuracy for authors? Should it be utmost caution, a high degree of care, reasonable care, or simply the duty to avoid harm? In the context of libel, it is clear that some statements, if false, will cause the subject serious harm. Others will not. It depends upon the nature of the charges and to a limited extent the position of the subject. A public official or candidate for office will obviously be subject to more harm by a false statement as to his or her criminal record than a person in private business. A false charge of criminality is more dangerous than a false charge of divorce. The risk and the foreseeability of harm are obvious facts about which juries and judges can reach sensible conclusions.

In all tort cases except libel, fault is determined by examining what the defendant has done. A motorist who negligently strikes a pedestrian is liable no matter who the pedestrian is. He or she may be number one on the FBI wanted list, a university president, an archbishop, or an unemployed derelict. The status of the plaintiff is irrelevant to the issue of the driver's fault. It will, however, materially affect the amount of damages.

In libel cases, on the contrary, the courts have focused not on the conduct of the author but on the identity of the subject. If the subject is a public figure, "actual malice" on the part of the author must be proved. If the subject is a private figure, a different degree of fault is required.[10] This doctrine is clearly unfair to both subjects and authors. It also provokes litigation because neither subject nor author can be sure in advance who is or is not a public figure. The test is elusive and inconsistent.

In November 1985, after more than fifty cases in which the Supreme Court has struggled with definitions of public and private figures, the Court was still divided over the issue. A public school teacher was accused by the local newspaper of lying at an Ohio High School Athletic Association hearing. The Supreme Court of Ohio held that the plaintiff was neither a public official nor a public figure. The United States Supreme Court denied certiorari.[11] Justice Brennan filed a blistering dissent pointing out that a public school teacher

is a public figure and that the disqualification of the school team was
a matter of public concern.

If fault is the test of liability, then it should follow that a reporter
who is negligent and whose false story causes harm should be responsible regardless of the identity of the plaintiff. Nor should the degree
of accuracy required be dependent upon the identity of the plaintiff.
But both the standard of duty and the degree of proof have been
made contingent upon the classification of the plaintiff as a public or
a private figure.

The Supreme Court has not elucidated its cryptic requirement that
an author (including the news media) must be at fault in order for
the subject to recover or the exact standards of proof to be met. But
these questions are inherent in all defamation cases. Instead of developing the answers on a case-by-case basis, promulgating novel doctrines that have no precedent, much difficulty would be avoided and
a measure of certainty achieved if the well-known standards of negligence were adopted in libel cases.

If these principles were applied to defamation cases arising out of
news reporting, the tasks of trial courts would be much simpler and
lawyers and litigants would be able to predict with some degree of
certainty the outcomes of cases. In determining fault or negligence,
the questions put to the jury would be the following: (1) Taken as a
whole, was the statement a false statement of fact or was it an
expression of opinion? (2) Was the defendant negligent? (3) Was the
plaintiff harmed thereby? The first question is often held to be a
matter of law to be decided by the judge. In my view this is a critical
question of fact that a jury is capable of deciding. If the jury were
instructed to consider the document as a whole in making this decision and not simply to rule on isolated phrases and paragraphs, the
decisions would likely be sensible. It is the rule in obscenity cases that
the book or article in question must be considered as a whole. This
rule is not followed in libel cases.

In *Herbert* v. *Lando*, [12] the Court of Appeals dismissed the charges
on remand because the substance of the article in question was not
false and defamatory. This case illustrates the confused doctrines and
interminable litigation characteristic of libel law since *New York
Times* v. *Sullivan*. Anthony Herbert, a retired Army officer, accused
his superiors of covering up atrocities that occurred during the Vietnam War. Barry Lando and Mike Wallace produced a television
program about Herbert's charges. Lando also wrote an article about
the subject that appeared in the *Atlantic*. Herbert sued for defamation, claiming that he was portrayed as a liar. He also sought, in the

language of the Supreme Court, "substantial damages to the literary value of a book he had just published recounting his experiences." The second issue was never addressed by the Court. The case turned on Lando's refusal to supply his notes and other documents sought by Herbert in discovery. He had requested any matter "relevant to the subject matter involved in the pending action." Because Herbert was a public figure, the defendant's state of mind under the actual malice test was of central importance to the plaintiff's case. The Supreme Court held that Lando had no claim of constitutional privilege under the First Amendment. Justice Powell concurred. Justice Brennan dissented in part, and Justice Marshall dissented. The four opinions total fifty-seven pages. The case was remanded to the district court and appealed to the court of appeals. The plaintiff declared that he would appeal to the Supreme Court a second time, even though the matter has been in litigation more than fourteen years.

Time, Inc. v. *Firestone*[13] has already been discussed. This case has been cited countless times in subsequent decisions. Had the Court employed the reasonable person standard instead of the public versus private figure test, the result would have been different and, I submit, protected responsible news reporting. Instead, the Court engaged in a detailed examination of the accuracy of the story. It was undisputed that a divorce had been granted. The reporter quoted verbatim from the decision of the trial judge who remarked about evidence "that would have curled Freud's hair." He did not elaborate on the evidence. The only possible inaccuracy, and that is somewhat questionable, is that the divorce was granted to the husband on the grounds of adultery. Adultery was one of the grounds for divorce alleged by the husband. Wife was granted alimony. By referring to Florida law, the Court concluded that despite the lack of clarity of the trial judge's order, the divorce could not have been granted on the grounds of adultery because if it had been the wife would not have been entitled to alimony.

The spouses had accused each other of lurid and salacious behavior. Obviously, such a story titillates large numbers of readers. The Supreme Court declared that the story catered to "morbid or prurient intrigue with scandal." In a free and democratic society a press has the right to provide its readers with exactly that kind of story, socially useless though it may be and regardless of "good taste." Censorship and the discredited bluestocking moral standards of Puritans such as Cotton Mather find their way back into the law by indirect means. Whether or not the story catered to prurient interest, gossip, or any other low tastes should have been irrelevant. Nothing in the story was obscene. It was a timely news report of a divorce that was deemed to be of interest because of the prominence of the individuals.

The Court engaged in a tortured analysis of whether the plaintiff was a public figure or a private figure. In applying the test of "public figure" promulgated ten years earlier, the Court had to decide whether the plaintiff had thrust herself into the public eye by being a party to a divorce action. Because one must go to court in order to obtain a divorce, it was held that she had not voluntarily placed herself in the public eye by filing for divorce. The Court might have as easily concluded that by marrying into a family in the public eye by reason of its wealth and position, the plaintiff had voluntarily assumed the role of a "public figure" or that her own behavior had brought her into the public eye.

I suggest that all these issues should be irrelevant to the First Amendment rights of a magazine to report a recent event that was obviously news. Under the negligence test here proposed the issues would have been (1) the negligence of the defendant, and (2) the harm, if any, suffered by the plaintiff as a result of the news story. Under the circumstances, was the reporter negligent? He had checked the dockets and accurately reported the order of the trial court and the allegations of the parties. *Time* is a weekly magazine. This was not a major story of great public concern. Was it reasonable to expect the reporter to research the law of Florida within those time constraints, bearing in mind the insignificance of the story and the very slight risk of harm to plaintiff against whom detailed charges of adultery had already been made public? I think most people would conclude that he was not negligent. If plaintiff had been required to prove harm to her battered reputation, I seriously doubt that a verdict of $100,000 would have been awarded or upheld. The Supreme Court remanded the case.

In *Rosenbloom* v. *Metromedia*, [14] previously mentioned, the Court also predicated its decision on the conclusion that plaintiff, who had been accused of selling obscene literature, was a private figure. In earlier cases, the Court had held that criminals are by that fact alone deemed to be public figures. At the time of the flash newscasts, plaintiff had been arrested. He was charged with crime. The fact that he was subsequently acquitted should not have changed his status of being a public figure at the time of the newscasts. The Court held that this was a matter of public interest and that the standard of proof required was "clear and convincing proof that the defamatory false-hood [was made] with knowledge that it was false or with reckless disregard of whether it was false or not." The Court concluded that there is no evidence to support a conclusion that defendant "in fact entertained serious doubts as to the truth" of its reports. That plaintiff was charged with a crime was undeniably true. Justice Black concurred, urging abandonment of *New York Times* v. *Sullivan* doctrine. Justice White concurred. Justice Harlan dissented, urging that damages be limited to actual harm reasonably foreseeable. Justices Marshall and Stewart dissented, expressing the view that in libel actions by private figures damages be limited to actual losses and that the standard of fault be left to state law.

Had this case been decided under general tort principles, the jury would have been instructed to decide whether the radio station acted negligently. Certainly as to the first broadcasts—hot news flashes—the defendant had no reason to doubt the accuracy of the police captain's information that plaintiff had been arrested for selling allegedly obscene books. It was, in fact, accurate. The repetition of the story two weeks later—before the court decided that the literature was not obscene—was also true. Whatever the district attorney's opinion was as to the obscenity of the materials, the charges had not been withdrawn. These were spot announcements, not lengthy stories. If, as several justices have suggested, the law limited damages to actual, provable harm it is unlikely that plaintiff could have proved any harm. Certainly, there was no outrageous behavior that would have justified any amount of punitive damages.

The case of *Gertz* v. *Robert Welch* [15] has provoked an enormous amount of academic discussion of the public versus private figure test. The case was tried three times. The Supreme Court justices found it necessary to issue six separate opinions. What abstruse, difficult legal problems could have engendered such an amount of intellectual ferment? The facts were simple and uncontested. The article falsely charged plaintiff with being a "Leninist" and "Communist fronter."

Under general principles of tort law, it is evident that in the political climate of 1969 these charges, if false, were seriously prejudicial. The risk was obvious and great. The article appeared in a monthly magazine. Defendant had ample time to investigate and verify the facts. There was no urgency in publishing this article as a hot news story. Defendant admitted that no effort was made to verify or substantiate the charges. Defendant's negligence was clear.

A jury might well have found that its conduct in failing to check a story where the risk of harm was so great was outrageous, justifying punitive damages. Whether Gertz was a public or private figure was really irrelevant to defendant's negligence.

If Gertz, in addition to being a practicing lawyer, had also been a member of a school board (many lawyers do serve on such public bodies with or without pay), the state legislature, or some public commission or agency, defendant's conduct would have been just as negligent and probably more harmful. But the test of liability would have been the subjective intent of the defendant: Did the editor or publisher act with reckless disregard of truth or falsity? Did they doubt the truth of the story? I submit that whatever the editor or publisher thought should be immaterial. Any reasonable person should have exercised care and verified these damaging allegations before publication.

Similarly, in cases of candidates for public office, the risk of harm of a false accusation is clearly very great. In *Ocala Star-Banner Co. v. Damron*, [16] the newspaper printed an admittedly false statement declaring that the mayor who was then a candidate for public office, had a criminal record. The defendant's only excuse was that he had had a temporary mental lapse. The plaintiff lost the election, sued the paper, and won. The Supreme Court reversed on the ground that he had failed to prove "actual malice." Similarly in *Monitor Patriot Co. v. Roy*, [17] the plaintiff was a candidate for public office. Just before the primary election, the defendant published a syndicated column in which plaintiff was characterized as a "small-time bootlegger." Plaintiff lost the election. He, too, sued for libel and won. Again the Supreme Court reversed. The case was remanded for a new trial. In both cases, I believe, the jury should have been asked to find whether the charge was false and, if so, whether the defendant was negligent in failing to check the facts. The Supreme Court declared, without giving any reasons or explanations that "application of tort law to the conduct of a political campaign is bound to raise dangers for freedom of speech and press."

It is apparent from the multitude of cases that the present rules do not protect freedom of speech and press or the legitimate needs of subjects. The test of whether the defendant acted negligently under all the circumstances would appear to give far greater protection to both subjects and authors and disentangle the courts from unworkable legal doctrines. The majority of the Court is clearly unwilling to adopt the absolutist position of Justices Black and

Douglas. The actual malice test severely prejudices public officials and candidates about whom admittedly false and damaging charges are made because, as Justice White declared, it puts a premium on the defendant's ignorance.[18] It also opens the press to harassment and invasion of privacy as plaintiffs pore through the notes of reporters and editors seeking evidence of "knowing" disregard of truth.

The category of "newsworthy" reports, as here defined, is different from "news" in that it does not involve recent events. It deals with matters of continuing interest and concern. Obviously, there are fewer, if any, time constraints on these reports and stories. The media have ample opportunity to check for accuracy. Liability for reports of newsworthy events would arise not only in connection with a subject's claim for libel but also for invasion of privacy. Most of the privacy actions have not been based on contemporaneous reporting of news but rather on the use of the incident at a subsequent time for a feature story, docudrama, or other treatment. It is proposed that in dealing with such claims a distinction be made between incidents that are merely news and those that are newsworthy.

Newsworthy is a more difficult concept than news. It is not time related. Obviously, some incidents and some persons are of only transitory interest. In a relatively short time, the event has ceased to arouse concern or even curiosity. The electronic media, the daily press, and the weekly and monthly periodicals, having reported the matter once or twice, drop it. The persons involved were of no interest before the incident, and they cease to be of interest afterwards. Such items are news. After a period of time they cease being newsworthy.

Other events and persons command much longer interest, some even enduring concern. Some matters require continuing reexamination and discussion. They may involve public issues such as foreign or domestic policy or matters of intellectual concern such as scientific discoveries and developments in the arts. The list of newsworthy matters is open-ended.

Webster defines "newsworthy" as something of general public interest. While this general statement is adequate for common understanding, as a legal standard a more precise definition is required. The critical factor in deciding whether a matter is newsworthy is not whether there is a general public interest but whether the interest of any segment of the public is more enduring than a brief period of several months. The general public may not have the slightest interest in the twelve-tone serial theory of music propounded by Arnold

Schönberg. But the subject is of continuing interest to musicians, musicologists, and music lovers. An article on this subject is newsworthy.

Many individuals because of their positions, their achievements, or their misdeeds are of more than passing interest. Artists, scientists, philosophers, and some academicians whose names are scarcely household words are of continuing interest to some segments of the public. Publications and media programs about them are newsworthy. Even the obsessively reclusive author, J.D. Salinger, by reason of his enormously popular and influential novel, *Catcher in the Rye,* is newsworthy.* Notorious criminals, such as the Boston Strangler, are newsworthy. The punk who robs a corner bar is news for a brief period of time, but is not newsworthy.

Although no reported decisions have been predicated on whether the statements that are the subject of the litigation are news or newsworthy, there is an implicit recognition of the fact that some speech involves more significant interests than others. This underlying assumption permeates the decisions that speak of giving the media "breathing space," and warn against the "chilling effects" of substantial verdicts that may lead to self-censorship.

This distinction, though couched in different language, forms the basis of the decision of the majority of the Supreme Court in *Dun & Bradstreet, Inc.* v. *Greenmoss Builders, Inc.* [19] That case arose out of an erroneous credit report on the plaintiff supplied to five customers of Dun & Bradstreet.† The Court there established the rule that in libel cases the trial court must apply an additional test of "public concern," so far an undefined term. The lack of definition and the addition of still another legal test to be met created more problems for trial courts, subjects, and authors. But the distinction between matters of general interest and of little interest is a rational one.

A pair of cases illustrates, without defining, the difference between newsworthy and non-newsworthy subjects. The rape of Ms. Cohn[20] was promptly reported in the press without mentioning the victim's name. Shortly thereafter it was again reported on the air, this time giving her name. Unfortunate though this rape was, this particular crime was of no interest to anyone except the family of the deceased victim and the criminal and his family. Under the public figure category, the Supreme Court denied recovery to the victim's family,

---

*Salinger's right to privacy and to enjoin publication of a biography of him is discussed in Chapter IX.
†The case is discussed in Chapter XI.

who surely suffered distress. The *Scottsboro* trial, in which a group of black youths were convicted of raping two white women on extremely suspect evidence, has been debated by the legal profession and the public for years as an example of race prejudice in the criminal justice system. Forty years after the trial, a docudrama about the crime and the trial was shown on television. The complainant in that case, who was still alive and leading a quiet private life as a respectable married woman, sued for invasion of privacy.[21] There can be no question that her privacy was rudely disturbed and that she suffered distress. But the *Scottsboro* case, unlike the rape of Ms. Cohn, is a significant historical event. The fairness of the trial has been debated by the legal profession and the public for more than four decades. The effect of the trial on perceptions of law and race prejudice will continue to be discussed for years. Whether or not the complainant "voluntarily" thrust herself in the public eye, she is forever a part of history.*

Compare Sidis, the child prodigy, with Alger Hiss. When Sidis was a child, his astonishing mental capacity was certainly a matter of news. Years later, his reclusive life was not news and of no general interest or public concern. Alger Hiss, a well-known former New Deal lawyer and director of the Carnegie Foundation, sued Whittaker Chambers for libel, alleging that Chambers had falsely called him a Communist.† Hiss was subsequently convicted of perjury. Some thirty years later, a docudrama on the trial was shown on national television. Hiss did not sue for invasion of privacy. If he had, the public figure versus private figure test might probably have yielded an unjust result. In the intervening years, Hiss was clearly not engaged in an activity that would qualify him as a public figure. But he, too, is a part of history. Any reading of the turmoil of the McCarthy era would be incomplete without the *Hiss* case.

Neither the complainant in the *Scottsboro* case nor Alger Hiss, however much they may desire seclusion and privacy, should have the right to claim redress from authors who choose to write about them and the events in which they were involved. Whether the author has a scholarly concern or simply seeks to exploit the continuing interest in these individuals should be irrelevant to the authors' First Amendment rights.

The test of newsworthiness in connection with privacy rights

---

*This is not to suggest that the producers of the docudrama had a right to change or fictionalize the facts without informing the audience.
†This case is discussed in Chapter II.

should be whether there is a continuing interest in the subject or in the event with which the subject is inextricably linked. Even criminals should have some rights of privacy. A person who is convicted of crime, serves his sentence, and establishes himself as a law-abiding citizen should have the right to be free of publication or revelation of past misdeeds unless he chooses to run for public office, apply for public employment, or work in a place of public interest or concern. But, some criminals like Ernesto Miranda have become part of legal history.[22] If Miranda were alive, he should not be able to claim a right to privacy.*

The public versus private figure test with the correlative requirement of proof of actual malice is, I believe, unworkable and unfair to both subjects and authors. But there is a bright line between public officials, including candidates for public office, and the rest of the population. The first plaintiff to whom the doctrine was applied was unquestionably a public official. By expanding the doctrine to apply to that amorphous category, "public figures," the courts have become enmeshed in deciding who is and is not a public figure. Many persons such as crime victims whose activities have nothing to do with matters of government or even matters of "public concern" have been included.

The distinction between public officials, candidates for public office, public employees, and all other persons is clear. These two categories are simply defined. Judges and juries can easily decide in which category the plaintiff belongs. The rights and responsibilities of public officials and the limitations on their conduct differ drastically from those of all other persons no matter how prominent or influential they may be. Public officials and employees give up many rights when they win or accept office or accept public employment, whether paid or unpaid. They have chosen public life rather than private life. They knew or should have known that certain burdens and restrictions are concomitant with privileges, perquisites, and powers of office (e.g., federal employees and most state employees are barred from engaging in certain kinds of political activity; many are required to make public disclosure of their assets;† some public

---

*In this seminal case, the Supreme Court held that before a defendant in police custody may be questioned he or she must be informed of the right to counsel and the right to remain silent or the accused's confession will be excluded from evidence.
†But see Denoncourt v. State Ethics Commission, 504 Pa 191, 470 A2d 945 (1983) holding that requiring disclosure of financial interests of family members of public officials unconstitutionally violated the privacy rights of such relatives.

employees are prohibited from striking). These conditions are not imposed on others. Indeed, they might run afoul of constitutional rights.

Public service exposes office holders and employees to criticism, both just and unjust. President Harry Truman pithily observed, "If you can't take the heat, stay out of the kitchen." Whenever I am attacked in the media, which happens from time to time, I recall this sage advice. If the criticism is too unpleasant, one can always resign. But the alternative, to muzzle authors who disagree with public officials and employees, would transform a democratic government into a bureaucratic dictatorship.

Many lawsuits against the media arise out of vigorous investigative reporting of alleged public corruption and waste of public funds. This kind of muckraking, if you will, often leads to grand jury investigations, indictments, and convictions. Without the disclosures by the media, it is likely that these derelictions of public duty would never be revealed.

Although the Supreme Court held that Senator Proxmire could be sued for defamation on the basis of his "Golden Fleece" awards,[23] they have accomplished great public good and many reforms. Senator Proxmire lists among savings to the taxpayers the following items:

> Funding for an 800-foot limestone copy of the Great Wall of China in Bedford, Ind., was halted following my Fleece, and plans for a Great Pyramid of Egypt never got off the ground. Savings in the hundreds of thousands.
>
> The Fleece on wasteful construction projects on Guam led to criminal prosecutions and a Department of Interior audit to foreclose future unauthorized spending.
>
> The Health Care Financing Administration stopped allowing podiatrists to cut the toenails of Medicare patients at a cost of $45 million annually after my Fleece of that program.
>
> Following my criticism in a Fleece award, the General Services Administration stopped the renovation of an old train station in Nashville, Tenn., and turned it over to the city with a savings to the taxpayers of $13 million.[24]

Investigative reporting of government officials and employees by the media and freelance writers has saved the taxpayers enormous sums of money and uncovered corruption. The convictions of Chicago judges and Philadelphia police officers, as well as many other

public officials and employees, are probably directly traceable to
media reporting. Until suspects are arrested, indicted, tried, and
convicted, no one can state with any certainty whether they are
innocent or guilty. These are not the kinds of defamatory statements
that can be proved or disproved until after the criminal trial and all
appeals are decided. If the subjects are convicted this is clear proof
of guilt. If they are acquitted, it is by no means clear that the authors'
statements were false. Criminal conviction must be by proof beyond
a reasonable doubt. Even if truth or falsity of defamatory statement
is required to be proved by clear and convincing evidence, this is a
materially lower standard of proof. The statement may be found to
be true in a civil action, and the accused may be acquitted in a
criminal prosecution. The criminal law also presumes that a suspect
is innocent until proved guilty. This salutary presumption should
not, however, foreclose disclosure of suspicions and suspicious circumstances. If authors risk substantial verdicts for undertaking such
reporting, the loss to the public will be severe.

If in 1919 the Supreme Court really meant that seditious libel was
dead, then an absolute privilege should be given to authors, including
the media, who criticize the actions of government officials, employees, aspirants to public office, and recipients of public funds.

Much of the public and judicial concern with the right of the
media to report news has focused on investigative reporting, the
glamorous and essential task of uncovering governmental and corporate skullduggery. Here the media act as agents for the public to
inform and expose so that the electorate can perform adequately the
difficult task of self-governance. These articles are clearly of public
concern whether they are timely news stories or more leisurely publications concerning newsworthy incidents and issues.

The media also perform another significant function, what has
been called "the bulletin board." Particularly daily and weekly newspapers give access to persons who wish to communicate with the
public. This can be done through paid advertisements, letters to the
editor, and pieces on the Op Ed page. The author in these instances
is not the reporter or newspaper but the person or persons who sign
the letters, articles, and ads. It is apparent that the media do not and
cannot vouch for the accuracy of these pieces. Nonetheless, in a
number of cases they have been sued for repetition or reporting of
libel. The complaint in *New York Times* v. *Sullivan* was based on a
paid advertisement.

The law, I believe, should limit responsibility for libel to those who
write such allegedly libelous signed statements, letters, articles, and

advertisements, and relieve from responsibility the publications that simply report that such accusations have been made or allow the authors space in the publications with or without charge. The contrary view forces the media, in effect, to censor all ads, letters, and personal expressions. If the media are to be held responsible in libel actions for the content of these communications, they must exercise control. Such control unwisely gives the media the right to censor paid advertisements, letters, and signed columns. Placing responsibility on the media for these pieces ignores the essential role the press plays in providing access to the public and segments of it to exercise their rights of free expression.

The Supreme Court has acknowledged that First Amendment rights are seriously implicated when government seeks to control or limit advertising by lawyers and other professionals,[25] and to restrict campaign expenditures by candidates for public office.[26] If the media foreclose access to the public by rejecting advertisements because of fear of libel suits, this will be yet another example of limitation of First Amendment rights by the private sector. Not only are those who wish to communicate denied access but also the vast unrepresented population that may wish to read these opinions and statements are denied that opportunity.

The Soviet Government purchased a full page ad in the *Washington Post* at the regular rate of $27,984.[27] Should the *Post* be responsible in damages if the ad contains false, libelous statements? Even if the editors have reason to believe that the statements are false and libelous, is it not a proper function of a free press in a free society to permit the Soviet Government to publish its statement? I believe it is. But under the actual malice standard, the *Post* would be responsible for damages (without proof of harm) if sued in libel.

Anti-abortionists, pro-abortionists, the Palestine Liberation Organization, the Anti-Defamation League, the proponents and opponents of apartheid, the proponents and opponents of Star Wars, and all the other controversial issues of the day should, I believe, have access to the media to present their opinions even though many may believe that such views are misguided or false or even dangerous. Justice Holmes's metaphor of the marketplace of ideas is an appealing fiction. But the marketplace is not free except to letter writers whose missives the press chooses to print and to persons who are able to appear on radio and television talk shows. Advertisements are often the only means by which persons in moderate financial circumstances can enter that marketplace.

If the media are held responsible for libelous statements by those who sign their letters, articles, and advertisements, and who appear on talk shows, it will seriously limit access to the public and correspondingly restrict the public's ability to read and hear any voices other than those vetted by the media. The lawsuit by Lillian Hellman against Mary McCarthy, Dick Cavett, and the television network indicates the dangers to this form of expression of opinion by libel suits. Those who favor libel suits to curb the power of the media ignore the indisputable fact that making the media responsible in libel actions for all material printed or aired will inevitably result in censorship by the media. In a letter to the *New York Times,* Reed Irvine, chairman of Accuracy in Media, Inc., asks, "What is wrong with chilling any propensity of journalists to defame with reckless disregard of the truth?"[28] I doubt that Mr. Irvine would want to authorize the *Times* or any other newspaper to censor or ban his communications to the public.

The letters to the editor columns of the press permit any individual to address a wide readership for the price of a postage stamp. Few special interest groups, no matter how well supported, are in a position to publish their own newspapers. Those who do subsidize journals to air their views rarely reach a general readership. By purchasing space in a newspaper or time on the air anyone who can pay the rate is able to reach an enormous audience. Open access as a First Amendment right should be fostered not limited. Those who believe they have been libeled by letters, Op Ed pieces, and advertisements, can always sue the authors and recover whatever damages a judge or jury chooses to award within the financial capacity of the defendant. The libeled individual is thus treated in the same way as any other tort victim. Persons injured in accidents or by dangerous products who recover substantial verdicts against those who have injured them have no guarantee that they will collect the judgment. That depends on the wrongdoer's ability to pay. If the wrongdoer files for bankruptcy, the injured victim is left with an uncollectable judgment.*

In the bulletin board function, the press is in the same position as cities, states, and the federal government with respect to highways. The governments own the streets and roads, but they cannot exclude licensed vehicles and drivers. When motor vehicle accidents occur on these highways, the governments are not responsible for the negligence of the drivers nor do they guarantee the payment of judgments

---

*Compare the asbestos plaintiffs who are unable to recover substantial verdicts against Johns Manville Corporation because it has filed for bankruptcy.

entered against such drivers. The only time a government or governmental agency is held liable for motor vehicle accidents is when it
is at fault in constructing or maintaining a dangerous condition on
the highway. In like fashion, when the media provide access to the
public by giving or selling space or time they should not be held
responsible for the libelous use of that space or time. I see no reason
in law or social policy for making the media, in effect, the guarantors
of judgments entered against those who utilize the media as a means
of open access to reach the public.

The media are frequently held responsible for repeating a libelous
statement made by another party. When a well-known individual
charges another with falsehood, crime, or some kind of defamatory
misconduct and the media report the charge, that is news. The media
do not report the libelous statement as a fact; they report the charge
because such an accusation is news.

Edwards v. *National Audubon Society,* [29] illustrates this type of
report. Naturalists opposing the use of the pesticide DDT believed
that bird count data were being misused by proponents of DDT. The
editor of the Audubon Society's publication, *American Birds,*
pointed out that the fact that larger statistics on the bird population
mean that there are more "birders," not more birds. He wrote,
"Anytime you hear a 'scientist' say the opposite, you are in the
presence of someone who is being paid to lie, or is parroting something he knows little about." A *New York Times* reporter interviewed Audubon officials who gave a list of persons to whom the
statement referred. The reporter contacted these people and wrote a
story reporting the charges and denials. The persons named sued the
author, the Audubon Society, and the *New York Times.* A jury
verdict against several of the defendants, including the *Times,* was
reversed. The court of appeals declared, "We believe that the *New
York Times* cannot, consistently with the First Amendment, be
afflicted with a libel judgment for the accurate reporting of newsworthy accusations made by a responsible and well-noted organization like the National Audubon Society." The Supreme Court declined to hear the case.

The decision may be read as a victory for the press. I suggest that
the implicit requirements of neutral reportage and the responsible
character of the organization making the charges are too restrictive.
Obviously if John Doe makes an accusation that is not news. When
ordinary citizens express the opinion that Ghadafi is paranoid or
crazy, as many people have done, that is not reported. It is not news.
When President Reagan calls Ghadafi a "flake" or a "mad dog," that

is news. These comments were widely reported in all the media. Should they have to defend themselves if Ghadafi should decide to sue? The media cannot question Ghadafi as to his mental status. There can be no "neutral" reportage, only a repetition of an unverified charge.

The Reverend Louis Farrakhan has made many irresponsible charges against groups and individuals that have been widely reported by the media. Is he a "responsible" person? The BBC broadcast in the United States a report from Moscow declaring that the "CIA cooks all sorts of reports. . . ."[30] Certainly such a serious charge is news. What the Soviets say about the CIA is a matter of public concern. The head of the CIA could claim that the report was of and concerning him, that it was false and defamatory, and published with actual malice because the BBC and the local American stations that broadcast the report had reason to doubt its truth.

Another example of the repetition of libel was the news report that Governor Edward D. Prete had called for the resignation of Chief Justice Joseph A. Bevilacqua of Rhode Island on the basis of reports that he associated with members of organized crime.[31] Bevilacqua resigned from the bench. If he had fought the charges, and had been successful, then he might have claimed that they were false and defamatory and sued the press for libel. The fact that such charges are publicly made against a public official is news that should be reported. The media do not vouch for their truth. In my view, there should be no liability for a truthful report that a named individual has made charges, whether or not those charges are ultimately proved to be false.

It is advisable again to refer to general principles of law when examining the role of the media that publish or air such charges. Under the law of agency, a principal or employer is liable for the wrongful acts of the agent or employee committed in the course of that relationship. Clearly the Audubon Society writer was not the agent or employee of the *New York Times.* He would be considered an independent contractor who has to bear responsibility for his own misconduct. Certainly the Moscow World Service was not the agent or employee of the BBC or any American radio stations. When the press or electronic media repeat a defamatory statement, this is in the nature of a hearsay statement. They do not represent that the accused scientist is fraudulent, or that the CIA falsifies reports. They merely report that those charges were made by named individuals or organizations.

Under the law of evidence, it is clear that when, for example, policeman A testifies that citizen B told him that the accused shot the victim, the policeman's testimony is hearsay. The policeman did not see the shooting. His testimony is admissible not to prove the truth of the charge but to show that the defendant was legally arrested. A policeman has probable cause to arrest when he sees a wounded victim and is told that the defendant was the assailant. When the media report that an author for the Audubon Society charges that plaintiffs are ignorant or paid to lie, they are in the position of the policeman who testifies that B said the defendant shot the victim. The only representation of truthfulness the police officer makes is that he or she is accurately reporting what was said. Should the officer be held to have libeled the accused on the basis of truthfully repeating a statement? I think not. Similarly, when the media truthfully report that X made a libelous statement about Y, that is hearsay with respect to the truth of the statement but not as to the fact that X made such a statement. When the media accurately report the defamatory statement clearly identifying it as the statement of another there should be no responsibility because the media have not made a libelous assertion.

Although all lawyers and judges agree that occasionally "the law is a ass," on the whole, legal doctrines reflect reality and provide sensible rules to resolve conflicting rights of parties. If the rules as to agency and hearsay were applied to cases based on repetition of libel, the falsely libeled person would be entitled to recover damages from the party at fault, the one who made the false and defamatory statement. The media, which never vouched for the truth of the libel, would be held to be privileged, and summary judgment would be entered in their favor.

Two elusive questions have not been litigated and, under the present state of the law, may not be justiciable for want of a plaintiff with standing to sue. They are the voluntary suppression of news by the media and the deliberate refusal of information by the government.[32] Both are the obverse of seditious libel. Rather than courting sanctions for criticizing and exposing government policies and actions, all too often the press has remained silent. The failure promptly to report the Bay of Pigs invasion is an example of voluntary suppression. The government blackout of information of the Grenada invasion exemplifies government withholding of information.

The media themselves often withhold information or present information prepared by government and private pressure groups. In 1980, the State Department and Mobil Oil Corporation tried successfully to persuade the Public Broadcasting System to cancel *Death of* *a Princess,* a fictionalized account of the execution of a member of the Saudi Arabian royal family for adultery. It was said to offend an ally that is a major oil supplier.[33] In 1986, ABC Entertainment postponed a program, *Amerika,* depicting life in the United States after a fictional Soviet takeover. Moscow warned that ABC's news operations could be jeopardized,* but ABC indicated that it would air the show.[34] Neither program was news. But both incidents indicate the dangers from pressures on the media.

Significantly, the Public Broadcasting System chose to air a program on Vietnam prepared by Accuracy in Media to refute the prize-winning series on Vietnam earlier aired by PBS. This is another example of the forces of privatism controlling the news.

These issues are of enormous importance to a democratic society. Doubtless they will be debated for years. The failure of the *New York Times* to report the planning of the Bay of Pigs invasion has been justified as a wise and responsible use of editorial discretion. It has also been criticized as self-censorship and an infringement of the now discredited concept of the public's right to know.

With hindsight one could conclude that the government and the American people might have been spared a humiliating disaster and the unnecessary loss of lives if the planned invasion of the Bay of Pigs had been reported before it occurred. The Congress would have had an opportunity to debate the underlying foreign policy as well as the use of military might without a declaration of war. But who among the many reporters who must have known of the government's decision would have had standing to sue the *Times* for deliberate withholding of news? Under what theory could a court have compelled the press to print what it chose not to print? These are significant legal issues that should be debated.

Under old English law, the attorney general had powers *parens patriae* to represent the public interest and could file suit. That power has been used in the United States chiefly to compel charitable trusts to function in the public interest. In the context of withholding news, the attorney general is a part of that government administration that wishes the information withheld. There is no representative of the public to serve this function.

England does not have a written constitution or any statutory or common law remotely resembling the First Amendment. In the face of government censorship, the media resorts to self-help. For exam-

---

*Ironically the Soviets are seeking to purchase the program for telecast in the Soviet Union.

ple, when the government interfered with a planned BBC program on conditions in Ireland, the employees did not rush to court; they went on strike.

In Scandinavian countries, the ombudsman, who is not a part of the government administration, is a special functionary to whom the duty of oversight is entrusted. The office of ombudsman* has been used to a limited extent in a number of states to oversee the operations of the police, public institutions, and other government agencies. Whether some similar representative of the public could or should be entrusted with the duty of compelling the disclosure of news is an interesting and hitherto unexplored question. Perhaps some voluntary agency might be established to investigate withholding of news and to alert the public when the media fail to do so.

The deliberate cutting off of information with respect to the Grenada intervention raises the specter of covert operations carried out in violation of congressionally imposed limitations or clearly articulated legislative policy.† The courts have not addressed this question principally because the media failed to litigate it. Such an action might be difficult to frame. Questions of standing to sue, the usual judicial refusal to consider political questions, and the threat of clear and present danger to the national safety and welfare would inevitably be raised. Even assuming that a plaintiff could be found to bring an action against either the media or the government and a justiciable issue could be framed, the matter could not be brought to trial for at least six months to a year. The harm from suppression would have occurred before the courts could act. At present, the only parties that can protect the public interest in disseminating all the news, whether fit to print or not, are the media. They are ill served by interpretations of libel law and the First Amendment that result in thousands of lawsuits for defamation and verdicts of millions of dollars.

---

*Professor Gilbert Cranberg of Iowa University suggests an ombudsman to deal with complaints against the press (*Time,* August 19, 1985, p. 55). The concept of an ombudsman to compel disclosure has not been discussed in the literature of freedom of the press.

†The belated revelations of aid to the Contras fighting the Nicaraguan government in violation of federal law exemplifies the public need to know that can be supplied only by the media.

·VIII·

Criminals, Victims, and Authors

. . . I wanted to write what I called a nonfiction novel—
a book that would read exactly like a novel except that
every word of it would be absolutely true.

—TRUMAN CAPOTE

STORIES about crime are as old in human memory as Cain and Abel. Psychiatrists and sociologists may ponder the dark reasons for the allure that violence, deceit, and death have for peaceful, law-abiding persons. Whether the armchair sleuths and parlor crime afficionados get sexual thrills from reading about dreadful deeds, whether this is healthy sublimation, or perverted voyeurism is not the concern of this book. Nor are literary merit and the motivations of the authors. The focus is on the legal rights of the criminals, the victims, and the authors, as well as the impact of the First Amendment on their conflicting claims.

Crime as a subject has attracted such masters as Dostoyevsky and Balzac and such producers of popular books about notorious criminals as Shana Alexander and the semi-anonymous "as told to" authors who produce scores of books about criminals.[1] A crime may serve as the opening scene of a "who dun it" detective story. It may be treated humorously as in *Sweeney Todd* and *Gaslight,* or with pretentious seriousness as in *The Executioner's Song.* Some authors, like psychiatrist Willard Gaylin, state the ideological purposes of their books. Gaylin's account of the slaying of Bonnie Garland[2] was written ostensibly to focus attention on the victims of crime and their families rather than on sympathy for the criminal. Other books on crimes are written simply because such books sell very well. None of these considerations or the motivations of the writer should be material to the legal rights of the three principal parties—the criminal, the victim,* and the author.

Prior to 1966, when Truman Capote's *In Cold Blood* was published, actual crimes had been treated by authors as the taking off point for fiction or for contemporary journalistic reports, sociological studies, and the like. Writers of fiction, by their art or craftsmanship, transmute the brief sordid facts of crime into novels. They do not purport to be giving the true stories of the people involved. Other uses by authors of actual crimes were primarily as research data. These books had a limited readership. They were not best sellers. The financial rewards of such authors were, on the whole, modest.

Capote created a new genre—"faction"—a nonfiction novel purporting to be a completely accurate and truthful account of real crimes, the criminals, the victims, and bystanders. Capote's book was an instant success, extremely popular with readers, critically acclaimed, and highly lucrative. It spawned an enormous progeny. During the succeeding two decades scores, if not hundreds, of books have been written about actual contemporary crimes. As soon as the criminal plunges his knife into the victim or fires his gun, avid authors are bidding for the story and various subsidiary rights.

The criminal, of course, is alive. The victim may be alive but if not is usually survived by family. The bystanders are fair game for anyone. The legal complications arising out of this new literary genre are novel, complex, and difficult. Because of the sudden appearance of this form of book and television program, there is little precedent for courts to be guided by and a lamentable dearth of jurisprudential discussion analyzing the conflicting rights, appropriate remedies, and the impact of the First Amendment. Unless there is thoughtful analysis of the legal rights of the parties and public policy, the courts will continue to flounder in uncharted seas. The unsatisfactory legal history of libel litigation will be repeated with equally disastrous results for litigants, the legal system, and the preservation of free expression.

This is a peculiarly contemporary problem. Prior to the advent of faction books and docudramas about living criminals, books about crime were not particularly lucrative. Many were sociological or criminological studies with a limited readership. Others dealt with notorious criminals who had been dead for many years. They rarely delved into the lives of the victims. There was little likelihood that

*The generic term "victim" as used here includes the families and friends of the victim and the bystanders who are caught up in crime as witnesses and sources of information. They are the plaintiffs who sue authors, publishers, and the media for invasion of privacy and libel.

the criminal or the author would profit substantially from the crime. There was not the unseemly spectacle of criminals and authors reaping hundreds of thousands of dollars from royalties while innocent victims and their families subsisted in poverty and misery.

Again, general principles of law offer sensible precedent. It is a fundamental, morally sound legal principle that one may not profit from his* wrongdoing. The most common application of this rule is the denial of insurance benefits to a criminal. If an arsonist burns his property, he cannot collect the insurance benefits even though he has faithfully paid the premiums. This is the general rule of law even though there is no clause in the policy excluding arson from benefits. Courts have had little difficulty in ruling that such payments would be contrary to public policy. Similarly the beneficiary of an insurance policy who contracts for the murder of the insured cannot recover. There should be little conceptual problem for courts in upholding statutes that provide for the confiscation of the criminal's royalties, against claims of the criminals that these laws infringe their First Amendment rights.

The rights of the authors of these books involve more difficult legal issues. In considering these novel questions, there are many competing rights and interests. Authors claim freedom of expression and property interests in the fruit of their labors. Crime victims claim statutory rights of reparation. The public interest requires enforcement of the principle that crime must not pay.

It is indisputable that these faction books do profit from the commission of crimes. Many profit enormously. It is also true that authors invade the privacy of living persons—the criminals, the victims, their families, and the bystanders. They depict the bloody horrors of the crimes in chilling detail. They are page turners because they use the techniques of the novel to make the story build to a climax and hold the attention of the reader. In addition, they have a peculiar fascination because they claim to be true. The authors meticulously amass detailed information about the criminal (or the accused, if not yet convicted) and all the people, including the victim, with whom he or she came in contact. Authors spend years accumulating detailed information. Readers are led to believe that they have an absolutely faithful picture of the criminal, the victim, and the cast of supporting characters. This, of course, may give rise to legally cognizable rights on the part of the people depicted.

*The masculine pronoun is used for convenience and because approximately 85 percent of all crimes and delinquent acts are committed by males. Significantly more than half of the victims, however, are females.

These books resemble the studies of sociologists like Oscar Lewis. Most scholars do not disclose the identity of their subjects. When the names of the family depicted in Lewis's *The Children of Sanchez* were revealed in the Mexican press, however, there was an outcry. It was charged that the portrait was not accurate. When the book does not purport to be a scientific study but claims to be a true portrait and is a highly lucrative best seller, the resentment is much greater.

Despite the careful, minute descriptions of the external details of the lives of the criminal and all the other people, including their day by day activities and the purported reproduction of conversations, curiously the reader rarely identifies with either the victim or the criminal. Gary Gilmore, the killer in Mailer's *The Executioner's Song,* is no Raskolnikov in whom the reader recognizes an essential human kinship. Jeffrey MacDonald, the subject of Joe McGinniss's *Fatal Vision,* is not a Jean Valjean whom one can pity. Each is a case study of a stranger from whom the reader feels safely distanced. There is that comforting gulf between them—the criminals—and us —the law-abiding people. The victims are simply pawns, accidents of fate or bad luck.

When I was a practicing lawyer, I represented many persons accused of heinous crimes. A good many of them had killed, robbed, raped, and embezzled. I knew them and their families intimately. I also got to know the victims and their families. As a judge I have presided over hundreds of criminal trials. When the accused is convicted, it is my unhappy duty to impose sentence. Before doing so, I get presentence reports that give me a great deal of information about the background of the offender: his family, his school record, his past employment, if any, his leisure activities. I also get a record of his IQ and a neuropsychiatric evaluation. The accused himself, if he is literate, often writes to me as do his family and friends. My picture of most law violators is vastly different from that of the writers of crime "faction." Some of these authors take the part of the criminal, often despite his or her admitted guilt. Of course, it is often the criminal's purpose in talking to an author to obtain this kind of extra-legal support for acquittal, a new trial, or a lenient sentence. Other authors of crime faction become extra-legal prosecutors, using the confidences of the criminal as additional evidence of guilt. I wish that the authors of books about criminals would present their protagonists as I see them: pitiful, essentially unloved and unlovable people who have outlawed themselves from society. They recognize their inadequacies but rather than seeking to help themselves, easily lapse into self-pity, bravado, and idle fantasies of power that they translate into reality by means of a readily available gun or knife. They are not such stuff as dreams or heroes are made of. Columnist Bob Greene, in writing about Gary Gilmore, commented on this new cult. He wrote, "[I] knew it would be only a matter of time until Gilmore took on mythic proportions—*The Executioner's Song* has been broadcast with an audience in the tens of millions—Max Jensen, Ben Bushnell [killed by Gilmore] . . . maybe someone will make a movie about them some day. Don't hold your breath."[3]

Although some of these books are hailed as literary masterpieces, many are sleazy potboilers written solely for the purpose of cashing in on the public taste for crime. Ironically these books are at the height of their popularity at the very time that the public sternly demands the death penalty and severe sentences for street criminals. Neither the literary merits of these books nor the social good or harm that they do should have any bearing on the rights of the parties.

The legal problems cannot be ignored. The number of books about crime is already enormous. More are being written and contracted for every day.* For example, the widow of James Oliver Huberty, who killed twenty-one people and wounded nineteen others at a McDonald's in San Isidro, California, was reportedly attempting to auction the rights to her story of life with a killer. She is quoted as saying, "I'm going to need money. I got to thinking, 'why be stupid?' To give it away is dumb."[4]

John W. Hinckley, Jr., who shot President Reagan and several others, has agreed to help George Campozi write a book about him and his exploits for 25 percent of the profits.[5] His parents collaborated on a book, *Breaking Points*. They are reported as being interested in mental health problems and saying ". . . we're trying . . . to make something good come of it."[6] This appears to be a disingenuous comment by persons actively promoting a book.

Gordon Liddy, one of the Watergate felons, commands a minimum of $3,000 per lecture and is in demand.[7] John Ehrlichman and Charles Colson, also Watergate felons, have written popular books. These works by criminals have commanded far more attention and reaped more profit for the authors than the book by Judge John Sirica, who presided over the Watergate trials and wrote a lucid and interesting account of the crimes and prosecution.[8]

---

*It is reported that Colonel Oliver North who allegedly was involved in "Irangate" and the transfer of arms to the Nicaraguan contras is negotiating for the sale of book, TV, and film rights to his life story.

R. Foster Winans, the reporter for the *Wall Street Journal* who was convicted for his part in a scheme to trade advance information on stocks, is getting bids from publishers for a book on his criminal activities. Prosecutor David J. Carpenter referred scathingly to Winan's "effort to cash in on the scheme by auctioning off his story to the highest bidder."[9]

Mary Ann Garton Bass, who married her son and was convicted of incest, is reported to be considering offers for film and book rights to the story of her crime.[10]

John Z. DeLorean, who was acquitted of drug conspiracy charges, has reportedly sold the rights to his story for $1.3 million.[11]

With such large sums involved, inevitably there will be suits and countersuits by criminals and authors as well as victims. In addition, there are disputes between competing authors and suits between authors, their publishers, and their insurers. Consider the charges and countercharges made by Jonathan Coleman, author of *At Mother's Request,* and Shana Alexander, author of *Nutcracker.* Both books are about Frances Schreuder, who allegedly persuaded her son Marc, to kill Frank Bradshaw, her millionaire father. Coleman has charged Alexander with "check book journalism," in that she paid for the interviews with the victim's widow. According to book reviewer, J. Anthony Lukas, Alexander stated, "I do not buy material . . . It's been my principle . . . But I couldn't turn down material like that." The material was allegedly purchased by her publisher, Doubleday & Company. As Lukas comments, "Thus she has it both ways, high minded disdain for the practice, yet full enjoyment of her publisher's poisoned fruits."[12]

Joe McGinniss, author of *Fatal Vision,* the story of Captain Jeffrey MacDonald who was convicted of killing his pregnant wife and two children, entered into a contract with MacDonald before the trial for 40 percent of the royalties. MacDonald is suing McGinniss, whose book unmistakably points to MacDonald's guilt. He charges fraud, breach of contract, breach of the covenant of good faith and fair dealing, intentional infliction of emotional harm (including "anxiety caused by hate mail . . . difficulties in relating to and dealing with prison personnel and fear and anxiety regarding physical well being due to adverse inmate reaction . . ."), and he seeks $10 million in damages. McGinniss is counterclaiming, and the government wants the proceeds under the Crimes Code for the victim's compensation fund.

Another unhappy subject is the widow of John Belushi, who cooperated with author Robert Woodward when he wrote *Wired* about Belushi's life and death from drugs. She complains of the lack of compassion in the book.[13]

There are also conflicts between criminal and victim over the literary spoils of the crime. Cathleen Crowell Webb, whose testimony led to the conviction of Gary Dotson for raping her, has written about her recanting of that testimony in *Forgive Me*. Dotson is reported to be working on his book about the events, but his attorney complains that Webb's book will cut into the profits for Dotson's book.[14]

This small sample of claims and counterclaims arising out of books dealing with contemporary crimes indicates the multiplicity of legal issues involved and the flood of litigation about to inundate the courts.

The perception that crime is a commodity to be sold to the highest bidder apparently affects the attitudes of criminals, victims, authors, and the public. So long as the price is high, such transactions will occur.[15] It is widely assumed that victims as well as criminals sell their life stories and profit from their unfortunate experiences. A resident of New Bedford, Massachusetts, when interviewed about a notorious gang rape that occurred there in 1983, stated that he did not feel sorry for the victim of the crime because she would get a lot of money for her story. In fact, one of the youths shot in the New York subway by Bernhard Goetz promptly sold the rights to his story to the *National Enquirer* and then complained that he had been cheated. Neighbors and friends also use the crime as a commodity and sell interviews and their impressions of the criminal.

Many authors view crime as lucrative, ready-made subject matter. Few reveal their attitudes toward the criminal and the victim so frankly as Shana Alexander. But it is evident that many exploit crime without regard for the needs or rights of either the criminal or the victim. In an interview, Shana Alexander explained her reaction to the news about Jean Harris's killing of Herman Tarnower, the well-known diet doctor and author of *The Scarsdale Diet*. Said Alexander:

> The TV was playing and I heard that a doctor, someone I knew, had been shot. I didn't know him very well but the name is rather unusual so when I heard "Tarnower," I remembered him a little bit. It said he had been shot and killed by the headmistress of the Madeira School. I certainly knew the Madeira School. It was all quite unlikely. I've been a journalist all my life; I mean you know that has to be a good story. . . .

Watching Harris on television, Alexander was struck by the similarity in appearance between herself and Harris—same hairdo, same shoes.

> I said, "This is fantastic, this is the greatest story." And then the lawyer came on right away. Obviously he was the lawyer because he had a hat and a cigar. All the reporters were gathered around. He was on the steps of the police station. He said, "Wait a minute fellows, you don't understand my client. She's very much a lady."
> I said, "Oh, my God, I think that's the title!"[16]

Alexander described Harris most sympathetically. Indeed, one might consider her book a brief on behalf of Harris to the appellate court. The book appeared after the conviction, but before the appeal was decided. Either those judges did not read the book or they were not impressed. Diana Trilling's book on Harris reached the opposite conclusion. Did it affect the courts? No one will ever know. Both Trilling and Alexander exploited Harris and Tarnower. If Tarnower had not been a wealthy bachelor but a married man of moderate means who left a widow and children, the inherent unfairness of permitting authors to profit at the expense of victims would be apparent. One might also ask whether Trilling and Alexander had any obligation to Harris.* Apparently neither had a contract with her. Although Alexander had spoken to Harris, Trilling states that she did not even interview Harris and obtained all her information from public records.

The three major parties concerned in litigation arising from crime "faction" are the author, the criminal, and the victim. The victim has received the least attention from the legal system. One reason is that few victims have gone to court to seek redress. Those who have attempted to assert claims of privacy have usually been unsuccessful. The public figure/private figure dichotomy established by the Supreme Court impedes rational discussion of the victim's claims. It may be helpful to examine the legal status—the rights and remedies —of the victim, without reference to precedent and consider what is fair to the parties and what is consonant with public policy.

Certain attributes of each individual are so inextricably and inte-

*Harris subsequently wrote her own story of the crime. She may be subject to laws confiscating the royalties of criminals who write about their crimes. She claims, however, that she wants to give her royalties to charity and contends that the law is unfair (*New York Times Magazine*, December 28, 1986, p. 42).

grally a part of personhood that, as I have urged in Chapter V, they should be entitled to constitutional protection under a general right of persona. These attributes should include, at a minimum, bodily and psychic integrity and privacy.

Criminal conduct invokes the heavy hand of the state. For the general welfare of society some, but by no means all, individual rights are restricted. Victims of crime are subjected to many invasions of time, economic hardship, and some loss of privacy. Crime victims and those who report crimes must give at least one and usually several statements to the police. Victims and any eyewitnesses must appear and identify suspects. Victims must testify at a preliminary hearing and again at trial. On both occasions they may be subject to sharp and unpleasant cross-examinations during which defense counsel try to discredit the testimony. A child victim of sexual abuse described the situation of a prosecution witness in a criminal case accurately. Defense counsel asked the obviously uncomfortable and hostile little girl, "Why don't you like me?" She replied, "Because you're going to make it look as if I'm lying." This is, of course, exactly what happens to witnesses and victims of crime.

In the trial of a criminal case under our adversary system, cross-examination is essential to protect the rights of the defendant. No matter how unpleasant or even painful this may be for the victim, it is essential for the fairness of the criminal justice system.

In order to maintain a reasonably safe and lawful community, it is also essential that victims of crime and eyewitnesses come forth and report crimes. If the crime is not reported, the police cannot attempt to find and apprehend the criminal. He will be free to prey on other victims.

After the trial and all the trauma attendant upon it, is a crime victim fair game for anyone who chooses to write about him or her? Victims of muggings, robberies, and burglaries as well as sex crimes, do not want to have to relive their painful experiences. They do not want their lives bared to anyone who chooses to be a voyeur.

The brutal disregard for the rights of victims and bystanders was initiated by Truman Capote in *In Cold Blood* and has been followed by his successors in this genre. Capote described the private lives of the members of the Clutter family who were killed by Richard Eugene Hickock and Perry Edward Smith. He gave a wealth of information utterly irrelevant to the crime itself and to the trial and punishment. Why should the fact, even if true, that Mrs. Clutter had been seeing a psychiatrist be aired to the world or the fact, whether

true or false, that as Capote wrote, "poor Bonnie— [was a] psychiatric patient for a half dozen years—sobbing behind closed doors"[17]?

The romanticizing of the two criminals is offensive to judges and
lawyers who must deal with such people and the terrible harms they
inflict on their victims, the families of the victims, their own families,
and all the people with whom they come in contact. It is, of course,
the privilege of any author to dramatize and heighten the qualities
of characters that are the creation of the author. When a book
purports to be "absolutely true," as Capote claimed, however, the
author may have some moral obligation to the reader to tell the
truth. I doubt that this should be a legal obligation. Courts should
not become involved with the subjective judgments and opinions of
authors, even when misguided, offensive, or blatantly exploitive.

The law must, however, be concerned with the treatment of both
the criminal and the victim. A civilized community simply cannot
permit murders, rapes, robberies, and other crimes to go undetected
and unpunished. If, in addition to the trauma and inconvenience of
the pretrial proceedings and the trial itself, victims and witnesses are
forever at risk of being exploited and of having their privacy invaded,
then they will be even more reluctant to report crimes and to testify.
It is estimated that only one-third of all crimes are reported.[18] The
problem is so serious that a mandatory crime reporting law has been
proposed requiring the bystander to notify the authorities.[19] Even
when a crime is reported, it is all but impossible to convict an
offender unless the crime victim is willing to cooperate and testify.
The fear of continuing intrusive publicity is a real, though difficult
to quantify, deterrent to successful criminal prosecutions.

Of equal significance, I believe, is the duty of the legal system to
protect victims and witnesses who wish to reclaim their privacy once
the trial is over. One means of protecting them would be to require
authors to get releases from their informants. A release is a useful
legal document designed to insulate the releasee from liability to the
releasor. This document has come under judicial scrutiny in many
contexts. As anyone who has had the misfortune of undergoing
surgery knows, a patient is required to sign a document releasing the
physicians and the hospital from all liability as a result of the surgical
procedures and associated care. The release will not be binding,
however, unless the patient gave a knowing and informed consent.
The patient must be informed of the risks, including the percentages
of failure associated with the surgery, all possible side effects, and the
existence of alternative procedures. Unless the patient was fully in-

formed and understood the risks, benefits, detriments, and options, and voluntarily consented, the release will not be upheld by the courts.

Many problems involving rights of victims and bystanders could be materially alleviated if the legal profession drafted standard detailed release forms. Those who wish to provide information to authors would be protected from their own ignorance and vulnerability. Authors would also be protected from claims by those who change their minds after the book becomes a best seller. I suggest that such releases be modeled after the standard waiver of jury trials required in most jurisdictions before an accused is permitted to give up his right to a jury trial. The defendant must be informed that he has an absolute right to a jury trial, what a jury trial consists of, the differences between a bench trial and a jury trial, the charges of which he is accused, and the maximum penalties that could be imposed if he is convicted. The defendant must state that he has not been threatened or coerced or promised any benefits for giving up his right to a jury trial and that he is satisfied with the advice of and representation by his counsel. Both the defendant and his lawyer must sign the waiver.

Releases by victims or bystanders should contain the statements that the releasors know: (1) that they have an absolute right not to talk to the author, (2) the nature of the book or other document that is contemplated, (3) the amount of compensation, if any, paid to the subject, (4) the extent of the rights released, including the author's subsidiary rights, (5) that the releasors have not been threatened or coerced or promised anything other than the payment agreed upon, (6) that they waive all rights to control the contents of the book and that there is no representation by the author as to the conclusions or inferences, as to guilt or innocence, motives or character of the releasors, and (7) that they have consulted counsel of their own choice and are satisfied with counsel's advice and representation. Such a release should be signed by the author and his or her counsel and by the victims and their counsel and be recorded in the county court.

Compare this careful procedure with what is reported to have occurred when Capote obtained releases for *In Cold Blood*. Clifford Hope, the Clutter family lawyer, describes Capote's technique in obtaining releases as follows:

> Bobby Rupp [boyfriend of the murdered Nancy Clutter] did not want to sign, and I didn't push it, because it was a tremendously upsetting

thing. Well, Truman got quite miffed about this, so he went and got another lawyer and talked Bobby into signing the release.[20]

The fact that parties enter into carefully drawn contracts when both are represented by lawyers does not, of course, ensure that there will be no litigation, as the suits and countersuits by MacDonald and McGinniss reveal. No self-respecting writer will permit a subject to exercise veto power over the book or article. Probably no subject is ever completely happy even with with a fulsome, flattering authorized biography. Few people are satisfied with their portraits or photographs. Each of us has a self-image nurtured to protect us from harsh reality. A book that purports to plumb the unconscious, to reveal hidden motives and desires may display the very characteristics we have spent a lifetime trying to camouflage. Robert Burns was wrong. We don't really want to see ourselves as others see us. Unlike Oliver Cromwell, most of us don't want the portrait painter to paint the warts. We really want a portrait that corresponds with an idealized self-image.

When the subject of a book is accused of a heinous crime that he or she denies having committed, that person risks dangerous revelations. It is easy to blame the author for disclosing damaging facts. The requirement of an informed consent and a legal release from crime victims and bystanders would accomplish several significant goals. One, it would protect those who wish their privacy to be respected. Second, it would enable subjects, if they so desire, to share in the profits realized from their misfortunes. Third, it would protect authors from lawsuits. Fourth, it would reduce the amount of litigation.

If crime victims and bystanders refuse to sign such consents, is the author precluded from writing about them? The crime and the criminal are, as it were, in the public domain. Authors are free to write about criminals with or without their consent, with or without their cooperation. Authors can base their books on public records, the testimony at the trial, contemporary news reports, and the statements of people who are willing to talk to the author. In such situations, I suggest that the author tell the reader that the victim does not wish to be identified or portrayed, that the portrait of the victim and/or certain bystanders is based on limited public information, and that beyond certain specified facts it does not purport to be a true or even partial likeness of the actual person. The use of disclaimers in all conflicts between subjects and authors is discussed more fully in the chapter on preventive law (Chapter XII).

Victims, like all other subjects, assert two rights: one personal and the other economic. The personal right is to privacy and seclusion, a right the law has largely ignored or brutally denied. The economic right to compensation has, in the past decade, begun to receive some recognition by legislatures and courts. In this area, legislatures responding to public demand have led the way, while most courts have reluctantly and grudgingly followed.

Victims' rights to share in profits from books about the crimes in which they were involved is a purely statutory creation of very recent origin. The only remote precedent may be found in Anglo-Saxon law, which required the criminal and his family or tribe to compensate the victims of his crime and their families or tribes.[21] Under this early tribal law, the distinction between crime and tort had not yet developed. Any wrong done by one person to another was avenged by the family or tribe of the victim. Such prolonged bloodletting gradually gave way to a system of compensation not unlike contemporary workers' compensation laws. Loss of certain bodily parts or functions were compensated at a fixed scale of payments. The death of an individual required payment to the family or tribe. This was known as the wirgild, or price of a man. With the passage of time, tribal vengeance was replaced by a system of law under which the state prosecuted the criminal. The victim and the family or tribe ceased to be parties to the prosecution. The victim was relegated to the status of a witness. The penalties exacted from the criminal were paid to the state, not to the victim or the victim's family.

The move to help crime victims was initiated in 1951 by Margery Fry, an English magistrate. In 1963, New Zealand passed the first crime victims' compensation act. The movement spread to the United States during the 1970s. The escalation of street crime, the widespread reporting of crime, and the rising costs of medical care all combined to make the idea of crime victims' compensation appealing. Under these state statutes, crime victims are compensated by the state from public funds. For some years, however, without statutory authority, a few judges have, as a part of the sentence imposed, required the criminal to compensate the victim to the extent of his or her ability. The Federal Crimes Code[22] also provides for victim compensation. Under some statutes, the criminal makes payments to the victim of the crime. Under other statutes, payments are made to a state compensation fund. Not many street criminals are wealthy or have great earning capacity. The greater part of the funds paid to victims come from public revenues. When the notorious killer known as "Son of Sam" entered into a contract for the sale of his life story, New York enacted a statute known as the "Son of Sam Law."[23] This law requires the payments of royalties to crime victims. Other states have enacted similar laws.

The rights of authors of crime books, like those of victims, are both personal and economic. By choosing to write about a living criminal, authors should not be deemed to have forfeited First Amendment rights or property rights. A New Jersey decision cast serious doubt on the validity of both rights. In that case the trial court ordered the profits on a book to be paid to the crime victims.[24] The author, Flora Rheta Schreiber, had contracted to give the subject, Joseph Kallinger, 12.5 percent of all profits on a book entitled, *The Shoemaker*. Kallinger was convicted of three murders as well as attempted rape and robbery. An appellate court reversed. It is unlikely that this is the final word on the subject.

Economics and free expression are inextricably entwined. Confiscation of earnings, as in the cases of those convicted of seditious libel, and the award of crippling libel verdicts in civil cases undoubtedly chill the authors' rights. When all royalties are confiscated, the authors' rights are not simply chilled, they are frozen.

Intellectual property is well recognized in American law. It is the basis of all copyright and patent law. Property cannot be taken without due process of law. Even statutory confiscation cannot prevail over this fundamental constitutional right.

It is an indisputable fact that a large part of the salability of books in this crime genre depends on the skill of the author. Even the most bloody, foul, unnatural crimes would be forgotten were it not for the art of a Shakespeare and a Sophocles. Certainly the craftsmanship of Joe McGinniss made *Fatal Vision* a best seller and a widely viewed docudrama. The facts of the crime alone would not have commanded the attention of so many readers and viewers. It is the skill of the author in combination with the facts that produces the royalties.

When the author makes a contract with the criminal for a share of the royalties, it is a simple matter for a court to order that the criminal's share be paid into a crime victims' compensation fund. The author's property is left intact. The criminal is prevented from profiting by his crime, and the victim receives some compensation.

It is an orderly, just, and easily administered solution to a peculiarly contemporary problem. Like all neat schematic solutions, it fails to comprehend the entire range of fact situations. First, there

must be a statute, either state or federal, that authorizes the confiscation of royalties or other profits derived by criminals. Some states do
not have such laws. Some statutes are badly phrased. Can the profits
be seized even after the offender has served his sentence? When I
require a criminal to pay the victim as part of his sentence or probation, my jurisdiction over him expires at the end of the sentence, even
though the victim's expenses and disabilities may continue long after.
Also, some statutes provide for payment to the victim rather than to
a victim's fund. What happens when the victim dies? Is the criminal
released from the obligation to pay? To make the victims' reparations
depend on the public interest in the criminal simply compounds the
unfairness of the victims' situation. Why should some victims recover nothing and others several hundred thousand dollars because
of the fortuity of the author's skill and the publishing business? A
federal statute would best regulate such problems, and prevent criminals from reaping profits from books based on their crimes.*

The drafting of such a statute to prevent criminals from profiting
from their crimes, if it is to reduce not promote litigation, will not
be simple. The definition of a contemporary crime would have to be
sufficiently broad to include all acts whether prosecuted timely or
not. MacDonald's wife and children were slain on February 17, 1970.
He was not brought to trial for nine years. He was convicted in
August 1979. Nor should authors simply be able to wait until after
the conviction and perhaps the execution of the criminal to avoid the
reach of the statute.

A simple definition of books "about a criminal and the crime"
would also be fraught with ambiguities leading to endless litigation.
The phrase "of or concerning" in libel has resulted in countless cases
that turn on whether the allegedly defamatory statement was clearly
understood to be about the plaintiff. These cases arise when the
actual name of the person is not used. If the book does not recount
the actual crime, will it be included under these statutes? Charles
Colson, a convicted Watergate felon, wrote a book ostensibly about
prison conditions. The book's selling point was the fact that it had
been written by Colson. John Ehrlichman, another convicted Watergate felon, has been busily writing novels. Although drawing on his
Washington background, his books are not specifically about his
crime. But much of the interest in his books is not as a result of their
literary qualities, but rather because of the notoriety of the author.
John Hinckley was found not guilty by reason of insanity. Would the

*The provisions of such a proposed statute are discussed in Chapter XV.

profit from the book he claims to be writing or the book his parents have written be subject to such a law? These are only a few of the problems of the drafters of such a statute. They are by no means insoluble.

A part of any criminal sentence can require the payment of a sum to the Crime Victim's Compensation Fund rather than to the victim of the crime. A number of state laws contain such a provision. It avoids the unseemly decision in the Mayflower Madam case in which the New York Supreme Court ruled that Sydney Biddle Barrows may keep the $600,000 she is making from two books and a television movie about her experiences running call-girl rings.[25] The basis of the court's decision was that she was guilty of a victimless crime. Under a crime victim's statute, any earnings or property of the criminal obtained during the period of the sentence, including any probationary period, would be applied to the sum fixed at sentencing and paid to a Victims' Compensation Fund, not to a particular victim or victims.

A well-drawn statute can comprehend most of these situations. But no matter how carefully crafted the statute, inevitably some criminals will profit by their crimes if they are not actually convicted. Some guilty felons become prosecution witnesses to avoid conviction. Some plead guilty to minor charges in return for withdrawal of prosecution on the major crimes, the subjects about which any book would focus. Henry Hill, a typical example, is the subject of Nicholas Pileggi's book, *Wiseguy: Life in a Mafia Family.*[26] Hill, who faced a life sentence for narcotics, entered the Government's Witness Protection Program. Hill's attorney approached the publisher Simon and Schuster about a book on Hill's criminal activities, with a share of the profits to go to Hill. All aspects of this sordid transaction can be justified on utilitarian grounds. By dealing with Hill, the government was presumably able to convict more important and dangerous criminals. By obtaining funds for Hill through royalties, the burden on the government to support Hill was lessened. And, of course, the author and publisher were able to profit from Hill's life of crime. The fact that some persons will continue to profit from their misdeeds does not militate against the desirability of eliminating this distasteful practice insofar as possible.

A statute prohibiting criminals from profiting from their misdeeds need not violate the rights of authors who are simply plying their trade and supplying the public with the kind of reading matter that is highly popular.

The alternative to a clear, precise, comprehensive statute is decades of litigation in which courts grope for guidance and litigants spend hundreds of thousands of dollars of their money and countless months of court time subsidized by the taxpayers seeking solutions that could more readily and satisfactorily be obtained by legislation.

Not all problems and litigation can be avoided by legal documents and/or statutes. Rights to privacy and seclusion of victims and by-standers can be created by statute. Whether they will prevail over the First Amendment rights of authors is an issue that only the courts can resolve. But an expression of legislative intent usually carries great weight with courts.

Another difficult constitutional question arises out of the impact of such books, movies, and television programs on pending cases. This question is generally subsumed under the rubric of free press versus fair trial. Whole libraries of learned volumes are devoted to this subject. The nineteenth-century cases arose out of the abuse of the contempt power by high-handed judges who attempted to close the courts to the press. At least since mid-twentieth century, the Supreme Court has ruled that not only trials but essential pretrial proceedings in criminal cases must be open to the public.* The Court has held that the very real dangers of press reports prejudicing jurors must be dealt with by the trial judges by less drastic means such as change of venue, sequestering (locking up) the jury, careful voir dire of jurors to ensure that they have not seen or heard prejudicial material, and even delay of the trial. These rulings are, I believe, sound and appropriate.

Trial judges also have considerable powers over the attorneys— both prosecutors and defense counsel. A judge can order them not to disclose the existence of inadmissible evidence such as illegally obtained confessions, the results of lie detector tests, and the like. The prior convictions of the defendant are a matter of public record and cannot be kept out of the press, even though the jury cannot be informed of these convictions. It is my practice as a trial judge scrupulously to avoid knowing the prior record of the accused even in a jury trial lest in some subtle way I may prejudice the jury. Although these precautions are troublesome and time consuming, they do not present major difficulties. It is possible to preserve both the First Amendment rights of the press and the due process rights of the accused.

---

*Sealing depositions and other evidence disclosed in pretrial proceedings and made part of the court record is a dangerous practice that should not be extended.

The Supreme Court has not, as of this writing, had occasion to consider the all-pervasive effects of national television docudramas on the defendant's right to a fair trial. My faith in the process of jury selection has not been shaken in criminal trials, but I have had some misgivings as a result of jury voir dire in asbestos cases. In the 1980s, it is inconceivable that any adult living in urban America has not heard of the perils of asbestos exposure. But any number of potential jurors testified that they had never heard of asbestos, or if they had heard of it, they were unaware of any health risks associated with asbestos. One wonders if such ill-informed or stupid people would make good jurors.

Jurors who were possibly prejudiced by reading books and seeing movies can be excused for cause; for example, I automatically excused anyone who saw the movie *Silkwood* from sitting on an asbestos case. But the effect of national TV docudramas is unknown and dangerously prejudicial. The docudrama *Fatal Vision* was shown on television while the motion for a new trial was pending. Although McGinniss had written to MacDonald on September 11, 1979, saying, "Total strangers can recognize within five minutes that you did not receive a fair trial," the unmistakably clear conclusion of his book was that MacDonald was guilty, that he did kill his wife and two children. My quarrel is not with McGinnis's conclusion although there are those who disagree.[27] A jury found MacDonald guilty, and an appellate court refused to reverse. The more subtle question is whether MacDonald could have received a fair trial if his motion for a new trial had been granted. It would have been extremely difficult, indeed, well-nigh impossible to have found a juror who had not heard of the TV docudrama. Forty-seven percent of the nation's television sets that were turned on when *Fatal Vision* was shown were turned on to it. The radio news flash announcing that MacDonald's appeal had been rejected described him as "Captain Jeffrey MacDonald of *Fatal Vision.*" There is a vast difference between reading a book about a crime and seeing it reenacted, as it were, on television. The old Chinese proverb, a picture is worth a thousand words, certainly applies to television. The skill of the actors, their physical resemblance to the actual people, the use of their own words all create an impelling impression on the viewer that he or she has actually witnessed the crime.

The law sensibly assumes that judges can and will put out of their consideration inadmissible evidence that they have heard. We do it every day. In the course of most trials, counsel will make a sidebar offer of proof. Attorneys will tell the judge out of the presence of the jury certain evidence they wish to introduce. The judge will rule either that it is admissible or it is not. Meanwhile the judge has heard the proferred evidence. This occurs also in non-jury trials. Judges are trained to make these distinctions. Jurors do not have this training and experience. It would be difficult for the average person who saw the compelling docudrama to distinguish between that presentation and the evidence presented in court. No matter how fair and even-handed authors try to be, obviously they select from a mass of material what seems to be most significant. The issue is not the "fairness" or neutrality of the author or producer, but the prejudicial effect of a docudrama on the litigational process.

I suggest that it is seriously prejudicial. The better the show is, the more people will see it and hear about it, and the more prejudicial it will be. Because of the immediacy and pervasiveness of national television, it presents far graver dangers to a fair trial than any printed matter. Therefore, it is proposed that such docudramas not be aired until the final appeals have been heard and decided.[28] Because appellate courts are not under the time constraints of the speedy trial provision of the Sixth Amendment and the implementing state and federal rules of court, the interval between verdict and final appeal may be several years. Such a delay, of course, prejudices the financial interests of authors. It also impinges on their First Amendment rights. Undue postponement may indeed prevent the docudrama from ever being shown. But in the balancing of rights, the likelihood of trial prejudice is so great as perhaps to warrant a reasonable delay.

A wise solution would be the adoption of a speedy appellate rule requiring appeals to be heard and decided within six months unless exigent circumstances require further delay. Criminal cases must be tried within six months of indictment or arrest, no matter how hard-pressed the trial courts are. A similar appellate rule should not cause undue hardship to the courts. It would protect the rights of all parties. Of course, if a new trial were granted, the showing of the docudrama would have to be further delayed.

Not all crime docudramas prejudice the rights of the accused. The *Atlanta Murders* docudrama clearly inferred that Wayne Williams, who had been convicted, was not guilty. If his case is reopened, the docudrama will have benefited him. Nonetheless, had it been shown before the trial or while the appeal was pending, it would have prejudiced the prosecution as seriously as *Fatal Vision* would have prejudiced MacDonald's defense had a new trial been granted.*

The desire for books about lurid crimes is probably not a passing fad. Such books have always had a substantial allure. Judges cannot simply hope that the spate of cases involving criminals, victims, and authors will simply disappear. Many lawsuits have been filed. More will undoubtedly follow. The courts will have to hear and decide this multitude of complex problems.

The manner by which a justice system treats criminals and victims is a hallmark of the society. The cognizance accorded to the First Amendment rights of authors of every type of writing has importance for everyone's rights to free expression. Efforts to curb authors arise when the ideas presented are unpopular or the financial rewards are tempting. Neither lack of social importance of this genre nor lack of concern for the individuals involved should militate against a thoughtful, just, and constitutional resolution of their conflicting rights.

*The actions threatened by the Georgia prosecutor and the state alleging defamation by docudrama fall within the category of seditious libel—criticism of government and government officials that should be privileged whether the alleged defamation is in writing or by means of docudrama.

·IX·

To Whom Does a Life Belong?

A biography is something one invents.

—LOUIS-FERDINAND CELINE

"WHOSE life is it anyway?" was the plaintive title of a moving play advocating the right of an individual to control his own life and death. This chapter discusses the right of individuals to control the depiction of their lives and accomplishments. It asks, "Is there a right to biography?"

Some legal scholars have urged that such a right be recognized.[1] This is another novel legal theory. It may be considered a logical extrapolation from the right to privacy. If one has the right to seclusion, to be free from the intrusions not only of government but of prying authors pandering to public curiosity, prurience, and vo-yeurism, should one not also have the right to control what is written about him or her? What could more uniquely belong to an individual than his or her own life story?

This desire to control not only one's own actions but the perceptions others have about one may be seen as a concomitant of the much-deplored contemporary narcissism and the demands of the "me generation." Many sociologists and psychiatrists perceive this concentration on the self as an undesirable egotistical trend.[2] It may, however, be viewed as a development of the democratic ideal, the notion that all persons are autonomous and have the right to control their own destinies, that they are not the creature of the state, the church, or even the family. The tension between autonomy and responsibility is being widely discussed in both political and legal terms.[3]

Rights of subjects as they affect biography conflict with rights of authors and the public in much the same way as do all claims of subjects against authors. The asserted rights of both subjects and authors are predicated on two basic interests—one is freedom, the other economics. With respect to biography, subjects assert the right to exclusive control over their own life stories, including the right to prevent anyone from writing about them, to choose the biographer they wish, and to write their own autobiographies. Subjects want to fashion their own images like artists who paint self-portraits. They also want to exploit for profit the public interest in their lives that they have created by their achievements and/or notoriety. This financial interest of the subject may be a very substantial asset.

Many persons treat their bodies and their skills as salable assets. Boxers sell shares in themselves. Marlene Dietrich insured her legs. All persons, famous or anonymous, can insure their bodies, their lives, and their earning capacities. All persons have both libertarian and financial interests in their lives and careers. Not all people are sufficiently well known or significant that others are moved to write about them. Some persons are delighted by the attention given to their persons, their achievements, or their ideas. Others are ambivalent. They have no objection to being the subject of a biography, but they want to dictate what the book shall contain, or they want to realize the profits that will accrue from a biography, or both.

Authors claim that they have the right to choose whatever subjects they wish to write about. Even under the most restrictive reading of the First Amendment, so long as authors do not write falsely defamatory material or obscene matter or present or create a clear and present danger, they may write what they please. Under copyright and contract law as well as common law principles, authors, like all other laborers, have the right to obtain and retain the fruits of their work. Literary labors have never been excluded from this general legal principle regardless of literary form. Every kind of writing from poetry to scientific studies is copyrightable and may be sold for profit if there is a willing buyer.

The interest of the public in all intellectual work is inchoate, difficult to define, and almost impossible to assert in a court of law. It is extremely unlikely that any potential reader would have a legally cognizable interest in demanding the publication of a biography, whether of pop music star Bruce Springsteen, or of a world-famous figure like Albert Einstein. Members of the public can assert rights by opposing the banning of a book from a public library. But it must be recognized that when an author is prevented from publishing a book, the public is inevitably prevented from reading that work.

The sudden surge of litigation and legal literature arising out of asserted rights of biography is undoubtedly due to the dramatic increase in the number of biographies about living subjects and the financial success of many of these books. When biographers confined themselves to subjects who were safely dead and buried, they were most unlikely to find themselves haled into court to defend against civil claims or criminal changes. The fears of biographers in earlier times were only unfavorable reviews or, even worse, no reviews at all.

Until the twentieth century, biography was considered a slightly musty, scholarly pursuit, not unlike archeology. The typical biographer was pictured as poring through old letters and documents seeking to reconstruct with fidelity the life of a subject, famous or infamous, who most often had been dead for decades or centuries. When the subject is a living person or one recently deceased, the biographer faces many problems. As author Primo Levi explains: "Finding oneself portrayed in a book with features that are not those we attribute to ourselves is traumatic, . . . For this and for other more obvious reasons, it is not a good practice to write biographies of the living. . . ."[4]

There are two recognized classes of biography: the authorized and the unauthorized. The former is usually a sycophantic, adulatory, flattering, and frequently untrue portrait. Writers of such books were for years generally conceded to be commercial hacks writing for pay rather than engaging in scholarly pursuits. Unauthorized biographies, far more numerous and significant, attempt to achieve both accuracy and that elusive goal, truth. With the rise in popularity of psychohistory, biographers have taken greater latitude in imagining the thoughts of their subjects and attempting to recreate, as it were, their inner souls.

Biographers, even those who write old-fashioned books adhering to documentary evidence, have often had disputes and difficulties with the families and friends of their subjects who refused access to letters, manuscripts, and other research materials. But even hostile or uncooperative family members, friends, and colleagues of the subject rarely go to court to enjoin a biographer from writing a book and generally do not sue to demand the destruction or banning of

a biography. Criminal prosecutions, even for seditious libel or obscenity, were rarely if ever brought against biographers. It has long
been established law that libel is a personal right available only to
the libeled person, not the heirs or estate of the deceased.

Actions for injunction, destructions of books, and criminal prosecutions have been brought against biographers in the 1980s. This is
an ominous development. A few cases do not create a trend, but these
lawsuits coupled with jurisprudential theories promoting the concept
of a right of biography require discussion of the subject and its
impact on First Amendment rights and values.

Three cases illustrate these types of lawsuits. Movie star Elizabeth
Taylor filed suit against ABC to prevent the production of a docudrama about her life.[5] All copies of a biography of President Valery
Giscard d'Estaing of France by Jean-Bedel Bokassa, a former leader
of the Central African Republic, were burned pursuant to the order
of a French court.[6] Antoni Gronowicz, the author of a biography of
Pope John Paul II, was prosecuted for mail fraud on the grounds that
statements in his book are false.[7]

The *Taylor* case reveals the mingling of issues of free expression
with financial interests and the preferment of financial claims over
First Amendment rights. Elizabeth Taylor claimed that she owns her
own life story; she asserted a right of publicity to profit by her own
life to the exclusion of other authors. She further claimed that any
production in which she would be portrayed by another actress
would present her in a false light. Harvard Law Professor Arthur
Miller is quoted as describing the *Taylor* case as "a goulash of
rights." Among the ingredients he sees are "the public's right to
know, her own rights to privacy, her property rights, and the need
to give the creative act some license."[8]

The issues, as I see them, are different and far more complex and
significant. The right to privacy claim is manifestly without substance. Elizabeth Taylor has been a well-known and highly publicized actress since she was a child. Her life, her loves, her multiple
marriages, her illnesses, and almost all the activities she has engaged
in have been widely reported in countless magazines and newspapers.
Having willingly led her life in the glare of publicity, it is disingenuous on her part to claim a right to seclusion and a reclusive life.

The right to publicity, to profit from one's own accomplishments
and career is, at first blush, an appealing argument. Nothing could
be more intimately one's property than his or her own life or life
story. Under the Anglo-American legal system, civil rights and

harms are translated into terms of money damages. The wrongdoer compensates the victims for emotional harms and physical harms in terms of dollars and cents. If there is a property right in one's life, it should also be paid for in money when it is infringed. In the case of Elizabeth Taylor, her life story would be worth a great deal of money because of her popularity and the enormous interest she generates in herself. Why should anyone else profit from her life? The argument is simple and appealing. It is too simple.

This is another example of the confusion of money with free expression. Taylor certainly "owns" her life to the extent that she is free to do as she pleases so long as she does not violate the law. Difficult questions of the rights of individuals to control their own lives and bodies against the claims of the state to interfere with that control have been raised dramatically in abortion and euthanasia cases. ABC, however, did not interfere with Taylor's right to lead her own life or her unquestioned right to publish her autobiography. What she claimed is an *exclusive* right to profit by and control any biography of her.

Under the Supreme Court's definition of a public figure, an individual who, like Elizabeth Taylor, is constantly in the news, would certainly be classified as a public figure. Under the category of newsworthy subjects here proposed, she would certainly be held to be newsworthy. Neither the public figure nor the proposed newsworthy classification that would apply to standards for libel and privacy sheds light on the claim of a right of biography. To date, no one has suggested that a biographer, including an autobiographer, has an exclusive claim to a subject. Notable and notorious individuals have been the subjects of many biographies. For example, more than fifty biographies have been written about Isaac Newton and more are being written. In the genre of biography, no author can claim to have the last word.

Taylor also asserted that she would be presented in a false light by whichever actress "impersonating" her.* A drama, even a biographical docudrama, cannot claim to present a photographic portrait with absolute fidelity. The process of selection and editing inevitable in even a straightforward news story is expanded when an

---

*The subject of a biography who is presented falsely, i.e., by stating verifiable facts incorrectly should, I believe, have a right of action under the right of persona. But, in one of the few cases involving a claim for falsity, the court held that unless the biography was not only false but also defamatory the subject could not recover (Spahn v. Julian Messner, Inc., 18 NY 2d 324, 221 NE2d 543 [1966], app. dismissed 399 US 1046 [1969]).

author transmutes facts into drama. The dramatist selects incidents and perhaps rearranges them to fit the constraints of time, the stage, and the attention span of the audience. The dramatist must also build conflict, suspense, tension, and character development to achieve the dramatic aim of catharsis. Few lives follow such a logical pattern. Even the most adventure-filled life requires editing and selection to develop a theme and build to a dramatic climax, to say nothing of compressing a lifetime into one or two hours. In addition, the actor or actress who plays the role of the protagonist inevitably contributes to the subtle process of interpretation. All actors and actresses put something of themselves into the part. No two Hamlets are ever the same. To adopt Taylor's argument prohibiting impersonation in literature or drama would be to eliminate all living persons from the realm of literary and dramatic material.

To accord the status of property to certain attributes of the individual may not constitute an advance in human rights and freedoms. The notion of a right of biography is one that gives me pause. This purported right differs radically from the right of privacy, which protects the values of seclusion and tranquility as well as avoidance of unwanted publicity. Rather the right of biography in most instances is essentially a fight over money, a contest between subject and author similar to the right of publicity.

Recent judicial decisions dealing with the right of publicity bear directly on the right of subjects to control their biographies. Most of the cases have turned on narrow interpretations of property rights without considering the impact of the First Amendment. Courts inquire as to whether subjects have previously exploited their lives by writing about it and whether they have established themselves as authors. These are, it seems to me, peripheral and irrelevant questions. If persons have an exclusive right to publicize their own lives, then it should not matter whether they have previously exercised that right. They may wish to do so in the future. Nor should it matter that they are not professional writers, biographers, or dramatists. Subjects can always write an "as told to" autobiography with the help of a professional. Or they can collaborate with a professional writer. Lee Iacocca's autobiography, which has been a best seller for more than a year, carries the byline "by Lee Iacocca with William Novak." Regardless of formal acknowledgments of assistance, it is well known that most public officials, such as former presidents and secretaries of state, utilize staffs of researchers and writers. So do many authors of best-selling novels, like James Michener.[9] To be a professional writer it is not necessary to work alone in a garret typing on a battered old Remington. Just as the large well-equipped laboratory that employs scores, if not hundreds, of scientists has made the solitary inventor working in his cellar or garage an anachronism, so the tape recorder, the word processor, and the research team may soon supplant the solitary author. Certainly any definition of author must include those who write books individually as well as those who produce them as part of a group effort.

Putting aside the definitions of author and issues of right of publicity and exploitation, the courts must grapple with the question of whether subjects can legally control the portraits of themselves that an author chooses to present.* To date, most decisions have turned on the financial interests of subject and author. But note the recent case brought by J.D. Salinger to stop Random House from publishing a biography, *J.D. Salinger: A Writing Life,* by Ian Hamilton, because it contains private letters that Salinger allegedly did not authorize for publication. Salinger has shunned publicity and lived an almost obsessively reclusive life. He has not published for twenty years. He is the author of the acclaimed novel, *The Catcher in the Rye,* considered a modern classic. Salinger wrote to Hamilton, ". . . It has always been a most terrible and almost unassailable wonder to me that it is evidently quite lawful . . . to break into the privacy not only of a person not reasonably suspected of criminal activity, but into the lives as well, however glancingly, of that person's relatives and friends. I've despaired long ago of finding any justice in the common practice."[10] Salinger is a person of enormous and probably enduring interest. I submit that he should not have a right to prohibit the publication of a biography about him provided that it is substantially accurate.† His claim that the letters that he did not authorize for publication cannot be published raises a different and equally difficult issue as to ownership. Author Hamilton claims that the use of copyright material is "minimal and insubstantial."

Everyone who has ever had his picture taken believes that cameras

*It is most unlikely that any biography would be published about a person who is of no public interest.
†A temporary injunction restraining distribution of the book was entered by U.S. District Judge Pierre N. Leval in early November, 1986. *New York Times,* November 8, 1986, p. 11. As of mid-January 1987, the book had not been released. This kind of prior restraint has been held unconstitutional in a long line of cases. See, e.g., the *Pentagon Papers* case discussed in the Introduction. Of course, there is no claim of any clear and present danger threatened by the distribution of a biography of a novelist.

do lie. Most persons are honestly convinced that the pictures do not do them justice. They believe that they are better looking, or younger looking, or more charming, or more impressive, or more kindly, or more trustworthy, or all these qualities than their pictures reveal. Portrait painters have disagreed with their subjects for centuries. Even when painters are famous and skillful artists, the subjects often disagree with the images of themselves created by these artists. The portrait of Lyndon Johnson by famed artist Peter Hurd was rejected by the president as "the ugliest thing I ever saw." The portrait was both scathingly criticized and fulsomely praised. The law has rarely taken cognizance of these differences of opinion. When an artist is paid the contract price, it is assumed that all legal rights are satisfied even if the portrait is relegated to a warehouse or destroyed.

If a book or a painting is to be treated like a pumpkin or a bushel of potatoes, then the rights of the parties will be governed by the law of sales. When a grocer delivers the goods the purchaser has ordered and the purchaser pays the agreed-upon price, the grocer's rights have ended. The purchasers can exercise total dominion over the goods. They can eat the pumpkin, give it away, use it as a jack o'lantern, or throw it in the garbage can. Grocers may deplore this waste of good food, but they cannot use the law to force the purchasers to eat the pumpkins or to serve them to their guests.

Can the purchaser of a painting hide it in a closet, alter it, or destroy it? These are significant questions that the law has not adequately dealt with. Diego Rivera's mural in the Prado Hotel in Mexico City contained as an integral part of the picture the words "Dios no existe." From time to time as the political climate changed, the word "no" was removed and then restored. Did Rivera have a right to prevent the mutilation of his work? This issue was never raised in Mexican courts. Rivera's mural in Rockefeller Center was destroyed in 1934 shortly after it was completed. No action was brought by Rivera in American courts. Had such a suit been instituted, it is far from clear what the result would have been.

In an interesting lawsuit, I sued the trustees of the Barnes Foundation, which has a priceless art collection but had banned the public from viewing the pictures.[11] There was no question that the foundation owned the pictures. The founder had bought and paid for them. Did the foundation have the right to keep them locked away from public view? I successfully claimed that because the foundation was tax exempt the public had to have reasonable access. In response to the assertion that possessors of property have the right to do with their goods as they choose, I argued that the owner of a masterpiece, such as the *Mona Lisa,* does not have the right to destroy it, that some goods, although privately owned and subjects of purchase and sale, have such an intrinsic public value that this transcends the claims of private ownership. The court did not decide this question, although it ordered that the collection be open to the public two days a week.

Even though individuals have a right to exploit themselves for their own profit, does the concept of property transcend the rights of others also to utilize the individual as a subject of a portrait or a biography? Artist Andy Warhol has created famous valuable pictures that depict Campbell Soup cans and Marilyn Monroe, as well as other famous people. The Campbell Soup Company did not claim the exclusive right to the use of its logo or to a share of Warhol's profits from the use of this well-known object. Nor did Marilyn Monroe claim a right to exploit her own image.

Warhol's picture of Marilyn Monroe is a faithful depiction of her, closely resembling the face seen on thousands of movie screens. Other portraits do not create a photographic likeness of the subject. Most great artists seek not merely to depict the facial features of the subject, the hair, the clothes, and the jewels, but to reveal the subject's character and personality, his very soul. History does not accord what Fillipe Archinto, Archbishop of Milan, thought of Titian's portrait of him. The viewer sees a worldly, cynical, crafty old man. Would the archbishop have preferred to be pictured as a saintly, compassionate, kindly shepherd of his flock? Which version would be true? Most great biographers also seek to portray not simply the external facts of the subject's life but the individual's character, motivations, and aspirations.

Whether subjects of portraits have a right to "touch up" the portraits of themselves or compel the painter to do so is an interesting question analogous to the issues raised in this book. Whether subjects of a biography, play, or docudrama can compel the author to rewrite it to their satisfaction is not a fanciful or academic problem dreamed up by a law school professor of torts. It is one of the many contemporary conflicts between subjects and authors that are now being settled or litigated.

One example of this struggle involves an NBC television film based on the crime of Mary Evans, an attorney who helped her client, Timothy Kirk, to escape from prison. Evans was convicted. Certainly, under any definition, she is a public figure. She deliberately thrust herself into the limelight by her criminal conduct. Court proceedings are a matter of public record. They are privileged and cannot be the subject of libel. Evans was not a victim like the Hill family whose privacy was invaded by the crime and the docudrama *Dangerous Hours* based on it. The docudrama about Evans and Kirk was scheduled for presentation in the fall of 1985. Neither Evans nor Kirk was to be mentioned by name. Nonetheless, Evans threatened suit claiming libel and invasion of privacy.

NBC yielded to the threat of a lawsuit and changed some aspects of the play. Sue Grafton, coauthor of the script, claimed the right to dramatize or fictionalize without interference by Evans. Grafton is quoted as saying, "Just because one woman broke one guy out of prison doesn't mean that she can control the rights to every story of a woman helping a man escape from prison."[12] In this instance, Grafton certainly appears to be right. Evans is not identified by name. Even though the actress resembles her, she is not a "look-a-like." This is an entirely different situation from an advertiser who uses a model unmistakably made up and intended to resemble Jacqueline Kennedy Onassis in order to get the commercial benefits accruing from her image.

Even if the film had been explicitly about Evans and Kirk and had used their names, should these subjects have the right to control what a biographer chooses to say about them? NBC's discretion certainly may be the better part of valor. A long, bruising lawsuit, appeals, and perhaps the establishment of undesirable precedent was avoided by changing the film. Whether Evans was glamorous and confident or timid and put upon is undoubtedly a matter of interpretation. Certainly it is not the kind of objectively verifiable fact that is susceptible of proof by clear and convincing evidence. Such abortive lawsuits do not decide the question of the right of subjects to exclusive ownership of their life stories or their right to control an author's portrayal of them.

The *Elizabeth Taylor* case is of particular concern because Elizabeth Taylor sought to use the injunctive power of the courts to prevent the showing of a television program. Although the distinction between prior restraint and subsequent punishment by criminal penalty or damage suit fails adequately to protect the author, nonetheless, prior restraint is far more damaging to the public. Had the Court enjoined the publication of the *Pentagon Papers,* the public would never have had access to this critical information. A subsequent damage suit would certainly have harmed the *New York Times* and perhaps had a chilling effect on future disclosures, but in the meantime the information could be published. This is a significant difference to the public.

The basis for an injunction in all civil cases is the threat of irreparable harm and the absence of an adequate legal remedy. Even when a teachers' strike closes the public schools for weeks or a transport workers' strike shuts down public transportation for long periods of time, courts rarely issue injunctions. Obviously, the school children and their families are seriously prejudiced. But the courts reason that the children can make up lost time by ordering more days of school after the strike is over. Though seriously inconvenienced by a transport workers' strike, the public can find alternative methods of travel. When a business seeks to enjoin a competitor from engaging in unfair trade practices, the usual remedy is not an injunction but the award of monetary damages for lost business. Applying these general principles to Taylor's claim for the exclusive right to exploit her own life, it seems clear that if she should have such a right, an award of damages, perhaps measured by a share of the profits on the book, would be an adequate legal remedy.

Even though persons may not, and as I argue, should not have an exclusive right of biography, do they have a property interest in their own life stories that may be enforced either by money damages or by compelling editing of nondefamatory passages in a biography? If a writer and subject choose to contract for the subject's life story and the subject is not a criminal, there is nothing in law or social policy to forbid the parties from making such an agreement. It is done every day. For example, William J. Schroeder, the artificial heart recipient, sold his life story to *Life* magazine.[13] The wife of writer Neal Cassady received more than $70,000 for her interest in the film about her husband.[14] Many well-known individuals and members of their families have entered into substantial contracts for the right of biography for books and movies. Such agreements have not, however, obviated litigation. Albert DeSalvo, known as the Boston Strangler, was paid for a release of all interests in his life as well as a waiver of tort claims. Nonetheless, he, like Jeffrey MacDonald, brought suit.[15]

The precise nature of the interest of the heirs and estates of well-known persons in their life stories is a legal question to which there are no clear answers. If there is a legally cognizable and enforceable property interest in the life story of a parent or next of kin, in many cases this would be a substantial asset in the six- or seven-figure bracket. Kinship to a famous person raises sensitive questions of rights and obligations that accrue on the death of that person.

Margaret Mead's daughter, Mary C. Bateson, commented perceptively about the problems and obligations of the family of a famous
person. It was evident that immediately following Margaret Mead's
death a horde of scholars as well as journalists would find the anthropologist an interesting and salable topic of research and biography. Bateson asks what obligation, if any, does the family owe to
such persons? Is it right or fair to favor certain prospective biographers over others? She writes:

> We talk in this country about property rights, but we rarely talk about
> the shares people have in each other's lives . . . requests from biographers,
> book writers, and film makers continue to come in. I could devote myself
> full time to responding to these requests and to the claims of those who
> want some important project strengthened by being associated with my
> parents' names.
>
> What then are the obligations laid on me by the rights that others feel
> they have? What do I do when a notorious star of a TV series decides
> that she was born to portray Margaret Mead. . . . How do I respond to
> the biographers who assume that their interest in my parents gives them
> a natural right to my time? Do the ethics change when the second such
> writer comes along, or the third and does it make a difference if they have
> studied anthropology or knew Margaret and Gregory [her father, also a
> distinguished anthropologist] in their lifetime?[16]

These are significant moral questions. The legal questions are also
important and far from clear. Bateson resolved her problems, in part,
by writing a biography of her mother. Bateson's book was widely
reviewed in tandem with the biography of Margaret Mead written
by Jane Howard, not always to the advantage of Bateson. One does
not know which book was more profitable, nor which is more useful
and enlightening to anthropologists and the public. It is a question
that the courts would be wise to avoid. If Bateson were not herself
an author, would she have a claim as the legal heir of her mother to
a right of biography against other authors? To date, this sticky issue
has not been decided.

Others have also avoided the legal issue of right of biography by
arranging for their life stories to be told in their lifetimes in order to
control the content and, perhaps, also to reap the profits. The well-
known sex therapists, William Masters and Virginia Johnson, sold
their life stories to television for a docudrama. As Johnson commented, "I began to feel that the film would eventually be done with

or without our cooperation and I decided it might be a good idea to give the public a more accurate view of what we are doing in our work."[17]

Cosmetics doyenne, Estee Lauder, outraged by a forthcoming biography of her by Lee Israel, rushed into print with her own autobiography. The Israel book, *Estee Lauder: Beyond the Magic,* had a first printing of 75,000 copies. Mrs. Lauder's book had a first printing of 100,000 copies and was a Literary Guild alternate selection perhaps because of the avalanche of publicity preceding publication.[18]

Another subject who has used her own life story and the life and death of her mother as profitable assets is Betty Rollin, a TV correspondent. Rollin describes how she helped her mother to commit suicide. Aiding and abetting, if not procuring, a suicide is a crime. As of this writing, no criminal prosecution has been brought against her, and there is no indication that the government will seek to confiscate her royalties.

In the subject's rush to anticipate the use of himself or herself and family by potential biographers, the subject may garner some of the profits. But the success of any book, even about as glamorous a subject as Elizabeth Taylor or as well-known a figure as Margaret Mead, depends in large part on the literary skill of the author and the merchandising skill of the publisher.

Interest in Elizabeth Taylor and Estee Lauder is transitory. If the public is denied another story about their lives, no one will be affected other than the subject and the potential author who must find a more available topic for the next book.

Most of the great body of biographical literature deals with people of more enduring interest: political figures, scientists, artists of all kinds, persons whose ideas and contributions are of sufficient importance to warrant the years of research and study that a good biography requires. Dumas Malone has devoted a lifetime to the study of Thomas Jefferson. Leon Edel has spent a major part of his professional life writing about Henry James. Although such scholarly biographies are often called definitive, each generation rewrites the lives of famous people to suit its own needs, in conformity with current ideas of history, psychiatry, and economics.

Since Plutarch wrote his *Parallel Lives* in the first century A.D., there have been countless lives of Julius Caesar and Alexander the Great, as well as many of his other subjects. Undoubtedly there will be more. Plutarch wrote about subjects who were his near contemporaries. Such books have a special value that can never be captured by later biographers. The irreplaceable source materials are the knowledge, opinions, and impressions of the friends, enemies, and colleagues of the subjects. Today, as in Plutarch's time, public officials who have played a leading role in national and world politics are natural topics for biographies by historians, political scientists, journalists, and protagonists and opponents of their positions.

The novel concept that presidential papers belong to the president as an individual, that they are his private property to use, destroy, or profit from is another distressing example of the extension of property concepts to limit freedom of expression and publication. Former President Richard M. Nixon entered into an agreement with the General Services Administration, a government agency, under which he deposited presidential papers and the controversial tape recordings with the proviso that neither the administration nor Nixon could have access to the documents without the consent of the other party for three years, that after five years the administration would destroy the tapes in accordance with Nixon's directions, and that they would be destroyed at his death or the expiration of ten years. An act of Congress incorporated this agreement. The Supreme Court upheld the statute.[19] I believe that such information should be in the public domain, available for use by any and all persons, subject only to necessary limitations of time, space, and logistics. The idea that such documents can be kept from public view at the whim of the public official intrudes the concept of private property into what has hitherto been considered public information.

Many subjects of biography who are not public officials or involved with governmental actions are persons of enduring and significant public interest. Sigmund Freud is such an individual. People will probably write about him for centuries to come. Disputes about Freud, both the man and his theories, have raged in scientific and popular literature since his first controversial paper. Undoubtedly Freud knew that following his death the differences of opinion would continue. To protect the great body of Freud's papers, his daughter and long-time assistant, Anna, appointed as archivist, K. R. Eissler, a devoted Freudian analyst. Many of Freud's letters and documents had never been disclosed until Eissler gave permission to Jeffrey Masson, a Sanskrit scholar and amateur Freudian, to read the papers carefully preserved in the Freud home in London. Masson concluded from his perusal of these papers that Freud had "betrayed" the truth when he revised his theory of seduction. In essence, Masson's theory may be stated as follows: Freud's study of a number of so-called hysterical young women patients revealed that these women claimed they had been sexually violated by their fathers. At first, Freud accepted the statements of these patients as factually true. Some time later, Freud concluded that the rape or seduction—the physical act of incest—had not occurred, but was the wishful fantasy of the patient.

Long after the fact, when many of the patients and Freud himself are dead, it is impossible to establish by standards of proof required in a court of law whether Freud's initial conclusion was correct or whether his revised position was sound. When Eissler learned of Masson's conclusions, Masson was removed from his position and ordered not to use these materials. According to Masson's own account, he acquiesced in these demands and then promptly breached his agreement, claiming an obligation to higher truths to reveal the information he claimed to have discovered. Despite his agreement, Masson wrote a book, *The Assault on Truth: Freud's Suppression of the Seduction Theory,* using the information he had obtained from the archives and presenting his own conclusions and his reasons as to why Freud had so radically revised his theories. The implications of Masson's charges could, under American law, be deemed to be defamatory. Charges of willful lying, unprofessional behavior, endangering the life of a patient, and similar accusations, explicit or implicit, could certainly give rise to an action of libel if Freud were alive.

The trustees of the papers of a famous or notorious individual are in an unenviable position. Their legal duties are far from clear. Are they to carry out the wishes of the deceased regardless of the consequences to science, history, and what are sometimes pretentiously called higher truths? Do they have a duty to consider what is loosely called the public's "right to know?" In other words, should the trustees destroy papers or seek to prevent their publication when such matters may place the individual who appointed them in an unfavorable light? Are the trustees the acolytes of the deceased, or do they hold the papers in trust for the public benefit?

Literary executors are often faced with this dilemma: to follow the wishes of the deceased or to preserve works for posterity. Evelyn Waugh is one of many authors whose wishes have been disregarded. In 1945, he wrote a preface to a collection of his earlier travel writings, *When the Going Was Good,* stating:

The following pages comprise all that I wish to preserve of the four travel books I wrote between the years 1929 and 1935—*Labels, Remote People, Ninety-two Days,* and (a title not of my choosing) *Waugh in Abyssinia.* These books have now been out of print for some time and will not be reissued.

Regardless of his wishes, Methuen republished in full *Waugh in Abyssinia* and Duckworth republished in full *Remote People.* [20]

If Eissler and Anna Freud had been aware of the potentially damaging nature of the papers, one can speculate that they might have been tempted to destroy them, or at least prevent Masson and others from reading them. Well-meaning family and colleagues have been known to destroy or expurgate material they deemed to be prejudicial to the deceased. If papers are destroyed, no court can repair the loss. If executors or trustees agree that papers should be destroyed, who can stop them? An employee or another colleague who is aware of the existence of the documents might wish to take action to prevent their destruction. Under the present state of the law, however, it is difficult to see what standing to sue such persons would have or what theory of property rights a court could invoke to grant a remedy.

Julian Barnes has written an amusing fictional work about the French novelist, Gustave Flaubert, *Flaubert's Parrot.* In the novel, Barnes describes the destruction by a "scholar" of a group of Flaubert's letters that shed significant light on Flaubert's life and attitudes. The scholar bought the letters; they were his property. Did he have a right to destroy or mutilate them? It seems to me that any papers of a deceased famous person are in the nature of a national treasure, like historically certified buildings that are by law protected from destruction or alteration despite the loss of substantial potential profits to the owner. Despite legal title to such papers, the owner should not have the right to bowdlerize or destroy them.* No one will ever know how much political and literary history has been "miswritten" as a result of expurgation of documents by surviving relatives of prominent persons and trustees of their property. The only way a person of public interest can be sure that his or her papers will be destroyed is to do it while alive.†

---

*This issue is not included in the proposed statutory remedy discussed in Chapter XV. It is, I believe, worthy of further discussion and probably an appropriate federal statute.

†The analogy to a living will is not farfetched. A person may instruct his family and physicians not to treat him, to let him "die with dignity." He cannot compel them to commit a crime by hastening his demise.

The dispute between Freud's executors and Masson has not rip-
ened into litigation. Masson published his book without any effort by
Freud's associates to restrain publication. To date no reported action
has been brought for breach of the oral agreement not to use the
material. The following scenario of what might have occurred if all
the parties involved had decided to sue each other indicates but a few
of the legal and moral issues inherent in the use of materials by
biographers:

Freud's executors might have sued Masson for breach of contract.
If the precedent of the *Snepp* case were to be followed, it is possible
that a court might have found that the Masson book was published
in violation of a contract and the proceeds of the book could have
been ordered to be paid to the estate.

The executors might have sued Masson for unauthorized use of
the documents. Clearly the papers "belonged" to the executors under
Freud's will. Papers are recognized as property that can pass by sale,
will, or the laws of descent. What is far from clear is whether title
to this property exists only in the actual documents, the pieces of
paper, or also in their contents. In a technological age, when not only
written documents but also recordings of music and dramatic performances are capable of easy reproduction and reuse by anyone, what
protection does the law afford the owner of such "property"? Masson's entire book was based on the unauthorized use of Freud's
letters. It could not be said that they were only a minor or peripheral
part of the book. Decided cases offer little precedential guidance
when a book involves wholesale use of material without consent of
the "owners" of the documents.

Masson might have sued Janet Malcolm for appropriation of his
intellectual property and for "scooping" him. Before Masson's book
was published, he was interviewed by Malcolm. Malcolm's account
was serialized in the *New Yorker* and was widely read. In it, she
reviewed Masson's contentions, explained the history of his connection with the Freud estate, examined Freud's theories, and concluded
that Masson's charges were unwarranted. She also gave a full and not
very flattering account of Masson's life and character. Her book, *In
the Freud Archives,* and Masson's were published at about the same
time. Hers sold far better than his. The entire basis of Malcolm's
book was Masson's work. Was this a commercial appropriation of
his work and intellectual property? There is no indication that Masson had any contractual relation with Malcolm or that he was paid
for his cooperation in agreeing to be interviewed. It is highly unlikely

that Masson would have talked so freely with Malcolm if he had anticipated her unfavorable treatment of him.

Masson may have a valid claim for libel against Malcolm. He did file a suit against her and her publisher seeking $12,000,000 in punitive damages and $200,000 in special damages.* One can understand and, indeed, sympathize with a person who bares himself to a reporter and then learns to his chagrin, like Jeffrey MacDonald, that he is depicted as a cold-blooded murderer, or like a Masson, an opportunist rather than a scholar. But these remarks are, in the main, expressions of opinion and not false statements of verifiable facts. Expressions of opinion should not subject the author to liability. Public officials have learned to exercise extreme caution in speaking with reporters even when it is "off the record." Surely anyone should know that a journalist interviewing a subject will do more than repeat verbatim the remarks of the interviewee. The journalist's impressions, background information, and conclusions are what make an interview meaningful.

When a subject consents to be interviewed, the simple rule should be, "Let the subject beware when speaking to an author." But too much caution or refusal by those who have intimate knowledge of well-known or significant persons would close off valuable resources to responsible biographers.

Unless there is a discrete, verifiable, false, and defamatory statement of fact, courts should not permit themselves to be used as referees in these acrimonious disputes involving interpretations and opinions.† One can logically infer that Masson welcomed the opportunity to create interest in his book through a lengthy *New Yorker* multi-part article. This is a typical case in which a subject (who is also an author) willingly used another author for his own purposes and found himself hoist by his own petard. Masson intended to profit from Malcolm. Instead, she profited from him. These are the chances that all persons take who agree to talk on or off the record. As John F. Kennedy stated, "Life is unfair." The courts cannot and should not attempt to provide redress for this kind of unfairness.

A recent case in which the Supreme Court considered tangentially the nature of property interests in documents involved the right of the owners of copyrighted performances shown on TV to prevent

*As of this writing the suit has not come to trial.
†See the bitter criticism of John Rawls, author of the widely acclaimed book, *A Theory of Justice* by Baker Sandels in Sandel on Rawls, 133 *University of Pennsylvania Law Review* 895 (1985), and Sandel's criticism of Rawls in his book, *Liberalism and the Limits of Justice*.

home viewers of beta max and similar devices from recording and replaying these performances without paying for the privilege of viewing them again. Any order to limit the rights of home viewers from doing what they want in their homes or to require them to pay would have been almost impossible to enforce. The Court wisely rejected the claims of the owners and producers of these shows.[21]

Publication without permission of letters of famous or notorious individuals owned by their heirs was involved in the case of *Meeropol* v. *Nizer.* [22] In this case, the sons of Julius and Ethel Rosenberg, who were executed for espionage, sued attorney Louis Nizer for using letters of their parents without their permission in his book, *The Implosion Conspiracy.* The facts were essentially undisputed. Nizer had used the letters without permission. The sons were probably motivated to sue Nizer because they did not like the book, which presented their parents most unfavorably. The *Rosenberg* case, involving the only peacetime execution of persons convicted of spying in American history, roused considerable controversy. At the time, passions ran high. More than a quarter century later, there are both ardent protagonists and opponents of the Rosenbergs, their trial, and sentence. The case has been the subject of much legal commentary and many books addressed to the general public. The court readily conceded that Nizer's book had little literary or scholarly merit. It might well be called a potboiler. It was financially successful.

In *Meeropol* v. *Nizer,* the court sidestepped the unresolved legal issues as to the extent of quotation permitted under copyright law and whether the owner of a document has title to the piece of paper only or also its contents, by holding that the letters constituted only a minor portion of the book. Judgment was entered in favor of Nizer.* Probably the number of words quoted without permission was as great as the number of words quoted by the *Nation* from Gerald Ford's book. Even though the *Nation* quoted from then unpublished material, the case was decided under copyright law, which protects both published and unpublished works that have been copyrighted.

Biographies are not written about gas station attendants, grocers, and sales clerks unless these people do something, either good or bad, that provokes sufficient interest to make a biography salable. It takes the art of a Jane Austen to make Elizabeth Bennett interesting, or

---

*Compare the pending action by J.D. Salinger, based in large part on the unauthorized use of letters.

the imagination of a Flaubert to transmute Emma Bovary from a bored housewife into a tragic figure. Those who do capture sufficient attention to be the subjects of biography must, like public officials, endure the slings and arrows of authors and critics. Virginia Woolf called Edmund Gosse a "dapper little grocer." It was a snide and untrue remark. He was neither little nor a grocer. This remark, like Alice Roosevelt Longworth's description of presidential candidate Thomas E. Dewey as "the little man on a wedding cake," may be nasty and unkind but such comments should not be actionable.

Not only heirs but also institutions closely connected with the subject of a biography assert rights to control publication. It is reported that Harvard University is stalling publication of Colin Simpson's *Artful Partners,* a nonacademic biography of the late Bernard Berenson, noted art scholar and critic.[23] Berenson willed his Florentine villa, I Tatti, and his papers to Harvard University. The Simpson book reveals business deals between Berenson and art dealer, Lord Duveen. Much of this information had already been published by Meryl Secrest and Mrs. Berenson's granddaughter, who reprinted her grandmother's letters.* The ostensible grounds for Harvard's concern is not the forthcoming authorized biography of Berenson but the unauthorized use of materials to which Harvard owns the copyrights. Harvard, Salinger, Gerald Ford, and others are relying on claims of property interest to defeat First Amendment rights.

The use and reuse of materials that are not plagiarized should, I believe, not be restricted. Quotation with or without permission but with attribution is a necessity for continuity of literary, political, and scientific discussion. No author writes on a clean slate. Sounds from the past echo in many books, giving a depth of understanding. Property concepts when used to prohibit or punish quotation seriously impede freedom of expression.

Should heirs have the right to control what is said or written about their illustrious or infamous forebears? The few cases raising this question have upheld First Amendment rights over the claimed right of publicity of heirs. Noted mystery writer Agatha Christie's heirs attempted to enjoin a biography of her, claiming that they had a right of publicity.[24] The heirs of movie idol Rudolph Valentino, claiming a descendable property right, sued for damages from a television

*See the article in *Newsweek*, September 29, 1986, p. 66, giving a brief account of these rather sordid dealings.

program based on his life.[25] They did not succeed. A contrary ruling would remove from the realm of comment, biography, and even fiction the lives not only of the living but of the dead. Every author who chose to write about the famous or infamous would be subject to a strike suit by the heirs of the subject. The preposterous nature of these claims is revealed in a cartoon. A client consults his lawyer and asks "I'm a relative of Ichabod Crane. Is it too late to sue Washington Irving?"

Since at least the reign of Elizabeth I, Anglo-American law has carefully limited restrictions on the alienability of real property imposed by will on the sensible theory that each generation should have the right to control and use property without being restricted by the "dead hand" of some former owner. Intellectual property in the form of letters, documents, literature, and works of art should also be available to future generations without restrictions imposed by previous owners. In the ongoing quest for enlarging rights of ownership, the law should be chary of acknowledging new, unprecedented property rights that infringe upon this principle.

More serious than the numerous civil claims for damages is the novel use of the criminal law to punish authors for alleged inaccuracies in books. An author's subjective awareness of truth and falsity has become a litigable issue as a result of the Supreme Court's promulgation of the "actual malice" standard in libel suits. Authors have been held in contempt for refusing to disclose their notes. Not all courts have required such information in the face of shield laws.[26] But except for seditious libel and obscenity, no author in the twentieth century had been criminally prosecuted for the contents of a book until the case of Antoni Gronowicz, the biographer of Pope John Paul II.[27]

After accusations by the Vatican charging that Gronowicz falsified information and faked interviews with the Pope, a federal grand jury at the instigation of the government was convened to investigate whether the author had committed criminal fraud. Such claims by any other subject of a biography would result in a libel suit. The author would be put to enormous expense defending the charges. The biographer and his publishers might find themselves faced with a verdict of millions of dollars, all of which would chill the willingness of other biographers and publishers to commit themselves to possibly controversial books.

A criminal charge is of an altogether different magnitude. Again one must wonder at the impact not only of politics but also of money on this extraordinary action. At stake were a $700,000 contract for movie rights to the book. The publisher, Richardson & Snyder, withdrew the book, and brought suit for the $60,000 advance paid to Gronowicz. Does the loss of perhaps a million dollars or more transform possible misstatements in a book into a crime? If the subject were not the Pope and if the author had received a modest advance of $10,000 with no subsidiary rights, it is unlikely that the might of the government would have been arrayed against him.

Political considerations also loom large. Cardinal Krol had endorsed the book. In a letter to Gronowicz dated December 27, 1982, he wrote, "I am not engaging in flattery when I say that your book is a masterpiece—different and better than anything I have read." The cardinal subsequently retracted his endorsement, claiming that he had not read the book.[28] One wonders who was engaging in fraud.

The government demanded, among other documents, Gronowicz's notes, papers, travel records for the past five years, including credit card slips, air tickets and passports, and all records of dealing with his publishers. Gronowicz refused to turn over the documents. A federal court imposed a $500 a day fine for civil contempt for disobeying a court order. But this decision was subsequently reversed by that court sitting en banc. The majority held that, "False statements intentionally made receive no First Amendment protection." After the court upheld the right of the government to prosecute an author for fraud, Gronowicz died. The prosecution has, therefore, been dropped. The propriety of the court's ruling cannot be appealed. This decision thus represents the latest statement of the law and, until a contrary ruling is made by another court of appeals, it constitutes a precedent that will be difficult to ignore.

Whether Gronowicz actually met with the Pope the number of times he claimed to have done so is a fact not an opinion. Could he have subpoenaed the Pope to testify in an American court of law? And if the Pope refused to respond, what could a court have done? Under the Sixth Amendment, an accused is entitled to confront his accusers. This salutary provision was adopted to abolish the nefarious English practice of convicting on the basis of documentary evidence. An accused cannot cross-examine a piece of paper.* Other

---

*In the reign of Elizabeth I, Sir Walter Raleigh was convicted and executed on such evidence. Raleigh was accused of high treason and tried in 1603. The indictment charged that he had conspired to deprive King James I of his government, to bring the Roman Catholic religion (described as Roman superstition) into the realm, and to procure foreign enemies to invade the kingdom. The entire trial consisted of documents and the repetition of charges, what would

books, fictional but referring by name to actual Popes, have been highly unflattering.[29] Can such authors be accused of crimes?

Many prominent political officials are the subjects of controversial books. Friends of the late Congressman Allard Lowenstein charged that a biography[30] of him is false. The book declares that Lowenstein was a CIA agent. Members of Congress who knew Lowenstein refute that statement. They have published a book denying the charges.[31] Threats of suits and countersuits were made. Again, a trial judge can only wonder how such an assertion could be proved or disproved in court. Would the CIA respond to subpoenas? Friends could at best testify that they did not know of Lowenstein's CIA connections, but such testimony would, like most attempts to prove a negative, be unconvincing. Again, self-help in the form of another book refuting the charges is probably the best and least costly remedy available to the maligned individual and his or her friends.

Another controversial book that could give rise not only to civil suits but also criminal charges of fraud is the autobiography of Arkady N. Shevchenko, who claims to have been a spy who came in from the icy tundras of the Soviet.[32] Author Edward Jay Epstein claims that, contrary to Shevchenko's assertion that he was a CIA mole, he was in fact a minor party functionary.[33] With a wealth of detail, Epstein purports to prove Shevchenko was not in the places at the times he said he was there and that other assertions by Shevchenko are absolutely false. A great deal of money is also at stake in this book, including substantial payments to ghost writers, as well as huge royalties from a best seller and subsidiary rights. Is Shevchenko a fraud as Epstein asserts? Did he con *Time* magazine and "60 Minutes" into giving him priceless publicity on the basis of willfully false statements? If those allegations are true, should Shevchenko also be prosecuted for fraud?

Columnist Anthony Lewis suggested a not too farfetched scenario in which Woodward and Bernstein, authors of *All the President's Men* were prosecuted by Attorney General Mitchell for fraud.[34] He headlined the column, "The Big Chill."

One can only surmise that prosecution of Gronowicz hastened the demise of the septuagenarian author. It was also a disaster for his

---

be deemed hearsay in any American court. There were no witnesses whom Raleigh could cross-examine. He complained bitterly, "You try me by the Spanish Inquisition, if you proceed only by the circumstances without two Witnesses." Under the then law of England, treason had to be proved by two witnesses. Nonetheless, Raleigh was convicted. He was hanged on October 29, 1618 (II, *Cobbett's Complete Collection of State Trials,* p. 1).

publishers who promptly repudiated him. Authors and publishers who are both endangered by damage suits and criminal prosecutions should in self-defense close ranks and present a united front against the enemy, whether it be the subject of the book or the government. Sometimes, the publisher cuts his losses and flees, leaving the author alone to bear the costs of his defense, slowly twisting in the wind. Other publishers defray the cost of defense unless the charges are "finally sustained."

Publishers may argue that authors have deceived them and that they are rightfully enraged by the fraud. Such a position appears to be disingenuous. Publishers, except for small houses like Pushcart Press, are sophisticated corporations. They have firms of lawyers on retainers. They have insurance policies. They have staffs of researchers and editors. They should investigate the bona fides of their authors and the accuracy of the manuscripts. Epstein reports that Shevchenko had a $600,000 contract with Simon and Schuster for a book on his spying experiences and that Simon and Schuster rejected the book and successfully sued Shevchenko for the $146,875 it had advanced. Certainly if those charges are true, Knopf knew or should have known of these prior abortive literary efforts of Shevchenko.

Except for the "actual malice" test in libel, the law holds parties responsible not only for what they actually knew but for what they should have known, what a reasonable person under those circumstances would have deemed prudent to investigate and what such a person would have learned. This sensible standard of responsibility would not restrict First Amendment rights. A publishing firm that issues a book under its name makes an implied warranty to the reader that the book is not a meretricious fraud. Readers can't recover the price of the book if they are dissatisfied. The good old legal maxim, "caveat emptor," let the buyer beware, precludes them from recovering. But the publisher should not be completely absolved from responsibility if it is the instrumentality through which lies are disseminated and fraud perpetrated.

This gets back to the fundamental questions, can a book, even if riddled with lies, constitute a criminal fraud? I see many extremely difficult legal problems in the use of the criminal process to punish authors who may have lied, even deliberately planned and written a book created from a tissue of lies. A crime must be created by the legislature. The criminal conduct must be explicitly defined. Under American law, crimes cannot be created ex post facto, that is, after an act has been committed, the legislature cannot then pass a law making that prior conduct illegal.* All these well-recognized principles appear to have been ignored in the Gronowicz prosecution. One must also ask what was the fraud? Was it a scheme to cheat the purchasers of the book? On its face this is a preposterous claim. Who has been harmed? If it is a crime, it is a victimless one. Or is the government seeking to protect from mental contamination those who might read a book containing false statements or one that is based on unsubstantiated evidence? This is a strange paternalistic attitude on the part of a government of a democracy predicated on the assumption that the citizens are capable of self-governance. I suggest that writing and publishing books and articles cannot and should not be deemed criminal acts. The threat to First Amendment rights is explicit. The crime of seditious libel was presumably buried by the Supreme Court in 1919. It should not be disinterred.

Many biographical works, like many books about crime, are sleazy and sensational. They are based on unverified gossip and often cause the subjects considerable unhappiness. In my opinion, such a book was *The Brethren* by Woodward and Armstrong. It purported to give an inside account of the Supreme Court based on information received from unidentified law clerks. The portraits of the justices were, in some instances, savage. The net effect was to mislead the public, to cause all judges and justices to be much more guarded in their relations with their law clerks, and to make a great deal of money for the authors and publisher. Even such a dismaying example of biography does not induce one to believe that there is or should be a legally cognizable and enforceable right of biography. Clearly, the Supreme Court is always a subject of great interest. Not only lawyers but also the general public want to know about the individuals who hold this great power, what kind of people they are, and how they think and act.

Several justices were disturbed by the book. Justice Blackmun wrote a very temperate and judicious article in the *New York Times* explaining how the Court really functions. There was never any indication that a criminal prosecution of the authors of *The Brethren* was contemplated. But a false and misleading group portrait of the Supreme Court is as politically dangerous as a false portrait of the Pope.

---

*Cf. the English case of Shaw v. Director of Public Prosecutions, 1962 A C 220 House of Lords in which the conviction of the publisher of a phone book listing the names of prostitutes was upheld even though there was no law making such a publication criminal. The government conceded that the publication was neither libelous nor obscene.

Other biographers have also written unfavorably about their subjects and made damning charges. Australian anthropologist Derek Freeman[35] attacked the truth of Margaret Mead's studies posthumously, especially her fieldwork in Samoa that formed the basis of her highly popular and successful book, *Coming of Age in Samoa*. It is now agreed by a respectable number, but by no means all anthropologists, that Mead's work was seriously flawed, that Samoan girls did not lead happy guilt-free lives characterized by promiscuous sexual relations. Should Mead have been prosecuted for fraud? If Mead were alive and had sued for libel, should the courts even attempt to decide the truth or falsity of the different versions of sex life in Samoa fifty years ago? The task would be impossible.

Even assuming there is an implied warranty of the truthfulness of a book, the remedy for breach of warranty is a civil action. If Ford or General Motors or Chrysler manufactures a defective automobile, even one unsafe at any speed, the remedy is a civil action for damages. Even when pharmaceutical companies violate specific statutes by selling dangerous drugs that actually cause many deaths, corporations are prosecuted and pay fines. The officers rarely go to jail. Is a book to be classified as a dangerous substance?

A basic difficulty for the courts in such cases is the question of fact finding. Unless centuries of criminal law are to be overturned, the government must establish criminal charges by proof beyond a reasonable doubt. The prosecution must present witnesses who can be examined and cross-examined. The defendant has a similar right to subpoena witnesses and to compel the production of documents and records. Any claim to a right of privacy withers in the heat of a criminal trial. Is the fraud one or a hundred false statements, or is it the contents of the book as a whole? Does the fraud consist of lies extrinsic to the book such as the number of interviews with the Pope or the quality of the research? Are courts to be in the business of taking expert testimony to determine the generally accepted standards of care and accuracy in research? Courts would be embroiled in impossible trials lasting months and months.

The answer to lies, even if they can be proved, is truth. But if the author of a counter-attack also risks criminal prosecution, it is most unlikely that deception will be disclosed. The attack on Shevchenko's book by Epstein is a more effective method of revealing literary deception than a criminal or civil trial. But if Shevchenko sues Epstein for libel, what will be the result?

The best account of the dangers of criminal prosecution of authors

was given by the prosecutor in the *Gronowicz* case. U.S. Attorney
S.G. Dennis, Jr., said in his argument to the Court:

> The power to investigate and the power to prosecute is the power to
> intimidate, it's the power to disrupt and it is certainly the power, perhaps,
> to intimidate an author from not publishing a book. . . . I think that it
> is always a risk that a government agency could abuse its authority for
> purposes of expressing ideas and thoughts that might be dangerous to the
> current administration or that might displease government officials.[36]

He then suggested that, of course, that was not the intent of the
government in the *Gronowicz* case.

The search for truth and the fear of ideas have been uneasy com-
panions throughout human history. Men feared witches and burned
women. Governments fear ideas and burn books. There are always
individuals and groups who seek to suppress expression under whatever guise is effective at the moment. At some periods in history,
heresy was the most potent tool for suppression of ideas. At other
times, sedition, disloyalty, and obscenity have been the particular
bêtes noirs used to punish expression. In 1985, a group of congress-
men condemned grants to poets who write "obscene" verse. One is
reminded of the pathetic plaint of Cinna in Shakespeare's *Julius
Caesar.* As the soldiers, presumably fighting against dictatorship,
stab Cinna, he cries in vain, "I am Cinna, the poet, I am Cinna, the
poet."

A citizen replies, "Tear him for his bad verses."

In the 1980s, the claim under which not only poets but also biographers, journalists, and other authors are punished is "falsity." If
either the government or the subjects of books can claim falsity, then
the protections of the Constitution are swept aside. Instead of robed
ecclesiastics sitting as solemn tribunals to ferret out errors of
thought, to determine guilt and pronounce sentence, robed judges
are expected to decide whether the author has made false statements
and to render verdict. Among the penalties imposed by the Inquisition were the confiscation of the heretic's goods. Confiscation of
royalties and substantial damage awards are not dissimilar.

·X·

Fiction, Fantasy, and Fun

*That is what I mean when I say his life became his fate
—he had the same attitude to his life as a sculptor to
his statue or a novelist to his novel.*

—MILAN KUNDERA

THE desire for stories is probably as old as human speech and
begins almost in the cradle. Does anyone know of a time when a child
did not ask for the miracle of a story, the tale of a life not his own?
Children and adults long to hear about the life of a hero, one who
is wiser and cleverer or stronger or braver than the teller of the tale
and the listener. The desire for a story transcends the age and conditions of life of the hearer. Chaucer's pilgrims came from all walks of
life, sacred and profane, rich and poor. The longing to go on a
journey may be strongest in the springtime when flowers, fields, and
strange places beckon. But the wish for tales is not bounded by the
calendar or the clock.

Perhaps 20,000 or more years ago, while a painter in the Lascaux
caves by the uncertain light of a smoky fire worked his magic depicting the might of the terrifying beasts of the forest and the prowess
of the puny ancestors of man, the tribe gathered to watch and to
listen. Undoubtedly they asked the elders for stories of animals and
the wily men and women who managed to outwit or snare or slay
their enemies. Some stories probably were reports of the events of the
day. Others may have described recent or long-past episodes. For
centuries, tellers of tales and writers of fiction and drama have used
history and current events as source material as well as imagination.
They also borrowed from legends and well-known tales and ballads.

The distinctions between news, history, and fiction were of little significance to the storytellers or their audiences.

The same desire for a story animates people today. In many parts of the world, the bard has been supplanted by the radio and the flickering TV screen. I have watched villagers along the banks of the upper Nile sit transfixed by the sounds emanating from a radio hung on a wooden pole, the principal link between the timeless village and the restless outside world. Even in the mountain vastnesses of Nepal and the steaming banks of the Irawaddy River in Borneo, people are drawn to the ubiquitous television by the enchantment of a story and of information about the world beyond the viewer's own experience.

Nowhere is the production and consumption of news and entertainment greater than in the United States. American writers, publishers, and the electronic media create and distribute both news and entertainment not only to our own population but also to the rest of the world. The demand for programs to fill the television channels every hour every day is so enormous that it is difficult to meet simply with the usual complement of new literature and drama, historical figures, and the reuse of old fiction and movies. In the search for material, authors increasingly turn to episodes from the lives of living people. Truth is not only stranger than fiction; it is more compelling. A true, real-life story has immense appeal. Whether this interest is pejoratively described as voyeurism, vulgar curiosity, or a Peeping Tom syndrome, the popularity of books, dramas, feature stories, and TV programs about real people cannot be doubted. There is nothing novel in writing about real people. But lawsuits brought by the subjects of such printed material and programs are a new phenomenon.

Not only do subjects who are identified by name and whose life stories are admittedly being used bring suit, but also individuals who believe that fictional characters are based upon them or incidents in their lives. Writers of fiction have for centuries used the lives of their families, friends, and acquaintances as source material for their novels and dramas. This was a well-understood and accepted practice. Indeed, students in "creative writing" classes are urged to write from their own experience. The best-selling book (which was later dramatized), *I Remember Mama,* describes the young author's use of real-life material. Innumerable stories, novels, and dramas drew their inspiration from an actual event. The use of family members, friends, and acquaintances as the prototypes of fictional characters is not new. What is new is the spate of lawsuits by persons who believe that they are the subjects of fictionalized treatment.

The line between biography and fiction is often thin, but it constitutes a legal continental divide. On the fiction side of the great rift, the author may likely be held responsible for portraying an imaginary character that inaccurately depicts a real person; whereas on the biographical side, an author may be relieved of liability for inaccurately depicting a real person. Such fantastic legal doctrine is not merely illogical, it puts at risk an enormous number of writers who are following centuries-old literary traditions, and it fails to protect those whose names, identities, and lives are being held up to public scrutiny.

Libel law as applied to fiction, satire, and cartoons has not been widely discussed in the media.[1] Usually these authors are not engaged in political comment. The United States government has little interest in their works. But whether novelists choose as their subjects life in a Russian Gulag or life in an Upper East Side penthouse, they should be entitled to the protections of the First Amendment. The law should not, I believe, be used to punish monetarily or restrict publication of books, regardless of subject matter.

Everyone knows that fiction is a story, as the dictionary describes it, an "invented story." It does not purport to deal with actual people. How, then, one must ask, can an imaginary invented tale defame a person? Obviously, unless an author is writing about extraterrestial aliens, invented creatures like Hobbits, or the unearthly characters of Doris Lessing and science fiction books, fictional characters will bear some relation to real people. The art of the greatest novelists is that readers recognize themselves in the fictional characters. This recognition of human emotions transcends gender, age, nationality, and socioeconomic status.

Most authors use as source material their own lives, their families, friends, enemies, and acquaintances. Drawing on their understanding of real human beings, they are able to invent characters that ring true. Of course, there are similarities between the prototype and the fictional character. But readers understand that a novel does not purport to portray a real person.

Novelists frequently find the germ of the book in an actual episode. Italo Calvino described the process by which a great author transmutes fact into fiction. He explains that in 1946 when Carlo Emilio Gaddo started to write *That Awful Mess on Via Merulana,* Gaddo intended to write not only a murder novel, but a philosophical novel as well. The murder story was inspired by a crime that had recently been committed in Rome. The philosophical inquiry was based on a concept announced at the novel's very outset: "Nothing can be explained if we confine ourselves to seeking one cause for every effect."[2]

Gaddo did not intend or purport to describe the actual people involved in the murder that gave rise to his novel. Neither the murderer nor the relatives of the victim sued Gaddo for defamation, invasion of privacy, or right of publicity. American authors are not so fortunate.

Let us examine not Gaddo's story but a hypothetical story by a hypothetical American novelist. Our author, a well-known and popular writer whose books sell in the hundreds of thousands and are subsequently made into movies and TV mini-series, reads in the press an account of a lurid crime. A woman, let us call her Carla Colson, was accused of murdering a policeman whom we shall call Martin Smith. Because there may somewhere in the United States be a woman named Carla Colson and a policeman named Martin Smith, I hasten to disclaim any knowledge of anyone named Carla Colson or Martin Smith or any incident such as the purely hypothetical incident I am about to describe. As we shall see, even such a disclaimer might not immunize me or the hypothetical novelist if sued for libel.

In this hypothetical case, the author read an item in the daily press reporting that Colson had allegedly shot Smith with his police gun in her apartment shortly after midnight. Colson's defense at the trial was that Smith was apparently answering a call for help from another apartment. When he knocked on her door and announced "police," she refused to open the door because, she said, she feared he might be an intruder. Smith broke down the door and entered with drawn weapon. In the ensuing struggle somehow Smith was shot.

Carla was prosecuted for murder. In the course of the trial, it was brought out that Carla Colson was, in fact, expecting a boyfriend with whom she had had a quarrel. Smith had had a series of girlfriends and was known to treat them with violence. A former girlfriend testified that she had felled Smith with his nightstick on one occasion to ward off a beating. Both Mr. Colson and Mrs. Smith testified that their respective spouses were models of faithfulness, chastity, and kindness. The jury acquitted Carla. Mrs. Smith received Smith's pension since there was insufficient evidence to show that he had been guilty of misconduct on the job.

Whether or not justice was served was a question raised by the irate prosecutor. In fact, both families were satisfied with the results of the case. It was a one-week wonder in the local press. The bare bones of the story were reported twice by the national wire services, once at the time of the arrest and the second time when the verdict was rendered.

Our best-selling novelist was being pressured by his agent and publisher for another blockbuster book, one that would be picked up by the national book clubs, the movies, and TV. After fourteen novels in twenty years, the wells of his inspiration were running dry. He had plundered his own past and the life stories of friends and relatives. He had even looted the pages of history looking for a combination of sex, violence, human passion, and conflict in a setting that would give scope to his not inconsiderable powers of description. He believed that the story of Carla and Martin would provide the armature on which he could construct a vibrant tableaux of unrequited passion, male fears of sexual inadequacy, and female childhood sexual abuse. All the popular and salable stock of issues, motives, and passion were utilized to flesh out this bare and tawdry story.

A year and a half after the trial, the book appeared. It sold even more widely than the author had hoped, and was sold to the movies and TV and translated into more than a dozen languages. Both Mrs. Martin Smith and Mrs. Colson read the book and claimed to recognize themselves in the novel. Both filed suit for invasion of privacy, defamation, right of publicity, right of biography, and our new category, right of persona.

The author, who had already made more than a half million in royalties, indignantly cried freedom of press, right of intellectual property, and the "higher truths" of fiction.[3]

The publishing company consulted its insurance carrier and its lawyers. The cautious insurance company suggested that the irate plaintiffs be paid off to the extent of the publisher's deductible, perhaps $50,000. If the plaintiffs accepted this sum, the insurer would be relieved of the not inconsiderable expense of defending the suit. The matter would be quickly and quietly resolved. The publisher blamed the author. The author had represented that the story was fiction. He, not the publisher, should be liable. The author is not insured other than under the publisher's insurance contract. At this point, questions of money became confused with honor, literary reputation, standing in the community, and the First Amendment. The outraged author, who had long since forgotten the little news clipping, demanded that his attorney countersue, charging frivolous abuse of process. Author and publisher became antagonists. Each engaged separate counsel.

Some two years later, the case comes to trial. I am the judge. Forty citizens are plucked from the privacy of their homes to be on the jury panel from which twelve will be chosen to serve as jurors and two more as alternates.* The process of jury selection takes more than a week. It is apparent from the beginning that the trial will last at least a month. A self-employed barber bursts into tears when he hears that he may have to serve for weeks. He explains that he will lose his shop, his family will have to go on welfare, and asks "who will take care of his sick wife"?† Counsel agree to excuse him.

A public school teacher who teaches English literature in high school is eager to serve. She is not the least concerned about what will happen to her classes. The thought of being in the presence of a great author thrills her. To her dismay, plaintiffs' counsel strike her. They do not want anyone on the jury who will be impressed by the author's fame. We exhaust two panels of forty and part of a third panel.

Slowly, one by one, ninety-four people are questioned. The author's lawyer will not accept as jurors any relatives of police officers or firefighters. They may be too sympathetic to the plaintiffs. A police officer earns about $30,000 a year. The lawyers reason that such jurors will wonder why an author whose life is never endangered by robbers, muggers, and the world of crazies should earn millions. They may be tempted to put into effect a share the wealth plan through a substantial verdict for the plaintiffs.

On the seventh day the jury is complete. It consists of three postal employees. They will be paid their salary by the government no matter how long the trial lasts. Certainly the case will be a relief from the tedium of their regular jobs. Two jurors are retired. They, too, are bored and eager for jury duty. One woman is a bank clerk. Her favorite reading matter is the romances of Barbara Cartland. One male juror says he reads only the sports page and the stock market. One never knows whether potential jurors frame their answers to avoid jury service or perhaps in rare instances to get on the jury.

---

*In New York and several other jurisdictions, civil cases are heard by six-person juries. It is far from clear whether this is a sufficient number of jurors to arrive at a fair verdict. In many jurisdictions, the judge conducts voir dire and asks only a limited number of perfunctory questions.
†This actually occurred during voir dire in a case tried before me. The responses and backgrounds of other jurors are a composite of actual panelists.

Although all these people have sworn to tell the truth, after a number of years, a judge becomes slightly wary. Truth can be shaded when potential jurors face the loss of a month's earnings, or when they are looking for some occupation to relieve the crushing boredom of idleness.

Assuming the prospective jurors answered the questions truthfully, there is not one person on the jury who has more than a high school education or a year or two at the local community college. One juror, a steel worker who has been laid off and is eager for the $10 a day he will earn as a juror, has a son who is a college professor. The juror says he rarely sees his son. None of the parties is happy with the composition of the jury. But I, the judge, press them for action. Hundreds of accused people are locked up in jail awaiting trial. Some of them may be innocent. While this laborious selection of the jury is taking place, at least a half dozen routine criminal cases could have been tried. There are also civil litigants who have been awaiting trial for four or five years. Some of them are badly injured. They cannot afford skilled nursing care or further surgery unless they recover damages from the parties who have allegedly caused their injuries.

Nonetheless, both the Colson and Smith families are entitled to their day in court and the chance of a lifetime to grab the brass ring of a share of the author's wealth. Under the present state of the law, I cannot grant the defendants' motion to dismiss the action. It is admitted by all parties that the characters in the book are not named Carla Colson and Martin Smith and that as described they do not resemble Carla and Martin. But the principal episode in the book is the murder of a married policeman by his jealous girlfriend. Even though Colson's defense was that she did not know Smith, and the jury evidently believed her, this jury in the libel case must decide the factual question as to whether the novel was "of and concerning" the plaintiffs.

The jurors are all nice, conscientious people. By the end of the six-week trial, even though we are not permitted to speak to each other, I feel that I know and like them. On my birthday they put a bunch of flowers on the bench with a card, "best wishes from your jurry [sic]."* When the trial is over, two of them thank me for the wonderful experience, as most jurors do. They say they will remember it forever.

---

*This actually happened in a civil case not involving libel.

But what are these nice people expected to do? The result of the case will depend, in part, as it always does, on the skill of the lawyers and the personality of the parties. Do the jurors like the author? Do they think he is an arrogant, heartless bastard or a nice man caught in an accidental dilemma? Do they think the plaintiffs really care about their reputations, or are they just trying to get a windfall? Finally, and most importantly, the result will depend on the statement of the law that the judge gives them, the instructions they have sworn to follow. These are complicated and numerous. Again and again I shall tell them that if you find that A is what happened then you must return a verdict for the plaintiffs; if you find that B is what in fact occurred, then you must find in favor of the defendant.

In order to give these instructions to the jury, the judge must consider a multitude of cases, none of which is exactly the same as this one, and he or she must seek to draw general principles that are lucid and comprehensible. Common sense would dictate that, unless a real person's name was used in a story actually describing that individual, there should be no recovery for defamation. But this is not the law, even though much of literature is based on a retelling of stories about real people. All the historical plays of Shakespeare purport to deal with fact. So do all historical novels. But since the characters in historical works are safely dead, courts do not have to consider whether they have been maligned.* When persons claiming to be the characters in fiction are alive and in court, the legal principles are confusing and bear little relation to the actual process of writing fiction.

Until the present time, it would have been unthinkable for anyone to base a libel claim on a novel in which the real name and identity of the person on whom a fictional character was based was not used. Few situations in literature are so bizarre and unusual that there is not some counterpart in real life. It is assumed that a novelist takes a simple situation from fact or perhaps from another book and invests the characters with new insights and dreams and longings. The *Joseph* trilogy by Thomas Mann is an elaborate reworking in three volumes of a brief passage in the Old Testament. One can only wonder if E. M. Forester in writing *A Passage To India,* had in mind an actual incident regarding a charge of rape made by an English woman against an Indian. Undoubtedly, during the course of the

---

*Paul Murray Kendall and other scholars attempted to rehabilitate the reputation of King Richard III, but he will continue to be known to most readers as the evil crookback of Shakespeare's imagination.

British Empire, a number of such charges were made. In our hypothetical case, the novel, a six hundred-page blockbuster, was an elaboration on a news item of three paragraphs.

New York Times v. *Sullivan* was intended to free the media from the old limitations of defamation actions in order to ensure the rights granted by the First Amendment. But courts adhering literally to words in the opinion have applied the "actual malice" test to writers of fiction. Clearly such authors not only disregard truth, they do not even purport to present reality. The case of *Bindrim* v. *Mitchell*[4] illustrates the fantasy world of defamation law as applied to fiction. The author of a novel entitled *Touching* enrolled in the group therapy course of a Dr. Paul Bindrim. In her novel, she described the nude therapy practices of an ostensibly fictional psychiatrist called Simon Herford. The physical description of Herford was very different from that of Dr. Bindrim. Bindrim is not the only nude therapist in California. Therapeutic modalities are not patentable. Doctors and therapists are free to practice all kinds of treatment. Some believe that patients should scream. Others believe they should touch. Some elicit confessions; others wait for the patient to speak voluntarily. Mitchell's portrait of the psychiatrist she called Dr. Herford and his methods was unfavorable. Bindrim brought suit against Mitchell.

Bindrim made two claims: breach of contract and libel. Before being admitted to the group therapy program, Mitchell had signed a contract that read in pertinent part, "The participant agrees that he will not take photographs, write articles, or in any manner disclose who has attended the workshop or what has transpired. If he fails to do so he releases all parties from this contract, but remains legally liable for damages sustained by the leaders and participants." The court struck the contract claim on the grounds that a therapist cannot by contract or otherwise prevent a patient from reporting the treatment she has received. Since Mitchell's treatment was part of a group encounter, the court found that she could also write about the group sessions. It is apparent that this contract was ineptly drawn. Bindrim, like author Joe McGinniss who also attempted to protect himself by contract in his dealings with Captain Jeffrey MacDonald, should have had a more comprehensive and carefully worded agreement.

As for the libel claim, Bindrim produced several witnesses who testified that they found that the therapy sessions described in the novel were the same as those practiced by Bindrim. The court held that it was a question for the jury to decide whether a reasonable person reading the book would conclude that Dr. Herford was in fact the plaintiff. The jury also had to determine whether the descriptions of the therapy session were, in fact, true. Bindrim recovered on the libel count $50,000 in compensatory damages and $25,000 in punitive damages against the publisher only. The verdict was upheld by the California courts. The Supreme Court refused to hear the case, leaving in effect the award. The author who had made no assertion that the description of the therapy sessions was factual and truthful was held liable because the description was false and defamatory. Under this ruling, fiction must conform to fact or the author will be held liable. How can a novelist assert truth as a defense when he or she is writing a work of imagination?

On the other hand, meticulous accuracy in descriptions of real people will prevent them from recovering for invasion of privacy. As Justice Douglas remarked in another connection, "This stands the First Amendment on its head."

Let us see how these rules would apply to our hypothetical case of Carla Colson. The character in the book was named Evelyn Richards. She was described as dark, lissome, and seductive. Carla Colson was short, blond, and overweight. The character in the book was described as a sexually promiscuous, lustful nymphomaniac who had been brutalized as a child by a series of rape-incest incidents. There had been no suggestion of a history of rape-incest in the reports of the murder. At the murder trial, Carla had presented evidence that she was a faithful wife, a model of virtue. If the character, Evelyn Richards, was intended to describe Carla Colson, obviously it was defamatory. The only defense to defamation the novelist could present under the law is truth. But clearly he was purporting to write not truth but fiction.

In our case, the first question the jury would have to decide is whether the novel is "of and concerning" the plaintiff, Carla Colson. As we have seen from the *Bindrim* case, the differences in names and physical descriptions are insufficient to protect the novelist. The jury must make its determination on this crucial question, not on what the author intended or the obvious designation of the book as a novel,[5] but on whether a reasonable person would have believed that the novel was "of and concerning" Carla Colson. In our case, Carla would certainly be able to bring in half a dozen friends who would testify that when they read the novel, they thought it was about her. The fact that Colson had killed a policeman and that the fictional character had also killed a policeman might be sufficient to convince the jury even though, unfortunately, many policemen are killed in the line of duty.

If the jury found that the book was about Colson, there is little doubt that it was defamatory. The description of a person as a murderer and as having committed incest would clearly be defamatory.* After a finding of liability, the jury would have to consider the question of damages. Colson would testify that she had been embarrassed, humiliated, and emotionally distressed by being portrayed as a nymphomaniac, a lewd woman, and a victim of rape-incest.

The jury would have to be given two confusing instructions, one on malice and the other on "actual malice." In order to find that the novelist had portrayed the plaintiff with "reckless disregard for truth," it would probably be sufficient to present the news story announcing the acquittal of Carla and the trial testimony in which she was described as a model of virtue. If the jury found that the novelist acted with "reckless disregard for the truth," it would be easy for a jury to find that he also acted with common law malice, i.e., evil intent or reckless disregard for the rights of others.

When a court instructs a jury on the question of punitive damages, the plaintiff is entitled to present evidence as to the defendant's wealth and earning capacity. Punitive damages are for the purposes of punishing and deterring reckless wrongdoers. A verdict of $250,000 will deter even the most reckless author and publisher. Since our hypothetical author had written a series of best sellers, it is likely that the jury, composed of people from the same community as the plaintiff, would award very large sums both for presumed damages and for punitive damages against a wealthy New York, cosmopolitan writer.

Although this is a hypothetical case, it tracks closely cases that have already been decided. It indicates that the First Amendment as interpreted by the courts is, at best, a fragile paper shield for novelists. It is this very uncertainty of the law under the "of and concerning" test that lays authors and publishers open to defamation suits.[6]

Novels by their very nature do not purport to describe real people and real incidents. They do not report fact. They do not overtly discuss politics. Their ostensible purpose is not to inform the public with respect to facts but to entertain or to provoke thought by the use of imagination. Some novels do involve, at least in part, real facts

---

*The fact that the character was an innocent child victim of incest rather than a voluntary participant in criminal acts would be immaterial to the claim of libel. It is presumed that such a charge is defamatory.

and discussions of political and philosophic concern. *War and Peace* discusses not only actual battles, which may or may not be accurately described, but moral values and social mores. Santayana's *The Last Puritan* is a philosophical novel. Books like Orwell's *Animal Farm* and Swift's *Gulliver's Travels* can be read on one level as fables for children; on another level, they are perceived as profound comments on the human and political condition. Kafka and Koestler wrote in the form of novels what were intended to be and were understood to be political statements, if not manifestos.

Dictators seem to understand that literature, music, and the arts can be as politically destabilizing forces as overtly political speech. Consequently they have denounced jazz, impressionist paintings, novels, and poetry as "revisionist" or "bourgeois" or have used other pejorative terms. Works of imagination have been burned as dangerous to society. Overt suppression of novels would probably not be countenanced today in much of the Western world and certainly not in the United States unless they are found to be obscene. But defamation actions have been used to suppress publication and to punish the hapless authors of fiction and comedy.

Free expression by writers of fiction and fantasy and by cartoonists are endangered by libel suits and the chilling fear of such litigation. The number of novels that are part of our recent literary heritage and that contain thinly disguised portraits of real people is legion. Thomas Wolfe's character, Esther Jack, who appears in *Of Time and the River* and is a central figure in *The Web and the Rock,* is widely believed to be a transparent mask for Aline Bernstein. Indeed, all Wolfe's novels were peopled by his family, friends, and acquaintances.* There are no reported cases of libel brought against Wolfe although many of the portraits are unflattering. Eugene O'Neill's *Long Day's Journey* gives a harsh picture of his family.

Sylvia Plath in her prose and poetry made no secret of the fact that she was writing about herself and her own experiences. Her mother and her husband, the poet Ted Hughes, might well have complained of the way they were depicted. They did not do so. Plath's psychiatrist, Dr. Jane V. Anderson, however, brought a libel and invasion of privacy suit based on a 1979 movie version of Plath's novel, *The*

---

*See Richard Walser, *Thomas Wolfe: An Introduction and Interpretation,* Barnes and Noble, Inc., N.Y. 1961, in which the names of the real persons are supplied in parentheses. He writes, "The scoundrels she introduced him to were, he convinced himself, the most despicable of rotten imposters: charlatans like Van Vleeck (Carl Van Vechten) and Rosalind Bailey (Elinor Wylie) and Seamus Malone (Ernest Boyd)," p. 100. Could Walser's identifications be deemed libelous?

Bell Jar, which was published in 1961.[7] Plath committed suicide in
1963. The character in both the book and the movie that Anderson
claims is "of and concerning" her is called Joan Gilling. Plaintiff
asserts that her reputation has been damaged because the character
is depicted inferentially as a homosexual. She is also described as
being physically unattractive. Plaintiff does not allege that "she has
lost patients." Although the book was popular in the sixties, the
movie was not a great success. One might conclude that if the plaintiff has not suffered any economic loss from the allegedly defamatory
movie, the damage, if any, to her reputation is the result of her own
identification of herself with a fictional character. Any significant
loss of privacy that Anderson has suffered is due primarily to the
publicity attendant on the lawsuit, including a front page item in the
New York Times, not the film. These sensible arguments do not
constitute a valid legal defense to a libel or privacy suit. However,
in other tort cases a plaintiff who is at fault, in whole or in part, in
causing the harm complained of is either barred from recovery or the
damages are diminished proportionate to the plaintiff's fault. If Anderson is deemed to be a public or a limited public figure, it will be
extremely difficult for the defendants to show the mental processes
of a deceased author and her lack of "actual malice." The defendants, who are producers of the movie and executor of Plath's estate
and who sold the book to the film company, did not substantially
alter the general outline of the narrative. Did they know the plaintiff? What was their intent? These are only a few of the legal issues
that a judge and jury will have to decide.*

President Reagan's daughter, Patti Davis, has written a novel,
Home Front,[8] describing the coming of age of a president's daughter.
This book reveals the problems facing courts if they are to consider
literary merit, relationship between subject and author, and motivation. One critic suggested that Davis "may have written this book as
much for catharsis as for money."[9] In addition to such unverifiable
questions, should a judge or jury be required to sift through the
personal lives of people to determine whether they were truthfully
or falsely portrayed? It is an impossible task. Moreover, the novelist
would be the first to admit that the book does not purport to be
literally true to life. The author is thus put in the impossible position
of attempting to prove as a defense to a charge of defamation that
fiction is fact.

---

*This case was settled. A settlement does not constitute legal precedent. However, the fact that
plaintiff did receive compensation undoubtedly will encourage similar libel suits based on
fiction.

In the eighteenth and nineteenth centuries, it was a popular convention to disguise political criticism by the device of changing the locale. Montesquieu's *Letters from the Persians* was written to describe contemporary French social and political practices. Gilbert and Sullivan's *The Mikado* is set in Japan, but no one in England failed to recognize Pooh Bah as the Lord Chancellor. Verdi used exotic settings to criticize contemporary Italian government and society. The heavy hand of the censor was stayed by such transparent and well-understood fictional devices.

It was equally well understood and accepted that some novels and even poetry were written about or addressed to real people although their actual names were not revealed. Four centuries of literary sleuths have been seeking the identity of the dark lady or dark man, perhaps, of Shakespeare's sonnets. The roman à clef has a long and honorable history. The real characters in such novels rarely, if ever, sued for defamation.

When fictional characters are placed in actual contemporary settings, they will undoubtedly bear some resemblance to real persons. If characters did not have common human traits of love, jealousy, ambition, fear, and hatred, they would not hold the reader's interest. All stories, including formula fiction like murder stories and romances, must have characters that the reader will respond to. Even animal stories endow wild creatures with human feelings. Lovable Bambi, little Br'er Rabbit, the vicious pigs in *Animal Farm* and the Houyhnhnms in *Gulliver's Travels* are depicted as having motivations and responses that human beings can identify with.

Of course, the characters in some books bear a closer resemblance to real people than others. The witty English novel, *Small World,* by David Lodge uses actual settings for the meetings of his band of roving, lustful scholars. The surroundings are described with meticulous accuracy. The conversations and academic discussions wickedly mimic the worst traits of academia. The uninitiated read the book as a joyous farce. The cognoscenti claim to recognize their colleagues. To date, no one has sued Lodge. Perhaps the real models, if they exist, would defame themselves by acknowledging the similarity.

Book reviewers often inform the public of the identity of the individual who is presumably the model for a fictional character. *October Blood* by Francine du Plessix Gray was reviewed by Judith Viorst who commented that readers "may note a certain similarity between Best's guidelines for the chic and Mrs. Vreeland's edicts, urgings, and outrageous 'Why Don't You column'. . . ."[10] Uninitiated readers may never have heard of Diana Vreeland, former editor of *Vogue.* They probably are not interested. It is the story and skill of the writer that induce most people to read novels. Within the world of fashion chic, readers may recognize Vreeland. After this book review they will certainly look for similarities. Will Vreeland sue Gray? Vreeland could allege defamation, right of publicity, and right of biography. Vreeland has written her own memoirs, *DV.* Probably she could not succeed in a claim for invasion of privacy since she herself has presumably "told all." But Gray's book may cut into her sales. The author has probably taken liberties with Vreeland's life and personality to make the novel more interesting, sexy, and compelling.

Does Gray or any other author have the right to write about people in the fashion publication world? The common sense response is "Why not?" *Vogue* is not the only fashion magazine. Vreeland is not the only doyenne of this world, although she may be the best known. Should she have a monopoly on the subject? Obviously not.

Defamation suits in fiction are perhaps the natural extrapolation of the law as to biography. If the law were carried to its logical conclusion, most of contemporary life would be off-limits to novelists. This is not a fanciful projection. A brief review of cases reported in the press reveals that novelists, like journalists, are being sued with increasing frequency. Nora Ephron's amusing novel *Heartburn,* about the divorce of two "yuppies," is widely believed to be autobiographical. Her former husband, Carl Bernstein, coauthor of *All the President's Men,* sued her for libel. Bernstein is not mentioned by name in the novel. Nor is the wife identified as Ephron. The intrinsic evidence, the book itself, gives no indication that it is "of and concerning" Ephron and Bernstein. "Of and concerning" is the legal test established by the Supreme Court for plaintiffs in libel suits.

An invariable rule of evidence in all criminal and civil cases, other than libel, is that a written document constitutes the best evidence. Unless it is ambiguous on its face, the parties are not allowed to introduce extrinsic evidence as to the intent of the parties or background evidence as to the circumstances giving rise to the document. But unless evidence is presented to the jury showing that the Ephron and Bernstein divorce is similar to the divorce described in *Heartburn,* a judge or jury would have no way of concluding that the story of a husband who has an affair while his wife is pregnant is based on Bernstein. Why should such evidence be admissible in a libel action? Probably most jurors would conclude that allegations of such conduct on the part of a husband are defamatory. If a jury were to find that *Heartburn* is "of and concerning" Bernstein, then Ephron's only defense would be that fiction is truth. Without knowing the facts of the personal lives of these two well-known individuals, it is reasonable to assume that a professional writer like Ephron would not adhere closely to facts. She would undoubtedly make the characters more definitively good and bad, the incidents more outrageous and funny, in order to transform a routine divorce into an extremely amusing novel in which the jilted wife comes out ahead. This would be especially true if the novel were addressed to a female readership. By the same token, the real husband would undoubtedly be annoyed and discomfited. Again, one must ask if annoyance and discomfiture rise to the level of legal wrong that is entitled to judicial protection, particularly in the face of First Amendment rights.

Bernstein could, of course, also claim invasion of privacy. Ephron and Bernstein are not simply writers. Like Norman Mailer, they are well-known personalities who have thrust themselves into the public view. Although this book disapproves the public figure test, both Bernstein and Ephron would undoubtedly be held to be public figures. The courts would then be faced with the as yet undecided question of whether public figures have a right to privacy in the nonpublic aspects of their lives.

Bernstein is not the only disgruntled husband who has sued a novelist wife. Adrian Antoniu, a New York investment banker who pleaded guilty to insider trading charges, sued his ex-wife, Francesca Stanfill, for libel. He alleges that her novel, *Shadows and Light,* is a distorted account of their marriage. He claims that he is falsely portrayed as a "rapist and sodomist, as an embezzler, compulsive gambler and liar, as a man whose only motives for marrying . . . were to defraud . . . and enhance his social position." Again, the description of the fictional character if it applies to the Antoniu is clearly defamatory. To defend the suit, his ex-wife would have to prove that he is a sodomist.

In contrast, the court allows biographers much latitude, as evidenced in the case of *Spahn* v. *Julian Messner.* [11] In this biography of a well-known athlete, there were numerous but not defamatory inaccuracies. Spahn sued because he wanted to be presented truthfully. The court held that he could not recover. In *Koussevitzky* v. *Allen Town & Heath, Inc.,* [12] the courts held that minor inaccuracies in the portrait of the orchestra leader did not transform a biography into fiction and denied recovery.

Some cases have sensibly denied recovery when the book in question was clearly fictional. The novel *Compulsion,* based on the notorious Leopold-Loeb murder, was held to be "evidently fictional," and recovery was denied.[13] Similarly, the novel, *Anatomy of a Murder,* was held to be clearly fictional and recovery was also denied.[14] The court pointed out that although the setting of the novel and the locale of the actual trial on which it was based were the same, the plaintiff was only a minor character in the novel. The court further stated that "No average reader of the book would remember the very minor subplot in which plaintiff had a place." Plaintiff's daughter also played an inconspicuous part in the novel. Her daughter at the time of the trial was nine years old. She was a legitimate child. The character in the book was a sixteen-year-old illegitimate child. The court further declared that "suggestion is not identification." These cases antedate *Bindrim* v. *Mitchell.* Although technically the refusal of the Supreme Court to hear a case does not constitute an approval of the decision of the lower court, most lawyers conclude that when an issue is clearly important and will affect countless other cases, the inaction of the Supreme Court sends a strong message. Until *Bindrim* is overruled, it will continue to be open season for lawsuits against novelists for alleged fictional portrayals of real people.

In a case subsequent to *Bindrim* v. *Mitchell,* the highest court of New York dismissed the appeal of a young woman who sued her former boyfriend for libel based on a novel, *State of Grace.*[15] A minor character in the novel is Lisa Blake, a prosperous prostitute. Unlike the protagonist in *Touching,* however, this character closely resembled the plaintiff. They had the same first name, same height and build, same fluency in French, same Manhattan street address, same academic record, and the same liking for ski weekends. Nonetheless, the court held that the similarities were insufficient to sustain a claim in libel. The court may have been influenced by the fact that only 3,981 copies of the novel were sold, and thus it had come to the attention of only a very small number of people. Also, the plaintiff's demand of $160 million in damages was clearly preposterous.

If the major character in a book is based on a real person, there is reason to believe that the courts will follow the decision in *Bindrim* v. *Mitchell.* A statute giving a rebuttable presumption to a disclaimer of truth and a clear statement that the characters are fictional appears to be the only protection for authors of fiction, and even a disclaimer may be ignored by the courts.

Significantly, when a subject sues on the basis of copyright infringement, he or she is less likely to succeed than when the suit is based on libel. The author of a book entitled *Fort Apache,* which is about crime and police activity in the Bronx, sued the film maker of *Fort Apache, the Bronx.* The judge noted the dissimilarities in the characters of the two police officers who were the protagonists of the book and film and held that despite the similarities of the incidents, the subject was fair game for anyone.[16]

If those who claim to be the subjects of novels are really interested in their reputations rather than their pocketbooks, the wiser course is not to sue. A novel, *The Greek Tycoon,* about characters who resembled Jackie Kennedy, Maria Callas, and Ari Onassis, was published and generally ignored. Had suit been brought, the book would undoubtedly have been more successful.

When outraged or avaricious subjects do sue, trial courts are faced with protracted cases and unclear legal doctrines. There is some precedent for examining the motives of the author. In *Binns* v. *Vitagraph,* [17] in which a movie was based on an actual event and used the real name of the subject, the court allowed recovery, finding that it was "designed for selfish, commercial purposes." This use of commercial motives in libel actions is unrealistic and requires courts to plumb the mind of the author. Only writers with secure literary reputations would dare to admit that their motives for writing a book were selfish and commercial. But it is obvious that a professional novelist, like a professional lawyer or doctor, must work for money unless he or she is independently wealthy. Even writers like Judith Krantz, who have made millions on books, continue to write others and earn even more money.

Some critics of libel law as applied to fiction, like the scholars defending the First Amendment as applied to political speech, assert the usefulness of fiction. They claim that the "higher truths" of fiction should be protected. Such a standard puts courts in the inappropriate position of deciding literary merit and redeeming social importance. Others seek a new and more specific legal standard than "of and concerning." One critic suggests that "An 'of and concerning' test that inquires into the clarity with which a fictional portrait refers to the plaintiff and into the conviction that a portrait prompts in the reader seems the best way to determine whether a work of fiction resembles a factual report sufficiently to damage a plaintiff's reputation."[18] While this reads well, a trial judge would find that a jury charge based on such a definition would differ only fractionally from the present "of and concerning" test. The standard of proof might be raised to "clear and convincing evidence," but so long as the jury is permitted to hear the friends of the plaintiff testify that they instantly and unerringly identified the fictional character with the plaintiff, such a change in verbiage would be meaningless.

Some works of fiction purport to be factual but are not although they are based on real events. This is nothing new. Defoe's *Journal of the Plague Year* published in 1722 reads like a contemporary record but is a work of fiction. *Robinson Crusoe,* an enduring work of fiction, was based on the actual adventures of Alexander Selkirk. Selkirk himself told Defoe about his experiences and gave Defoe his papers. Had Selkirk sued for defamation, what should a court have done? *The Confessions of Nat Turner* by William Styron is clearly a work of fiction, but it is based on the life of a real person. Fortunately for Styron, Turner is dead and cannot sue. If a lawsuit were brought based on a right of publicity, which clearly is a property right that belongs to the estate or heirs of the subject, what should be the legal standard? As previously noted, this writer believes that the right of publicity is an undesirable legal doctrine that should be abolished. When journalists present fiction as fact, as occasionally happens, there is no defamed subject who can sue. Usually the publication in which the false report appeared prints a disclaimer. Mario Vargas Llosa, the great Latin American novelist, claims that fiction is the art of lying. He explains, ". . . in everything I've written, I began with experiences still vivid in my memory and stimulating to my imagination and then fantasized something that is an extremely unfaithful reflection of that material."[19] Vargas Llosa's first novel was burned because it allegedly slandered the Leonicio Prado Military Academy. His wife believed that she had been slandered by one of his other novels. We who are geographically and culturally removed from Vargas Llosa can see the folly of expecting literal, factual accuracy in his novels. To ask for truth in fiction is an oxymoron, a contradiction in terms. So long as the law refuses to recognize that writers of fiction, whether the product be masterpiece or potboiler, are not engaged in journalism or biography or history, then it will continue to apply inappropriate standards.

Much of the present legal difficulty arises from two causes: (1) the refusal of the law to classify types of written and spoken communication, and (2) the melding of what had hitherto been fairly well-defined types of writing—fiction and nonfiction. The mixture of fact and fiction in many types of writing and electronic media production poses new legal problems that the courts have not yet addressed.

Shall these hybrids be treated as fact or fiction, or should new legal doctrines be devised to meet the special problems they pose?

Mailer, in his sprawling book, *Armies of the Night*, gives it the subtitle, "History as a novel, the novel as history." This should put the reader on notice not to expect an accurate account of the event. It is the author's subjective impressions for which there can be no objective standards of truth or accuracy. The so-called "New Journalism"[20] also uses new and novelistic techniques, as well as borrowing from sociology, psychiatry, and economics. Does the reader have a right to expect accuracy, or simply the journalist's opinion? If so, should not the reader be put on notice?

The most prevalent form of the hybrid of fact and fiction is the docudrama. These are among the most widely viewed television programs. Any number of docudramas have given rise to lawsuits. To date, no satisfactory legal doctrine has been developed to deal with these singular and unprecedented problems. Among the many popular docudramas are *Pack of Lies* and *An Englishman Abroad*, dealing with actual British defectors. *The Falcon and the Snowman* describes two Americans who sell military secrets to the Soviets. *Concealed Enemies* takes as its subject Alger Hiss. No lawsuits have been brought because the subjects are either in the Soviet Union or have been convicted of crimes and could scarcely claim loss of reputation.* Some critics object to what they consider the unduly sympathetic treatment accorded to liars and traitors.

Unresolved legal problems implicit in docudramas arise because these dramas purport to depict fact accurately. This is manifestly impossible. Dramatists, like novelists, must shape their material simply to heighten dramatic effect and to make an essentially sordid tale interesting. Abby Mann, the writer and producer of the *Atlanta Child Murders*, claims that he "bent over backward" to give an accurate portrayal.[21] This claim of accuracy is patently impossible to sustain. No trial lasting many days can accurately be compressed into a two-hour drama. Inevitably a great deal of evidence is eliminated. The process of selection may be "fair," but it cannot claim to be accurate. Such an allegation cannot be sustained. One is reminded of Irving Younger's unsuccessful plea to the jury in the *Tavoulareas* case that every word in the allegedly libelous article was true. Reasonable fairness is the most one can expect of journalists.

Another docudrama based on an actual lawsuit, this time not a

---

*Docudramas based on crimes have been discussed in Chapter VIII.

criminal prosecution, was *Reckless Disregard*. It used the libel suit
by Dr. Carl Galloway against Dan Rather as its basis. That trial
arose out of a broadcast on "60 Minutes" in 1979 about California
medical insurance fraud. The program described nineteen separate
visits to a clinic by a suspect in a fraudulent medical claim. A bill
bearing the name of Dr. Carl Galloway was referred to. Galloway
claimed that his name was forged. He lost the suit. As of this writing,
his appeal in that libel action is pending. Much of the dialogue in
Reckless Disregard was lifted from the trial. But fictional elements
were introduced. The producer, Mark Tarlov, is reported as stating
that the film was intentionally simplified for dramatic reasons.[22] A
love interest was also added. The show purported to discuss the
difficult questions of privacy and libel, to which whole libraries of
books, including this one, have been devoted. Obviously, neither the
legal intracies nor the social and policy reasons could be adequately
explored within the time limits and the constraints of dramatic convention. Whether the producer and author intended to be "even-
handed" and fair or whether they were presenting a biased point of
view should not be determinative of the rights of the subject. For a
court to decide "fairness" on the basis of content would not only be
an almost impossible task, but it would involve the courts in a form
of censorship, with the court awarding damages to the subject if it
found the program to be unfair, but not awarding damages if the
program presented arguments pro and con. Such a rule of law would
protect neither subject nor author.

The sword that will cut the Gordion knot is specific disclosure. So
long as the docudrama is clearly labeled fiction, the public is not
misled. The real subject who has been fictionalized should have no
claim against the author for a misleading or untruthful presentation
that is labeled as fiction rather than fact.

A program presented as fiction or drama "based on a true incident" is the most that a dramatist or film producer of a docudrama
should claim to offer. As a *New York Times* editorial succinctly
declared ". . . the license to fictionalize requires giving up the license
to claim reality."[23]

As I see it, writers, even of TV docudramas, need no "license."
The First Amendment should guarantee their rights to fictionalize
and dramatize any incident so long as they do not claim to be
presenting a factually accurate report about a real incident involving
real people and do not use the names of the individuals involved or
advertise the program as being based on those persons. If the viewer

or reader notes a resemblance to a real incident, that synapse should not be the basis of legal liability.

It is claims of fidelity and accuracy that caused the difficulties in the *Westmoreland* case. How could a jury know what the true facts were when historians and the persons involved cannot agree? The "counter" program "Television's Vietnam: The Real Story" shown on public television* makes similar impossible claims. No one can ever know the "real story" about a historical event. The participants may lie in their accounts. They may honestly believe what they say but be misinformed. Their perceptions may be faulty. Every trial lawyer and trial judge can cite countless cases in which truthful, honest, unbiased witnesses identified the wrong person. These witnesses were on the scene. They saw what was happening. Their eyesight was not defective. They were honestly mistaken. Often one witness will testify that the defendant was wearing a green shirt. Another will say he was wearing a blue shirt. The witnesses are not colorblind. The color of the shirt may be irrelevant to the case. Unswerving accuracy about simple matters is difficult to obtain. It is infinitely more difficult in complicated matters such as the Vietnam War. A program rushed to production to refute another program would be well advised not to claim truth, reality, or accuracy, but merely a point of view based on available evidence.

Even scholarly historians with no ostensible political biases disagree. Thomas Jefferson, safely dead for a century and a half, has been the subject of countless biographies. Many disagree in their interpretations. Readers must exercise their own judgment. Does one believe Dumas Malone or Fawn Brodie with respect to Jefferson's relationship with a female slave? Both claim documented truth. If subjects are alive and litigious, it is well for authors and commentators to moderate their claims of truth and accuracy.

Humor presents more difficult problems of proof. What strikes one person as hilarious often fails to strike another as being at all funny. Queen Victoria is reported to have said, "We are not amused" upon seeing an imitation of herself by the Honourable Alexander Grantham Yorke, Groom-in-Waiting to the Queen.

Everyone knows how difficult it is to "catch a joke" in a foreign

---

*The influence of government on programming of public television is beyond the scope of this book. Needless to say serious dangers to free expression are implicit. Private commercial advertising intruding into the performance of such quasi-public events as the Metropolitan Opera and the Fourth of July celebration of the centennial of the Statue of Liberty also raise issues that should be addressed by legal and social policymakers before they ripen into litigable issues.

language even when the hearer is reasonably fluent in the language. American readers of *Punch* and English readers of the *New Yorker* often find themselves agreeing with Winston Churchill that these two nations are divided by a common language.

The most likely subjects for parody are obviously stuffy, self-righteous individuals. The joke is the incongruity between the character of the real person and what he or she is depicted as doing by the author or cartoonist. One cannot parody an unknown or obscure individual unless it is a stock figure such as cartoonist's Helen Hokinson's clubwoman or Pete Arno's grouchy capitalist in his wealthy club. Unlike fiction and drama that can be enjoyed as works of imagination without knowing the identity of the person on whom the novel or drama was based, the identity of the individual is crucial to parody. The popularity of libel suits in the 1980s and the large verdicts awarded, as well as the confusion of legal doctrine, have resulted in some unfortunate decisions. The Reverend Jerry Falwell sued *Penthouse* magazine for libel on the basis of a parody depicting Falwell as an incestuous drunkard. Falwell claimed he had been besmirched and so had the memory of his dead mother. The judge dismissed the privacy claim. The jury held for the defendant on the libel claim but awarded $200,000 damages for "intentional infliction of emotional distress" and the Court of Appeals affirmed.[24] Usually an award for emotional distress is part of the damages when the defendant has been found responsible for a substantive wrong such as negligence, products liability, or invasion of privacy. An award of damages without a basis of substantive wrongdoing is anomalous. Hurt feelings do not usually constitute a grounds for liability.

Humor that does not strike the subject as funny has given rise to a number of lawsuits. The showing of a movie, *John Goldfarb, Please Come Home*, which used the name of Notre Dame University, was permanently enjoined as was circulation of the book on the grounds that it capitalized on the name and property rights of the university.[25] The opinion does not refer to *New York Times* v. *Sullivan*. Whether such a sweeping order could stand today is questionable. The obviously humorous elements of the film were given little consideration.

Humor is a characteristic of American life. The Gridiron Banquets in which the press ridicules important public figures is an annual event in Washington. Despite the rather merciless barbs, skits, and songs, to date there are no reported libel suits based on the Gridiron entertainment. But many libel suits have been brought on the basis of humorous writings and cartoons.

In the 1980s, a spate of lawsuits arising out of parody or satire have been instituted. In Vermont,[26] a proposal to use treated effluent for snowmaking prompted bumper stickers reading: "Killington: Where the Affluent Meet the Effluent." Killington sued the Barre-Montpelier *Times Angus* newspaper over a cartoon showing skiers carrying toilet plungers. The caption read, "Looks like the snowmaking machines are clogged again."

L.L. Bean, Inc., the Maine store that sells sporting goods by mail order catalogue, sued *High Society,* a magazine that bills itself as "American's Hottest Sex Magazine." *High Society* printed a parody of the L.L. Bean catalogue featuring the "L.L. Bean's Back-to-School Sex Catalog."[27] The format closely resembled that of the Bean catalogue. It featured among other items a "Swiss Army Knife and Pocket Dildo" and a "Tartan Jock Strap." L.L. Bean was not amused, although others may well have found the parody funny.

Trademarks have long been a subject of litigation. The law is reasonably clear that a business may not simulate a competitor's logo or name and get a free ride on a well-known name or design. Parody, however, is different. *High Society* magazine is not a competitor of L.L. Bean. If anything, it is giving L.L. Bean free publicity rather than taking its business away. The distasteful nature of the parody, being sexually explicit, should not, however, influence legal conclusions although it clearly looms large in the thinking of the subject who is parodied. L.L. Bean took no action against a "clean" parody, *Items from Our Catalog,* that unmistakably poked fun at the Bean catalog.

A number of other suits have been filed. At this writing none has been decided. Pulitzer prize-winning cartoonist, Tony Auth, reports that in 1986 eight libel suits against him were pending. Paul Szep, the award-winning *Boston Globe* cartoonist, was a defendant in a $3.6 million libel suit brought by former Massachusetts Governor Edward King. A Massachusetts court awarded a summary judgment on all counts in favor of the newspaper. Former Philadelphia Mayor Frank Rizzo is suing Rob Lawlor, formerly of the *Philadelphia Daily News.* Mr. Rizzo alleges that a Lawlor cartoon caused him "severe emotional distress and mental anguish." Milt Priggee of the *Dayton* [Ohio] *Journal Herald* is being sued for $12 million. The suit was filed by James Celebrezze, a former justice of the Ohio Supreme Court, over a cartoon satirizing a dispute with the Ohio Bar Association. The drawing shows a bunch of gunmen in a car labeled "Celebrezze" riddling the bar group with bullets. According to the *Wall Street Journal,*[28] Priggee maintains the cartoon wasn't aimed at James Celebrezze at all; the cartoon involved his brother, Frank

Celebrezze, the current Chief Justice of the Ohio Supreme Court, who isn't suing Mr. Priggee.

The legal doctrines on which a subject predicates a lawsuit against the author of a parody or cartoon are invasion of privacy, libel, right of publicity, and the anomalous novel theory—intentional infliction of emotional distress. Whether or not courts adopt the public/private figure dichotomy or look to older law on privacy, it is clear that only well-known individuals and institutions are the subject of this type of humor. Jane Doe and Richard Roe, whatever their real names, are essentially anonymous. Jokes about them would be pointless unless they were used as prototypical characters, in which case, the allegedly offensive material would not be "of and concerning" that individual. Widespread public recognition of the character of institutions and individuals is the basis of parodies and cartoons. Clearly any name that is sufficiently well known to be instantly recognizable has lost whatever privacy the institution or person may have had.

Books that mingle real people with fantastic episodes, like Heller's *Good as Gold* and Coover's *The Public Burning* depend on the fact that readers will know the identity and public persona of the individuals depicted in fantastic and ridiculous ways.

The nature of parody is to hold a person up to ridicule. That is also the test of libel. But for more than two centuries, truth has been a defense to libel. The obverse of the defense should be that the libel must purport to be true. No reasonable person could believe that the statement in *Hustler* magazine that Jerry Falwell had sex with his mother and a goat was intended to be true. Accordingly, it should not be deemed to be libelous.

Are parodies and cartoons intended to inflict emotional distress? I believe they are. The purpose of this kind of humor is to prick bubbles of conceit, arrogance, and self-righteousness in an amusing way. The old Chinese proverb, "one picture is worth a thousand words," underlies all cartoons. They are a shorthand expression of a more complicated idea. The punch of a cartoon depends upon the viewer's tacit recognition of the elements in the cartoon without verbal explanation.

In the case of *Girl Scouts of the United States* v. *Personality Posters Mfg. Co.,*[29] the Court refused to enjoin distribution of a poster showing a pregnant girl wearing a Girl Scout uniform with her hands clasped over her large abdomen. Beside her is the Girl Scout motto, "Be Prepared." The Court properly held that this was "satirical expression" and protected by the First Amendment. No reasonable person would conclude that the picture of the pregnant girl was that of a real Girl Scout or that the Girl Scouts as an organization advocated or condoned teenage pregnancy. The humor, if any, depended on viewer recognition of the Girl Scout uniform and slogan.

It is proposed that the legal test for libel in humor be: Does the cartoon or parody purport to be a true statement with respect to the individual or institution depicted?" This test is easily understood and can be readily applied by courts and juries. The best and only evidence needed would be the document itself. Such cases could be tried fairly and expeditiously. "Actual malice," truth, public/private figure tests, and other complicated legal doctrines would be irrelevant. If such literature or pictures purported to be truthful statements about an individual and if untrue were defamatory, then the law should protect the subject. But if the clear purport is not a statement of fact but satiric, ironic, or humorous comment, then the subject has not been defamed. Satire, parody, cartoons, and all forms of humorous expression, whether verbal or visual, are entitled to First Amendment protections. The fact that feelings are hurt, as in the case of Jerry Falwell, should be irrelevant to the right of free expression. As has previously been pointed out, persons in the limelight should not expect the law to protect their bruised egos.

The award of damages for emotional distress was designed to compensate adequately those who had been injured by the fault of another when damages for out-of-pocket expenses and loss of earnings are inadequate to to cover the harm done—a girl whose face is scarred as a result of an accident, a man who is lamed by defective machinery, and a mother who sees her child killed by a drunk driver have all been harmed. The girl and the man may not have lost any earning capacity, but the scar and the limp cause emotional distress that should be compensated by the wrongdoer. Emotional harm to the plaintiff that does not result from some fault on the part of the defendant is not compensable under principles of tort law. If the parody or satire is not false and defamatory, there should be no recovery even though the plaintiff's feelings were hurt.

The Last Hurrah, a novel by Frank Connor, contained a scathing portrait of an Irish Catholic Democratic political figure. The book was set in Boston. It was lively, amusing, perceptive, and popular. Most readers assumed that the model for the protagonist or antihero was the late Mayor Curley of Boston. David Lawrence, a contemporary of Curley, was also a powerful Irish Catholic Democratic politician. He had been mayor of Pittsburgh and later governor of Pennsylvania. Many ward heelers in Pittsburgh thought the book was about David Lawrence. It is of some significance that these politicos did not find the portrait offensive. Had they been asked the question posed to witnesses in defamation cases, "Would you want to associate with a person who behaved like the character described?" their answers would have been resoundingly "yes."

This incident also reveals the flimsy basis for the conclusion that a person's reputation has been damaged from fiction or satire or that he or she has been held up to contumely.

Libel and obscenity should not be confused. Falwell is reported to have sued *Hustler* in order to "punish" the magazine. Despite what Falwell may see as his role in society, under the law he has no higher standing than John Doe. Prosecution for obscenity and actions to enjoin the distribution of obscene materials are the duty of the state not the individual citizen, just as prosecution for any other crime must be undertaken by the government not the victim of the alleged crime.

If one examines the law of defamation, not in connection with *Hustler, Touching,* or other contemporary publications, but as it would apply to recognized works of fiction and satire, appropriate legal principles are more easily discerned. The character of "stinking Lizavetta" in the *Brothers Karamazov* by Dostoyevsky is a poor, ignorant, dirty creature. Perhaps there was a real person named Galena on whom Dostoyevsky patterned Lizavetta who was part of a household he visited from time to time. He may have actually been acquainted with her. Her friends and family, if literate, recognized her as the prototype of this fictional character. She could prove by them that the character of Lizavetta was "of and concerning" her. Would Dostoyevsky then have to prove that she was in fact "stinking" in order to avoid a substantial damage verdict? Making her stinking was clearly a literary device to heighten contrasts and to make more vivid a fictional presentation. Should her recovery and Dostoyevsky's liability turn on proof of whether she was in fact clean or "stinking"?

Mr. Gradgrind is the prototypically stupid, venal, brutal schoolmaster. Doubtless Dickens had visited or heard of some English boarding school in which conditions were horrible. There were many such institutions at the time. Indeed, it was the verisimilitude of Dickens's descriptions as well as the tear-jerking pathos of his stories that contributed to his popular success. In today's litigious climate it takes little imagination to posit a lawsuit by a schoolmaster, let us call him Smythe, who would claim that he had been defamed. It would not be difficult for such a plaintiff to find a number of friends to testify that on reading the book they recognized Gradgrind as being "of and concerning" Smythe. Smythe would assert that the portrait was false; he did not beat the boys or starve them. If Dickens had actually visited the plaintiff's school, a verdict against Dickens would be almost inevitable under the state of libel law in the United States. A description of one boarding school is much like that of another. An author wishing to show the evils of the school naturally exaggerates. Similarly, one wishing to show the stupidity of nude therapy by means of fiction would also exaggerate.

With respect to both serious and humorous fiction, it must be remembered that all authors will consciously or unconsciously base their characters on real people. The principal character may indeed be the author. Flaubert declared, "Emma Bovary, c'est moi." In other books the characters are derived from real people not overtly identified by the author. Perhaps the law should adopt another caveat, "Let the friend of a writer beware."

This danger of seeing one's self in the fiction of a friend or acquaintance was amusingly described by David Lodge. He depicts Desiree, a female writer, and Ronald, a male author, both married to other persons, going to bed together. This dialogue ensues; Desiree to Ronald:

"I was thinking."
"It occurred to me . . ."
"Sorry."
"Sorry."
"What were you going to say?"
"No, please . . . you first."
"I was going to say," says Desiree, in the darkness, "that before we go any further, perhaps we ought to come to an understanding."
"Yes!," says Ronald eagerly, then changes his intonation to the interrogative, "Yes?"
"What I mean is . . ." Desiree stops. "It's difficult to say without sounding as if I don't trust you."
"It's only natural," says Ronald. "I feel the same."
"You mean, you don't trust me?"
"I mean there's something I might say to you which might imply that I didn't trust you."
"What is it?"
"It's . . . it's hard to say."
"I mean," says Desiree, "I've never done it with a writer before."
"Exactly!"
"And what I'm trying to say is . . ."

"That you don't want to read about it in a novel one of these days? Or see it on television?"

"How did you guess?"

"I had the same thought."

Desiree claps her hands. "So we can agree that neither of us will use this material? Whether its good or bad?"

"Absolutely. Scout's honour."

"Then let's fuck, Ronald," says Desiree, rolling on top of him.[30]

It is likely, despite these vows, that two years later Ronald will read a romance by Desiree with a caddish character named Robert, who he recognizes bears a similarity to himself. And Desiree will read a farce by Ronald in which she recognizes with dismay a bossy female novelist named Daphne.

Both rush to court. They do not claim breach of contract but defamation.* I suggest that since both works were clearly labeled fiction that the judge should enter summary judgment for both defendants.

---

*If these hypothetical authors should sue for breach of contract, it is clear that they had entered into a valid, binding agreement. The promise of each constituted consideration for the promise of the other. Since both had breached the contract, that count would be dismissed. If only one had breached the oral contract, the measure of damages would be the profits made on the book.

·XI·

Economic Interests and
the First Amendment

*A man must serve his time to every trade
Save censure—critics are all ready made.*

—LORD BYRON

COUNT BAZAROV in Turgenev's *Fathers and Sons* declared, "I agree with no man's opinions; I have some of my own." Most of us have opinions about people, goods, events, and ideas. When airing these views the last thing we expect is to be served with a complaint in libel. Most non-lawyers assume that defamation refers to a scurrilous, false statement about an individual and that, except for such remarks, they are free to express their opinions about any subject. If they think that an employee or colleague is lazy or incompetent, if they believe the products they have purchased are substandard, if they conclude sadly that their doctors or lawyers are less than able, most Americans believe they have a right to say so. After all, this is a free country, isn't it? The First Amendment is supposed to protect everyone's right of free expression.

Lawyers and judges who read decisions in libel cases must conclude that this belief in the free-wheeling right of expression of opinion is misplaced. This chapter discusses the extension of First Amendment rights to what are essentially commercial transactions and the correlative limitation on freedom to criticize. Although there is a broad spectrum of fact situations to which the courts have recently extended the concept of defamation, the four principal areas involve product disparagement, advertising, employment, and the sale of information.

The unprecedented expansion of defamation to commercial interests can be traced again to the equation of money and freedom of expression. This is most apparent in the election law cases. Congress attempted to make the electoral process more open and democratic by limiting the amount of money that can be expended by candidates for federal office. The need to curb the trend toward an elected oligarchy is clear. In 1984, the forty-three newly elected members of Congress had an average minimum reported wealth of $252,292. One-third were millionaires.[1] The Supreme Court held that restrictions on the amount of money that could be spent in election campaigns violated First Amendment rights.[2] Whether the legislation was wise or practical is a debatable question. But confusing freedom of expression with the issue of access to the media through the expenditure of money creates conceptual problems. The recognition that money is often required in order to reach an audience does not logically impel the conclusion that such expenditures must be protected under the rubric of freedom of expression. The freedom of expression of those who do not have equal access to funds is inevitably curtailed by the preferment of those who do.

Cases involving essentially commercial relationships to which First Amendment doctrine has been applied have often led to suppression of criticism, thereby protecting those being criticized. But the courts have not engaged in an analysis of the competing rights of subject and critic. As a result, manufacturers sue critics of their products, students sue professors, professors sue their colleagues and universities, customers sue purveyors of erroneous information, and government censors advertising. In all these situations, what is really at stake is the financial or economic interests of the parties. But the courts are mired in applying the difficult doctrines enunciated in *New York Times* v. *Sullivan* and its progeny because one or both parties raise the tattered banner of the First Amendment.

Whether one accepts the instrumental approach to the First Amendment advocated by such civil libertarians as Professors Thomas I. Emerson and Zachariah Chafee or the absolutist approach of Justices Black and Douglas,[3] it seems clear to most people that these cases do not involve the issues of self-governance, criticism of government, access to information, and freedom from the heavy hand of the censor—the First Amendment issues that American courts have wrestled with for two centuries. In the many cases that do involve freedom of expression, the Supreme Court has recently disparaged the claims and defenses of those who seek the protection

of First Amendment rights because of the imputed commercial motives of the authors in question. In this curious *Alice in Wonderland*
world of law, publication of excerpts of Gerald Ford's memoirs is
denigrated because of the assumed commercial motives of the author.[4] But overt advertising of products has been held to be protected
speech.[5] The recent cases involving commercial interests, relying on
New York Times v. *Sullivan*, repudiate long-standing precedent denying First Amendment rights to commercial speech—the distinction previously made by the Supreme Court between "talk for profit
and talk for other purposes."[6]

A number of lower court cases have attempted to limit the test of
commercialism when dealing with expression of ideas, literature, and
entertainment. As one court wisely observed, "Everything that appears in a magazine is placed with the intention of increasing sales."[7]
But it also pointed out that if commercial use is so broadly construed
it would intrude upon important constitutional freedoms. Conversely, if the First Amendment is so broadly construed as to cover
every disparagement of parties or products in commercial transactions, the essential purposes of freedom of expression are lost in a
welter of cases involving monetary interests that can adequately and
fairly be protected under commercial law.

Injurious falsehood or trade disparagement is a tort well recognized in the law. It consists of the publication of matter derogatory
to the plaintiff's title to property or to the plaintiff's business and
products of a kind calculated to interfere with plaintiff's relations
with others. To prevail in such an action plaintiff must prove: (1) a
false statement communicated to others, (2) that such statement
induced others not to trade or deal with plaintiff, and (3) the pecuniary losses resulting therefrom.[8] This is the rule that prevails in all tort
actions, namely that the plaintiff must prove a wrongful act on the
part of the defendant, a causal relationship, and harm suffered. In
trade disparagement cases, plaintiff is required to prove that the
statement was false by objectively verifiable standards. If it was
simply an opinion, there could be no recovery. This particular aspect
of the law of torts was not troublesome. Lawyers knew the rules and
advised their clients accordingly.

In 1984, this settled law was radically changed by the Supreme
Court in the case of *Bose* v. *Consumers Union*.[9] The difficult doctrines of libel law and First Amendment rights were held to be
applicable to what was at best a case of trade disparagement and,
under a more cautious reading, an expression of opinion for which

no liability should attach. Plaintiff alleged that it had been libeled. One must wonder if the case had been brought under the rubric of trade disparagement whether the courts would have become involved in these complicated questions.

The action arose out of an item in *Consumer Reports* evaluating loudspeakers. The allegedly libelous statements are as follows:

> Worse, individual instruments heard through the Bose system seemed to grow to gigantic proportions and tended to wander about the room. For instance, a violin appeared to be 10 feet wide and a piano stretched from wall to wall. With orchestral music, such effects seemed inconsequential. But we think they might become annoying when listening to soloists.

After stating opinions concerning the overall sound quality, the article concluded:

> We think the Bose system is so unusual that a prospective buyer must listen to it and judge it for himself. We would suggest delaying so big an investment until you were sure the system would please you after the novelty value had worn off.

The trial judge denied defendant's motion for summary judgment.

Consumer's Union is one of several well-known organizations that rate products. It should be obvious that there are legitimate differences of opinion about most products. Is Coca Cola better than Pepsi Cola? Is a Ford safer than a Chevrolet? Is a Zenith television better than a Sony? Does the Philadelphia Orchestra have a better sound than the Chicago Symphony? Is Robert Redford a better actor than Dustin Hoffman? The committees that award Emmys, Obies, and Oscars disagree among themselves. The media critics disagree with the committees. And the public makes its own choices. Had this case come before me, I would have granted the motion for summary judgment following the oft-repeated ruling of the Supreme Court that there is no such thing as a false opinion, a statement that was again repeated by the majority in the *Bose* decision.

Many difficult cases could be easily resolved if courts adopted E. B. White's definition of the word, "fact": "Use this word only of matters capable of verification, not matters of judgment. That a particular event happened on a given date, that lead melts at a certain temperature are facts. But such conclusions as that Napoleon was the greatest of modern generals or that the climate of California is delightful, however defensible they may be, are not properly called facts."

This definition was obviously not controlling in the *Bose* case. Following a nineteen-day trial, the judge entered an order in favor of the plaintiff, finding that the statement that the sound tended to or seemed to wander along the wall was false, that it was disparaging, and that the defendant published it with "actual malice." The trial court found that plaintiff was a "public figure." Is every manufacturer of a well-known product a public figure? If so, the only manufacturers who can be deemed private figures are those that are unsuccessful. Plaintiff was awarded $115,296.00 plus interest for eleven years. The court of appeals reviewing the record found there was no "actual malice." The Supreme Court affirmed on the ground that in First Amendment cases appellate courts "must exercise independent judgment and determine whether the record establishes actual malice with convincing clarity."

Justice White dissented on the ground that the court of appeals erred in reviewing the record "de novo," that is deciding for itself on the basis of the record rather than confining its review to whether the trial judge was "clearly erroneous." Justices Rehnquist and O'-Connor also dissented on the issue of standard of review. All nine justices apparently agreed that an allegation of trade disparagement should be tried under the same rules and principles as libel cases against the news media and other authors and that manufacturers of goods are public figures.

Consumers Union was ultimately relieved of liability, but the doctrine established in this case will haunt the courts for years. One is reminded of T.S. Eliot's famous apothegm:

> This is the final treason,
> To do the right thing for the wrong reason.

The difference between sound wandering "along the wall" or wandering "about the room" is vague at best. Acoustics is not an exact science. If it were, there would not be so many unsatisfactory concert halls and theaters. Even among the cognoscenti, there are differences of opinion as to whether sound is dull or clear, whether or not there are dead spots, and whether the string and the wind sections of an orchestra are properly balanced.

I believe the decision is wrong because the report is an expression of opinion as to which there can be legitimate differences. I believe it is also wrong because in trade disparagement and other commercial cases, First Amendment freedoms are not at issue and the standard of "actual malice" is inappropriate. It is also wrong because under this doctrine plaintiff does not have to prove damages. There was no evidence that Bose lost any customers because of the report. Any award of damages would be based on rank speculation.

Let us examine a hypothetical case that involves an actual misstatement of fact, like the erroneous statement that the mayor had a criminal record—a discrete, verifiable fact that is either true or false. Assume that Consumers Union published a report that the brakes on a particular automobile would not stop a vehicle going at 50 m.p.h. within 500 feet. E. B. White would consider this a statement of fact. It can be verified by testing. The tests can be replicated. It does not depend on the individual perceptions of the tester. Assume that the statement was erroneous and that it could be proved that as a result of the report potential purchasers did not buy this particular vehicle. Assume also that Consumers Union had hired a new, unskilled person to make the test and failed to supervise the work. Why should a commercial company engaged in supplying information not be responsible if the information is erroneous and the plaintiff is harmed as a result of the error? The "actual malice" of the commercial company is irrelevant. In my view, companies in the business of supplying information warrant its accuracy and should be held to a high standard of responsibility. But when they proffer opinions, there should be no liability.

Rating of products is usually an expression of opinion even when those who publish the opinions claim some expertise. Jurors are always instructed that the testimony of expert witnesses must not be accepted as a fact but treated as an opinion that they may accept or disregard. The weight to be accorded an expert opinion depends upon the training and experience of the expert, his or her care and skill in making the tests and observations on which the opinion is based, and the expert's credibility. Companies that publish such ratings do not usually disclose the identity or expertise of those who actually make the tests and evaluations. The readers can accept or reject these ratings and make their decisions based on their own observations, the opinions of friends and acquaintances, the persuasiveness of the seller, the price, or any reasons, or simply a hunch. There can be no warranty of accuracy as to an opinion.

It is an everyday fact of life that competitors producing similar products assert that their own goods or services are better than those of their rivals. Every product advertised—from pain relievers to fried chicken—is claimed to be better than its competitors. If all these companies sued for libel, the courts would be so overloaded with cases that they would grind to a halt. For years courts dismissed criticisms of businesses, products, and performances as expressions of opinion. When a restaurant owner sued a guidebook to New York restaurants for giving his establishment a bad review, he won a $20,000 verdict in compensatory damages and $5 in punitive damages. But this was overturned by the court of appeals.[10] The court held that, with the exception of one item, the allegedly libelous statements were expressions of opinion not fact. Among these statements were that the "dumplings, on our visit, resembled bad ravioli . . . chicken with chili was rubbery and the rice . . . totally insipid. . . ." Obviously, it would be impossible to prove the nature of the food served at that particular meal. What is tender to one palate may be rubbery to another. The one misstatement of fact, that the Peking duck ·was served in one dish instead of three, was in my opinion, a minor and insignificant part of the entire review. Had the review of the restaurant been considered as a whole (the law in obscenity cases), this small misstatement of fact would have been treated as de minimis. That is a well-established doctrine requiring that minor matters not be considered by the courts. In this case, the court held that the restaurant was a public figure and had failed to prove actual malice. Without discussion, the definition of public figure was expanded to include almost every business that serves the public. This is another example of the unsatisfactory nature of the distinction between public and private figures. This decision antedates *Bose* v. *Consumers Union.*

Americans expect critics to be vigorous, indeed vituperative. A famous example of terse, devastating criticism is Dorothy Parker's review of *I Am a Camera.* She wrote, "No leica." George V. Higgins in reviewing the NBC film, *Peter the Great*, in the *Wall Street Journal* called it an "assault on reason." He concluded, "But pity above all the soul of poor Peter: If he didn't go to hell 260 years ago for all his murders and sins, this is punishment enough." One can imagine the chaos that would ensue if criticism were subject to libel law. No one would dare to review a book, a play, an opera, a concert, or a movie. Intellectual discussion of the arts would have to take place behind closed doors, with only intimate friends and after a careful sweep for listening devices. Scientific discussion would be fraught with danger. The land of the free and the home of the brave would be an enormous silent gulag patrolled not by government agents but by private persons, potential libel plaintiffs. This horrifying scenario is not an imaginary fancy. It is a logical extrapolation from the *Bose* decision.

That case was tried without a jury. After reading the multiple opinions of the Supreme Court, I wonder how I shall try similar trade libel cases when one of the parties demands a jury trial. The best evidence would be the machine itself. The trial judge in *Bose* relied principally on the testimony of experts, particularly the one who tested the speakers. In contrast, when a book is alleged to be obscene or libelous, the judge and jury read the book. Although they also hear experts who give opinion testimony, the triers of fact ultimately rely on their own judgment of the book. Should a judge who may have a tin ear listen to the speaker and decide? Should a jury listen to a series of records played through the speaker in question? Or perhaps the same records played through a different speaker? If a jury is to decide such a case, what should its composition be?

The problems of jury selection in trade libel cases will be formidable. In federal courts judges customarily conduct voir dire (questioning of prospective jurors). In most state courts counsel question prospective jurors extensively. I favor the state practice. Careful questioning often reveals disabilities of panelists, such as stupidity and prejudice, that are not disclosed by simple yes or no responses to a set series of questions asked by the judge. In a case like *Bose* involving phonograph equipment, the plaintiff might want lovers of Mozart on the jury. The defendant might prefer rock afficionados. Should the court permit inquiry on voir dire as to the musical sophistication of prospective jurors and the kinds of recording devices they have? I can foresee that plaintiff's counsel would strike all jurors who don't know a tweeter from a woofer and defendant's counsel would strike all musicians. If the judge limited voir dire, the jury would decide, as they do in many cases, on the basis of expert testimony. Very few truthful experts could give an opinion with reasonable scientific certainty. It would be similar to asking a jury to decide whether a piece of sculpture by Brancusi is a work of art. In the 1920s, customs inspectors imposed duty on Brancusi's *Bird in Flight* on the value of the metal. They concluded that it was not a work of art. Art is duty-free regardless of the value of the materials of which it is composed.

If the restaurant case had gone to trial before a jury, would the jurors be permitted to have a meal in the restaurant? In land damage

cases, juries actually go and view the premises and decide for themselves the value of the property even though they hear the testimony
of experts.

A legal doctrine following the sound distinction between fact and
opinion would obviate these absurd legal issues. Investors, actors,
playwrights, and a host of people involved in the production of a
dramatic performance lose a great deal of money as a result of an
unfavorable review. But should the reviewer be required to pay
damages because he or she wrote an unfavorable, or even spiteful
review? If, as the Supreme Court has repeatedly declared, the First
Amendment gives breathing space to expression, certainly an expression of opinion as to merit, value, or competence, no matter how
misguided, should be protected. It must be remembered that what
is heresy in one generation often becomes orthodox wisdom in the
next. When courts adopt theory as fact, the results are often undesirable and appear shocking to later generations. A signal example is
the widely prevalent belief at the turn of the century that mental
defectiveness was hereditary. Accordingly, the Supreme Court
upheld the legality of compulsory sterilization of weak-minded
women.[11]

Nonetheless, trial courts are now bound to deal with opinions as
if they were facts. In trade disparagement cases and a host of other
commercial matters when claims of First Amendment rights are
asserted, courts will have to decide truth or falsity as well as applying
the complicated rules and standards developed in the media cases in
order to protect freedom of the press. Confronted with such litigation, I feel that I have been cast in the improbable role of a Don
Quixote when I am really a Sancho Panza. I know that the lusty
wench, Dulcinea, is not a damsel in distress. Bose Corporation and
the plaintiffs who appear before me complaining of inaccurate bank
and credit reports are not suing because their honor has been besmirched, but because they have lost sales and profits. The defendants and other commercial institutions are not embattled fighters for
freedom of the press. They are businesses that wish to recover lost
profits and to avoid liability for their errors. I know that my spavined
bench is not a noble steed carrying me to defend the ramparts of the
Bill of Rights. But these are the doctrines and rules under which a
wide variety of commercial cases will now have to be tried and
decided.

For centuries under Anglo-American law, a plaintiff's right to
recover even for the grossest injury depended upon the use of the

right words. If a party mistakenly filed the wrong writ, no matter how meritorious the claims or defenses, that party could not prevail. A writ of scire facias instead of writ of fieri facias would put the hapless plaintiff out of court.* The rise of equity in the fifteenth century was an attempt to mitigate the rigidity of the law and to promote a just result. Faced with the intransigence of the King's Bench Court, equity, a second system of courts, was established so that the chancellor could ignore harsh and anachronistic legal rules. New axioms were used to promote a more just result. *Cessante ratione, cessante lex.* When the reason ceases the law ceases. Equity will presume that what should have been done was done. Many doctrines such as clean hands were devised to prevent a wrongdoer from recovering despite a valid legal claim. All these developments were necessary to bring the law into conformity with perceptions of justice.

In the early twentieth century under federal law and the laws of most states, equity and law were merged. Simplified code pleading was adopted. The plaintiff had only to state the facts on which the claim was based and the relief requested. The defendant could raise preliminary objections or file an answer. The substance rather than the form of the documents was deemed to be of paramount importance. It was expected that judges would be freed from technical restrictions and could rule upon the facts as they were proved in court. To a great extent these hopes of the legal reformers were realized. But these sensible measures have failed to bring libel into conformity with general concepts of law and fairness. Courts continue to ignore the substance of the claim and deal with the form of the complaint. Judges must now decide whether the manufacturer of a warped wicket is a public or private figure or a limited public figure. They must also determine whether a business corporation that released erroneous information should be held to a standard of actual malice or some other degree of fault, the degree of proof, and all the other complicated, ill-defined requirements established to guard freedom of the press.

Any individual, corporation, or association can bring a complaint in libel against any party no matter what that defendant's occupation or enterprise may be. The range of such legal actions is apparently limitless.

---

*Fieri facias is a writ of execution on the goods of a judgment debtor, whereas scire facias is a writ of execution after a levy has been made but the judgment has not been paid.

Employment rights provide a fertile source of libel cases. Such litigation involves a confusion of property interests and free expression. In these cases, the job applicants and seekers of job advancement sue for libel. They name as defendants the institutions and the individuals they believe are responsible for denying them the positions or preferment they sought. Any individual or institution hiring an employee, whether the task to be performed is monitoring nuclear weapons or mopping floors, seeks references. When a job applicant is not hired or an employee is not promoted, the disappointed individual may well conclude that he or she has been defamed by the references. Disappointment becomes disgruntlement and escalates to outrage and then to litigation. These libel plaintiffs usually target wealthy corporations and institutions as defendants. Their actions are based on allegedly defamatory statements that they claim injured their trade, commercial, or professional interests.

Academic squabbles give rise to many such libel suits. A typical case was brought by a professor who was denied tenure. He sued the university and the faculty committee.[12] As part of the pretrial proceedings, the plaintiff sought discovery of his files. Under a California statute[13] providing that letters of reference are private and may not be disclosed, the request was denied.*

Another California case[14] involved a feud between two faculty members. One sued the other for libel and joined the university as a defendant. Plaintiff was obviously seeking a deep pocket defendant. He demanded all the files of the defendant faculty member as well as his own file. The university resisted producing these files, claiming that release of such information would destroy collegiality. Certainly if faculty members who must vote on granting promotions and tenure thought that their reports and discussions would be made public or shown to the subject, there could not be free and frank discussion of teaching abilities, moral character, and scholarly attainments. Such chilling of expression of opinion would not only destroy collegiality, which is often breached in other contexts, but would certainly lead to a lowering of academic standards. The ultimate losers would not be the faculty and trustees, but the students, who would have inferior teachers, and the public, who would have a less well-educated citizenry and cadre of professionals.

Many significant intra-academic and intra-corporate disputes arise

---

*Compare shield laws designed to protect reporters' rights to confidentiality. Despite such laws it is not uncommon for reporters to be jailed for protecting their sources while persons accused of crime are free on bail.

out of whistle blowing by students and colleagues who discover that their superiors are misusing funds, engaging in dishonest or sloppy research, or failing to report errors. Professor Alan Westin has compiled numerous horrifying case histories of such whistle blowers, the substantial errors they uncovered, and the reprisals taken against them.[15] Not only did they lose their jobs and standing, many also found themselves defendants in libel suits.

The number of libel cases brought against critics of government, corporate, and academic employees and officials increases year by year. Libel lawyer Bruce Sanford estimates that probably a thousand such suits brought by disgruntled public officials and corporate executives were pending in 1985. There is no limit to the categories of disappointed persons who sue for libel. Judicial aspirants found to be "not qualified" by bar associations have brought libel suits.[16] Lawyers who objected to press comments about the quality of their legal arguments have sued for libel.[17] A doctor sued his colleagues for defamation when they expressed a lack of confidence in him.[18] An employee who was fired for not being "cooperative" sued for libel, and the court found that the statement was capable of a defamatory meaning.[19]

As a result of these suits, corporations and individuals are increasingly reluctant to give information to prospective employers. Even failure to give information may result in a suit for defamation. As one lawyer commented, companies asked for references must walk an "ultra-thin line" to avoid suits for defamation by former employees and prospective employees who, when denied jobs, obtain through discovery statements as to why they were not hired. Some discharges are unjust and motivated by spite, jealousy, or ill will. These people have rights that should be adjudicated. But the gravamen of their complaints should be denial of due process, not libel. Many courts sensibly refuse to hear these cases and grant summary judgment for the defendants.[20] Whether they can continue to do this under present legal doctrine is dubious.

The fact is that many universities and admission boards do not have fair procedures for hearing complaints. A case before me revealed the muddled thinking, high-handed actions, and yielding to public pressure characterizing much institutional behavior that gives rise to litigation. In that case,* a fraternity was put off campus on charges of a "gang rape." The district attorney and local police

---

*This case was settled and, therefore, not reported.

investigated the incident and concluded that there was insufficient evidence to prosecute for rape, indecent assault, or any other crime. Meanwhile, pressure from students, alumni, faculty, and women's organizations mounted. The university authorities felt impelled to do something. An ad hoc committee was convened to hear charges against the individuals and the fraternity.

The university had a legal staff. The fraternity and members retained counsel. When the hearing began, someone asked what rules of procedures would be followed. A distinguished professor of physics replied, "We'll make them up as we go along." Rank hearsay testimony was admitted. A written report by a pharmacologist as to the effects of ingestion of drugs on behavior was admitted and was a critical item relied upon by the board even though there was not a scintilla of evidence that anyone allegedly involved had used drugs. An investigator who presented the most damaging hearsay evidence sat on the adjudicating committee. None of the persons present during the alleged incident was permitted to testify although there were several known eyewitnesses who were not members of the fraternity or friends of the alleged victim and who were presumably neutral, unbiased, and reliable.

I found that the suspended students and fraternity had been denied due process. I did not hear the substantive charges but gave the university a reasonable period of time to conduct a fair hearing and specified minimal rules of procedure. Instead of holding the hearing, the university "settled" the case by paying compensation to the alleged victim and reinstating all the students and the fraternity. This solution satisfied no one. But the students had run out of money and could not afford to continue the legal battle to clear their names. Whether the university misused funds in paying the alleged victim was an issue no one raised.

I have also heard many cases involving expulsion of students from public schools and discharges of teachers and other personnel. I have never decided the substantive charges but instead required the school board to give the students and teachers a fair hearing. In most states, boards of licensure for such trades as cosmetologists and undertakers are established by statute and required to conform to administrative procedure laws in deciding disputed issues involved in granting and revocation of licenses. Similarly, statutes or regulations govern procedures with respect to unions and other job-related organizations. There are countless complaints of improper conduct, lack of qualifications, and the like. These matters are heard by properly constituted boards under prescribed rules. Although the losing party has a right to appeal to the courts, few such cases are appealed. When the individuals have had a fair hearing and the facts have been brought out before a panel of experts, both sides are satisfied, if not happy, regardless of the result.

Whenever I read press reports of warfare in academia, charges and countercharges of false scholarship, faked laboratory reports, denial of tenure because of spite and the like, I fear an impending lawsuit.

Stanford University has charged that Steven W. Mosher, a student, lied about his use of grant funds. The faculty voted to expel him from the doctoral program in anthropology.[21] Mr. Mosher, who spent some time doing research in China, has published several accounts of his findings, including rural poverty and governmental pressure on women to have abortions. It is reported that Peking officials accused Mosher of improper behavior. These charges and countercharges have been aired in the media. Are they appropriate issues for a court to decide?

It is reported that Mosher has retained counsel. If he sues Stanford, he would certainly demand discovery of all communications the university has had with Chinese officials, minutes of all faculty meetings, reports by faculty members evaluating his work, and other relevant information. Stanford would undoubtedly resist. Both parties would probably claim First Amendment rights—Mosher to say and publish whatever he wished about his China experience without fear of reprisal; Stanford on behalf of its faculty to assert their rights to express their views on professional matters without fear of litigation. In such a hypothetical case, I believe both parties are right. Both the student and the faculty members have rights to free expression. Such lawsuits should not be treated as libel actions but suits for employment and professional rights. The student wants his degree, which is really a union card for academic employment. The faculty and university want the right to control the degree-granting process. The student who has invested years of study has a property interest in getting his degree. Faculty members also have a strong property interest in maintaining professional standards. The value of their positions and their degrees is lessened if unqualified or less-qualified persons are admitted to their ranks.

If such a hypothetical case were prosecuted as a libel suit, both parties would suffer regardless of the final outcome. The case probably would not be decided for a decade until all appeals or funds were exhausted. If the case came to trial, the judge or jury might well have to decide the following questions: Is the student a public figure, a private figure, or a limited public figure? Is the question of "public concern"? Did the university act with "actual malice"? And most important, and impossible of proof: Were the statements false? The court would have to decide on the basis of fragmentary and unreliable evidence whether China pressures women to have unwanted abortions. This is an issue as little susceptible of legal proof as the body count in Vietnam. American scholars may not know for years, if ever, whether the Chinese government compelled women to have abortions under coercive threats.*

Day after day I must decide whether a person accused of crime gave a statement to the police freely and voluntarily or under coercive conditions. The accused and the police officer are in court. Both testify under oath. Even though I see and hear both of them give diametrically opposite testimony and even though I am intimately familiar with the practices and procedures of police in taking statements from suspects, such decisions are difficult and fraught with possibility of error. To decide whether a vast number of unknown women in China were or were not coerced into having abortions is an impossible task.

Not all academic cases involve such arcane factual issues. But regardless of the alleged basis of the denial of degree, promotion, or tenure, such lawsuits are prolonged and bitter; they rarely repair the damage done to the aggrieved party or the university. If the plaintiff is ultimately reinstated, the situation will be an unhappy one. These questions are better decided within the institution or profession.

Most such cases come to court because the institutions and professional associations, relieved of the constraints of statutes and union contracts, fail to provide fair and proper grievance procedures. Many bar associations and state courts now provide confidential hearings for those accused of unprofessional conduct.

Special committees hear charges against allegedly malfeasant judges and lawyers. These are not open hearings. If the evidence does not support the charges, the accused is spared the opprobrium of publicity. If it does, the matter ultimately goes to court.

Many bar associations have established procedures for hearing fee

---

*It might, of course, be possible although difficult to produce evidence in court that a number of Chinese women were coerced into having unwanted abortions. Whether such instances constitute evidence of a pattern of government policy or were simply anomalous cases, however, would be even less susceptible of the kind of rigorous proof demanded by the law in most cases.

disputes between lawyers and clients. Before there were such procedures, it was my unhappy lot to hear several of these cases. All could have been decided with less acrimony and damage to reputation through professional grievance procedures.

Some issues like racial and sexual discrimination in universities had to be litigated in court in order to establish legal rights. In the 1970s, many leading universities did not have even one full tenured professor who was a female or a member of a racial minority. But once the law was clearly established, questions involving professional competence could more easily be handled through administrative hearings than court trials.

Medical malpractice litigation is now causing much consternation because of the high cost of malpractice insurance. Had the medical profession itself taken action to police its members, much litigation could have been avoided. Any number of malpractice cases I have tried were brought against doctors who had been sued for negligence a number of times before. Despite incontrovertible evidence presented in the course of those trials, no action had been taken against any of the doctors by medical associations or boards of licensure. It was not until the insurance companies cancelled their policies, that incompetent and careless physicians were put out of practice.

After one particularly shocking case before me in which a patient had been blinded, an official of the local medical association told me how happy he was that the defendant doctor's insurance had been cancelled and he would no longer be able to practice medicine. "The doctor was a disgrace to the profession," he declared. "If you knew that, why didn't you take action before he mutilated so many patients?" I asked. That case was reported in the local press. If the insurance company had not cancelled the policy, the doctor would undoubtedly have sued for libel.

This is not an anomalous case. The Public Citizen Health Research Group reports that in 1983 state medical boards took disciplinary actions against only 563 physicians, although an estimated 136,000 to 310,000 instances of medical malpractice occurred.[22]

Under such circumstances malpractice suits are inevitable. It is also inevitable that many of those sued will bring actions for libel. Statements made in pleadings and in the course of litigation are privileged. But often adversely critical and allegedly defamatory statements are made outside court proceedings. Such libel suits are really ancillary to the malpractice cases. The gravamen of these suits is not the besmirching of reputation, but the charge of malpractice.

The issues are different. The legal rules and doctrines are different. The question is not the "actual malice" of the patient, who may well be motivated by real spite, ill will, and a desire for revenge, but the competence of the physician.

Doctors are not the only professionals who are subject to bitter criticism. Lawyers and judges frequently get an unfavorable press. An article charged that a State Supreme Court justice was influenced by friendships and campaign contributions in certain decisions and that he used his influence to obtain a job for his son. The justice sued the paper. The trial judge held that the article was subject to a defamatory meaning and refused to dismiss the suit.[23] The trial judge is subject to the supervisory powers of the Supreme Court. Under these circumstances, how can the press get a fair trial?

There are many other problems with such a lawsuit. Even though the article is subject to a defamatory meaning, it involves inferences and opinions, not facts. How can anyone know the elements that influence a judge's decision? When a litigant is a friend, most judges wisely recuse themselves to avoid the appearance of bias. When a judge hears a case involving a friend, that judge has an unenviable Hobson's choice. If he or she decides in favor of a friend or campaign contributor, it will be inferred that the judge favored the litigant. If the judge decides against the friend or contributor, the unhappy litigant may claim that the judge leaned over backwards to prove judicial virtue.[24]

With respect to charges of nepotism, there is really nothing the accused can do. How can one prove either that the job was given as a result of subtle, tacit pressure, or that it was not? No one can determine the unexpressed motivations of another person. Nepotism is not a crime. Certainly it is not even frowned upon in private enterprise. Helping members of one's family is as American as apple pie. Why should such an allegation, whether true or false, constitute an actionable tort?

Comments about the competence of lawyers are often devastating.* The *American Lawyer* published a lengthy and highly critical article about Dan Burt, General Westmoreland's lawyer in his libel suit. It reported, "Burt created *Westmoreland* v. *CBS* and rode it to national prominence. Then, when the going got tough, he abandoned

---

*The Court of Appeals for the Seventh Circuit has ruled that comments concerning an attorney's performance in oral argument are not libelous per se (Quilici v. Second Amendment Foundation, 769 F2d 414 [7th Cir., 1985]). Whether this decision will be appealed is not known as of this writing. However, only a definitive decision by the Supreme Court or a statute limiting such actions can halt the proliferation of lawsuits by disgruntled professionals.

the case and negotiated his client's unconditional surrender."[25] The article clearly implied that Burt was incompetent. It also inferred that he negotiated a settlement without the approval of his client. Such conduct would be a breach of professional ethics. As of this writing, there is no reported libel suit by Burt against the *American Lawyer.* But that article is capable of a defamatory meaning. If the *Gertz* decision is controlling, Burt is a private figure. If the burden of proving truth were on the defendant, Burt could possibly succeed in such a lawsuit.

Again I envision with dismay the problems of the judge who would have to try such a case. There would be a mighty battle of experts, some claiming that Burt's legal tactics were wise and competent; others the contrary. In a legal malpractice case before me, defense counsel asked for a continuance even though the trial date had been set months in advance. Counsel claimed more time was needed to find an expert witness. Opposing counsel protested. "Judge," he declared, "you know that with enough time and money anyone can find an expert to support any claim." One can predict more battles of legal experts in the suits against the *American Lawyer* brought by judges who were included in that publications' list of "worst judges." Whether a judge is the best, worst, or "most mediocre" is, in my view, an expression of opinion not susceptible of proof of truth or falsity. These judges have not been impeached or removed from the bench. Although their feelings have been wounded, I do not think they should have cognizable claims either of libel or job-related injuries.

An interesting Michigan case indicates that almost any communication can give rise to a libel suit.[26] In that case, a lawyer for an insurance company defending a medical malpractice suit wrote to several lawyers suggesting a defense theory. The doctor who was being defended by the insurance company sued the lawyer charging that the letter had a "defamatory" meaning.

Society is the loser no matter who wins these lawsuits. All of us suffer when incompetent or dishonest people are employed in the private and public sectors and are elected and appointed to public office. Job security is important in both the public and private sectors. Civil service, tenure, and union contracts were designed to protect employees from being fired for prejudice or politics. But they were never intended to shield unqualified persons from scrutiny or to prevent future employers from making an objective assessment of persons seeking employment.

The shocking reports of abuse and molestation in child care centers, old age homes, and other institutions have forced these organizations to adopt more rigorous employment practices. They now require references from former employers; they seek information not only from police records but from neighbors and associates. If such people risk libel suits when giving their opinions, important information will be foreclosed to the detriment of society. Most child abuse reporting laws contain provisions holding harmless those who report in good faith. Whether such laws protect against libel suits is an open question. No reported cases have raised this issue.

Opinions and evaluations of job qualifications are, in my view, important aspects of freedom of expression. They also provide helpful information that protects society. Of course, there are dangers to the persons who lose jobs or advancement and never know why. The unverified FBI files, replete with hearsay and gossip, have caused immeasurable harm to many innocent individuals. Disclosure of unfavorable reports with the names of the reporters deleted would provide the job applicant with an opportunity to rebut such reports without destroying the rights of those who do report.

Attempts to stifle or palliate criticism do, I believe, interfere with the First Amendment rights of the critics. A signal example of this suppression of opinion was Harvard University's action halting publication of *Cue,* a university-financed survey of student opinion of faculty.[27] The university objected to such words as "arrogant" and "condescending" used to describe faculty members. But if an opinion is solicited, or even if it is volunteered, it should not be altered or suppressed.

Some measures can be taken to protect whistle blowers and those who in good faith give their honest opinions as to candidates and prospective employees. The Federal Civil Service Reform Act[28] prohibits government agencies from taking reprisals against whistle blowers. The greatest protection for the public, the whistle blowers, and those who give opinions as to prospective employees and office seekers is for courts to follow the long line of authority that holds that there can be no such thing as a false opinion and grant summary judgment in favor of the defendants.

Advertising is frankly commercial speech. Individuals, groups, and businesses spend money to advertise products and to present opinions and information. The Supreme Court held unconstitutional a state statute regulating advertising that is not false or misleading,[29] recognizing that commercial speech is entitled to First Amendment protections, although perhaps of a lesser degree. This presents a radical and much needed advance in the law. Formerly ordinances prohibiting distribution of flyers were upheld.[30] Recent decisions hold that advertising of drugs[31] and abortion services,[32] although commercial speech, are entitled to First Amendment protections because the information is a matter of public interest. In a series of cases dealing with advertising by professionals, the Supreme Court recognized both the rights of the advertisers and the public. Lawyers may now advertise their services provided that the advertisement is truthful.[33] In other contexts, the Court has established stringent tests for admittedly commercial speech.[34] The Court has avoided hard questions* with respect to the right of the federal government to regulate publications under statutes designed to protect the investing public.[35]

The Court has sustained the right of the government to prohibit the distribution of election campaign leaflets on a military post.[36] This is precisely the kind of information necessary for self-governance that the First Amendment should protect. That decision comes perilously close to both prior restraint and punishment for seditious libel. There was no suggestion that distribution of these leaflets constituted any danger, much less a clear and present danger, to the national welfare or security. These cases reveal more instances of the preferment of commercial speech to political speech.

A new and potentially enormous area of litigation involving commercial communications was opened by the decision of the Supreme Court in *Dun & Bradstreet, Inc.* v. *Greenmoss Builders, Inc.* [37] This case arose out of an admitted error in a credit report. It was tried and decided under legal principles enunciated in *New York Times* v. *Sullivan* and its progeny.

The facts are simple and uncontested. Dun & Bradstreet erroneously informed five of its regular customers that plaintiff had filed a voluntary petition in bankruptcy. The error was committed by a seventeen-year-old high school student employed by defendant. Apparently no one checked his work. Many judges would have treated this as a commercial case. Defendant was clearly negligent. Plaintiff should have recovered whatever losses it incurred as a result of the dissemination of the erroneous information. Under this doctrine, a jury would have been instructed that if the defendant was grossly negligent and acted with reckless disregard for the rights of the

---

*These sensitive questions of government regulation of communication are beyond the scope of this discussion that is focused on the rights of subjects vis à vis authors.

plaintiff, punitive damages could be awarded in the discretion of the jury in order to punish defendant for its conduct and to deter future gross negligence. In awarding punitive damages, the jury would be permitted to consider the defendant's assets, but the award would have to bear some relationship to the actual damages. For example, if a plaintiff could prove that it probably lost a contract on which it would have made a profit of $10,000, it would recover $10,000 in compensatory damages. An award perhaps of $20,000 in punitive damages would be unreasonable.

Because the complaint alleged libel, this simple case that could have been tried in two or three days bedeviled the trial judge, the Vermont Supreme Court, and nine justices of the Supreme Court. They labored mightily and brought forth not a mouse but a three-headed monster.

The jury returned a verdict of $50,000 in presumed damages and $300,000 in punitive damages. The Vermont Supreme Court upheld the verdict. It concluded that the precatory language with respect to punitive damages in *Gertz* was applicable only to media defendants. Justice Powell, writing for a plurality of the Supreme Court consisting of himself and Justices Rehnquist and O'Connor, held that matters not of "public concern" are entitled to "reduced" First Amendment protections. Although public concern had been mentioned in prior cases, it had not been a critical test of liability. Chief Justice Burger and Justice White concurred but urged that both the *Gertz* and *Sullivan* cases be reexamined. The clear implication is that they would like to overrule these decisions. Justices Brennan, Marshall, Blackmun, and Stevens dissented, pointing out the difficulties in using a test of "public issues" or "public concern" and the fact that each future case would have to be decided by the trial courts on an ad hoc basis.

Had this case originally come before me I would have treated it not as a question of libel but as a tortious interference with a contract or a contract for sale of goods or services. An interference with prospective contractual relations is a recognized tort. In order to recover in such cases, a plaintiff has only to show that it probably would have entered into contracts with one or more of Dun & Bradstreet's customers to whom the report was sent and the probable profits it would have made on those contracts. In this case, correct information was promptly supplied to the customers and the plaintiff did not lose any business. It suffered no compensable damage under doctrines of commercial law. The annoyance caused by having to get the report corrected was certainly not worth $50,000.

The information supplied by Dun & Bradstreet, since it appears in printed form, could also be treated as a product or as a service. In either event, Dun & Bradstreet was not engaged in expression but in a commercial sale of information. It would not have required any "stretching" of the law to find an implied warranty of accuracy.

Certainly Dun & Bradstreet's customers purchased the credit rating service relying on its truthfulness and accuracy. The fact that this was a contract between Dun & Bradstreet and its customers to which Greenmoss was not a party would not present any obstacle to recovery if the plaintiff had been harmed. It has long been held that a third party who is reasonably in contemplation as a user of the goods produced by the seller and sold to the buyer is entitled to recover if it is harmed by the product. Dun & Bradstreet, like all credit reporting companies, should have known that businesses that are the subject of its credit reports will be affected by those reports. The favorable reports will be advantageous. The unfavorable ones will be highly prejudicial. They also know that their customers will rely on the reports. There is no question that Dun & Bradstreet was negligent. Although the term *res ipsa loquitur,* the thing speaks for itself, is no longer in use in many jurisdictions, no proof of failure to exercise care should be required in this case. There really is no excuse for this kind of error. The fact that a seventeen-year-old was employed and his work was not checked, would be ample proof of negligence if such were needed.

A false credit report is dangerous—dangerous to the subject of the report and dangerous to the customer who relies on it to his detriment. If the situation were the reverse and Greenmoss had been deeply indebted and the purchasers of the services were erroneously notified that its financial position was good and in reliance on that report extended credit to Greenmoss and suffered losses, there is little doubt that they could recover from Dun & Bradstreet. Freedom of the press has nothing to do with the sale of a commodity or sale of a service.

With respect to damages, the courts found themselves in a tangle of inappropriate verbiage. Greenmoss was unable to prove any loss suffered as a result of the erroneous report. Under ordinary principles of commercial law, there is no presumption of damages. Damages are a fact that have to be proved like any other fact. Nonetheless, an award of $50,000 in presumed damages and an award of $300,000 in punitive damages were upheld.

A plurality of the Court recognizing the difference between media and non-media defendants refused to use this fact as a basis for finding liability. Instead, they relied upon still another complicated test: Is the subject matter of "public concern"? Public concern was not defined. It is the vaguest of concepts. Is the report of a run of the mill crime of public concern? It may be that a crime is of public interest, but is the identity of the victim? What concern does the public have in a novel, allegedly about a person who is not a public official and who is not engaged in public life? If the "public concern" test were to be applied to past libel cases, many media defendants would have been unable to sustain a First Amendment defense. What possible public interest was involved in Mr. Gertz's claim that he was falsely dubbed a Communist? He was a lawyer in private practice. What public interest was there in the arrest of Rosenbloom, an alleged small-time smut peddler? On the other hand, there was considerable public interest in the false report about the mayor's criminal record involved in *Ocala Star-Banner Co.* v. *Damron.*

I have tried many cases involving false or erroneous credit reports by banks, stockbrokers, and others engaged in finance. Although some plaintiffs included a libel count, these cases were not decided under libel law but under appropriate commercial law. The issues in deciding liability were: Has the bank breached its obligations under the banking code? Has the broker tortiously interfered with prospective contractual obligations? These issues were not difficult to frame or to decide. When information is clearly erroneous, it is not hard to prove negligence. The real problem is proof of damages.

Credit information is essential to commercial transactions. Most people use credit cards. If a store is erroneously informed that a customer's credit has been cancelled, this is embarrassing and inconvenient for the customer. Often it causes real harm. Until the matter is corrected, card holders cannot make purchases using the credit card. They may be unable to go on a trip, buy an automobile, or make settlement on the purchase of a house. Such card holders who are thus compelled to breach agreements may be subject to substantial penalties. Most commercial enterprises rely on a line of credit from a bank. If credit is erroneously cut off, even for a brief period, a business may fail.

Other erroneous information causes untold harm. When a driver is stopped for a traffic violation and is not carrying an owner's card, the police officer usually checks to see if the car is stolen and if the driver has a criminal record. It occasionally happens that a person with the same name is wanted on a serious criminal charge. The careless driver is then held in custody until the correct identity can be established. To date, no one has suggested that this erroneous information constitutes an actionable libel.

When a governmental agency furnishes criminal information to another agency, it is providing a service. When a commercial enterprise provides credit or other information, it is engaged in a sale of a commodity. Neither the commercial company nor the government agency is engaged in communication of news, entertainment, or opinion. These are the types of expression traditionally entitled to First Amendment protections.

With the widespread use of the ubiquitous computer, more and more different kinds of information are for sale. Advertisers, charitable organizations, hospitals, theaters, and others buy lists of potential customers and donors. Governmental agencies and industry use computerized information to check on employees, customers, suppliers of goods and services, and a host of other legitimate purposes. If the information is erroneous, as will inevitably occur sometimes, should this be treated as libel by computer simply because the product supplied consists of words rather than tangible goods or traditional types of services?

Most inventions present novel legal problems when first used. Courts have to struggle to pour new wine into old bottles of traditional doctrine. Often statutes are needed simply because unprecedented situations cannot adequately be dealt with under existing law. Before the invention of automobiles, there were no requirements for a driver's license. Anyone big enough and strong enough to control a horse was deemed fit to drive a carriage. It soon became apparent to legislators that government had to exercise control over drivers in an attempt to prevent physically unfit, mentally disabled, and repeatedly careless individuals from driving. More recently, compulsory insurance laws have been enacted to protect victims of vehicle accidents.

The purchase and sale of verbal information has spawned a large industry. Inevitably many legal problems arise. The use of sophisticated equipment enables this material to be quickly and cheaply available. But the basic data are supplied by fallible human beings. The machines are designed and programmed by equally fallible individuals. If the computers on billion dollar spaceships malfunction, it is not unreasonable to expect that those used for routine, mundane affairs will also occasionally malfunction, sometimes with unfortunate results to individuals and institutions. The legal responsibilities of suppliers of information present many difficult problems. But the blanket application of libel law to misinformation appears to be unwise and unnecessary. The only constitutional right of anyone who alleges that he or she has been harmed by another is due process. If the other is at fault and the one harmed is properly compensated for the harm done, the constitutional requirements are met. If redress is more appropriately available under principles of contract or warranty than defamation, there is no constitutional inhibition with respect to the choice of legal doctrine. It is irrelevant whether the right not to be defamed is deemed a liberty interest or a property interest. Under either theory, the Constitution requires due process of law, not a specific legal doctrine.

One may read the Constitution as Justice Brennan does as setting forth basic principles that are to be applied by living judges to contemporary problems. Or one may read it as Attorney General Meese does, as being a document fixed in time to be read as it was written two centuries ago. Under either interpretation, it is difficult to find that the First Amendment covers the sale of credit information. Justice Harlan wisely pointed out in a dissenting opinion in an antitrust case, "[it] is one of those cases familiar in treble damage litigation where injury resulting from normal business hazards is sought to be made redressable by casting the affair in antitrust terms."[38] The application of libel doctrine to commercial disputes appears to be both inappropriate and unwise. Obviously it provides a vehicle for large recoveries that would be unobtainable under any other legal theory. It is the thesis of this chapter that the legal doctrines and policy considerations that guide courts in the trials and decisions of these cases involving economic or commercial interests should reflect the realities of the controversies rather than legal nomenclature.

·XII·

Preventive Law

*As a litigant I should dread a lawsuit beyond almost
anything else short of sickness and death.*

—LEARNED HAND

BETWEEN the extremes of litigation fought to the point of financial and emotional exhaustion and the supine surrender to calumny and lies, there is a median position of reasonable conduct for both subjects and authors. Many of the conferences and articles devoted to the problems of libel and free expression, however, fail to consider the option of preventive law. The learned symposium commemorating the 250th anniversary of the *Zenger* libel trial[1] typifies many of these discussions. It focused on *New York Times* v. *Sullivan* and its progeny. The participants included journalists, publishers, lawyers, academics, and judges. In the course of lively debate, the following irrelevant matters were discussed: the high rate of illiteracy, the declining number of newspapers, the malign and pervasive influence of television, the cost of air time, public hostility to the media, and popular disaffection with First Amendment rights. Brooding over the meeting like a Holmesian omnipresence in the sky was the fear that changes in the composition of the federal courts would drastically and adversely affect free expression. Holmes, Madison, and Jefferson were invoked as the lares and penates guarding the shrine of the First Amendment. No one mentioned the fact that the gods in this pantheon of free expression explicitly excluded libel from the rights they so eloquently defended. And no one discussed the role of the private sector in limiting free expression although it is these lawsuits by private subjects that now constitute the most serious and prevalent dangers.

The subjects raised in the symposium are not insignificant, but they have little relevance to the problems of free and untrammeled reporting of news, airing of programs, and publication of books and articles. The high rate of functional illiteracy among adults is variously estimated from 13 percent to 52 percent, depending upon standards of competence.[2] Yet, two centuries ago when the Bill of Rights was adopted, there was no compulsory public education. There were very few free schools. The majority of people in that agrarian society were probably illiterate. But they were able to function adequately. The number of newspapers has been steadily declining throughout the twentieth century. The growing monopoly of sources of news and opinion may well constitute a threat to the political process. But the the widespread phenomenon of the one-newspaper city long antedated 1964 and the spate of libel cases. The extraordinary role of TV and radio as the global schoolhouse and now the primary sources of news cannot be ignored. The fact that many people prefer "Dallas" to the pontifications often heard on public broadcasting is a fact of life. But one must recall that in the nineteenth century people avidly read "penny dreadfuls" in preference to the classics. They also eagerly read Dickens. Public taste is scarcely a litmus test of First Amendment rights.

The public attitude toward the First Amendment is not a verifiable fact. The answer depends upon which pollster one reads and how the questions are framed. Whether juries, as representatives of the public, are hostile to the First Amendment cannot be ascertained by the simple sociological numbers game, counting the cases in which verdicts were for or against the media. Except in extraordinary cases, juries follow the instructions of the judge as to the law on liability. The cases of Peter Zenger, William Penn, and recently Clive Ponting (the British civil servent who gave information about the Falkland Islands War to a member of Parliament), are signal examples of juries that defied the courts when they believed the law was unjust and inappropriate.

In my opinion, the problems with libel law are not public illiteracy, monopolistic media, or majoritarian hostility to free expression, but the law itself. The focus for remedial action should, therefore, be on the law of libel, not the legal system, trial by jury, or any of the large philosophical questions propounded in learned articles and discussions.

I begin with several simple premises: Everyone should have access to the courts for redress of wrongs, including the award of monetary damages. The First Amendment guarantees not a privilege to express one's self, but a right. Since error in all human enterprise is inevitable, the law should provide a method of correction. Litigation should be the last resort, not the first or sole remedial action for subjects who claim their rights have been infringed.

The idea of preventive medicine has captured the attention of doctors and public health officials around the world. Would it not be better, they argue, to avoid the painful and costly treatment of diseases through less expensive and more effective means of prevention such as immunization, proper nutrition, and improved methods of sanitation and safe water supply? The obvious answer is yes. It is better for the individuals and better for the society that must bear the burdens of heroic and extraordinary treatment of ailments that could be prevented.

Any one who has followed the tortuous and costly litigation of the many conflicts between subjects and authors should be moved to consider the possibilities of preventive law.* The trial of complex cases is not only very costly to the litigants, even those who are insured, it is also an emotional ordeal. The costs to the public are not inconsiderable.

I propose three simple preventive measures: apology, retraction, and disclaimer. The use of one or more of these devices will not eliminate all libel litigation. But each could avoid many unnecessary and costly suits for inadvertent errors.

I do not deplore all litigation as being unduly costly or an improper use of the courts. The entire administration of justice, including the elaborate American system of courts, exists for the peaceful resolution of disputes according to legal principles and for the fair and lawful prosecution of those accused of crime. Litigation is appropriate and necessary when there is a dispute over the facts or the law and when the public interest is involved.

In many libel cases the facts are not in dispute. The parties are not interested in legal rights but in vindication of "honor." Often the allegedly libelous statement is only marginally inaccurate. The plaintiff objects to inferences that impugn his or her integrity. The defendant may be willing to concede that the statement was overbroad, that

---

*Banks, savings and loans, and other lending institutions in an effort to prevent litigation are using carefully worded documents rather than relying on oral communications (The *Legal Intelligencer*, December 2, 1986, p. 3).

the implication objected to was not intended, or even that the facts were, with hindsight, erroneous.

The case of *Dalitz* v. *Penthouse International Ltd.*[3] presents an extraordinary example of the usefulness of a procedure for apology. In 1975, La Costa resort and its officials filed a $522 million libel suit against *Penthouse*. More than ten years later, after *Penthouse* had expended $8 million in legal fees and La Costa had also expended enormous sums, the suit was settled. Counsel for the parties issued a joint statement declaring in pertinent parts: "The toll has been punishing and arduous on both sides. . . . It appears that if the case were to continue through yet additional court proceedings, whoever would ultimately win would enjoy a Pyrrhic victory at best. . . ." The statement also lauded La Costa for its civic and philanthropic contributions and *Penthouse* for its professional awards.

Reasonable people must ask why this sensible solution was not reached much sooner. There is no legal doctrine or constitutional mandate that bars apologies, retractions, and disclaimers as means of avoiding litigation. Apology is the simplest procedure. It is used every day in countless activities that could lead to litigation.

Courtesy and good manners are not trivial concerns of the wealthy as to the right fork, or the right wine, or proper attire. Civility is what makes the ordinary irritations of daily life tolerable. "Please," "thank you," and "pardon me" may be routine phrases, but they are not meaningless. They reveal that the speaker recognizes the other as a human being entitled to at least a modicum of respect. Particularly in an urban society where innumerable contacts with strangers are inevitable, these common expressions of courtesy prevent minor contretemps from escalating to confrontations, fist fights, and court battles. Every time someone inadvertently steps on another's foot or jostles a fellow pedestrian on a sidewalk or a passenger in a subway, the possibility of a lawsuit exists. Under the common law any offensive, unprivileged touching of another is a crime: battery. It is also a tort. Most of these daily encounters conclude with a mumbled apology and the parties go their separate ways. Occasionally an apology is not forthcoming. Hostile words are exchanged. Then blows. And sometimes a stabbing or shooting ensues. One reads of the murder of a person preempting a parking place. Fortunately these violent episodes are the exceptions not the rule.

Visitors to England are impressed by the fact that no one "jumps the queue." People wait their turns in line. Similar courtesy prevails in Russia, where waiting in line for almost every purchase is a way of life. These adjustments to necessity make urban living possible.

Every day in the United States countless automobiles collide. The drivers examine their vehicles and see that little or no damage has been done. They apologize and go their respective ways unless one is seeking to get a dishonest windfall by falsely claiming damages. Such cases do occur, and little can be done to prevent them or other instances of fraud and cheating. The difference between these cases and libel suits is that the automobile owners must prove the damages to the cars and the injuries to themselves and their passengers.

I have tried several such fraudulent cases. Neither judges nor juries are easily persuaded that an old car was badly damaged when the other vehicle was not damaged at all or that the passengers all suffered back injuries from a little bump. But plaintiffs in libel cases do not have to prove damages. Hence there is every incentive to sue in the hope of getting a windfall verdict from a judge or jury.

The statement made by CBS to Westmoreland and accepted by him in order to terminate the trial can be viewed as an apology. Apparently the defendants were willing to make such a statement at the inception of the litigation without admitting legal culpability. I doubt that it would have terminated the litigation at an earlier point, because of pride or pique and the not inconsiderable expenses already incurred. But would it not have been a gracious and decent thing to do?

In the case of author Lerman whose topless photo was published without her permission, it appears clear from the opinion of the appellate court that the photograph was published unintentionally and without knowing that it was in fact a picture of her. When this fact was called to the attention of the defendants, why didn't they immediately make a public apology without admitting liability? Was she interested in establishing her good name and reputation as an author who does not pose topless for publication, or was she interested in obtaining substantial monetary compensation? This is a question that can be answered only after an apology is tendered.

It may be argued that only the threat or fear of substantial monetary damages induces carefulness and caution on the part of defendants. But inaccuracies and mistakes are inevitable in all human activities. Even the use of sophisticated modern technology such as the computer does not eliminate error. The difficulties of the IRS in collecting taxes and making refunds give ample testimony to the fact that unintentional error occurs despite careful procedures and good intentions. The IRS belatedly apologized to the tens of thousands of taxpayers who were inconvenienced by these errors. Such common courtesy is still a part of the American ethos.

A public apology, made in the same manner and with the same amount of publicity as the original act or words complained of, would restore the good name of the plaintiff. It would ease hurt feelings. It would not provide compensation. If the multitude of defamation cases are really brought to protect the subjects' legitimate interest in their reputations, not for monetary compensation, that interest can be protected by an apology or retraction without the necessity of a lawsuit.

Prevention is practiced not only in medicine but also in industry. Most factories and other work places have safety equipment either by the compulsion of statutes or simply to avoid harm and attendant litigation. Manufacturers recognize that collisions are an inevitable concomitant of automobiles even when drivers are careful and sober. To minimize harm arising from unintentional, accidental collisions, automobiles are equipped with bumpers. The correction of error or retraction is a kind of legal bumper to minimize harm done inadvertently.

Retraction is not an untried remedy. Lord Campbell's Libel Act of 1843 provided that the defendant could plead retraction in reduction of damages.[4] Retraction is peculiarly appropriate when the fact alleged by the author with respect to the subject is conceded to be false or erroneous. In the case of the mayor of Philadelphia who, it was conceded, was falsely reported to be under federal investigation for alleged wrongdoing, a retraction would certainly have been appropriate. In those defamation cases in which the facts are susceptible of actual proof, the defendants usually concede the error. Unless the charge was made willfully and spitefully, the old common law meaning of malice, then a prompt retraction as widely publicized as the false and defamatory charge should provide ample redress for the harm to reputation and good name. Nothing in the law prevents the media from publishing a correction. Many responsible newspapers do regularly publish corrections of inadvertent errors.

The principal obstacle to a retraction by a defendant who knows that the defamatory statement was false or overbroad is the fear that such an admission will make it more difficult to defend a libel action. If suit has not been filed, a retraction may convince the plaintiff that he or she has a sure chance of winning a substantial verdict. Under the adversary legal system, a defendant rarely offers to settle until the plaintiff has made a demand. After a due interval during which the parties through counsel take the depositions of all the important potential witnesses and make demands for all relevant and irrelevant documentary evidence, the defendant makes an offer. Demand and offer define the parameters of the measure of damages insofar as the parties are concerned. What juries, who know nothing of these negotiations, will do is unpredictable. Offer and demand also set the limits, in a practical sense, for the judge or any third party who attempts to settle or mediate the dispute. Regardless of the merits, no one is going to suggest more than the demand or less than the offer.

What usually ensues at this point may be likened to a purchase and sale of a commodity in a Turkish bazaar. The demand is always in excess of what the plaintiff really expects, and the offer far less than what the defendant is willing to pay. An experienced judge can usually find a figure to which both parties agree. By such means, the vast majority of civil suits are settled without ever reaching a verdict. If they were not settled, the court system would be unable to function from the overload. Attorney Elmer Gertz, the plaintiff in the much-cited case *Gertz* v. *Robert Welch*, in advising lawyers how to win libel suits cautions, "The law in this area is in a state of flux—new court rulings are likely. So counsel must check what the Supreme Court and lesser courts are saying. . . ."[5] This very uncertainty militates against settlement.

One reason that most cases can be settled is that the lawyers for both parties know the law and are able to make reasonable appraisals of the likely outcome of the case. Because the law of defamation is so unsettled, it is almost impossible to make such an appraisal with any degree of assurance. One never knows what decision will be handed down the next day or week that may alter the rights of the parties. Few people are willing to bet when the odds keep changing.

Another obstacle to settlement is that defamation suits usually involve not only money but also pride. The plaintiff has asserted under oath when filing suit that his or her reputation has been tarnished by the false charges of the defendant. The defendant has the pride of authorship, the reputation of being a fair and scrupulous reporter or author. The publisher or member of the media also has a public reputation for fairness and integrity to maintain. Instead of dealing with parties who are fighting only about money, counsel and the court find themselves involved with the egos of prima donnas, parties who have convinced themselves of their own rectitude and virtue and the belief that they have been treated unfairly. It is difficult to see what even the most skilled and patient judge, mediator, or conciliator could do to resolve disputes when neither party is sure of his rights and both are convinced of their respective virtues.

It may be argued that retraction is an inadequate remedy because the truth never catches up with falsehood. Admittedly there is no way to ensure that every person who read or heard the false and libelous statement will see or hear the retraction. But no legal remedy is absolutely complete. The aim of the law in awarding damages is to place the injured party in the same position he or she or it would have been in if the wrong had not occurred. In a breach of contract case, a wronged corporation can be awarded the profits it would have made if the contract had been performed. Of course, this is a rough measure. The company might have had a strike and lost money on the contract. If the contract had been performed, the company might have gotten additional business from others who had been favorably impressed by its services or products. But damages based on the profits that the plaintiff expected to realize if the contract had not been breached provide a reasonably fair remedy.

In a negligence case in which the plaintiff suffered a broken arm because of the defendant's negligence, the plaintiff is awarded a sum of money to cover medical expenses, loss of earnings, and pain and suffering. A fractured arm is never quite so strong and free of pain as one that has not been injured. In such cases, the law recognizing that perfect justice is impossible in an imperfect world provides a roughly fair approximation of the plaintiff's losses.

Retractions can provide a similar imperfect, rough justice for those defamed by erroneous reports. Government cannot compel the media to publish corrections or retractions. The Supreme Court has held that a statute requiring space for reply constitutes an impermissible interference with freedom of the press.[6] There is, however, no law or legal doctrine that prevents the media from voluntarily publishing or airing a retraction. Nor is there any legal principle that would prohibit a requirement that as a prerequisite to filing suit for libel the subject must make a demand for a correction or retraction statement. A demand as precondition to a legal claim is not unknown in the law. When suing for breach of contract, the plaintiff is required to allege that a demand for payment has been made and refused. If the defendant chooses to pay, litigation is avoided. If the defendant does not pay and the court finds that the contract was breached without legal justification, interest will run from the time of the demand. This is a strong incentive for a defendant to pay.

In a defamation case, the subject should be required to make a prompt demand on the author for a correction or retraction. If the author issued a prompt correction or retraction giving an equal amount of exposure on the air at a comparable time or equal space in comparable location in the publication in which the defamation appeared, the defendant should by statute be relieved of further obligation and liability unless the plaintiff could prove that actual harm occurred in the period between the libel and the retraction. In other words, the subject could not collect either presumed or punitive damages. Any special damages would have to be proved. The retraction would be evidence of lack of common law malice, and thus preclude an award of punitive damages. If freed from the dangers of legal admissions, the device of retraction would constitute an inexpensive and tactful solution to many libel cases. It would restore to the subject the good name inadvertently tarnished by the defendant. It would permit the defendant to admit error without conceding incompetence or lack of professional standards. And it would avoid bruising and costly litigation.

If libel plaintiffs were given the choice of prompt retraction or bruising and costly litigation, it is likely that the usual cost/benefit calculus that prevails in most litigation would impel a large number of libel plaintiffs to avoid expense and settle for vindication. Moreover, if the offer of retraction were made and rejected, the plaintiff's likelihood of recovering punitive damages would be extremely slight. The amount of compensatory damages that could be proved in the limited period between publication of the alleged libel and the offer of retraction would also be limited. Defendants would also be moved by economic self-interest to offer apologies or retractions except in cases in which truth was absolutely unassailable.

Apology and retraction are appropriate remedies for erroneous and libelous news reports and some commercial libels. They do not affect biography, fiction, comedy, or docudramas. The preventive device readily available to authors of these genres is the disclaimer. Many novels bear the standard legend: "The characters in this book are fictitious. Any resemblance to living persons is purely coincidental."

To date, such a disclaimer has been only a paper shield against real, ravenous tigers seeking what cannot too melodramatically be called blood money. A disclaimer should be more than a device to shield authors from liability. It should be a notice, a warning to the reader and the viewer with respect to the material being presented.

Does it purport to be fact or fiction? People have a right to know what it is that they are reading, hearing, or seeing.

In 1938, the nation was panicked by Orson Welles's program, "War of the Worlds." Those who tuned in late thought they were hearing a news program. While audiences are probably more sophisticated in the 1980s, they should be told explicitly the kind of program or printed matter that is being offered to them.

By law or by custom the public is put on notice in many common transactions of everyday life. Packaged food is labeled as to weight and contents. Drugs are also labeled as to content. Dangerous products carry warnings. Cigarettes have warnings on the packages. Securities cannot be sold publicly without full disclosure of the financial status of the issuer.

Persons accused of crime must be informed of their legal rights before they can be questioned by the police. Patients must be told in detail of their medical conditions, the proposed surgical treatment, and the risks involved. Purchasers buying goods on the installment plan must be informed in detail of the transaction: the amount of interest, the right to repossess, the notice that must be given.

Disclaimers are a variant of the principle of truth in labeling. The law recognizes that members of the public have a right to know the ingredients of the food and drugs they ingest. They have a right to know whether the clothing they are buying is made of wool or synthetics. They have a right to know the financial condition of the companies in which they invest their money. Albert Shanker, president of the American Federation of Teachers, proposes statutes requiring full disclosure of the qualification of teachers so that parents will know whether or not the teachers assigned to their children are qualified to teach these subjects.[7]

"Sunshine laws" that require meetings of public councils, commissions, and other bodies to be open to the public and press are predicated on the sound principle that the public has a right to know what elected and appointed public officials are doing. In his *Utopia*, Sir Thomas More required all public affairs to be planned in the Senate or at public occasions in the belief that open meetings would make it difficult for officials to oppress the public. A number of states and municipalities have adopted such laws in an effort to curb corruption and misuse of power. The belief that public access to information is an essential prophylaxis in a democratic government is not unfounded. Similarly, truth in labeling of verbal material, whether printed or disseminated over the air, is a salutary principle. The reader or hearer should know whether the material being presented is fiction, fact, or opinion.

Newspapers have long made a clear distinction between what is presented as news and what is presented as opinion. Editorials, columns, and the Op Ed page are clearly understood to be the opinions of the writers. What appears in the news columns is supposed to be factual. This distinction is not so clearly maintained in magazines and in presentations on the air. Are "in-depth" analyses of the news fact or opinion? Thoughtful readers and viewers probably recognize that any analysis requires the exercise of judgment and is, of necessity, opinion or comment. Frequently it is not so labeled.

Blurring of the line between fact and fiction occurs most blatantly in the docudrama. Its very name indicates that it is a dramatic performance and a documentary. The two aims are mutually incompatible. The most telling example is a court trial purportedly reproduced in a docudrama. As has been noted, most trials consist of hours of rather tedious testimony, objections by lawyers, and rulings by the judge. In order to condense a trial of several weeks into a dramatic presentation of an hour or two that will hold the viewers' attention, there must be selection. Much will, of necessity, be omitted. What is retained is often highlighted for dramatic effect. Not every point made by every witness can be included. The story line must not be broken. It is difficult for actors to avoid the telling gesture or facial expression that infuses neutral words with implicit meanings which may or may not be those that were expressed by the real-life character being portrayed. In print, an editor or author may rigorously adhere to recorded fact. Once the incident is removed to the stage or screen, however, the personalities of the director and the actors shape the character. Inevitably the picture is skewed.

Another serious problem in presenting a trial that occurred years ago as a documentary is the failure to point out changes in the law. Frequently standards of proof have changed. Material that was admitted in evidence twenty or forty years ago would now be excluded. The legal standards of fairness have been changed. If that very trial were held today, under current rules of evidence and in accordance with newly promulgated standards of due process, the results might well be different.

With the rigid time restrictions of TV and the need to maintain viewer interest, it is not possible to explain these subleties. The average viewer whose attention is riveted on the unfolding story probably does not stop to make these mental adjustments. The viewer feels, if the presentation is dramatically skillful, that he or she is present at the historical incident.

Particularly in the presentation of docudramas, a disclaimer would be useful. The public should be informed that the program is a dramatic reconstruction of events, that it is not historically accurate or complete in all details. Although living persons who were participants in the episode and who believe that they were not presented fairly or truthfully would probably still feel aggrieved, they would know that the viewers would not be under the misapprehension that the portrait was factual. The author's right to make use of material essentially in the public domain and to have the necessary artistic liberty to shape the material for dramatic presentation would be protected.

The British play, *Tom and Viv,* is based on the lives of T.S. Eliot and his wife. Like any book or play about a marriage, it presents the leading characters from a point of view. Was the husband fair to his wife? Did she help or hinder the great man's career? Did he adapt, adopt, or appropriate her ideas and words? These are subtle distinctions that perhaps owe as much to the eye of the author as to the actual, probably unknowable private behavior of the subjects themselves. If *Zelda,* the biography of F. Scott Fitzgerald's wife by Nancy Milford had been published during his lifetime, a libel suit would have been likely. The author charged that Fitzgerald published his wife's fiction as his own. Similar charges were made with respect to William Wordsworth, who was alleged to have appropriated his sister's poetry. A striking illustration of the possibilities of legitimate differing points of view about husbands and wives is revealed in *Parallel Lives: Five Victorian Marriages* by Phyllis Rose.

Were Eliot and/or his wife still living, it is not unlikely that one or both would sue for libel. Under the present state of American law, artistic liberty to deviate from documented facts has not been recognized. The charge that Eliot's wife was insane or mentally ill is, under traditional common law libel, defamatory. If the dramatist were required to prove the truth of the charge, that would be an almost impossible burden to sustain. In the trial of John Hinckley, Jr., the man who admittedly shot President Reagan and pleaded not guilty by reason of insanity, the battle of the psychiatric experts lasted thirty-nine trial days. It is reported that Hinckley's parents and the government each spent more than a quarter million dollars for expert witnesses.

The jury's finding that Hinckley was legally insane raises the question of whether such an issue is susceptible of proof. To muddle libel suits with an attempt to prove the truth of a charge of insanity would prolong and complicate cases that are already too lengthy and complicated. The charge, explicit or implicit, that Eliot forced a sane wife into a mental institution to be rid of her is also clearly defamatory. To determine whether she was or was not insane, a jury would have to speculate on the basis of conflicting opinions of experts on issues that are ill defined by law.

It may be argued that in any personal injury case that is what juries do. The plaintiff's expert testifies that in his or her opinion the plaintiff suffered a serious injury. Defendant's expert reads the same X rays and testifies that plaintiff was not injured or had a preexisting injury. Physical ills can be defined with reasonable precision. The concepts are not difficult, although the evidence may be highly technical. The difficulties of proof inherent in psychiatric problems are infinitely greater because there is less consensus, both legal and medical, on definitions.

In literary, dramatic, or journalistic presentations of behavior and motivations of people, issues of truth or falsity are infinitely more difficult. But under libel law, the rights of subjects and authors are predicated on such findings.

The disclaimer, or truth in labeling, if applied to fiction, reports, dramas, and docudramas based on real people would avoid many of those insoluble legal problems.[8] It would give the reader or viewer the truthful information that fidelity to fact was not intended. Litigation to decide whether fictional or dramatic treatment, what formerly was called "poetic license," presents a true or false portrait of the subject would be avoided.

The basis of truth in labeling statutes and requirements for informed consent is the sound legal presumption that people are reasonable, that if they are fully informed of the facts they can then make intelligent decisions. This is a median position between government irresponsibility and paternalism. The former is characterized by laissez-faire economics and the law of caveat emptor. Paternalistic governments, whether monarchies or dictatorships of the left or right, exercise tight control of production of goods, availability of services and information and entertainment. This censorship is always justified as being in the interests of the people, to protect them from religious, economic, or political heresy. American court decisions upholding censorship have been premised on the analogy between drugs and ideas: because the government has the right to protect people from poisonous drugs, the Court concluded that it can protect the public from poisonous words and thoughts.[9]

This median position of labeling is particularly appropriate in the realm of ideas where dangers of the heavy hand of censorship are omnipresent. It is reasonably clear that government control by overt censorship of the contents of speech, printed material, and matter distributed by the electronic media is now prohibited under the First Amendment. The greater danger to free expression is presented by nongovernmental pressure groups that seek to control textbooks, radio, television, and all forms of publications, as well as rock music and the visual arts. Proponents of both private and government censorship argue that children, vulnerable people, and the public in general should not be exposed to material that some find offensive. The responsible answer to these objections is truth in labeling.

Most television channels now carry information with respect to sexually explicit material and violence at the beginning of a program. Viewers are put on notice of what they are going to see. If they believe such shows are offensive, they can switch the channel. This is not censorship. It is another form of truth in labeling.

The trial of the Scottsboro boys was an important event in American law and history. It changed public perceptions. A docudrama based on the trial added fictional elements with respect to the complainant. The presentation of the trial was also altered. If the producer of the docudrama had informed the viewers of the fictional elements, the alleged rape victim would not have been so seriously affronted. The effectiveness of the program would not have been impaired. It is impossible to know whether such a disclaimer would have avoided litigation. But fairness and decent treatment of subjects and honesty to viewers should mandate an accurate statement declaring that the program is a fictionalization and not historically accurate. Even though the alleged rape victim was held to be a "public figure," and denied recovery,[10] she should have a right either to be presented truthfully or to have the viewers told that the presentation was fictionalized.

The *Westmoreland* case probably would not have lasted months, if the program had carried the statement that it was based on the best evidence available but did not purport to give the entire "truth," since that could only be established by exhaustive research and documentation beyond the capacities of a television series. It might also have carried a statement that General Westmoreland denies that he altered or falsified the body count. When controversial programs about an individual are presented, the public should be told that the subject disagrees. I do not believe that every subject is entitled to equal time to rebut charges.* But if the public knows there is a contrary view, those who are interested can pursue their own inquiries.

In fiction, satire, and comedy, labeling is particularly appropriate. Probably 99.44 percent of the readers of *Hustler* would have recognized that the piece on Jerry Falwell was a farce even without the disclaimer "AD PARODY—NOT TO BE TAKEN SERIOUSLY." *Hustler* sued Moral Majority, Inc., under copyright laws for republication of the piece without permission of *Hustler*. The court held that Moral Majority's dissemination of the piece to further Falwell's stand on moral and religious issues was a fair use of the copyrighted material. The free press issues involved in *Harper & Row* v. *Nation* were not discussed. Had Falwell sued for libel, the labeling of the piece as parody should have protected *Hustler*. A statute giving a strong presumption to such labeling by the author would avoid much litigation.

The author of *Touching* could have included the usual disclaimer that any similarity between characters in the book and real persons was purely coincidental.

Warnings, disclaimers, and releases are given effect in all other aspects of the law except libel. An accused who is told he has a right to remain silent and, nonetheless, makes an incriminatory statement, cannot successfully claim that he was coerced unless the circumstances under which the statement was taken were, in fact, coercive. An unfortunate investor will not recover if he claims fraud when the stock labeled "high risk" proves to be worthless. A patient who is informed that there is only a 50 percent likelihood of a successful result of surgery, and who still decides to have the operation, will not prevail in an action against the surgeon following an unfavorable result unless serious negligence is proved. A purchaser whose goods are repossessed will get short shrift when the contract clearly specifies the seller's right to retake the goods after default.

Courts do not probe the mind of the manufacturer who truthfully labels the product, or the mind of the policeman who reads the warnings to a criminal suspect, or the doctor who obtains the informed consent of the patient. If the party who was warned or

---

*The dispute over the fairness doctrine of the Federal Communications Commission is beyond the scope of this book.

notified appeared to be normal and to understand what was told him or her, the obligation is fulfilled.

The person who was informed or warned has a heavy legal burden to show that the consent or the statement was not voluntary or informed or that the warning was insufficient to put the party on notice of danger. It is only in libel cases under the "actual malice" test that the author's mental processes become a legal issue enabling the subject to obtain discovery of private documents and to question the author's thoughts. This tortuous process that invades the privacy of the author would be largely eliminated by truth in labeling laws.

Most lawyers do not undertake to represent clients in cases that cannot be won unless the client adamantly insists upon bringing suit and advances substantial fees.[11] Lawyers, like doctors, get informed consent. They tell their clients of the probabilities of success and failure before instituting suit.

If a statute gave legal effect to disclaimers and created a rebuttable presumption that the writing or program was, as labeled, fact, fiction, or a fictionalized presentation based on a true incident, a great many potential libel suits would be aborted. Most reasonable people do not pursue expensive losing causes.

Another aspect of disclaimer is the consent obtained from a subject who is interviewed. These interviewees are subjects of books, movies, and docudramas. They frequently sue for libel. Some of this litigation could be avoided or aborted by the use of appropriate contracts or waivers. Radio and television stations routinely obtain the consent of an interviewee to the interview and all uses of the program. The subject waives or releases whatever rights he or she may have to profit from the program or to use it. Most careful authors also obtain releases from the subjects they utilize. Whether these releases qualify as informed consent is a matter of opinion. Not many have been tested in the courts.

A release is a form of contract that must be supported by consideration, some quid pro quo. The author gets the interview and the story. Unless the subject is paid for the interview, there is a question as to the consideration received by the interviewee that supports the contract. In many instances, the person interviewed wants the publicity. Authors of books blatantly huckster on talk shows. Authors, politicians, and persons promoting various causes give their time in return for the publicity that they desire. Such nonmonetary rewards are sufficient consideration to make a contract enforceable.

Trafficking in life stories, the sale of one's privacy to provide material for an author, is for many a distasteful business. Others are willing to barter the most intimate details of their lives for cash or a moment in the limelight. Others whose misconduct has brought them brief notoriety seek to cash in on it.

Those who are reluctant to reveal their lives, who have no wish to expose themselves or sell their stories are, I believe, entitled to legal protection. To date, the law has taken little interest in assuring that their consents obtained under all sorts of conditions and frequently at a time of great emotional upset, are indeed voluntary. A mother's consent to the adoption of her baby, sometimes obtained before the birth, but usually immediately after the baby is born, is voidable for a period of six months in most jurisdictions. The law recognizes that in making such an irrevocable decision, a person needs to be in unimpaired physical and mental condition and should have time to reflect.

The decision to barter one's life story is, of course, not comparable. But it may have lasting and deleterious effects. Some rules should be established to protect both subjects and authors. There are many kinds of contracts between authors and persons accused of crime. In one instance, the accused paid a stated sum to the author on condition that if the author concluded that the subject was guilty the book would not be published. If the author concluded the subject was innocent, then the author was free to sell the book to any publisher. The subject released all rights to edit, review, or censor the manuscript in any way. Many publishers enter into contracts for books about a particular crime specifying that if the accused is acquitted the book will not be published.

Writers, until suit is actually filed, usually assume that they will be protected by their agents and publishers. It is not a safe assumption. Subjects on the whole rarely have counsel until they decide to sue. There is little opportunity for them to engage in preventive law.

Since all the parties involved in endless libel litigation are ill-served by the present law of libel, common sense would dictate that the communications industry establish some guidelines and standard forms of contracts and releases designed to minimize, if not eliminate, the most prevalent types of lawsuits.

At a minimum, subjects and authors should each be represented by counsel before signing any waiver, consent, or contract. The author should clearly retain control of the manuscript, including a provision that the subject waives all rights to read, review, or revise the manuscript. Before interviewing any subject, including authors like Jeffrey Masson, the author-interviewer should obtain a carefully worded comprehensive release and waiver of all rights, including the right to sue for libel.

Because the question of damages in libel suits is so difficult, and enormous verdicts are likely, a provision for liquidated damages in the event the contract is breached would be desirable. Under such a provision, the parties would know in advance the price of violating the contract. Trials would be simplified and considerably shortened. The likelihood of appeals would be substantially reduced.

Standard form contracts are common in many commercial transactions. Because the provisions have been carefully drafted, tried and tested, much litigation is avoided. Eric Rayman of Simon and Schuster suggested that authors and editors work closely together and that contracts be written more carefully. He urges that legal action not be the first but the last step taken. These are wise, easily implemented suggestions for preventive law.

Because authors, editors, and publishers are literate, and most subjects are also literate and reasonably intelligent, the arguments often used to avoid contracts would not prevail in these disputes. It would be difficult to claim that either of the parties to such a contract could not read or understand it because of functional illiteracy or educational deprivation. Nor could it successfully be argued that one of the parties was coerced into signing such an agreement. Except in extraordinary cases of bad faith or unconscionable behavior, courts would give full effect to waivers obtained with informed consent and to agreements entered into by counseled parties.

I also suggest, not entirely in jest, that counsel for eager plaintiffs provide their clients with a copy of Harold Laski's poignant account of his experiences as a libel plaintiff. After being accused of advocating revolution, Laski brought a libel action. After a long and bruising trial, the jury returned a verdict for the defendant. An unpublished article entitled "On Being a Libel Plaintiff" was found among Laski's papers after his death. It reads in pertinent part:

> . . . The defendant's advocate, under the guise of a pleasant suavity . . . no doubt intended to impress the jury . . . seems to have three major objectives. He is anxious to confuse you if he can. He mobilizes all the practised ingenuity of years to catch you in some contradiction. With one eye on the jury and the other on the judge, he seeks to rate your motives as plaintiff at their most base, eager, if he can, to make you lose your temper, when he hopes to have you in that psychological condition where

emotion has become the master of your reason. He will be gentle, rude, browbeating, ironical, all within half a dozen questions. He will try to make you say "yes" or "no" to questions not one of which is likely to permit an answer of this kind. He will preface his questions by some brief sentences which, as he explains so smoothly to you, are intended to make you feel why he is asking them, but are, in fact, quite obviously intended to sow in the jury's mind some carefully devised thought intended to denigrate you. If your answers do not suit his purposes, he shrugs his shoulders and looks at the jury with an air which seeks to combine the conviction that you are a halfwit with the implication that, in any case, you cannot be telling the truth. . . .

When your cross-examination is over, you subside into the position of being yourself a spectator. You may see your witnesses bullied and scorned and confused; your only part is, nevertheless, silence. And silence is still your part when counsel for the defense makes his final speech to the jury. He has one object only . . . to make you appear an impossible person, abject, arrogant, contemptible. He suggests every sort of dubious motive as the ground upon which you brought the case. He hardly makes even an effort to weigh the evidence that has been put in . . . on both sides . . . for the consideration of the jury. His main concern is to create the kind of atmosphere that reduces something that, for you, is at the very base of all your future life, to the kind of amusing trifle which can have "laughter in court" placed after it in brackets by the reporters. . . . [The trial casts] a painful burden on the jury, the members of which were so tragically troubled with the need to think about the matters they had to understand. . . ."[12]

Publishers and producers of television, radio, and dramatic performances can also take preventive action by prefacing every publication and program with a statement of the nature of the contents: fact, fiction, satire, biography, fictionalized biography, fictionalized drama based on a true incident, and the like. These simple, traditional legal devices can easily be utilized in the multifarious relationships between subjects and authors to the benefit of both parties and the avoidance of much litigation.

If courts give full effect to waivers obtained with informed consent, much litigation could be avoided. Subjects presented with such documents may become wiser and warier. It may be that some books will not be written because subjects refuse to cooperate. They have such rights. Books may be written without purporting to reveal the subject's words and thoughts. It can scarcely be argued that the public will be the loser if subjects are more cautious. The First Amendment will be the winner if such contracts are enforced.

·XIII·

One Nation: Fifty Laws of Libel

*When the highest court of a state has reached a
determination [with respect to the First Amendment] we
give most respectful attention to its reasoning and
conclusion, but its authority is not final here. Were it
otherwise the constitutional limits of free expression in
the Nation would vary with state lines.*

—PENNEKAMP V. FLORIDA

THIRTEEN fractious, quarreling colonies were fused into one nation in the crucible of conflict. The result was compromise. Certain
powers were reluctantly ceded to the weak fledgling government.
Under the Tenth Amendment, all authority not specifically granted
to the federal government was retained by the jealous, powerful
states. After two centuries of geographical expansion, population
growth and demographic changes, wars, depressions, and recessions,
it is obvious that the United States is one nation not a confederation
of states. Although there are race, class, and economic differences
among this heterogeneous people, they are bound together not only
by language and government but by economic, industrial, financial,
and social institutions. Among the potent unifying forces are the
national media. Some regional differences linger in the arts. But they
pale in significance compared with national similarities.

The legacy of confederation persists in the dual systems of government—federal and state. State governments deal primarily with issues and problems within their geographic boundaries. National and
international problems are confided to the Congress and the president. In the actual day to day operations of government, there is little
serious conflict between the states and the federal government.

The dual system of laws and courts, however, is a source of conflict
and difficulty in many situations. Nowhere is this more troublesome
than in litigation between subjects and authors. The founding fathers

probably never anticipated a nation in which most significant legal issues would ultimately be decided by the United States Supreme Court. In 1789 and for some time thereafter, most litigation was conducted in the state courts. John Jay, the first Chief Justice of the Supreme Court, complained that the Court had too little work. In the 1980s, Chief Justice Burger insistently complained that the Court was overworked.

The division of jurisdiction between the federal courts and the fifty state courts is rational and operates reasonably well with certain significant exceptions. All courts, both state and federal, are bound by the Constitution. State courts have exclusive jurisdiction over violations of state law, including crimes, and civil matters arising within the state. Lower federal courts have jurisdiction in three principal areas: matters involving interstate commerce, federal statutes, and suits between citizens (including corporations) of different states (known as diversity jurisdiction). Since 1938, federal courts are required to apply the law of the appropriate state in diversity matters.[1] There is no federal common law. Accordingly, all libel suits are decided under the law of one of the states regardless of whether the action is brought in a state or federal court.

Under the Fourteenth Amendment, the rights and immunities established by the Bill of Rights are applicable to the states.* Accordingly, any party who claims that constitutional rights, including First Amendment rights, were violated looks to the highest court of the land for a declaration and enforcement of those rights.

Communications and entertainment are national industries. National television and radio programs and national magazines and journals of all kinds and the great national newspapers have been instrumental in creating a national ethos and culture. Most books, other than regional books published by regional presses, are distributed nationwide. Printed matter, regardless of where it is sold or distributed, is protected by federal copyright law. Although there are many local radio and television stations that provide local programs heard predominantly within the borders of a single state, a vast proportion of these programs are also heard in other states. The national networks dominate prime time.†

---

*The suggestion of Attorney General Meese that this doctrine has not been followed is wrong. President Reagan's reference to the "unamended Constitution" may presage radical changes in the law. But as of this writing, there is no indication that any responsible court has adopted his view.

†The electronic media are subject to federal regulation. But libel suits against them are decided under state law. The sensitive issues of government control of programming such as the fairness rule are beyond the purview of this discussion.

Most of the libel cases brought against media defendants involve communications across state lines. Almost all suits against authors of books and magazine articles involve interstate communications. But despite the fact that the leading defamation cases have concerned national publications and national television, defamation has been treated by the courts as being exclusively a matter of state law, principally because there is no federal law governing the subject.

The landmark, seminal case of *New York Times* v. *Sullivan* was decided under Alabama law subject to the First Amendment. The Court took pains to point out that only 394 of a total issue of 650,000 papers were distributed in Alabama. Nonetheless, the case was decided under Alabama law. One can surmise that the reason the Court looked to Alabama law was the fact that there was neither a federal common law of libel nor a federal statute. Absent Alabama common law, Sullivan would have had no legal doctrine under which to assert a claim for injury to reputation, a property right. The Court would then have been faced with deciding whether denial of such a right violated the due process clause of the Fourteenth Amendment.

Time, Inc. v. *Firestone*, previously discussed, was decided under the law of Florida. *Keeton* v. *Hustler Magazine*[2] was decided according to New Hampshire law even though only 10,000 to 15,000 copies of the magazine were sold in that state. New Hampshire was the only state in which plaintiff's claim would not have been time barred.

The libel suit by President Hamaela DeRobert of Nauru against Gannett Publications is based on a single copy of Guam's *Pacific Daily News* that was mailed to this tiny Pacific Island Republic.[3] DeRobert is seeking $40 million in damages, claiming that articles linking him to an illegal loan of $675,000 by the government of Nauru to a separatist political faction in the Marshall Islands were false. His legal bills, estimated at more than $4 million, are being paid by the government. President Kabua of the Marshall Islands is suing for libel based on the same article. DeRobert brought suit in Hawaii. Every day cases against the national media and national book publishers are brought in all the states. Each will be decided in accordance with the requirements, rules of procedure, and substantive law prevailing in those states.

More than a century ago, Congress and the courts recognized the necessity of having one national law governing interstate transportation and subordinating state laws and regulations to federal law.[4] One recommendation of this book is that actions by subjects against authors involving communications distributed across state lines be decided in accordance with federal law. It makes no sense whatsoever for national organizations to be subjected to the peculiarities of the laws of fifty states.

The Supreme Court had the opportunity (which it did not take) in *New York Times* v. *Sullivan* to hold that, because the *New York Times* was engaged in interstate commerce, the imposition of Alabama libel law unconstitutionally hampered or impeded interstate commerce.

Prior to the decision in *Erie Railroad* v. *Tompkins*[5] overruling *Swift* v. *Tyson,*[6] it had been law for more than a century that cases in federal courts should be decided under federal law. *Erie Railroad* v. *Tomkins* required federal courts to look to the law of the state in which the action arose. Although the merits of the *Erie Railroad* case have been debated for half a century, its relation to libel law has not been seriously considered. With little discussion of the effect on interstate communications, these perplexing cases have been remitted to the vagaries of the laws of the fifty states.

The states have libel privilege statutes that vary considerably. California, for example, has twelve separate statutes dealing with libel privilege, immunity, and malice. Thirty-three states have libel retraction statutes, all different. Ten states have privacy statutes, all different. The statutes of limitations of the several states governing the time within which suit must be brought vary from one to four years.[7] A federal statute would establish the same statute of limitations for the entire nation. There would be no advantage to a plaintiff in suing in New Hampshire. There is also no reason why the taxpayers of New Hampshire should be saddled with the not inconsiderable costs of a lengthy trial and protracted appeals when neither the plaintiff nor the defendant is a resident of that state and only a minimal number of issues of the publication are sold in that state. While there is a basic similarity in the common law of all states except Louisiana, the decisional developments vary considerably. Authors, including publishers and the media, must be prepared not only to defend actions in the federal courts and the courts of all fifty states, but under fifty different bodies of law.

Under the present state of libel law, the plaintiff's first problem is to find a jurisdiction where the defendant can be sued. This is not a simple matter, as many separated and divorced spouses who seek alimony, child custody, and child support know. It can be a futile, expensive, and exhausting quest. In most libel suits, at least one defendant is a deep pocket corporation. It is much easier to sue a corporation than an individual who can move out of the state to avoid service.

Every state has some form of "long arm" statute that permits courts to take jurisdiction over corporate defendants that do business within the state without actually serving the complaint on the corporation or one of its officers. But individual defendants must be personally served. It is not necessary for a defendant to have an office in the state. A defendant doing business in a state can be sued in that state even though he or she has never actually set foot in the state.

If the defendant has been properly served, the court must decide whether to take jurisdiction over the case. A two-step inquiry is made. First, it must be determined whether the cause of action arose in the state, and second, whether the defendant has "minimum contacts" within the state. If the cause of action does not derive from the defendant's activities within the state, the plaintiff must establish that the defendant maintained "continuous and substantial ties" within the state.[8] A simple example explains the meaning of these rules. If a manufacturer or distributor physically located in state A advertises its products in state B and sells them there by mail or other delivery, that is sufficient. An occasional sale that represents only a very small percentage of the defendant's business will, in most instances, be insufficient to give the state court jurisdiction. Yet, in *Keeton* v. *Hustler,* only a small fraction of the total number of copies of the defendant's publication was sold in New Hampshire. Nonetheless, the Supreme Court held that New Hampshire had jurisdiction over the libel action. The customary test in commercial cases is a sensible one: Was the defendant's conduct such that he or she should reasonably anticipate being haled into court in that jurisdiction?[9] The question of jurisdiction may be of enormous importance. For example, if an action is brought for the death of an individual allegedly killed as a result of the wrongful conduct of the defendant, the state law applicable will be a critical issue. Some states limit recovery for wrongful death to $25,000; others to $100,000; and some states have no limitation on the amount of recovery. In libel actions the choice of law is also of great significance. The laws of several states vary considerably with respect to punitive damages. Some states recognize a right of privacy. Others do not.

With a federal libel statute, the parties to the action would frequently be saved considerable inconvenience and expense because there would be no advantage to a plaintiff to bring suit in a remote state where neither plaintiff nor defendant resides. To defend an action two or three thousand miles from one's home or regular place of business is a real hardship and entails considerable expense. It necessitates retaining special counsel in that state to work with defendant's regular attorney. The principal parties and witnesses have to travel great distances and lose considerable time from work and leisure activities. Documents are sent back and forth.

The doctrine of *forum non conveniens,* an inconvenient forum, was developed to permit courts to require that litigants sue in the place where most of the witnesses and parties reside. These questions often arise in transportation accidents. For example, a plaintiff who resides in New York purchases bus tickets in New York for a trip to California. The company has offices in New York. An accident occurs in Nevada. But the bus made a stop in Kansas. The witnesses and parties are all residents of either Nevada or New York. Why should the case be tried in Kansas simply because the plaintiff chooses to bring suit there? The defendant also does business in Kansas and many other states. Most courts will require that the trial take place either in New York or Nevada.

This does not end the legal questions. Which law shall be applied? If someone was killed in the accident and suit is brought by the deceased's estate or executor, the trial court will have to decide that question. In the hypothetical transportation case, the trial court would have to decide whether to apply the law of the place where the contract was made, New York, or the place of the accident, Nevada. The judge may decide that under the law of the trial jurisdiction the law to be applied is the law of the place of the accident. The judge then looks to the law of that state, which may provide that the appropriate law is the place of making the contract. This kind of round robin is known as renvoi. It plagues courts and litigants in many types of cases.

In a 1956 case involving the unauthorized telecast of a prizefight, the court held that it would have to apply the laws of four different states. The fight was broadcast from New York and Pennsylvania stations. The New York broadcast was visible only in New York. The Pennsylvania broadcast was seen in Pennsylvania, New Jersey, and Delaware. The court held that it would "look to Pennsylvania law (where the suit was brought) as to Pennsylvania injuries, under Pennsylvania conflict of laws rule as to what law to apply to Delaware and New Jersey and to the law of New York as to the New York telecasts."[10] The court had to apply the laws of four states with respect to both liability and damages. Imagine the confusion in charging a jury as to the laws of four different states.

In libel actions, courts have listed the following contacts as particularly relevant to the choice of law:

1. The state of plaintiff's domicile.
2. The state of plaintiff's principal activity to which the alleged defamation relates.
3. The state where the plaintiff in fact suffered greatest harm.
4. The state of the publisher's domicile or incorporation.
5. The state where the defendant's main publishing office is located.
6. The state of principal circulation.
7. The place of emanation.
8. The state where the libel was first seen.
9. The law of the forum.

These difficult and time-consuming decisions would be substantially avoided by a federal statute. Because all states would be governed by the same law, the rights of the parties would not depend upon the choice of forum by the plaintiff. Moreover, there would be little advantage to either party in choosing between suing in state or federal court.

Sometimes A sues B in the state court and B sues A in the federal court for claims arising out of the same transaction. I recall trying two cases in Scranton, Pennsylvania, a very inconvenient forum, involving the same parties and the same fact situation. The parties and witnesses lived in Philadelphia and New York. We lawyers rushed back and forth across the street from the county courthouse to the federal courthouse. Questions involving a testamentary trust that had been set up as a corporation were decided by the county judge and questions involving the rights of the shareholders of the corporation were decided in federal court. Usually what happens in such instances is a kind of Alphonse and Gaston routine. The state judge will defer action until the federal case is decided and the federal court will defer to the state court.

These problems frequently occur in defamation and privacy cases because most members of the national media have their principal offices in New York, Washington, D.C., or California. Their publications and electronic programs are distributed and broadcast in most of the states.* The Supreme Court considered these jurisdictional

---

*Manufacturers of products sold nationwide who are sued under products liability law for defective goods have similar problems.

questions in the suit brought by Shirley Jones, an actress, and her husband against the *National Enquirer.* [11] They sued for libel, invasion of privacy, and intentional infliction of emotional distress in California where they lived. The *Enquirer* is regularly sold in California. Plaintiffs also sued the editor and the author of the story, both of whom were Florida residents. The individual defendants moved to quash service on the grounds that they could not be sued in California. The trial court granted the motion, holding that in libel cases assertion of First Amendment rights requires greater than usual contacts with the forum state. The California Court of Appeals held that First Amendment concerns were irrelevant to the jurisdictional question and reversed, holding that the defendants caused a "tortious effect" in California. The California Supreme Court denied review, in effect holding that California had jurisdiction. The United States Supreme Court denied review, in effect upholding California jurisdiction. This is one of the rare instances of unanimity in a libel case. But compare *Dun & Bradstreet, Inc.* v. *Greenmoss Builders, Inc.,* [12] decided the following year, in which the plurality of a sharply divided Supreme Court held that in First Amendment cases the usual standard of review of a trial court's decision—was it clearly erroneous?—does not apply. It held that in libel cases the appellate courts should consider the evidence themselves. If that doctrine of review had prevailed in the *Jones* case, the question of jurisdiction might have been decided differently.

Many of these difficulties as to choice of law, jurisdiction, and damages in actions by subjects against authors and counter-suits could be avoided by a comprehensive federal statute. Despite the Supreme Court's oft-repeated concern about the chilling effects of libel suits, it cannot be disputed that the prospect of defending actions in fifty states under fifty different laws is a daunting prospect.

To minimize liability for libel, many book publishers now include in their contracts a guarantee on the part of the author that there is nothing defamatory in the manuscript. Other publishers reject manuscripts because they fear libel suits. Rita Lavelle, a former official of the Environmental Protection Agency, has written a book about her experiences in the Reagan administration that, she claims, "Tells all." She reports that she cannot find a publisher because all fear libel suits. [13] If that is, in fact, the reason her manuscript has been rejected, it gives cause for concern. Robert Coover's novel, *The Public Burning,* a satire on the execution of the Rosenbergs, was also reportedly rejected by a number of publishers who feared libel suits.

There is no way of knowing how many otherwise salable books have been rejected to avoid libel suits.

I do not suggest that all these unpublished authors are mute inglorious Miltons. Milton himself would undoubtedly have eloquently thundered against this kind of self-censorship as he did against licensing laws. This is another dangerous aspect of privatism. In effect, the subjects are given a veto power over publications and electronic media programs. In my view, it is immaterial whether Rita Lavelle's book is a responsible report or gossipy trash. If the book were banned by government action, what would be the legal basis for such a ruling? It is unlikely that a book about a government agency could be deemed to be obscene. The Environmental Protection Agency does not deal with espionage, military secrets, foreign policy, or high-level weapon technology. It is most improbable that the Lavelle book could offend any statute prohibiting disclosure of secrets. Because Lavelle purports to write about past events, her book could not possibly present a "clear and present danger" to the national security or welfare. The only foreseeable harm resulting from its publication would be bruised egos of subjects and the likelihood of litigation.

This potent and justified fear of litigation prevents publication of many books and articles and airing of TV and radio programs. A federal law would not, of course, eliminate the fear of litigation. It would, however, reduce the uncertainties created by fifty different bodies of law.

Certainty of legal rights and obligations permits potential defendants to conform their conduct to meet those requirements. Certainty also permits lawyers to restrict their case preparation to a limited number of issues and thus reduces the costs of litigation. The statute here proposed would permit the granting of summary judgment in many situations that now require prolonged and costly trials and appeals.

A federal statute governing defamation and privacy suits in which the allegedly offensive communication was transmitted across state boundaries would not oust the jurisdiction of state courts to hear these cases. It would require that state courts apply federal instead of state law. It is the general rule of interpretation of statutes that when federal and state law govern the same subject, the federal law preempts the field. With respect to libel suits based on interstate communications, the federal statute would undoubtedly supersede state law. In many cases involving interstate commerce, the Supreme

Court has held that federal statutes preempted the field and relegated the applicability of state statutes to purely intrastate transactions.[14] Because the vast majority of written and electronic communications do cross state lines, a federal statute would govern the overwhelming majority of such cases.

Probably most state courts would follow the federal statute even in purely intrastate libel cases not governed by such an act. It is a common practice of all judges to look for authority. By training and habit judges seek precedent rather than innovation. Despite popular complaints that the judiciary acts as a super-legislature, judges rarely assume a creative role. As Justice Cardozo pointed out, judges legislate interstitially only when there is no applicable statute or case law governing the problem at hand and then only because they have no other option. A trial judge cannot refuse to decide a case because there is no precedent. He or she must make the best-educated guess extrapolating from similar or analogous cases and statutes. On rare occasions, courts do make new law because the statute or prior case law is clearly outmoded or unjust or appears to violate constitutional rights.

But legislation is the most common and forthright means of obtaining relief from unfair common law doctrines. Both the Congress and the state legislatures have enacted numerous statutes for the purpose of repealing manifestly unfair legal rulings. For many years under the common law it was the rule that a plaintiff harmed by reason of the negligence of the defendant could not recover if the plaintiff himself had been negligent, no matter how slightly. After decades in which badly injured plaintiffs were denied recovery, most states enacted comparative negligence laws apportioning liability according to fault. If the defendant is 75 percent negligent and the plaintiff 25 percent negligent, the defendant is held liable for 75 percent of the damages.

When individuals and small businesses were at a gross disadvantage in suing railroads, Congress passed a law to provide for fairer treatment of all parties. The Cullom Report of the Select Committee on Interstate Commerce noted that a plaintiff "can go into court to enforce his right, but experience has shown that in most cases, he does not do so because he cannot on account of the expense, and especially because of the difficulty of making necessary proof to sustain his action."[15] Another reason impelling passage of the Interstate Commerce Act was that the legal enunciated doctrines by the Supreme Court unduly favored the railroads.[16] There is ample precedent for the enactment of statutes to change decisional law that is perceived by the public to be unfair or unworkable or both.

Rather than attempting to establish a constitutional right of persona through the long, costly process of litigation, a statute provides a far better method and more immediate means of protecting such a right. The likelihood of obtaining constitutional protection through the courts is remote. As recently as 1972 the Supreme Court, in rejecting a constitutional right to decent living conditions, declared: "We do not denigrate the importance of decent, safe, and sanitary housing. But the Constitution does not provide judicial remedies for every social and economic ill. . . ."[17] If, as I believe is the fact, the American people consider that privacy is a value entitled to legal protection, the obvious way to obtain that protection is by means of a statute.

A federal statute is not the only means of bringing order and certainty into the conflicts between subjects and authors. A slower statutory route is the promulgation of a model or uniform state statute. There are many such statutes. Usually they are drafted by a group of experts under the auspices of a prestigious body such as the American Law Institute. The several states then enact the law. State legislatures are frequently delighted to be spared the difficult, costly, and time-consuming task of drafting a complicated statute. The Uniform Commercial Code is a signal example of a successful state law governing complex transactions, many of which occur across state boundaries. Within fourteen years after the draft was completed, forty-eight states enacted the code with only minor variations. Unquestionably it has brought order and stability to numerous banking, sales, and other commercial transactions. It has eliminated an enormous amount of litigation as well as jurisdiction shopping.

Even when a state has not adopted a model act, the judges of that state look to the act as a standard to provide guidance as to which of many possible options to adopt when faced with difficult decisions. The model Child Abuse Reporting Law deals with a simpler but equally widespread problem. Within a decade of its promulgation, it was enacted by all fifty states. It provided a clear remedy for a problem for which the common law had found no satisfactory solution. Child abuse is primarily a local problem. Appropriately it was confided to state law and enforcement through state agencies. A related problem with interstate ramifications is that of runaway children and interstate kidnapping of children. These problems have been satisfactorily dealt with by a federal kidnapping law and interstate compacts on runaways.

Libel, privacy, and litigation between subjects and authors can, I believe, be more appropriately and speedily resolved by a federal statute because most of the communications giving rise to such litigation are distributed nationally.

A federal statute has many other advantages over the common law in dealing with specific areas of law. Most statutes contain what are called "legislative findings." Usually a well-drafted statute sets forth the need for a statute and the reasons impelling the legislature to favor the position taken. These findings based on hearings and committee reports provide invaluable compilations of facts. Hearings on a federal libel law would permit members of the media, authors, publishers, lawyers, and plaintiffs to testify as to their respective problems. A committee could take testimony with respect to the costs of litigation, the reluctance to publish news, novels, and biographies, as well as the special problems and needs of the electronic media. A congressional committee could also compile data as to the length of trials, the cost to the public of this litigation, and its effects on court backlogs.

Many statutes also contain a declaration of policy. This presents a clear statement of those interests the Congress wishes to protect. Because legislators are responsive to the views of their constituents, this presents the fairest and most reliable expression of the will of the people. When interpreting such a statute, courts do not have to grope for reasons to prefer one view over another. The legislature has spoken.

Under a federal statute, courts can properly consider national policy issues. State courts are not expected to consider questions of national policy in deciding litigation arising under state law. When interpreting a federal statute, such concerns are appropriate. On a case by case basis through the process of accretion, courts create a body of national law that interprets the will of the people as expressed by the Congress and the policy of those laws. When interpreting §301 of the Labor Management Relations Act, the Supreme Court declared that it would "apply substantive federal law which the courts must fashion from the policy of our national labor laws."[18] In the absence of a federal libel statute, there is no national law and no national policy on which the courts, state and federal, can build to fashion a body of law.

Many federal statutes provide for concurrent jurisdiction in the federal and state courts. Such concurrent jurisdiction recognizes the roles of both court systems and does not result in an overload of cases in the federal courts. It also avoids the unseemly spectacle of jurisdiction shopping and the dismaying results when similar cases are decided differently by courts of different jurisdictions.

Statutes are preferable to ingenious efforts by lawyers and judges to bring the claims of litigants within the rubric of constitutional rights. Many of the problems encountered in deciding libel cases arise from the fact that courts are bound by prior decisions based on constitutional rights and principles. Despite the vast spectrum of fact situations and the obvious differences between cases involving commercial transactions, fiction, biography, and news, all courts must attempt to follow or distinguish the long line of First Amendment cases. A statute provides a new baseline, a new beginning for courts. First they will look to the mandates of the statute.

Every enactment by a legislative body carries a presumption of constitutionality. Although a statute cannot abrogate constitutional rights, it can create new substantive rights and procedures.[19] It can give recognition to interests previously ignored.

The 1984 Federal Crimes Code, for example, reflected a growing public concern for the victims of crime. The Congress recognized the financial needs of victims of crime and made provision in the sentencing options available to the courts for restitution and reparations to be paid to crime victims and to crime victim compensation funds. As early as 1970, some judges had under old common law principles been ordering restitution to crime victims as a condition of a probationary sentence. The enactment of the Federal Crimes Code not only gave legitimacy to the practice but also provided counsel for the defendants the opportunity to request such a sentence. It gave the victims a legal basis on which to urge consideration of their needs by the sentencing court.

In privacy cases, a statute would give injured plaintiffs new rights. It would also clarify the rights of defendants. If such a statute expressly rejected a right of biography in those cases, it would permit defendants to obtain a summary judgment without the necessity of elaborate and costly pretrial procedures. Under the proposed statute, almost all cases could be tried more expeditiously and with greater certainty of the outcomes.

Statutes, unlike the Constitution, are not documents for the ages. Statutes do not purport to declare fundamental rights but rather to provide remedies for immediate problems and needs. They reflect contemporary perceptions. A statute can be amended or repealed if it becomes obsolete or unworkable. If any provision unduly infringes upon the rights of any party, that section will be held unconstitutional. In brief, a statute does not purport to be a permanent declaration of rights, but rather a temporary or transitory means of coping with a specific problem in accordance with well-understood principles of law.

A statute governing the rights and remedies of subjects and authors can give recognition and approval to concepts such as retraction, disclaimer, and truth in labeling that have not been widely utilized. These remedies could, with statutory authorization, provide substantial protections at minimal cost to both subjects and authors. If such provisions prove unworkable or too heavily weighted in favor of one party or against the other, modification by amendment is not too complicated or protracted a process.

Peter Mancuso, a journalist for the *Boston Globe,* after interviewing leading libel lawyers for plaintiffs and defendants reports, "Both sides acknowledge that it could be years before the [Supreme] Court makes any significant clarifications in libel law and that plaintiffs and defendants alike would be better served if the system were changed to reduce the tension, cost and confusion of litigation."[20] A federal statute is the most available and expeditious means of bringing about change.

·XIV·

Other Options

Two roads diverged in a wood, and I—
I took the one less traveled by,
And that has made all the difference.

—ROBERT FROST

T HE widespread dissatisfaction with libel law has given rise to many proposals for change that deserve thoughtful consideration. In evaluating any suggested remedy, one must have a standard by which to appraise it. The harm or evil sought to be alleviated may be taken as a baseline. But it does not provide an ideal goal against which the remedy can be measured. The Rand Institute for Civil Justice postulates three criteria for measuring the success of any dispute resolution system: the system should be prompt, inexpensive, and fair.[1] Certainly these are desirable goals. Everyone wants speedy, cheap justice. In cases that involve only disputes over money,* these criteria are appropriate and sufficient. But in disputes in which constitutional rights are implicit, other considerations must take precedence.

Protection of First Amendment rights transcends the interests of the litigants. These rights affect the entire nation. All constitutional provisions to some extent define and shape our society. Their preservation and enforcement is a matter of concern to the entire public, not simply to the individuals claiming those rights. The treatment accorded those accused of crime, for example, is a measure of the civilization and humaneness of a society. It may well be that by his reprehensible or brutal conduct the accused has forfeited any claims

*These are the kinds of cases that were evaluated by the Rand Institute.

to compassion or mercy. But no one guilty of even the most heinous acts should be deemed to have forfeited rights to due process of law and presumption of innocence. A contrary view would make the reach of the Constitution vary depending on the character of the individuals attempting to assert their rights. More than eight centuries of legal doctrine stemming from the Magna Charta would be jettisoned by such an ad hominem interpretation of the Constitution.

In libel and privacy cases, far more is at stake than speed and convenience and economy for the litigants. Public access to information, opinion, and entertainment is directly affected by libel and privacy litigation. Thus, considerations of speed and cost, no matter how desirable, cannot be permitted to override the necessity to uphold the Constitution.

Referring again to criminal law, it is obvious that a due process trial in which an accused is afforded constitutional rights is neither speedy nor cheap. Non-lawyers, such as criminologist James Q. Wilson, who urge swift, certain justice for offenders ignore the obvious. Justice cannot be either swift or certain if constitutional rights are to be preserved. It is well to recall Justice Frankfurter's observation that the history of due process has largely been the history of procedure.[2] Procedural rights are significant not as ends in themselves but because procedural regularity has been, to date, the best means of ensuring that a just result will ensue. From time to time, shocking miscarriages of justice do occur. Most often the cause is not evil intent but failure to abide by the rules or failure to provide adequate counsel for the parties so that the adversary system can function fairly.

In litigation between subjects and authors, the most significant criterion for evaluating laws and procedures is whether they will effectuate the broadest possible rights of freedom of expression without infringing upon other rights. Certainty of the law is also a significant criterion. Certainty may be the most important factor in reducing expense and delay. If the law were reasonably clear and certain, it would also materially reduce the amount of litigation. The number of cases that authors must defend as well as the time and expense of defense are related to self-censorship.

The length of a trial directly affects the expenses of trial. Lawyers, like plumbers, are usually paid on an hourly basis.* The longer the

---

*In some instances plaintiffs' lawyers take the case on a contingent fee basis. Counsel receives as a fee a percentage of the plaintiff's recovery. If the plaintiff loses, counsel does not receive a fee. Defendants' counsel, with rare exceptions, are paid on a time basis regardless of whether the defendant wins or loses.

trial, the greater the out-of-pocket costs as well as the emotional wear and tear on the parties. The number of issues to be decided is a material factor governing the length and cost of trial.

Even with the most clearly defined statute, there are constraints on reducing time and expense because constitutional rights must be protected. Everyone recognizes that hasty guilty pleas in which poor defendants give up their rights because they cannot afford to assert them, even when provided with free counsel, are not consonant with the mandates of due process and the goals of a democratic society. This is true even though the accused *may* be guilty as charged. Similarly, some procedural shortcuts that are acceptable to subjects and authors in order to reduce their expenses may not be in the best interests of the public and the preservation of First Amendment rights for all Americans.

Much civil litigation is prolonged and costly. To reduce the amount of libel litigation, the incentives to sue must be reduced. But so long as authors use living subjects for their source materials in reporting news and writing fiction, biography, and docudramas, the potential for litigation remains.

"Justice delayed is justice denied" is an old and truthful aphorism. One reason for the delay in libel litigation is the disproportionately large number of cases that are appealed. Most of those that are heard by the Supreme Court are remanded for a new trial. Many libel cases are tried twice, and some three times. Attorney Gertz had to wait fourteen and a half years to collect his judgment. Herbert's litigation has continued for a decade. He is contemplating another petition to the Supreme Court.

A review of sixty-one libel decisions of the federal courts of appeal reveals that twenty-four were reversed.[3] This rate must be compared with a 19 percent reversal rate in all civil cases. I do not fault either the juries or the trial judges for the high rate of reversals. Most of the errors of the lower courts occurred because the rules are unclear and constantly changing. Gertz himself warns other lawyers prosecuting and defending libel suits that the law is in flux.[4]

The proposed changes in libel law range from eliminating all litigation to limiting the amount of damages recoverable. Examining these proposals from the viewpoint of a trial judge, I see serious flaws in many and some very sensible suggestions in others.

Elmer Johnson of General Motors takes the most extreme position, maintaining that there is no excuse for any civil litigation, that all cases should be settled.[5] If people are reasonable and they are simply arguing about money, they can resolve their disputes by the process of give and take. In fact, this is what happens in most civil cases. Plaintiff's counsel makes an exorbitant demand. Defense counsel refuses to make an offer. Both declare they are willing to litigate if it takes six months. At this point, most experienced trial judges suggest that the costs to the parties may be disproportionate to the results. Counsel, who really have no intention of going to trial, usually request the judge to place a figure on the case that they can submit to their clients. I usually give a range of reasonable amounts. If plaintiff is able to prove A, B, and C, then X is a reasonable sum. If plaintiff can prove only A and B, then Y is an appropriate figure. Counsel know the strengths and weaknesses of their respective positions. They go back and forth. Plaintiff lowers the demand. Defendant raises the offer until agreement is reached. This process occurs whether the settlement is for $10,000 or $10,000,000. I recall one particularly acrimonious discussion that lasted more than two days. When settlement was finally reached and both clients had happily agreed, one lawyer said to me, "Judge, do you feel as if you had just bought a rug in a Turkish bazaar?"

This procedure, though distasteful, was desirable and in the best interests of the parties and the public. An acrimonious six-month trial was avoided. Both parties were spared huge counsel fees and fees for scores of expert witnesses. By the end of the case, the litigants would have been extremely hostile. Regardless of the outcome, the loser would have appealed. The matter would have dragged on for years. It would have cost the taxpayers about $2,000 a day and added enormously to the backlog.

Some judges think every case should be settled. I do not. A small percent of civil cases involve constitutional rights that should not be compromised. Others involve significant legal issues that should be decided so that others with similar problems can know what the law is and conform their conduct accordingly. A very few cases involve factual situations that should be aired so that the public knows what is happening.* A small number of cases are simply strike suits. The plaintiff sues only for the purpose of obtaining a settlement not because he or she really has a good cause of action. In my opinion none of these cases should be settled even though it might be cheaper

---

*For example, in a case tried before me brought by one corporate officer against another, the evidence indisputably revealed that both plaintiff and defendant were looting corporate assets to the serious detriment of the stockholders. Fearing that the facts would become known, the parties settled their differences. The case was never reported in the press.

and easier for the parties. The vast majority of cases between subject and author in my opinion are susceptible of settlement but many should not be settled.

"Alternative dispute resolution" popularly known as ADR, has surged to the fore in the 1980s as a panacea for all civil litigation. The Center for Public Resources in New York City urges arbitration and other alternatives to litigation.[6] In essence, instead of courts of law that function in the open and duly elected or appointed judges, it substitutes private individuals who have been selected by the parties and who decide cases behind closed doors. This is a most alarming manifestation of privatism and antidemocratic principles. It betrays a distrust of public officials and the public that selects them. Although a very few of the 18,000 American judges have betrayed their trust and some are less competent than one would desire, there is no reason to believe that privately hired arbitrators and mediators would, on the whole, be superior or that they would be sensitive to public needs and constitutional mandates. The entire process of appeal and decision of significant issues by the Supreme Court would be aborted.

In California, private dispute resolution is called "Rent a Judge." In the Eastern states, it is known as "Judicate." Those who can afford to pay and wish to do so, in effect, buy their own legal system. These programs and many similar ones are operated by for-profit corporations. They are widely touted by those engaged in these businesses as offering quicker and more effective results. These plans have been lauded as "private settlement for the public good" and denounced as "secret justice for the privileged few."[7]

General Westmoreland is a vigorous and insistent proponent of a proposal to remove libel cases from the courts. He calls for a National News Council to arbitrate libel cases.[8] Aside from the fact that it is highly unlikely that most subjects and authors would agree to such a plan, it has serious flaws. Arbitration and mediation are available and have been for many years. Although many disputes are settled satisfactorily by professional arbitrators, a good many are not. If one party refuses to abide by the decision of the arbitrator, the case will ultimately come to court.

First Amendment issues, although frequently treated as disputes over money, involve serious public issues. These cases should be heard in open court, not behind the closed doors of a mediator's office. There is already an ominous trend restricting the right of the public to know what is happening in the courts. For example, in

Tavoulareas v. *Mobil Oil Co.,* the Court of Appeals for the District of Columbia held that the press has no right to see depositions that are part of the court record until after verdict.[9] Ultimately this information will become public. When cases are arbitrated or mediated, however, the record is never open to the public.

Unless the parties agree, it is difficult to see how anyone—individual or corporation—can constitutionally be deprived of access to the courts or denied the right to a trial by jury.

Another widely praised proposal is the suggestion by Professor Marc A. Franklin that an action for declaratory judgment be substituted for a suit for damages.[10] A bill has been introduced into Congress embodying this idea.[11] The gist of the proposal is that a plaintiff would forgo claims for monetary damages in return for a declaratory judgment holding that he or she had been defamed. The bill also provides for a one-year statute of limitations, prohibits punitive damages, and provides that the losing party pay the winner's counsel fees. All these provisions require critical analysis.

The declaratory judgment notion has been accepted by some as a panacea. Attorney Bruce J. Ennis suggests that " . . . plaintiffs would gain a speedy method of vindicating their names in return for freeing the press from the specter of huge costs."[12] This sweeping claim requires some skeptical review. The idea that libel plaintiffs are suing for honor not money is predicated on Professor Franklin's statistics. In response to a questionnaire, most libel plaintiffs stated that they had brought suit to vindicate their good names. I do not doubt that this is what they said. Most people ascribe to themselves nobler rather than baser motives. As any practicing lawyer and trial judge knows, most clients, like most other people, put the best foot forward. Persons suing for divorce always say they want to do what is fair and right for the spouse. Few jilted wives say, "I want to take that so and so for every penny he has." But that is what they proceed to do. Similarly, most husbands say they want to be fair and generous to the ex-wife. In fact, most will litigate interminably to avoid a fair settlement. Convicted offenders rarely admit their evil motives. Even when pleading guilty, most defendants claim some excuse or extenuating circumstances.

It requires a suspension of common sense and experience to conclude that a plaintiff who paid substantial legal fees and other expenses would be satisfied with a mere declaration of virtue and no monetary balm. Possibly a General Sharon or General Westmoreland would find a declaratory judgment sufficient. Yet, it must be remembered that each demanded millions of dollars. It was only after losing the trial that Sharon declared that he was vindicated. Until the money ran out, Westmoreland was unwilling to accept a statement vindicating his "honor."

The major fallacy is the premise that a declaratory judgment suit would be cheaper and quicker than an action for damages. The issues of public versus private figure, actual malice, and countless other questions would have to be decided. Authors also have honor. Few members of the press would be willing to concede that they had made egregious errors. It is unlikely that they would concede error even though they would be relieved of the possibility of monetary damages. As Ray Cave, managing editor of *Time* magazine explained in discussing the *Sharon* case, "The principle was, if you think your story is right then you better defend it."[13] With respect to fiction and commercial speech, difficult problems of proof, including "of and concerning," whether the statement was one of fact or opinion, and the knowledge of the defendant would still have to be decided.

Moreover, since good name is deemed to be a property interest, it would undoubtedly violate the constitutional requirement of due process to deny damages to a plaintiff who had been defamed unless the claim was waived. Despite these obvious flaws, the *American Law Journal* in January 1986, proclaimed that 1986 may be the year of the declaratory judgment.[14]

Other proposals have been made by many lawyers. Floyd Abrams, attorney for the *New York Times* and other media defendants, is an articulate and prolific author on the subject. It is difficult, however, to know exactly what his views are. In an article in the July 1985 issue of the *American Bar Association Journal,* Abrams comes out squarely for retaining the rule in *New York Times* v. *Sullivan.* [15] But in the July-August 1985 issue of the *American Lawyer,* Abrams stated, "Basically, where you come out is that the law as it now stands, if it is applied strictly and accurately by the judges works pretty well!"[16] This would seem to put the onus on the lower court judges for failing to apply the law strictly. But in September 1985, in an article in the *New York Times Magazine,* Abrams wrote, "The law effectively chills both the press and private citizens who wish to speak out on public issues."[17] He then made several proposals for change. These deserve thoughtful consideration.

Abrams endorses the declaratory judgment proposal. He urges retention of the Sullivan rule and the "harshest commentary" on those in power. Abrams suggests a fixed limit on damages. Certainly verdicts in the millions of dollars for hurt feelings are a travesty and promote litigation. This book suggests that damages be strictly compensatory and that the amount of damages should have to be proved —in other words, that the doctrine of presumed damages be abolished. Although from time to time, the Supreme Court has suggested that damages ought to be proved, notably in *Gertz* v. *Welch,* the Court has never implemented that proposal.

A monetary cap on damages is a widely urged remedy in all civil cases. Spokesmen for the Reagan administration urge limiting damages in civil actions against the government. Assistant Attorney General Richard K. Willard suggests that the legal system is out of control, the product of a "largely unelected judiciary imposing its risk preferences on the rest of society."[18] But the fact is that the vast majority of American judges are state court judges who are elected. They and the juries impose damages because the law requires it. Former Attorney General Griffin Bell proposes a cap on punitive damages and that they be paid to the government, not the injured plaintiff.[19] The Tort Policy Working Group, a Reagan task force considering the insurance problems raised in tort litigation, recommends limiting noneconomic damages to $100,000 including punitive damages.[20] The group did not address the problems of libel and privacy litigation, but it is likely that its recommendations will be seriously considered in connection with all tort litigation. The group also recommended a sliding scale of lawyers' contingent fees. Significantly, the task force explicitly stated that it did not recommend whether its proposed reforms be implemented "at the federal or state level or through legislative or judicial modification of the law." However, a panel of the prestigious and knowledgeable American Bar Association opposes putting a cap on liability awards.[21]

Any restriction on the amount of compensatory damages in libel suits raises serious constitutional questions. Good name is deemed to be a property interest. A plaintiff who has been defamed has a constitutional right to recover compensation for the damages to that property interest, whether the damages be one dollar or one billion dollars. It would appear that proposals singling out libel plaintiffs for a special limitation on property damages would also run afoul of the equal protection clause. In addition, any figure would inevitably be arbitrary and bear no relation to the damages actually suffered by any plaintiff.

Restrictions on plaintiffs' counsel fees are frequently urged by defendants. The recommendations in this book are not designed to favor either plaintiffs or defendants. Counsel fees are only one item, albeit a large one, in the total cost of litigation. Limiting counsel fees might make it more difficult for plaintiffs to obtain representation and thus indirectly prevent some plaintiffs from bringing suit. Although reduction in the volume of libel litigation is highly desirable, it should not be achieved at the expense of litigants and their counsel, who would, in many cases, be unable to present an adequate claim or defense if fees were severely limited. Moreover, a limitation on fees would not achieve any of the aims of protecting First Amendment rights, protecting privacy, or making the law more certain and just.

The proposal for change most frequently mentioned is one I believe to be essential and sound, namely giving effect to correction of errors. Of the eleven persons who presented views on rewriting the law of libel in the *American Lawyer,* five recommended the use of some form of retraction. They are Floyd Abrams, William P. Tavoulareas, Bob Woodward, William Thomas, editor of the *Los Angeles Times,* and Steven Brill, editor and publisher of the *American Lawyer.* Heath Meriweather, executive editor of the *Miami Herald,* also believes in retraction. He states, "We must be willing to correct errors."[22]

Another popular suggestion embodied in the declaratory judgment bill is adoption of the British practice of placing costs and legal fees of the winning party on the losing party. It must be remembered that English law and practice are very different from American law and practice. In a mock trial of a hypothetical libel case at the American Bar Association meeting in London in July 1985, the lawyers concluded that the plaintiff would win under English law but the media would win under American law.[23] Not only is there no equivalent of the First Amendment in England, there is a long history of licensing the press and judicial orders restricting publication of comment on pending litigation. Prior restraint of publication is permitted and occurs with frequency. England also has a "law of confidence" doctrine that recognizes a property right in documents.[24]

Despite forty years of postwar democratization of English society, the legal system is still largely the province of the upper classes. Little effort has been made to enlarge access to the courts by the poor. Contingent fees are prohibited both in England and Canada. While there may have been some abuses, the contingent fee has opened American civil courts to poor and moderate-income plaintiffs. The risk of having to pay the defendants' enormous legal expenses in libel suits would not merely chill the rights of some plaintiffs it would

permanently freeze them. William P. Tavoulareas and William
Buckley who have brought a number of libel suits would probably
not be deterred, but many potential plaintiffs with legitimate claims
would be denied access to justice.

Not all libel defendants are wealthy media moguls. Many individuals attempting to exercise their own First Amendment rights
are being sued. For these defendants and for many small publications, this additional burden if such a defendant lost in court could
make the difference between financial viability and failure. Such
papers and magazines perform significant public services not only to
their own communities but to the nation as a whole. The *Point Reyes
Light* of California, with a circulation of 3,500, won the Pulitzer
Prize for exposing Synanon, a California-based drug rehabilitation
program. Synanon was found to have perpetrated a fraud on the
courts by destroying tape recordings and documents. These materials related to violence, money, purchase of guns, legal terror tactics,
changing sex partners, coerced abortions and sterilizations. Synanon
was subsequently denied a federal tax exemption and was dismissed
as plaintiff in several libel suits.

I do not accept with equanimity the cavalier statement of British
journalist Harold Evans, "I know that many small newspapers do
give up doing investigative work. But they are more worried about
legal fees."[25] Of course, they are worried about legal fees. One hundred thousand dollars in legal fees, a modest amount in libel suits,
is a crushing burden for a small publication. In my opinion, the law
should promote free expression rather than discourage it.

There is little consensus with respect to other proposed remedies.
Defense counsel in general favor retention of the actual malice standard, whereas plaintiffs' counsel oppose it. Defense counsel oppose
punitive damages; plaintiffs' counsel favor retention of punitive damages. The public interest lies somewhere between these polar views.

I suggest a return to the common law rationale and standard for
punitive damages. Punitive damages were designed to accomplish
two ends: to punish a wrongdoer who committed an outrageous act
and to deter him from doing so again. The act that would warrant
punitive damages had to be outrageous in itself or done with personal
spite or ill will. A mistake, no matter how negligent, would not
warrant punitive damages.

None of the reported cases following *New York Times* v. *Sullivan*
that have been discussed herein involved either an outrageous act or
personal ill will. Under common law doctrine, there would be no

reason to impose punitive damages on a careless reporter or publisher. Certainly the underlying public policy expressed in the First Amendment, if not its actual mandate, should militate against the imposition of punitive damages except in the most extraordinary and egregious cases.

Some would remove libel cases from jury trial. But in England where jury trials in civil cases have been abolished, an exception is made for libel suits. I believe this indicates the importance of jury trials to protect both parties in these sensitive and difficult cases. The proposal, though frequently voiced, is really academic. The Seventh Amendment to the Constitution of the United States guarantees the right to trial by jury in civil common law cases.[26]

It is often argued that some cases such as products liability and antitrust are too complicated to be entrusted to juries. Significantly, those who make these arguments usually insist on a jury trial. A federal court has unequivocally declared that juries can effectively decide complex litigation.[27] Jury trials are, on the whole, longer than bench trials. But the cost differential in the overall budget is insignificant. This country can still afford justice.

It is easy to point to a case like *Huan* v. *NEC Microcomputer* in which a \$47.5 million verdict was reversed,[28] and conclude that juries are hostile to First Amendment claims. In that case, a former sales representative of the defendant, a computer chip manufacturer, sued for libel, fraud, and breach of contract. The California state jury awarded plaintiff \$64 million, of which \$2.5 million was for damages on the libel count, plus \$43 million in punitive damages, also on the libel count. This was the largest reported libel award. The California Superior Court reversed and ordered a new trial on breach of contract and fraud only, dismissing the libel charge. This case, like many other libel suits, really involves only a commercial issue. Plaintiff was discharged by the defendant. The libel claim arose out of a republication of an industry newsletter article about plaintiff's dismissal. Such decisions must be balanced against the verdict in *Lakian* v. *Boston Globe,* in which the jury awarded no damages.

Drawing distinctions between judges and juries is a popular pastime of authors of socio-legal studies. It is easy to count the number of reported cases in which jury verdicts have been reversed by appellate courts in libel cases. One statistic frequently cited is that 89 percent of jury verdicts in libel cases are for plaintiffs, but 75 percent of those that are appealed are reversed.[29]

All such statistics must be received with caution. Legal cases are not fungible goods. A verdict is based on many factors that differ from case to case. Among them are the actual facts involved, the strength of the evidence, the skill of the lawyers, and the response of the jury to the litigants. Appellate decisions are based on the record in the trial court and the law. In an area of law such as libel, where the rules change so drastically and with such rapidity, unless the same period of time and identical cases are tabulated, the results of the researchers will be different because their data as to facts and law are different. It is also difficult to know how to tabulate appellate decisions. Even the Supreme Court does not always have the last word. In many libel cases, the Supreme Court remands the matter for a new trial. The second trial court verdict is appealed. The appellate court decision is appealed, and the Supreme Court again remands the case for a third trial. The process goes on and on. Sometimes the appellate process is more complex. An intermediate appellate court will reverse the trial judge, and the Supreme Court will then reverse the appellate court.

Since libel law is rapidly changing, a high reversal rate in libel cases is not unexpected. It must be remembered that approximately one-third of all federal cases that are appealed are reversed. Most cases are not appealed unless counsel reasonably believes there is a good chance of winning. A recent study finds that 90 percent of libel plaintiffs lose on appeal.[30] But we do not know how many obtain substantial settlements to avoid a retrial.

Because most defamation actions are brought against corporate defendants, this apparent bias against the media must be tested against other civil suits brought against corporate defendants. A Rand study of jury awards in Cook County, Illinois, found that the average award against a corporation was $120,000, significantly greater that the $18,500 average award against individual defendants.[31] Considering the wealth of most media defendants as compared with other corporate defendants, the alleged public hostility to the media may be a misperception.

Most of those volunteering to rewrite libel law are representatives of special interests. They represent either those hostile to the media or are counsel for plaintiffs or defendants. No one speaks for the unrepresented public. One looks in vain to academia for this point of view. Professor Frederick Schauer of the University of Michigan Law School bases his critique on an unproved assumption of the people's "rather deliberate lack of interest in knowing."[32] He proceeds on an "admittedly nonmajoritarian view about what is necessary to have a good government." This Platonic, elitist notion of press freedom to criticize public officials does not advance the search for legal doctrine that protects subjects, authors, and the public.

All too often the academic point of view is trapped in what Professor Cass Sunstein of the University of Chicago Law School describes as "fine spun theory." There are attempts to draw distinctions between juries and judges. The former are perceived as majoritarian and the latter as antimajoritarian. As has been noted, almost all state judges are elected public officials and are as representative and majoritarian as legislators.* Federal judges are appointed for life. But, as Mr. Dooley aptly pointed out, the Supreme Court follows the election returns. Most federal judges are part of the political process and reflect the philosophy prevailing at the times of their respective appointments.

All these proposals for rewriting libel law are implicitly predicated on legislative action, although except for the declaratory judgment bill, no one has proposed a libel statute. Both Professor Lawrence H. Tribe of Harvard Law School, a vigorous civil libertarian, and Michael McDonald, general counsel for the American Legal Foundation, a conservative nonprofit law firm that often supports suits against the media, agree that libel law must be changed. Tribe declares, " . . . the purposes of a vigorous and free press are ill served by the current state of the law."[33] McDonald states, "The trials are bad for both sides. We've got to streamline the process."[34] A statute would, of course, resolve the qualms of those who fear antimajoritarian or imperial judges.

The proponents of these various remedies do not discuss specific mechanisms for reform; they have avoided proposing a statutory remedy. They do not consider whether the remedies should be by way of a federal or state statute.[35] It is obvious, however, that any changes in the foreseeable future must be made by legislation. Astonishingly, there has been little discussion of a broad act governing all aspects of libel and privacy law. Probably both plaintiffs and defendants want to retain those aspects of the law that are favorable to their respective positions. Academic critics have focused principally on language in Supreme Court opinions rather than examining how these doctrines affect the trial of cases. Phrases like "neutral report-

---

*According to the Rand Institute for Civil Justice, 95 percent of all tort cases are filed in state courts (Rand, *Civil Justice Round Table,* June 1986).

age" are used with little recognition of the problems in defining and applying such concepts.

The following chapter sets forth the principal goals and content of a federal statute governing the rights of subjects and authors under the First Amendment. It does not undertake the difficult and meticulous task of draftsmanship. That must await the democratic process of legislative hearings at which representatives of subjects and authors can present their views. From such differences of opinion, a consensus can be reached that does not unduly favor one side or another, but rather represents the public interest.

·XV·

A Proposed Libel Statute

Never judge particular cases by general laws.

—ARISTOTLE

DRAFTERS of remedial legislation can follow one of two paths. They may list the rules of law and decisions they believe to be unwise or unfair and seek to correct those particular evils. Or they may survey a branch of the law and attempt to provide a rational structure setting forth rights, procedures, and remedies. The former route proceeds on an ad hoc basis to attempt to undo decisional law that was also developed on an ad hoc basis. It may successfully deal with situations that have arisen in the past. It rarely provides a guide for future cases.

The latter course is more ambitious and somewhat daunting. It requires at the outset an understanding of the factual matrix from which the litigation has arisen, an educated guess as to future developments in the social and economic milieu, and a philosophical or policy goal that the legislation is designed to promote.

There are many dangers in promulgating a comprehensive statute or code. No matter how intelligent and learned, the drafters can never avoid some oversights or anticipate all contingencies. There will inevitably be lacunae. The Pennsylvania Crimes Code offers a good example of the pitfalls. It was a creditable effort to rationalize a multitude of statutes embodying old common law crimes and more recent offenses such as drug abuse, child abuse, and computer crimes. Some offenses were covered under several acts with different penalties. Lawyers and judges had to scan dozens of laws to determine under which provision the particular offense occurred. The code was a useful advance even though several offenses, such as battery and incest, were unaccountably omitted and some crimes were given inappropriate penalties. For example, theft is graded as a more serious offense than indecent assault. These flaws are relatively minor matters that can be corrected whenever the legislature chooses to do so.

The advantages of a comprehensive statute over a limited statute are considerable. A comprehensive act spells out rights and remedies. It can provide clear definitions. With a broad problem like rights of subjects versus authors that is governed by the laws of fifty states and the overlay of two centuries of American case law and almost a millennium of English case law, the benefits would be enormous. It would be of considerable help to subjects and authors.

The old maxim, "Ignorance of the law is no excuse," is a sound principle. People do know that killing, cheating, and lying are wrong, even though they may not know the precise definitions or penalties. The law presumes that most individuals and corporations will obey the law. The entire system of democratic government is predicated on this assumption. As Austin observed, the people are in a habit of obedience to the law. If any significant proportion of the population habitually violated the law, as occurred during prohibition, the entire system would fail to function. Those who habitually or intentionally violate the law are a very small percentage of the population. Generally they are career criminals, or parties who think they can escape detection or those who by reason of moral or political conviction deliberately violate the law and precipitate test cases.

Defendants rarely deliberately seek litigation. It is usually the subject not the author who goes to court. In some few instances, such as the *Pentagon Papers* case, the issue was of such transcendent importance that a test case was necessary. Some subjects and authors who believe their rights were violated or that the law as interpreted is wrong will insist upon a court determination of their rights. I believe the vast majority of litigants, however, would find a clear statement of the law defining rights and limitations to be enormously helpful in avoiding the prosecution and defense of a multitude of costly court cases.

The legal presumption that the public knows the law is a fiction when applied to street criminals. It is highly unlikely that semiliterate purse snatchers and muggers know the penalties for these crimes or that they would be deterred by the knowledge that if convicted the term of imprisonment would be ten years rather than two years.

The parties involved in defamation and privacy cases are literate. They act with forethought. Indeed, this anticipatory fear of litigation has led to the chilling effect the Supreme Court has unsuccessfully sought to avoid.

A statute would also significantly aid lawyers. Most lawyers are cautious. Although many like to litigate, they do not like to lose cases. Sometimes lawyers are unable to deter their clients from pursuing lost causes. But usually they do persuade them to settle rather than litigate when failure is fairly certain. A statute that puts litigants and lawyers on notice as to rights and liabilities is likely to deter fruitless litigation.

Judges find statutes very helpful. When there is an applicable statute, judges do not have to search for a statement of law among a welter of conflicting opinions, or to make policy decisions predicated on analogies and hunches. In a statute, the public intent, though often inartfully expressed, is manifest. A statute also provides a trial judge with the proper language with which to charge the jury. Most jury verdicts are reversed not because the jury was prejudiced or irrational but because the judge gave them wrong instructions as to the law. This is particularly true in libel cases. Trial judges must search through five and six opinions of justices of the Supreme Court in a single case seeking the precisely correct language. When a statute governs the rights of the parties, the task of the judge is much easier, and error is avoided. When I try a homicide case, I read the pertinent sections of the statute to the jury. In my experience, they have little difficulty comprehending these definitions. I know that the statement of the law is correct and that no appellate court will send the case back for a new trial because the language used in the charge was possibly misleading. Diligent lawyers will comb through a jury charge looking for a "must" instead of a "may" and an "and" instead of an "or" to find a basis for a new trial. When I charge a jury in a products liability case based on judge-made law, I must be sure that I have followed the very latest expression of the Supreme Court, not one from the preceding year. If, for example, a jury is instructed that the product is "unreasonably dangerous," the case will be reversed. The latest approved language, as of this writing is simply "dangerous." The language of a statute does not change from decision to decision.

The logical first step in rewriting libel law is to rewrite the definition of libel. The present definition—a statement that holds a subject up to hatred, contempt, or ridicule—is vague. Read with the gloss of centuries of interpretation it is anachronistic. The most recent textbook formulation of defamation as a statement that charges immoral or obscene conduct is both difficult to apply and obsolete. Contemporary standards of morality are elastic, to say the least. Homosexuality and lesbianism, once considered crimes, are now deemed to be matters of sexual preference for which job discrimination is prohibited in many jurisdictions. The enormous number of unmarried mothers is telling evidence of the fact that premarital female unchastity (under present law a clearly defamatory statement) is no longer considered a disgrace. Similarly, lying and cheating rarely result in loss of reputation or standing in the community.

It is proposed that defamation be defined as follows: a statement that taken as a whole makes a verifiably false charge that the subject committed a specific criminal or other degrading act. A criminal act needs no definition. One can simply refer to the crime codes of the states and the Federal Crimes Code. A degrading act is less easy to define, but it would include such matters as gross sexual misconduct, cruelty, and indecent treatment of others. Significantly, none of the recent Supreme Court cases has involved such charges.* Requiring that the statement charge a specific act would be enormously helpful to both plaintiffs and defendants. It would permit the parties to present proof of the truth or falsity of the charge. A criminal indictment or information is required to contain not only the facts that constitute the crime but the date and place at which the crime allegedly occurred. To say that a person is a liar, a cheat, and a fraud is difficult to prove or disprove. Note that these were the ineptly worded charges in the letter that gave rise to the case of *McDonald* v. *Smith* in which the Supreme Court upheld a libel verdict. Probably most people have told lies at one time or another. Many have "fudged" on their income tax returns or failed to return library books. These are forms of cheating. Countless persons have violated parking laws and driven over the speed limit. These are crimes. Limiting libel to specific charges of criminal acts would eliminate countless libel claims that are based on what can at best be denominated name calling. If a plaintiff did file such a charge, the defendant could immediately request a summary judgment. A protracted trial

---

*Satires, parodies, and other patently humorous pieces have involved such descriptions. Under the proposed statute, humor would be barred from libel actions.

on the issue of whether the charge was one of fact or opinion would be avoided.

A statute should also contain definitions of fact and opinion. It is proposed that fact be defined as a discrete, objectively verifiable statement of a specific matter. All other statements would be defined as opinions.

The test of truth like that of defamation should be based on the document as a whole and should be only substantial accuracy, not meticulous nit-picking verification of every detail. As Justice Rutledge pointed out, ". . . any standard which would require strict accuracy in reporting legal events factually or in commenting on them in the press would be an impossible one. . . ."[1] Meticulous accuracy in any kind of reporting when the reporter is under time constraints to meet a deadline is an impossible standard.

The question of reasonable accuracy is subsumed in the definition of fault. Fault should be defined as negligence, the failure to do what a reasonable person would have done under all the circumstances, or doing what a reasonable person would not have done under the circumstances. The circumstances would include the amount of time available to check and verify the accuracy of the statement, a reasonable appraisal of the likelihood that the statement was true, and the risk of harm to the subject if the statement was false. Although the Supreme Court has held that the defendant cannot be held responsible in libel without proof of fault, the definition of fault has been left to the laws of the fifty states. A national standard of fault for all statements disseminated in interstate commerce would enable both plaintiffs and defendants to know what their rights and responsibilities are. The tried and true standard of negligence is a fair one that judges and juries have little difficulty in understanding and applying.

Under these proposed definitions, it is probable that the jury in *Time, Inc.* v. *Firestone* would have found that the reporter was not negligent and that the report taken as a whole was not substantially false. Under such a statute, it is reasonably clear that Damron, the mayor who was falsely charged with having a criminal record, would have recovered. Any reasonable person would have checked to ascertain the truth of such a serious charge. Failure to do so would be neglience. Similarly, in the case of *Gertz* v. *Robert Welch, Inc.,* any reasonable person would have investigated before printing such serious charges. The entire question of public versus private figure could be avoided if the standard of fault were negligence.

Statements that do charge facts that can be proved or disproved would be actionable. Under the negligence test, it would be unnecessary to prove the state of mind of the defendant to determine whether he or she acted with "actual malice," the present test of liability for public figures. Elimination of both these troublesome, judicially created tests would avoid many lengthy trials and irrational and unfair decisions.

There is an old legal axiom frequently used to dismiss claims brought by plaintiffs who assert, often truthfully, that they have been damaged—*damnum absque injuria,* harm without legal injury. This doctrine should also apply to plaintiffs whose skills, performances, and products are the subject of unfavorable opinion even though such a plaintiff has actually suffered some emotional distress or monetary loss.

These definitions would also permit summary judgment in libel cases arising out of commercial transactions and employment. A statement with respect to a service or a product such as the hi-fi speakers involved in *Bose* v. *Consumers Union* would clearly be a matter of opinion. Statements as to the competence, integrity, and qualifications of employees and candidates for jobs and offices would also be deemed to be opinions and not actionable.

These definitions should also eliminate many of the libel actions now brought by public officials against citizen critics and the press. Under such a statute, a case like *Rosenblatt* v. *Baer* that was based on an oblique criticism of the management of a public ski facility would have been dismissed on a motion for summary judgment instead of having to be tried and appealed all the way to the Supreme Court.

I believe that a trial judge should read the allegedly defamatory document and decide whether it purported to state a fact or merely the writer's expression of opinion, albeit an expert opinion. If the court concluded that it was merely an expression of opinion, summary judgment for the defendant should be granted.

Under the present state of libel law, with the exception of particular state statutes, the parties must attempt to fit their claims within the narrow Procrustean bed of the Constitution. Congress can create by statute rights in addition to those predicated upon the Constitution. Of course, a statute cannot detract from constitutional rights, privileges, and immunities, but it can add to them.

At present the public as such has no rights cognizable in a court of law in libel actions. The Supreme Court has held that under the Constitution there is no right to know. A statute could clearly estab-

lish the public's right to know. Thus, whenever the media as agents
for the public wish to examine conditions in prisons, old-age homes,
institutions for children, and the like, or to look at court records,*
those denying access would have to establish some superior right or
privilege in order to do so. I believe that such a provision would be
enormously helpful to the public as well as to the media.[2] It would
recognize, contrary to present law, that the press has special rights
of access to enforce the public's right to know. It would be consonant
with the premise of the Freedom of Information Act and state sunshine laws. Such a provision would give access to public institutions
and governmental activities. Whether the military could be compelled to permit reporters to cover such events as the Grenada invasion is, of course, problematic. But the burden would be on the
government to prove a clear and present danger in order to deny
access.

The principal right conferred on subjects by the proposed statute
would be a right of persona. This would include the right of privacy,
the right of publicity, and the right of truthful depiction in works
that purport to be factual. Rights of privacy and publicity are the two
principal doctrines other than defamation that subjects can now seek
to utilize. These claims, however, depend upon the vagaries of state
statutes. A federal statute should recognize these three rights and
define their limits.

A number of states do have privacy laws. The New York statute
prohibiting the use of an individual's name or likeness for advertising
purposes without consent offers a satisfactory model to protect subjects from commercial exploitation. Absent such a statutory protection, subjects have no redress.

Privacy unrelated to advertising is a more difficult claim to enforce. As of this writing, most courts have not recognized such a
right.[3] A statute should specifically declare that all persons have a
right to privacy and a right to be let alone unless by their own actions
they may be deemed to have waived that right. If they have waived
such right, then authors should be free to write about them.

The multiple definitions of public figure, limited public figure, and
private figure promulgated in numerous Supreme Court opinions
have proved to be difficult to apply and qualified by numerous exceptions. A statute setting forth standards of waiver of privacy would
avoid these vague and ever-changing standards.

---

*Denial of media access in these situations has been upheld by the Supreme Court.

Definitions of classes of persons deemed to have waived rights of privacy should include the following:

1. Public officials, employees, and aspirants for public office and jobs and recipients of public funds and their spouses.
2. Those who by their own conduct have sought public attention.
3. For a limited period of time, those who are involved in matters of news, whether of "public concern" or not. (This difficult, vague concept would also be avoided.)

It is, I believe, essential to include spouses among those who should be deemed to have waived rights of privacy. The old fiction of identity of husband and wife has long been shattered. But even though marriage does not obliterate individual personalities and rights, the marital relationship is recognized in countless aspects of law, such as joint tax returns, community property, right of survivor, and the like. Public officials are now, under many statutes and regulations, required to make public reports of the income and property of themselves and their spouses. Use of a spouse's position to obtain business and favors is a fact. Marion Javits, wife of Senator Jacob Javits of New York, was severely criticized for doing business with Iranian officials. It was assumed, whether accurately or not, that because of the senator's position she received special advantages. Geraldine Ferraro's husband was subjected to searching scrutiny and censure. Had she not been a candidate for vice president, it is unlikely that either government authorities or the press would have inquired into his business affairs. Whether spouses of public officials and candidates should or should not be subjected to the white light of publicity is a philosophical and political question. But the fact is that spouses know or should know that they will be subject to close scrutiny and therefore must be deemed to have waived their privacy rights. In my view, such public persons cannot claim rights of privacy as to any aspects of their lives, whether sexual, financial, political, social, or artistic.

Others must also be deemed to have waived privacy rights by seeking the limelight. Such persons would include movie stars like Elizabeth Taylor, authors like Norman Mailer, artists like Andy Warhol, and quasi-political persons like Betty Friedan, all of whom have welcomed, if not courted, public attention.

Persons accused or convicted of crime must also be deemed by their acts to have waived all privacy rights at least for a limited period of time.

I do not believe that judges or jurors would have undue difficulty in making rational decisions as to those who have not waived their privacy rights.

Persons whose privacy should be protected include victims of crimes and accidents and their families and all those who have involuntarily become subjects of news. Once the news has been reported, these persons should be allowed to assert the privacy rights they never waived.

Those who wish to write books or present docudramas about these incidents could do so without fear of litigation by the use of several simple devices. First, the disclaimer. The author or producer should tell the public that the incident, though accurate in basic respects, has been fictionalized. Second, the real names of these people should not be used and their identities should be disguised. Most rape victims suffer severe psychological trauma. Many require years of therapy before they can lead relatively normal lives. Often these victims, as well as victims of other brutal crimes, move to avoid encountering people who know of the incident. They truly begin new lives. All of this painful effort is put to naught when a human interest story or docudrama years after the incident brings the matter to light again.

Much hostility to the media is engendered by tasteless and cruel intrusions into private grief. Does anyone really want to see a reporter thrusting a microphone into the face of a mother who has just seen her child killed and asking her how she feels while the cameras are grinding away? Most people are repelled by such conduct. Few reported cases have arisen from such unnecessary and heartless behavior. There is nothing to prevent the media from voluntarily refraining from such conduct while aggressively pursuing the real story, which is the cause of the crime or accident, and the identification of those who are responsible.

Many responsible reporters, newspapers, and members of the electronic media voluntarily refrain from publishing the names of rape victims and juveniles accused of crime. A statute should prohibit the release of the names and photographs of such persons. Although the Supreme Court held that a statute prohibiting the press from publishing the names of apprehended juveniles was unconstitutional because of underinclusion (it did not apply to the electronic media),[4] the concurring opinion of Justice Rehnquist strongly indicates that a comprehensive statute would be sustained. It is proposed that the statute prohibit the release by all the media of the names and photographs of crime victims and children accused of crime.

Rights of privacy have been recognized in other contexts. Congress has clearly indicated its belief that individuals do have significant privacy rights. Social security information and tax returns are zealously guarded so that personal information may not be disclosed whether defamatory or not.

A right of truthful though nondefamatory depiction of another has not been recognized, despite the fact that the Supreme Court has repeatedly declared that the Constitution does not protect a lie.

There is no legal inhibition against imposing liability for false statements when the author is at fault. There is no moral or legal principle that requires protection for false depictions of individuals. On the contrary, every ethical and legal tenet suggests that both truth and privacy are characteristics valued in our society and entitled to legal protection. Innumerable philosophers and judges have extolled the values of privacy and dignity. Justice Blackmun declared: " . . . we'll keep . . . some of the basic precious things such as privacy and the Bill of Rights."[5] But neither truthful portrayal nor privacy has been recognized as a constitutional right by the Supreme Court. A statute can give legal recognition and protection to both truth and privacy.

It is my contention that there is not and should not be a right of biography. Whatever bundle of attributes should be comprised in a right of persona, that right should not include an exclusive right to exploit one's life. Biographers are in the curious position of being accorded either total immunity from falsehood or being restricted by the threat of suit from publishing at all. Again I suggest a median position. As a First Amendment right, everyone should have the right to write biographies about any person living or dead. But the author should be held to a reasonable standard of accuracy. Falsehood, even though not defamatory, should not be privileged. In biography, as in libel suits, the standard of truth or falsity should be that promulgated in obscenity cases—that the writing or electronic program be considered as a whole. Thus, minor inaccuracies should not result in liability if the book, article, or program is a reasonably fair and truthful account.

A statute could ban the so-called right of biography. It could specifically prohibit the use of injunctive relief. Many statutes prohibit injunctions and remit the allegedly aggrieved party to an action for damages. If a biography was substantially false and the biographer was negligent, the subject could recover compensatory damages for such falsity. Authors would not be precluded from writing about people who simply prefer not to have books written about themselves or prefer to have only "authorized" or vetted biographies. A contrary position would remove from the ambit of free expression an enormous range of subjects, both living and dead,* to the detriment of authors and the public.

The law with respect to what is called "right of publicity" should also be clarified by statute. The term is too broad and vague. What is meant to be protected is an individual's property right in his own performance or achievement. It is akin to copyright. No one can steal or use another's intellectual property without the consent of the author, composer, or performer. Such use of another's skills is an appropriation of property rights. But a statute should define and limit the concept so that it is clear that individuals or institutions can be the subjects of books, movies, biographies, and television programs that are not false or defamatory. Copyright and patent laws are the appropriate protection for intellectual property, not suits for an alleged right of publicity.†

Among the important activities of authors, including all persons who write letters and make oral comments, that should be established by statute as rights entitled to protection are: (1) the right to criticize all public officials, employees, and candidates and aspirants for public office and employment; (2) the right to report defamatory statements made by others; (3) the rights of whistle blowers; (4) expressions of opinion as to qualifications and merits of individuals (this would be comprehended in the definitions of fact and opinion); (5) the rights of biographers to write truthfully about any person living or dead; (6) the rights of authors to publish fiction and present docudramas clearly labeled as fictional without fear of defamation suits unless the claim of fiction is patently a sham designed to avoid the statute; and (7) the rights of humorists, including cartoonists.

The public versus private figure test as applied by the courts has proved to be uncertain and evanescent. Neither subjects nor authors can know in advance who will or will not be declared to be a public figure. The exclusion of public employees from the definition of public figure on some undefined scale of job importance is irrational.

---

*Note the proposed New York statute that would permit the family of a deceased person to sue for libel for a period of five years after the death of the allegedly libeled individual (*New York Times,* June 28, 1986, p. 31). This bill was withdrawn but may be introduced again.
†Whether the format of public documents such as judicial opinions is copyrightable is open to question. See majority and dissenting opinions in West Publishing Co. v. Mead, 55 LW 2141 (1986).

All public employees should be subject to public scrutiny. Authors, including the media, should be entitled to examine the conduct of all public officials and employees without fear of litigation. A statute clearly establishing this right and excluding all others from the category of public figure would eliminate the problem of deciding who is a public figure. It would be a fact beyond dispute.

The repetition of defamatory statements by others correctly attributing the statement to the real author should be privileged as a legitimate report of news. The media should not be responsible for the defamatory contents of signed columns, letters to the editor, and advertisements. If this had been the law in 1964, the *New York Times* would have been entitled to summary judgment against Sullivan. Neither the press nor the electronic media should have to answer for statements made by others.

Whistle blowers perform a significant public service by calling attention to derelictions by public officials and by private individuals and corporations. As of this writing, courts have failed to protect whistle blowers from either reprisals or defamation actions. Congress has acted to protect whistle blowers in government service from reprisals by their superiors. Although a federal statute cannot protect employees of private enterprise not engaged in interstate commerce from retaliatory actions by their employers, it can give whistle blowers conditional immunity from libel suits for statements communicated across state boundaries.

Whistle blowers should be protected for two reasons: first, they, like all persons, have First Amendment rights of free speech; and second, they perform a valuable public service in alerting government authorities and the public to wrongdoing and dangerous conditions. One example illustrates the need to encourage and protect whistle blowers. More than twenty people died from taking the drug Selacryn. The manufacturer did not report these deaths as it was required to do under the law. Certainly some employees—including scientists, file clerks, and typists—after the first two or three deaths must have recognized that something was wrong. Had someone alerted the government, probably at least seventeen or eighteen deaths could have been prevented.

I suggest that whistle blowers who have probable cause to suspect wrongdoing should by statute be immune from suit for defamation. Most child abuse reporting laws provide immunity for those who in good faith report cases of suspected child abuse. These statutes have been extraordinarily successful in encouraging people to notify public authorities of dangerous situations and thus protecting vulnerable children. I do not recommend the good faith standard. Good faith is a subjective test difficult to prove or disprove. Probable cause is an objective standard. Long experience shows that judges and juries have little difficulty in understanding and applying the test fairly. In most criminal cases, the prosecutor must prove that the police had probable cause to obtain an arrest warrant or to arrest without a warrant. The question put to the courts is whether on the basis of the information available a reasonable person would have grounds to believe the accused *might* be guilty, not that he is guilty. In the context of a defamation suit brought against a whistle blower, the test would be whether a reasonable person having the information the whistle blower had and taking reasonable inferences would have believed that the subject was probably engaged in the activity charged. This is a lower standard of proof than falsity. It is a much easier test to apply than "actual malice," which requires an examination of the author's mental processes.

Probable cause is a moderate standard of proof. Criminal law requires proof beyond a reasonable doubt for conviction. In defamation cases involving private figures, the Supreme Court requires proof of falsity by clear and convincing evidence. Both impose a high burden on one alleging that the accused has committed a crime or that the defendant in a libel case has lied. They are appropriate for such serious charges. They are inappropriate for whistle blowers. A police officer who arrests an accused does not charge that the accused has actually committed a crime, but only that there is reason to believe that he has committed a particular crime. Similarly, most whistle blowers are not prepared to prove that the individuals or corporations mentioned have actually engaged in the wrongdoing alleged, but that there is reason to believe that they have done so. Whether the burden of proving truth is on the whistle blower or on the subject who brings the libel suit, the test should not be truth or falsity, but simply probable cause to believe the charge. To date no court has applied such a test. In the *Hepps* case, the Supreme Court has probably settled the question of burden of proof for private figures in libel actions. A statute should specify that, with respect to public figures suing whistle blowers, the burden of proof is on the plaintiff to prove that the whistle blower acted without probable cause or with spite or ill will. A statute establishing probable cause as the standard of immunity for whistle blowers in defamation actions would give courts a standard that is easy to understand and apply. It would permit those who have reasonable grounds for suspecting wrongdoing to inform the appropriate authorities and/or the public of the information they have without fear of defamation suits.

Fiction, comedy, satire, movies, drama, and docudramas are now treated much the same as any other allegedly defamatory communication. Courts engage in lengthy trials to determine whether the statement was "of and concerning" the unnamed subject, whether the piece was "straight" or satirical, whether the docudrama was true or false. The law, in my opinion, must recognize the essential difference between programs, books, and stories that purport to be fiction or humor and those that purport to be fact. This book suggests that the law establish a truth in labeling provision. If a novel is labeled fiction and does not mention the subject by name, then there should be a strong presumption that the work is not about the subject.

When a real person happens to have the name of a fictional character and the character does not resemble him or her, the courts have properly denied recovery. Mere fortuity would explain such an accidental use of a name.

When subjects sue on the basis of fiction or docudramas, courts should avoid the complicated and perplexing questions of truth, falsity, actual malice, and the public/private figure dichotomy. I suggest that in such cases, whether the suit is based on libel, invasion of privacy, or right of publicity or biography, the threshold question should be: Did the writing or program purport to give a true account of X, the real person? The jury should be instructed that if it did not, a verdict should be entered for the defendant. In deciding this question, the only evidence would be the book or program itself. What did the author say he or she was doing? Was the book or drama labeled fiction or fact? Was it a "straight" piece or a satire? Did the author tell the reader or viewer that the work was based on the life of X or the trial of X? If so, did the author make clear that it was a fictionalized version?

One of the great advantages of trial by jury is that we trust the common sense of the average citizen. If the legal question is something that the layperson can understand, there is no need for expert testimony. Even in a medical malpractice case, if the doctor amputates the left leg instead of the right leg (such instances have actually occurred), the plaintiff does not need to bring in an expert witness to testify that this conduct does not meet the standards of medical competence. In cases based on fictionalized or dramatized versions of real incidents, it would be unnecessary to take testimony as to what other people thought. Usually these witnesses are the friends of the subject and the friends of the author, scarcely unbiased witnesses. Instead, the jury should decide on the basis of the best evidence, the allegedly libelous book or drama.

Truth in labeling is required by statute with respect to food, drugs, and many commercial transactions. The Supreme Court has required truth in advertising of legal services.

When an author clearly labels a work fiction and states that any resemblance to persons living or dead is purely coincidental, that should raise a rebuttable presumption that the work is fiction. Such a presumption could be overcome only by clear and convincing evidence. Such a provision would largely eliminate the troublesome "of and concerning" test. Unless the work actually described the subject and unmistakably traced his or her life and experiences, the disclaimer should not only protect the author but put readers and viewers on notice that the work is not about the subject.

In my view, no statute should attempt to cover every possible contingency. The similarities of name, address, physical appearance, activities, and taste between the plaintiff in *Springer* v. *Tine** and the fictional character in the book should, I believe, have been sufficient for a court to find that the character was "of and concerning" her. But the court held for the defendant. The fact that the character was portrayed as a prostitute, a criminal activity, should have allowed recovery, even under the restrictive provisions of the proposed statute. Legislation cannot prevent judges from making wrong decisions. Appellate courts exist to correct manifest errors. On the other hand, the proposed statute should prevent recovery in a case such as *Bindrim* v. *Mitchell,* in which the protagonist in the novel does not resemble the plaintiff at all. It would also impose a higher burden of proof on any plaintiff seeking to recover for libel based on fiction or satire in which there was a clear disclaimer. A subject clearly used as the model for a fictional character should have a right of recovery under the proposed right of persona, not libel, unless the character was portrayed as engaging in criminal or degrading acts, in which case there would be a right of libel.

The suggestion that courts give a presumption of accuracy to the label that authors affix to their works, such as fact, fiction, fiction based on a factual incident, etc., is designed to protect the subject

*See the discussion of this case in Chapter X.

from the emotional trauma of being identified with a fictional character, to protect the author from the emotional and financial strain of a lawsuit, and to relieve the courts from a welter of difficult cases. It should carefully be distinguished from statutes requiring labels on literature, movies, and electronic programs. Recent cases in which the Justice Department claims the right to label as propaganda Canadian films dealing with nuclear war and acid rain in my view involve impermissible government censorship based on the content of the films.* Such a concept extended to printed material imported from other countries would embroil the government and the courts in deciding not only whether books and articles are factually accurate or matters of opinion—the basis of many libel actions—but also whether the opinion is to be designated as "propaganda"—a term as yet undefined by the law. A statute giving a presumption of validity to the author's designation of his or her own work as fact or fiction does not involve censorship or pejorative labeling by the government.

If the subject is interested only in protecting his or her reputation, such a statement is a far greater protection than a libel verdict holding that the fictional work does actually describe the subject. Such a disclaimer would also protect the subject's privacy.

An example of careful labeling was contained in an interview with Fidel Castro published by *Playboy* magazine. The magazine explained that the interview as published was not a verbatim unedited transcript and carried this warning: " . . . we want to let our readers know that even though this 'Interview' with Castro may well be the most faithfully rendered ever, it has undergone extensive cutting as well as interruptions to break up the text . . ."[6] Such a statement may well protect the magazine from charges of libel, false light tort, and other claims. It also properly puts the reader on notice that the "interview" has been extensively edited. Readers should know whether or not they are being furnished with the exact statements of the interviewee.

Similarly, if comedy and satire are so labeled, the subject would have to overcome both a presumption and a privilege to prove that in fact the piece was not satirical and that it purported to be a truthful portrait. Similar presumptions and privileges should be established for dramas and movies. If the work was only a barely disguised portrait of the subject, the presumption could be overcome.

---

*Several courts have reached different conclusions on this sensitive question. See *Philadelphia Inquirer,* June 21, 1986, p. 4A. Undoubtedly the issue will eventually reach the Supreme Court.

The purpose of such a federal statute would be to discourage "strike" suits, claims that have little substance but can be used to coerce a settlement. Strike suits are by no means limited to defamation actions. They abound in commercial suits and negligence claims. But in actions by subjects against authors, the strike suit has an impact on the First Amendment. By increasing the odds against success in such frivolous actions, the threats to free expression are correspondingly reduced without foreclosing those who have meritorious claims.

The peculiarly contemporary genres—the "factual novel" and the docudrama, a dramatized version of a real incident—place subjects and authors in numerous conflicts in which both have meritorious claims. Subjects assert that their privacy is invaded and that they are represented in a false light. Authors assert not only the right of free expression but also of artistic or dramatic license to shape the facts into a compelling, interesting presentation. The solution to this dilemma, I suggest, is a truthful disclaimer: a statement that the facts have been altered and that the author does not purport to give an accurate representation of the subject. Those who do not have a right to privacy would be protected from being falsely presented. The reader or viewer would know that there was no attempt to present an accurate portrait.

A statute should clearly recognize the difference between media and non-media cases. Commercial products and services and employment rights and entitlements should be treated under existing law that now provides, in most instances, adequate protections. Of course, a statute cannot remove from the ambit of the First Amendment parties and claims that the Supreme Court has upheld as being constitutionally protected. But a declaration of policy in the preamble to a statute can express the sentiment of Congress that it is the purpose of the law to protect the free, untrammeled flow of news, information, entertainment, literature, and the arts, and that commercial interests should be protected by contract law, including breach of implied warranties of accuracy. Although a statute cannot override the Constitution, courts give great weight to statutes and the expressed will of Congress.[7]

The non-media cases should, I believe, be decided on the basis of the commercial interests involved. If a bank or other institution sells or supplies information, it in effect warrants the accuracy of that information. Free expression is not involved. No one is attempting to interfere with the institution's right to disseminate information. The Supreme Court has declared countless times that there is no right to lie. Consequently, I see no constitutional barrier for not holding those who make false statements responsible for the harm done.

The employment cases can be treated appropriately by a provision in the statute giving a right of confidentiality to references and opinions as to competence, integrity, and qualifications.

Most critics of the present libel law advocate some provision for retraction. Correction of error given the same prominence as the original statement is, in my opinion, a far more sensible proposal than a declaratory judgment suit. If the author, when informed of what the subject considers to be the true facts, makes a correction, apology, or retraction the subject is vindicated without the necessity of retaining counsel and going to trial. This provides an expense-free, prompt vindication. The author is also spared the expense and trouble of defending a libel suit.

If the false defamatory statement is made in the press, the correction should be given equal prominence. A front-page story must also carry a retraction on the front page. Similarly, if the false, defamatory statement is made on prime-time news, the retraction should also be made at the same time. A false statement in a periodical can be corrected on a comparable page of a subsequent issue of the periodical. With respect to books, retractions and corrections present more difficulties. But it would not be unreasonable to require the publisher to pay for an ad containing the retraction or apology in all the periodicals in which the book was reviewed and advertised. Future editions would, of course, contain the correction.

The provision for corrections, retractions, and apologies is designed to protect the good name and reputation of plaintiffs and to spare defendants the costs of defending a lawsuit and paying damages. The choice of admitting error and paying these relatively minor costs of retraction rests with the defendant. The statute would not require it, but it would simply give the defendant that option, which if exercised would limit the plaintiff's recovery to provable damages incurred between publication of the libel and the retraction.

Probably the truth never catches up with a lie. But courts of law are unable to provide exact or perfect justice in any aspect of civil or criminal law. A prison sentence imposed on a mugger or a rapist does not psychologically or physically restore the violated victim of the crime. Five years in prison is not commensurate with the harm done to a mutilated victim of a crime. Nor is a life sentence. A civilized society simply does not impose equivalent harm upon a law violator. Similarly in civil cases, no amount of money damages will compensate a plaintiff who has been blinded or maimed by the negligence of the defendant. Justice Douglas declared that "The Federal Employers' Liability Act was designed to put on the railroad industry some of the cost for the legs, eyes, arms, and lives which it consumed in its operations."[8] Obviously the law cannot restore those limbs and lives. The most it can do is require the wrongdoer to pay an appropriate sum of money. The proposed libel act can only provide a reasonable approximation of equivalent publicity for corrections and retractions. If after examining the subject's evidence the author is still convinced of the truth of the statement, then trial is inevitable and appropriate. Subjects who believe they have been falsely defamed should pursue their legal remedies. If they are right, they should be compensated for the harm caused rather than having to spend money and time to obtain vindication without compensation. Authors who believe they have told the truth should not be coerced into falsely retracting. If they choose to defend an action and are proved to be wrong, they should pay for the harm they have caused.

The subject of damages should be specifically covered by any statute. The usual common law rule of damages that operates fairly in the vast majority of civil cases should, I believe, be applied to defamation and privacy actions. The plaintiff should recover for those harms, including emotional harms, actually proved, not presumed, that were caused by the author's fault. If this rule were followed, juries would have the usual criteria by which to measure damages. Trial judges would also be able to exercise their usual function of remitting damages in excess of what was proved. Trial and appellate judges would have a sound basis by which to measure the fairness of the verdict. Although juries will obviously know that the large target defendants are wealthy, there is no reason to believe that under proper instructions their verdicts against media defendants would be larger than verdicts against enormously wealthy non-media defendants.

The usual rule in punitive damages operates satisfactorily in most tort cases other than libel. It is the general practice at the close of the case for the court to decide whether taking the evidence in the light most favorable to the plaintiff a jury could reasonably find that the defendant's conduct was outrageous or that the defendant acted with personal animus or a willful, reckless disregard for truth. If the judge finds that the evidence would not support such a finding of outrageous conduct, the jury may not be informed of the extent of the defendant's wealth. Under these standard instructions, even plaintiffs who have been rendered quadriplegics by the fault of the defendant or who have endured long, painful terminal illnesses are rarely awarded more than $5 million. Such sums are usually based on the extraordinary cost of medical and other services such plaintiffs require. They are based on the evidence as to the plaintiff's life expectancy, loss of earnings, and expenses, as well as pain and suffering. It is most unlikely that jurors who award a twenty-five-year-old paraplegic with a dependent wife and two small children $1 million would award a libel plaintiff $10 million or $20 million if given the same instructions. It is even more unlikely that, in the event such a verdict was returned, the trial court would not reduce it. There is no constitutional inhibition against this proposal. The only right of a person harmed through the fault of another is due process of law.

In order for a court to give the jury an instruction on punitive damages, there must be evidence that the defendant knew or should have known that the conditions were so hazardous as inevitably to cause serious harm to persons such as the plaintiff. Some judges have allowed punitive damages against asbestos companies upon documentary proof that the companies in fact knew that the ingestion of asbestos fibers would cause asbestosis and cancer in a very high proportion of employees. This is the kind of outrageous disregard for human life and well-being that the law contemplates in the award of punitive damages, not a negligent misstatement of fact.

A federal libel and privacy statute should include a shield law for reporters and all authors who obtain information on a promise of confidentiality. At present the rights of such persons depend upon the laws of the states. Some have strong shield laws; others do not.

A comprehensive libel and privacy statute would put authors on notice as to the kinds of statements that are defamatory. If they publish statements that are clearly libelous if false, they should be required to use reasonable care under all the circumstances to ascertain whether the statements are true. A reasonable mistake would not result in liability. An unreasonable failure to investigate would, and in my opinion, should be actionable. But even such an error, if promptly corrected on demand and given equivalent publicity, would permit both parties to avoid litigation and give appropriate redress to the wronged subject by clearing his or her name. Such a proposed provision, permitting prompt retraction, would permit the author who was unreasonably careless to mitigate damages. Again, this is consonant with contract and tort law that permit the wrongdoer to mitigate damages by taking prompt action to save the plaintiff further harm.

A statute can also establish a rational system of classification based on the character of the communication. To treat an exposé of an alleged cover-up by public officials on "60 Minutes" and the release to five companies of credit information under the same rules and doctrines of law verges on the preposterous. But that is what trial courts are required to do. They must weave their tortuous way through a maze of Supreme Court opinions, concurrences, and dissents to find the appropriate refinements for a fact situation that has often not been considered or even contemplated by the Court.

Congress can survey the entire spectrum of conflicts between subjects and authors and make classifications on a broad, rational, conceptual basis without waiting for the aleatory process of litigation and appeal to bring these problems to the attention of the courts. Distinctions should be made among these basically different types of communications: news, newsworthy reports, crime stories, biographies, fiction, humor, whistle blowing, and commercial reports.

Some critics of the state of libel law in 1986 suggest that the media should not have a preferred status. They apparently assume that in the litigation between subjects and authors, all defendants are wealthy media corporations. That is far from true. Increasingly, defamation actions are being brought against individuals and small papers, journals, and radio stations who can ill afford the expenses of defense. Frequently, the subject is richer and more powerful than the author. Regardless of the relative wealth and power of plaintiff and defendant, every person, organization, and association should be entitled under the First Amendment to speak out and express opinions, no matter how unpopular or unorthodox. Everyone should be free to write and publish without fear of being haled into court to defend against a defamation charge.

The trouble, expense, and emotional trauma of defending a lawsuit, as well as the fear of an enormous verdict, are considerable burdens. Most people will think many times before expressing themselves at a meeting or in a letter or publication if they risk a lawsuit by doing so. Not many people, including professional writers, have insurance to defray these expenses. Even the media giants are in danger of losing their insurance coverage. Although plaintiffs' lawyers often take cases on a contingent fee basis, risking their time in the expectation of success, defense counsel require payment, often in advance. A plaintiff can cut his or her losses and withdraw suit when the going gets tough. A defendant cannot. There is no right to free legal services even for indigents to defend a libel action. Although few suits are brought against indigents, some defendants are indigent by the time of verdict.

Comparison of a recent case decided under present law with the procedures and likely results if it were tried under this proposed statute, reveals the advantages of such legislation. Frank Marcone, an attorney, sued *Penthouse* magazine in libel for a 1978 article entitled "The Stoning of America."[9] The jury awarded him $567,000. The article stated that Marcone, who represented motorcycle gangs and himself went on motorcycle weekends, was indicted in federal court in February 1976. The charges were withdrawn without prejudice in May 1976. The article stated as a fact the following:

> Frank Marcone, an attorney from the Philadelphia area, contributed down payments of up to $25,000 on gross transactions. . . . (Charges against him were dismissed because he cooperated with further investigation.)

The court of appeals set aside the verdict. The court first determined that the action was to be decided under Pennsylvania law, even though *Penthouse* is not published in Pennsylvania. It is a national magazine. The court listed the issues to be decided as follows:

1. The defamatory character of the statement, which was held to be a legal question for the judge not the jury.
2. The publication by the defendant.
3. The applicability of the statement to the plaintiff.
4. The recipient's (reader's) understanding as to its defamatory nature.
5. The recipient's understanding that it applied to the plaintiff.
6. Special harm to the plaintiff.
7. Abuse of conditional privilege.

None of the first six issues was really in dispute. The verdict was reversed because the court held that plaintiff was a limited public figure and failed to prove the defendant's "actual malice" by a preponderance of the evidence.

The real question, in my view, was whether the charges were withdrawn because plaintiff cooperated or simply withdrawn at the discretion of the prosecution, a not infrequent occurrence.

This was a fact that could be proved yes or no by the testimony of the prosecutor. Under the proposed statute, the plaintiff would have the burden of proving by clear and convincing evidence that the statement was false. If he failed to prove that, a verdict would be entered in favor of defendant. If plaintiff did prove that the statement was false, then plaintiff would have to prove fault, defined under the statute as negligence. *Penthouse* is a monthly magazine not a daily paper. It probably had ample time to investigate the truth of its story. A phone call could have verified or corrected the statement. If false, a jury would undoubtedly have found *Penthouse* was negligent. Plaintiff would then have to prove actual damages. At that point, the court would receive evidence as to his reputation, good or bad, and the financial and emotional harm suffered. It is most unlikely that plaintiff could prove damages of a half million dollars.

But if Marcone was falsely defamed, why shouldn't he recover for the harm done? First Amendment rights of *Penthouse* would not be chilled by an award of reasonable damages, perhaps $50,000 for a negligently false statement.

The Supreme Court refused to hear the case. Lawyers and judges can only wonder why attorney Marcone was subject to different legal standards than attorney Gertz who was held to be a private figure and recovered $400,000. Litigants must wonder what happened to the real question, the truth or falsity of the defamatory statement.

What will happen to the next lawyer who believes he or she has been defamed and sues? And what guidance will the trial judge who hears the case have? Should he or she follow Gertz or Marcone? If Gertz is the polestar, then the plaintiff will recover a windfall. If Marcone is controlling, the plaintiff will lose. This either/or conclusion is, I believe, unreasonable and unfair. The status of the law is more confused than before.

A statute would resolve this multitude of questions and many more. Because a statute would create a national law applicable to most cases in all state and federal courts, the practice of jurisdiction shopping would be largely eliminated. A statute could also provide that the plaintiff could bring only one action in libel or privacy based on one defamatory statement, no matter how widely it was disseminated. The old maxim that every person is entitled to a day in court should mean simply that a plaintiff has only one chance to prove his or her case. Since the applicable law throughout the nation would be the same, neither plaintiffs nor defendants would be unfairly prejudiced by such a restriction.* Under such a proposed statute,

---

*A repetition of a defamatory statement after the litigation was terminated would, of course, give rise to a new cause of action.

cases could be tried in the most convenient forum. Judges would not have to engage in the arcane pursuit of determining the applicable law. The rights of subjects and authors engaged in national dissemination of information by print or electronic media would not be subject to the vagaries of the laws of fifty different jurisdictions.

As of this writing, there is no reliable information as to why subjects sue for defamation or what changes in the law would reduce litigation without depriving subjects of their rights. But the aim of remedial legislation is the reduction of fruitless, unjustifiable, and costly litigation.

Professor Marc Franklin, who has examined every reported defamation case from January 1976 to June 1979, raises the following interesting questions.

> It would be illuminating to know more about why suits are brought under today's defamation law. Do perceived political or social pressures require that certain cases be pressed even if they appear hopeless? How are such cases financed? How much is expended in insurance and in self-insured legal defense expenses in comparison with the money that is transferred in these cases? . . .
>
> In any event, more knowledge about how defamation law actually operates will facilitate serious reflection about the adequacy of this important part of our legal system.[10]

No one can disagree with this conclusion. The reported cases are only the proverbial tip of the iceberg. At present there is no reliable comprehensive information with respect to the unreported cases that constitute the vast majority of all litigation or the still larger number of cases that are settled and claims paid even before institution of suit. A congressional committee could provide this sorely needed information.

George Orwell's *1984* presented a terrifying picture of a fearful, cowed society in which Big Brother (the government) was listening and watching the citizens day and night. No one dared speak even in a whisper. The threat and actuality of lawsuits resulting from a letter or a statement in a meeting present ominous examples of privatism in suppressing First Amendment rights. The fact that the defendant *may* be vindicated after a decade of bruising and costly litigation will not encourage free expression.

Although newspapers, magazines, the electronic media, and publishers of books are better able to defend lawsuits than individuals, many of these defendants are not wealthy. A verdict of $100,000, a modest sum in defamation cases, plus at least $100,000 in legal expenses, can mean the difference between viability and failure. Another voice is silenced. Even the wealthiest corporate defendants find the onslaught of defamation suits daunting.

While some plaintiffs are recovering what can best be described as windfalls for hurt feelings, others who have suffered real emotional trauma from intrusive reporters and authors who depict them cruelly or falsely are denied recovery.

All these decisions are predicated on precedents and language derived from other cases in which the fact situations were materially different.* No lower court judge who takes the oath of office seriously is free to ignore rules of law established by the Supreme Court no matter how unfair and undesirable they may appear to be. A statute is the only sword available to cut the tangled Gordion knot composed of fibers of actual malice, public and private figures, of and concerning, presumed damages, denial of privacy, and right to know.

Any comprehensive statute governing the rights of subjects and authors will have to be carefully drawn. It will require the goodwill and cooperation of the bar and the media, as well as the expertise of scholars. The challenge is formidable. The alternative is decades of chaos and public disillusion with the law. Such a federal statute should provide more adequate and certain protection to both subjects and authors and ensure a broader range of information, literature, and entertainment available to the public. Prompt legislation would forestall the adoption of drastic remedies whose effects would at best be problematic and at worst undermine long-established principles of jurisprudence and jeopardize the rights of subjects, authors, and the public.

*A statute establishing rights frees the court from the difficult and much-criticized task of seeking authority for individual rights arising out of problems never envisioned by the drafters of the Constitution.

Epilogue

We must not make a scarecrow of the law,
Setting it up to fear the birds of prey
And let it keep shape, till custom make it
Their perch, and not their terror.

—Shakespeare

OBSERVING the unseemly court wrangles between subjects and authors, the public is often tempted to cry, "A plague on both your houses." Demands of subjects for astronomical awards, intransigence of authors, and lengthy trials and interminable appeals are distasteful. The media are blamed for arrogance and insensitivity, lawyers are charged with unduly prolonging litigation, and courts are accused of obfuscating the issues. While finding justifiable fault with all involved in these cases, the public tends to overlook the notable contributions to American life made by both the legal system and the media.

Lawyers and judges have enabled the poor, the disenfranchised, the disadvantaged, and those subject to legal, social, and economic discrimination to obtain rights and redress for wrongs to an extent unequaled in any other nation at any time in recorded history. For more than two centuries, lawyers and judges have protected the press from the heavy hand of government censorship and reprisals. The law, with all its shortcomings, still protects the press and the public from government secrecy and reprisals.*

*The *Washington Post* revealed in the spring of 1986 that six times within a twelve-month period the federal government pressed the newspaper to withhold or alter an impending article (*New York Times,* May 18, 1986, p. 11). It is difficult for the public to know whether this practice indicates a trend or involves a justifiable concern with respect to a clear and present danger to national security.

The role of the media in alerting the public to dangers has been notable. Despoliation of the landscape, waste of resources, pollution, and harm from toxic agents have been brought to the attention of the public by fearless investigative reporting. Corruption in government —from the cop on the beat to the Oval Office—has been uncovered by the media.

One has only to compare the access of the American public to news with the limited official version of events disseminated by the controlled press in much of the world to realize the coverage and vigor of the media. With rare exceptions, Americans can read whatever they choose—from masterpieces to trash. When one travels to countries behind the iron curtain and China, people always ask for books and newspapers. In the United States, people can see all kinds of art and hear all kinds of music. In Spain during Franco's regime, Goya's *Los Caprichos* were labeled heretical. In many countries, modern art is disparaged as bourgeois, and contemporary music is forbidden.

The freedom to know and to enjoy is dependent upon a fearless press and a courageous bench and bar that resist any form of government censorship or control. It is, therefore, dismaying to see that these two great institutions—the press and the law—are perceived as adversaries rather than allies. It is even more disheartening to note the mistrust that the public expresses with respect to both professions.

Neither is blameless. Examples of insensitive and tasteless journalism abound. There are occasional instances of dishonesty. The award of a Pulitzer Prize to reporter Janet Cooke who presented a fictional story as a factual report and the misleading accounts in the *New Yorker* by Alistair Reid are two distressing examples. But, unlike the conduct of the Nixon administration in the Watergate fiasco, there was little attempt by either the *Washington Post* or the *New Yorker* to suppress the truth. They accepted responsibility for misleading the public.

Some lawyers have been derelict in their obligations to clients and the court. They have overreached and overcharged. But they have been disciplined by bar associations and by the courts. Some few judges have been corrupt. They have been convicted and sentenced by honest judges.

A vigorous press and a courageous bar are needed to maintain freedom and democracy. Both are predicated upon the protection of individual rights of privacy, dignity, and free expression.

Constitutional principles are inviolable. But laws and doctrines are not immutable. They can be revised to meet changed conditions and new problems. Many bitter conflicts between antagonistic interests in American society, such as labor and management, consumers and manufacturers, and landlords and tenants, have been resolved by the courts under appropriate statutes without adopting new and untried procedures incompatible with the American legal system. Legislation enumerating rights of authors, subjects, and the public and providing for fairer and more expeditious procedures can enable the courts to resolve the disputes between subjects and authors without infringing the rights of either party. Such a statute, if carefully drawn, would alleviate the chilling effect of litigation on the exercise of First Amendment rights.

Notes

INTRODUCTION

1. Rex v. Woodfall, 98 Eng. Rep. 914 (1774). Under the law of England in the eighteenth century the press was licensed. To publish without governmental approval was to court criminal prosecution. The English law of libel permitted recovery for truthful but defamatory statements.
2. 1 *Annals of Congress* 433.
3. New York Times v. Sullivan, 376 U.S. 254 (1964).
4. New York Times v. U.S., 403 U.S. 713 (1971).
5. See U.S. v. Progressive. AP report, September 5, 1980, Milwaukee. This case has not appeared in the official law reports.
6. U.S. v. Ginzburg, 338 F.2d 12 (3rd Cir., 1964).
7. Grand Jury Matter. In re: Gronowicz, 3rd Cir., decided June 24, 1985.
8. Snepp v. U.S., 444 U.S. 507 (1980).
9. *National Law Journal*, January 27, 1986, p. 26. See also the case brought by the President of Naura, a small island in the Pacific against the *Pacific Daily News* in which the paper was held not liable after seven years of litigation costing approximately $5 million. *National Law Journal,* January 6, 1986, p. S11. As of this writing, it is not known whether an appeal will be taken.
10. *Time* magazine, October 21, 1985, p. 72.
11. Dirks v. SEC, 463 U.S. 646 (1983).
12. *National Law Journal,* April 28, 1986, p. 46. See also Forer, *Money and Justice: Who Owns the Courts* (New York: W.W. Norton, 1984), p. 31, pointing out that with the exception of bankruptcies and prisoner petitions, the volume of federal, civil, and criminal litigation has declined. See also Galanter, "Reading the Landscape of Disputes: What We Know and Don't Know (And Think We Know) About Our Allegedly Contentious and Litigious Society," 31 *UCLA Law Review* 4 (1983).
13. Chafee, *Government and Mass Communications: Commission on Freedom of the Press,* (Chicago: University of Chicago Press, 1977), pp. 106–107.
14. Time, Inc. v. Hill, 385 U.S. 374 (1967).
15. Time, Inc. v. Firestone, 424 U.S. 448, 476 (1976). The case was remanded for the Florida courts to determine whether fault under Florida law had been proved.
16. Bindrim v. Mitchell, 155 Cal. 29 (1979); cert. den. 444 U.S. 984 (1979).
17. Ocala Star-Banner Co. v. Damron, 401 U.S. 295 (1971).
18. Hutchinson v. Proxmire, 443 U.S. 111 (1979).
19. McDonald v. Smith, 472 U.S. 479 (1985).
20. *National Law Journal,* May 27, 1985, p. 1. Bruce W. Sanford, a well-known libel lawyer, explains, "Given the lack of clarity that characterizes modern libel law,

well-conceived procedures for pre-publication review are the ounce of prevention that is worth the pound of cure." Sanford, *Libel and Privacy: The Prevention and Defense Litigation* (Washington, D.C. and New York: Law & Business, Inc., Harcourt Brace Jovanovich, 1985), p. 35.

21. See *Libel on Trial: The Westmoreland and Sharon Cases,* a BNA Special Report (1985).
22. *American Lawyer,* October 1986, p. 149.
23. William Safire, Essay in *New York Times,* October 27, 1986, p. A23.
24. See article by Gail Diane Cox of ACCN News Service, "Do prepublication letters stifle First Amendment?" *The Legal Intelligencer,* December 15, 1996, p.3.
25. *New York Times,* October 6, 1985, p. A56.
26. For such discussions see, for example, Franklin,"Winners and Losers and Why: A Study of Defamation Litigation," in Winfield, *Libel Litigation Nineteen Eighty-one* (New York: Practising Law Institute, 1981). Ashdown, "Of Public Figures and Public Interest—The Libel Law Conundrum," 25 *William and Mary Law Review* 937 (1984). Smolla, "Let the Author Beware: The Rejuvenation of the American Law of Libel," 132 *University of Pennsylvania Law Review* 1 (1983). Bollinger, "Free Speech and Intellectual Values," 92 *Yale Law Journal* 438 (1983). Koffler and Gershman, "The New Seditious Libel," 69 *Cornell Law Review* 816 (1984). Eaton, "The American Law of Defamation Through Gertz v. Robert Welch, Inc., and Beyond: An Analytical Primer," 61 *Virginia Law Review* 1349 (1975). Wellington, "On Freedom of Expression," 88 *Yale Law Journal* 1105 (1979). For a summary of American libel law prior to New York Times v. Sullivan, see Pilpel and Zavin, *Rights and Writers* (New York: Dutton, 1960).
27. Note that with respect to the perplexing legal issues involving surrogate mothers, Noel P. Keane who heads the New York Infertility Center says, ". . . we need laws that spell out these issues for us." In the novel and difficult issues involving the rights of subjects and authors, we also need laws that spell out the issues and rights of all parties.
28. Note the deference paid by the Supreme Court to an act of Congress in California Federal Savings and Loan Association v. Guerra, 55 L.W. 4077 (1987). Although the decision ostensibly turned on the question of whether the Pregnancy Discrimination Act of 1978 preempted state law, the Court recognized that Congress passed the act to reverse the decision of the Court in General Electric Co. v. Gilbert, 429 U.S. 125 (1976), holding that discrimination on the basis of pregnancy was not sex discrimination.The dissenters adhered to the view that granting disability leave for pregnancy unconstitutionally grants a preference based on sex.
29. Houchins v. KQED, 438 U.S. 1 (1978).
30. This book does not discuss theories of justice. There is a plethora of such literature. To date none of the well-known legal philosophers has addressed the questionable justice of libel law. I assume for the purposes of this book that a just legal system requires that one who has been harmed as a result of the fault of another should be compensated for those harms. I also assume that verdicts that bear no relation to the harm actually suffered are unjust.

CHAPTER I

1. Multimedia Entertainment, Inc., Donahue Transcript #06135, 1984.
2. *New York Times,* February 17, 1985, p. 19.

3. *New York Times,* February 8, 1985, p. 4E.
4. Justice White in his dissenting opinion in Gertz v. Robert Welch, Inc., states: "Several of them [newspaper owners] report yearly profits in the tens of millions of dollars after tax profits ranging from 7 to 14 percent of gross revenues." 418 U.S. 323, 390 (1974). Obviously, the majority of the almost 2,000 American daily papers, the weeklies, and the smaller periodicals do not have commensurate earnings or assets.
5. This is a very recent development. Note that the report by the American Civil Liberties Union on Civil Liberties Today, Dorsen, *Our Endangered Rights* (New York: Pantheon Books, 1984), does not mention the dangers to First Amendment rights from libel suits.
6. Baer, "The Party's Over," *American Lawyer,* November 1985, p. 69.
7. *New York Times,* February 17, 1985, p. 72. Nat Hentoff whose column appears in the *Village Voice* in an interview with *Publisher's Weekly,* April 11, 1986, p. 30, was asked: ". . . Would you say publishers, book or newspaper, are being more careful?" He replied: "Careful isn't the word. They're scared. I know Roy Cohn told me last year that whenever he sees in PW that a book is coming out about Joseph McCarthy, he writes a letter to the publisher saying you are now on notice that if there is anything in there about me that is defamatory, I am going to hit you with everything I've got. He says . . . I can't prove it . . . that some such letters have resulted in the removal of certain manuscripts. At newspapers, and I think this is also true of publishers, the lawyer in the newsroom is now commonplace. We have at least three or four lawyers who go over much of what appears in the *Voice* every week. And that's okay provided the lawyer doesn't step over his function and try to be so safe as to remove something just because it's questionable. I don't think James Madison had in mind that the lawyers should be in the newsroom or in the publisher's office."
8. *Wall Street Journal,* August 6, 1985, p. 17.
9. Tavoulareas, *Fighting Back* (New York: Simon and Schuster, 1986).
10. *Wall Street Journal,* December 11, 1985, p. 64.
11. Goldstein, *The News at Any Cost: How Journalists Compromise Their Ethics to Shape the News* (New York: Simon and Schuster, 1985).
12. Twentieth Century Fund Task Force Report for a National News Council, *A Free and Responsive Press,* 1973, p. 4.
13. *Harper's,* January 1984, p. 46.
14. Burnett v. National Enquirer, 144 Cal. App. 3rd 991, 193 Cal. Rptr. 206 (1983).
15. *New York Times,* July 2, 1983.
16. This verdict was reversed by the Pennsylvania Superior Court, August 1, 1986. Undoubtedly, the plaintiff will appeal.
17. *New York Times,* June 4, 1985, p. C25.
18. *New York Times,* February 10, 1985. The $11 billion verdict in *Pennzoil* v. *Texaco* dwarfs these verdicts. Such fights between corporate giants are not comparable to suits by individuals against corporations. In such actions for personal injuries the Rand Institute reports that verdicts averaged only $69,000 in 1975–1979 and in products liability cases (obviously against wealthy corporations) only $177,000. The Institute for Civil Justice, *An Overview of the First Five Years 1980–1985* (Santa Monica, CA: Rand Corporation, 1986), p. 23.
19. Buckley v. Valeo, 424 U.S. 1 (1976).
20. When a defamation action is brought on the basis of a book, article, radio or TV broadcast, often there are disputes between the actual writer or reporter and the publisher or media corporation. There are problems of insurance coverage. Is the publisher or the author responsible for the expenses of trial? Sometimes the reporter who may be blameless is fired or demoted. These

conflicts are beyond the purview of this discussion. But the refusal of publishers to provide legal representation for writers sued for libel effectively limits free expression. The demand of newspapers to have exclusive rights to publish books developed by their reporters also raises difficult questions. See the problems of reporter Severo of the *New York Times* who sold a book developed from a news report on "Lisa," a severely disabled patient, to another publisher. *Philadelphia Inquirer,* February 3, 1985, p. 6L. Many of these conflicts could be resolved by more careful and comprehensive contracts between reporter and newspaper.

21. Curtis Publishing Co. v. Butts, 388, 171 U.S. 130, 171 (1967).
22. Rosanova v. Playboy Enterprises, 411 F. Supp 440 (S.D. Ga., Savannah Div., 1976).
23. Brown v. Board of Education, 347 U.S. 483 (1954).
24. Baker v. Carr, 369 U.S. 186 (1962).
25. Gertz v. Robert Welch, 418 U.S. 323 at p.343 (1974).

CHAPTER II

1. Cooley, "History and Theory of the Law of Defamation," 3 *Colorado Law Review* 546 (1903).
2. Prosser and Keeton, *On Torts,* 5th ed. (Chicago: West Publishing Co., 1984), p. 771.
3. Pollock, *On Torts* (F.H. Thomas Law Book Co., 1894), p. 299.
4. Rabben, "Prewar Free Speech," 90 *Yale Law Review* 523 (1981).
5. Gilmore, *The Ages of American Law* (New Haven: Yale University Press, 1977). See, for example, Nimmer, *Freedom of Speech* (New York: Matthew Bender, 1984), in which the facts of a case are rarely discussed but the quotable phrases are repeated.
6. The masculine pronoun is used here advisedly. Until the mid-twentieth century, the number of female judges was so small that their influence on libel law was practically nonexistent.
7. Prosser, *On Torts,* 4th ed. (Chicago: West Publishing Co., 1971), p. 737 et seq.
8. Franklin, "Winners and Losers and Why: A Study of Defamation Litigation," in Winfield, *Libel Litigation Nineteen Eighty-one* (New York: Practising Law Institute, 1981), p. 493 et seq.
9. Pollock, *On Torts,* p. 286.
10. See McLane, *Spenser's Shepheardes Calender: A Study in Elizabethian Allegory* (Notre Dame, IN: University of Notre Dame Press, 1969), pp. 15–19.
11. Rex v. Barmondiston 473; 79 E.R. 404 (1618).
12. Lord Cromwell's case [Lord Henry Cromwell] 4 Co. Rep. 12b 76 E.R. 877 (1581).
13. Bushell's case 16 Cr. Pract. 279; 30 Juries 275; 38 Publ. Auth. 84 (1670).
14. Significantly, the Federal Communications Act gives the federal government the color of authority under which to grant, renew, or deny licenses to radio and television stations. This power can be used, in effect, to punish broadcasters whose views are inimical to the authorities. See e.g., U.S. v. McIntire, 365 F. Supp. 618 (DC N.J. 1973), in which a fundamentalist minister who had lost his radio license was enjoined from broadcasting from a ship on the high seas. Control by the FCC of the content of broadcasts and the fairness doctrine are beyond the purview of this book.
15. Ponting, *The Right to Know* (London and Sydney: Sphere Books, Ltd., 1985).
16. Many legal scholars looked upon the Supreme Court in the twentieth century as the defender of First Amendment rights. For a more critical view of the

history of freedom of the press, see Levy, *Emergence of a Free Press* (New York: Oxford University Press, 1985), a revision and reissue of *Legacy of Suppression,* published in 1960.

17. Patterson v. Colorado, 205 U.S. 454 (1907).
18. Gompers v. Bucks Stove & Range Co., 221 U.S. 418 (1911).
19. Lewis Publishing Co. v. Morgan, 229 U.S. 288 (1913).
20. Schenck v. U.S., 249 U.S. 47 (1919).
21. Fox v. Washington, 236 U.S. 273 (1915).
22. See Martin, *Harold Laski* (New York: Viking Press, 1953). Not all libel plaintiffs recover huge verdicts. William F. Buckley sued the Liberty Lobby that charged Buckley's *National Review* with being racist, pro-Nazi and pro-fascist for $16,000,000. The jury awarded him $1,001. The three-week trial cost Buckley more than $160,000. *New York Times,* October 28, 1985, p. A12.
23. See Marbury, "The Hiss-Chambers Libel Suit," 41 *Maryland Law Review* 75 (1981).
24. Brown v. Board of Education, 347 U.S. 483 (1954).
25. IV Blackstone 150.13.
26. See e.g. Branzburg v. Hayes, 408 U.S. 665 (1972); Herbert v. Lando, 441 U.S. 153 (1979); Application of Earl Caldwell, 311 F. Supp. 358 (N.D. Cal. 1970).
27. Dun & Bradstreet, Inc. v. Greenmoss Builders, Inc., 105 S. Ct. 2959 (1985).
28. Gertz v. Robert Welch, Inc., 418 U.S. 323, 395 (1974).
29. Time, Inc. v. Firestone, 424 U.S. 448, 476 (1976).
30. Curtis Publishing Co. v. Butts, and Walker v. Associated Press, 388 U.S. 130 (1967).
31. Rosenbloom v. Metromedia, 403 U.S. 29 (1971).
32. Gertz v. Robert Welch, Inc., 418 U.S. 323 (1974).
33. Time, Inc. v. Firestone, 424 U.S. 448, 476 (1976).
34. Lorain Journal Co. v. Milkovich, Sr., memorandum opinion 106 S. Ct. 322 (1985). Philadelphia Newspapers, Inc. v. Hepps, 54 L.W. 4373 (1986).
35. Harper & Row v. Nation, 471 U.S. 539 (1985); cf. Maxtone-Graham v. Burtchaell, 803 F2d 1253 (2nd Cir. 1986), holding that borrowing 4.3 percent of copyrighted work was not unfair. Would 5 percent have been unfair?
36. Buckley v. Valeo, 424 U.S. 1 (1976).
37. Federal Election Commission v. National Conservative Political Action Committee, 470 U.S. 480 (1985). See also Federal Election Commission v. Massachusetts Citizens for Life, Inc., 55 L.W. 4067 (1986), holding provisions of the Federal Election Campaign Act prohibiting corporate expenditures in connection with an election unconstitutional as applied to a corporate newsletter exhorting readers to vote for "pro-life" candidates.

CHAPTER III

1. *Philadelphia Inquirer,* July 26, 1985, p. 1.
2. *Philadelphia Inquirer,* August 6, 1985, p. A10.
3. The move to limit verdicts is not restricted to libel suits. In the mid-1980s, defendants in personal injury cases and insurers actively campaign for a cap on compensatory verdicts and abolition of punitive damages. Whether this is a well-orchestrated scheme by insurers to win public support based on misinformation about million dollar verdicts and settlements or a legitimate public concern is beyond the purview of this discussion. See *New York Times,* May 25, 1986, p. 18E. Whether punitive damages should be abolished in all civil cases is essentially a policy decision that should be made by the Congress based on full and accurate information.

4. Fuentes v. Shevin, 407 U.S. 67 (1972).
5. Restatement of Torts, §402 A.
6. Beauharnais v. Illinois, 343 U.S. 250 (1952).
7. Wynberg v. National Enquirer, 564 F. Supp. 924 (C.D. Cal. 1982) See Note, "The Libel Proof Plaintiff Doctrine," 98 *Harvard Law Review* 1909 (1985). See also Guccione v. Hustler 55 L.W. 2167 (1986), in which the Court of Appeals for the Second Circuit set aside a $1.6 million libel verdict holding that plaintiff, the publisher of *Penthouse,* was libel-proof.
8. Restatement of Torts, 2d, §591.

CHAPTER IV

1. Lerman v. Flynt Distributing Co., Inc., 745 F.2d 123 (2nd Cir. 1984).
2. *New York Times,* June 10, 1986, p. C17.
3. Curran v. Philadelphia Newspapers, Inc., Del. Ct. Pa. 76-13449. This case has not been reported.
4. *American Lawyer,* November 8, 1982, p. 1.
5. Sellars v. Stauffer Communications, Inc., 695 P. 2d 812 (Kansas 1985).
6. Rosenblatt v. Baer, 383 U.S. 75 (1966).
7. Anderson v. Liberty Lobby, Inc., 106 S. Ct. 2505 (1986).
8. Rand, *The Institute for Civil Justice, An Overview of the First Five Program Years: April 1980–March 1985,* p. 26.
9. *New York Times,* December 8, 1985, p. 41.
10. *Lawyers' Digest,* December 1985, p. 16.
11. *National Law Journal,* July 8, 1985, p. 39.
12. Pring v. Penthouse, 695 F.2d 438 (10th Cir. 1982); cert. den. 462 U.S. 1132 (1983). Although Miss Wyoming did not recover, her attorney has written a book about the trial and may recoup some of his losses. Spence, *Trial by Fire* (New York: William Morrow, 1986).
13. Forer, *Money and Justice: Who Owns the Courts?* (New York: W.W. Norton, 1984), p. 24 et seq.
14. Forer, "One Judge's View of the Split Verdict in Civil Cases," *Pennsylvania Law Journal Reporter,* August 31, 1981.
15. See Palsgraf v. Long Island R.R. Co., 248 N.Y. 339, 352 (1928).
16. I believe that most judges do feel constrained to follow the law regardless of their own inclinations. But the received wisdom of court critics is to the contrary. Typical is the comment of Professor Lee C. Bollinger who urges judges to restrain their personal beliefs and apply the law (Bollinger, *The Tolerant Society, Freedom of Speech and Extreme Speech in America* (New York: Oxford University Press, 1986). Bollinger, like many other commentators, sees the judiciary as undemocratic because they are not "tied to the electoral process." The fact is that elected state judges, including most justices of the highest state courts, are elected not appointed. The difficulty most judges have is in ascertaining what the law of libel is from a welter of conflicting opinions.

CHAPTER V

1. Ocala Star-Banner Co. v. Damron, 401 U.S. 295 (1971).
2. Zacchini v. Scripps-Howard Broadcasting Co., 433 U.S. 562 (1977). Earlier cases decided under state statutes prior to New York Times v. Sullivan and

subsequent Supreme Court decisions giving First Amendment protection to commercial speech, such as Virginia State Board of Pharmacy v. Virginia Citizens Consumer Council, Inc., 425 U.S. 748 (1976), are of little precedential value. The entire subject must be reexamined in the light of both the nature of the subject's claims and the constitutional rights of the defendant. For a discussion of the early cases see Gordon, "Right of Property in Name, Likeness, Personality and History," 55 *Northwestern University Law Review* 553 (1960). Cf Haelan Laboratories, Inc. v. Topps Chewing Gum, Inc., 202 F.2d 866; cert. den. 346 U.S. 816 (1953).

3. See Marsh v. Alabama, 326 U.S. 501 (1946).

4. Dissenting opinion Bazemore v. Savannah Hospital, 155 S.E. 194 (Georgia, 1930).

5. People Express Airlines, Inc. v. Consolidated Rail Corp., 495 A.2d 107 (N.J., 1985).

6. See Falwell v. Penthouse, Inter. Ltd., 521 F. Supp. 1204 (DC W.D. Va., 1981).

7. For an interesting discussion of rights of the person, see Radin, "Property and Personhood," 34 *Stanford Law Review* 957 (1982). The failure of law to protect a right of truthful presentation of an individual is revealed in Paul v. Davis, 424 U.S. 693 (1976). Plaintiff's picture was put on a flyer describing him as an "active shoplifter" even though charges against him had been dismissed. The court held that he had neither a liberty nor property interest under the civil rights law and that his claim was not within the protected zone of privacy. See also Prosser, "Privacy," 48 *California Law Review* 383 (1960).

8. Roe v. Wade, 410 U.S. 113 (1973). But see Dronenburg v. Zech 741 F.2d 1388 (CA Dist. Col. Cir., 1984), upholding the discharge from the Navy because the plaintiff was a homosexual. The court refused to recognize his claim to a right of privacy as to sexual preference.

9. Moore v. City of East Cleveland, Ohio, 431 US 494 (1977).

10. Warren and Brandeis, The Right to Privacy, 4 *Harvard Law Review* 193 (1890). See Prosser, "Privacy," 48 *California Law Review* 383 (1960). But see Kalven, "Privacy in Tort Law—Were Warren and Brandeis Wrong?" 31 *Law and Contemporary Problems,* 326 (1966), suggesting that the doctrine of privacy may be used to reform the law of defamation. It is evident in 1986 that unless privacy is recognized by statute as a protected right such reformation will not occur.

11. Stanley v. Georgia, 394 U.S. 557 (1969); Sony Corp. v. Universal City Studios, Inc., 464 U.S. 417 (1984).

12. Roberson v. Rochester Folding Box Co., 171 N.Y. 538 (1902).

13. N.Y. Civil Rights Act., 1903 McKinney 1976 §51.

14. Arrington v. N.Y. Times, 433 N.Y. Supp 2d 164 (1980).

15. As of 1985, the following states had such statutes: California, Florida, Nebraska, New York, Oklahoma, Rhode Island, Tennessee, Utah, Virginia, Wisconsin.

16. Zauderer v. Office of Disciplinary Counsel of the Supreme Court of Ohio, 105 S. Ct. 2265 (1985).

17. 5 U.S.C.A. §552(a) (1974). Note the continuing concern of Congress for protecting privacy. The Congressional Office of Technology Assessment reported the failure of the law to protect the privacy of communications in the computer age. *Legal Intelligencer,* October 25, 1985, p. 3. The Freedom of Information Act, 5 U.S.C. §555(b)(6) prohibits disclosure of records that constitute a "clearly unwarranted invasion of privacy."

18. *Personal Privacy in an Information Society* (Washington, D.C.: U.S. Government Printing Office, 1977), p. 8.

19. In 1939, the American Law Institute Restatement of Torts §867 recognized a right of privacy. The Restatement, though frequently cited by courts, does not have the force of law.
20. Onassis v. Christian Dior, 472 N.Y. S.2d 254 (1984).
21. U.S. v. Miller, 435 U.S. 435 (1976).
22. Wyman v. James, 400 U.S. 309 (1971).
23. Cal. v. Carney, 105 S. Ct. 2066 (1985). See also Cady v. Dombrowski, 413 U.S. 433 (1973).
24. California v. Ciraola, 54 L.W. 4471 (1986). See also Katz v. U.S., 380 U.S. 347 (1967).
25. Bowers v. Hardwick, 106 S.Ct. 2841 (1986).
26. MacLeder v. WCBS TV, New York Times, June 4, 1985, p. C25.
27. Blaustein, "First Amendment and Privacy: The Supreme Court Justice and the Philosopher," 28 Rutgers Law Review 41 (1974), p. 54.
28. Sidis v. F.-R. Pub. Corp., 113 F.2d 806 (2nd Cir. 1940).
29. Melvin v. Reid, 112 Cal. App. 285, 297 Pac. 91 (1931).
30. Philadelphia Inquirer, December 2, 1984, p. 13C. Note that Barrows has been permitted to keep the royalties on her book on the grounds that it involved victimless crimes. See Chapter VIII.
31. Time, Inc. v. Hill, 385 U.S. 374 (1967).
32. Cantrell v. Forest City Pub. Co., 419 U.S. 245 (1974).
33. Emerson, The System of Free Expression (New York: Random House, 1970), p. 556.
34. Wolston v. Reader's Digest Ass'n., 443 U.S. 157 (1979). But see the astonishing interpretation of "public controversy." In footnote 8 the majority states, "Certainly, there was no public controversy or debate in 1958 about the desirability of permitting Soviet espionage in the United States; all responsible United States citizens understandably were and are opposed to it." If consensus withdraws a subject from public debate, then courts will have to turn to opinion polls to determine what subjects may or may not be discussed with impunity.
35. Briscoe v. Reader's Digest Ass'n., 4 Cal. 3rd 529 (1971).
36. Cox Broadcasting Corp. v. Cohn, 420 U.S. 469 (1975).
37. Com. v. Wiseman, 356 Mass. 251, 249 NE2d 610; cert. den., 398 U.S. 960 (1970).
38. The use of public funds loomed large in Curtis Publishing Co. v. Butts, 388 U.S. 130 (1967), in which the Supreme Court held that because the University of Georgia football coach was paid by private funds he was not a public figure. On the other hand, in Hutchinson v. Proxmire (443 U.S. 111 [1979]), the Supreme Court held that the recipient of a grant of federal funds was not a public figure.
39. When similar arguments were made by members of the media who wished to film prison conditions following the death of an inmate, the Supreme Court found that the First Amendment rights of the media and public interest did not prevail over the intransigence of the prison authorities who refused to grant permission (Houchins v. KQED, 438 U.S. 1 [1978]. The privacy rights of the prisoners, if any, were not at issue.
40. Pajewski v. Perry, 363 A.2d 429 (Del. 1976).

CHAPTER VI

1. A move to cut off federal funds to poets accused of having written pornographic poetry was blocked by the House Committee on Education and Labor.

New York Times, September 15, 1985, p. 75. Other attempts to censor or impede free expression continue.

2. The Supreme Court granted Accuracy in Media, Inc., leave to file a brief amicus curiae, Edwards v. New York Times, Co., 434 U.S. 1002 (1977). But the Court held that the government could exclude the NAACP Legal Defense Fund from the combined federal employees charitable contributions. Cornelius v. NAACP Legal Defense Fund, 105 S. Ct. 3439 (1985). Recognition of the need to raise funds for political campaigns was ignored in this case, cf. Buckley v. Valeo, 424 U.S. 1 (1976).

3. Weems v. U.S., 217 U.S. 349 (1910).

4. Furman v. Georgia, 408 U.S. 238 (1972).

5. Gregg v. Georgia, 428 U.S. 153 (1976).

6. *The Works of Thomas Jefferson,* edited by Ford (New York: G. P. Putnam's Sons, 1904), pp. 464–65.

7. Meiklejohn, *Political Freedom, the Constitutional Powers of the People* (New York: Harper and Row, 1960 ed.), p. 21.

8. Emerson, *The System of Free Expression* (New York: Random House, 1970).

9. Bork, "Neutral Principles and Some First Amendment Problems," 47 *Indiana Law Journal,* 1, 20 (1971).

10. See Patterson v. Colorado, 205 U.S. 454 (1907).

11. Debs v. U.S., 249 U.S. 211 (1919).

12. Schenck v. U.S., 249 U.S. 47 (1919). See Smolla, "Let the Author Beware: The Rejuvenation of the American Law of Libel," 132 *University of Pennsylvania Law Review* (1983).

13. Abrams v. U.S., 250 U.S. 616 (1919).

14. Korematsu v. U.S., 323 U.S. 214 (1944).

15. Korematsu v. U.S., 584 F. Supp. 1406 (N.D. Cal. 1984).

16. Dennis v. U.S., 384 U.S. 855 (1966).

17. *Philadelphia Inquirer,* December 2, 1984, p. 24H.

18. Snepp v. U.S., 444 U.S. 507 (1980).

19. U.S. v. Ginzburg, 383 U.S. 463 (1961), rehearing den. 384 U.S. 934 (1966).

20. Haig v. Agee, 453 U.S. 280 (1981).

21. U.S. v. The Progressive, Inc., 486 F. Supp. 5 (W.D. Wisc., 1979).

22. Red Lion Broadcasting v. FCC, 395 U.S. 367 (1969).

23. Houchins v. KQED, 438 U.S. 1 (1978).

24. See Cook, *Maverick: Fifty Years of Investigative Reporting* (New York: G.P. Putnam, 1985).

25. C.I.A. v. Sims, 105 S.Ct. 1881 (1985).

26. Greer v. Spock, 424 U.S. 828 (1976).

27. Rosenblatt v. Baer, 383 U.S. 75 (1966).

28. McDonald v. Smith, 472 U.S. 479 (1985).

29. *New York Times,* January 14, 1985, B11. Few of these cases have come to trial and even fewer have reached the appellate courts. Reports in the press give incomplete and alarming information with respect to the growing prevalence of such suits by government officials against their critics. See *New York Times,* February 14, 1985, p. B11. See also Roberts, *The Silencing of Citizens, Human Rights* (American Bar Association Section of Individual Rights and Responsibilities) 28 (1985).

30. *Philadelphia Inquirer,* November 29, 1985, B1.

31. See Mill Service, Inc. v. Bolk, *Philadelphia Inquirer,* January 18, 1986, B1.

32. The opinion of Justice O'Connor in Harper & Row v. Nation, 471 U.S. 539 (1985), clearly suggests such an untenable distinction.

33. Dun & Bradstreet, Inc. v. Greenmoss Builders, Inc., 105 S.Ct. 2939 (1985).

34. See Branzburg v. Hayes, 408 U.S. 665 (1972); New York Times v. Jascalevich, 78 N.J. 259, 394 A.2d 330 (1978). But see U.S. v. Cuthbertson, 651 F.2d 189 (CA 3rd, 1981), restricting reporters' material to exculpatory evidence in criminal cases and requiring in-camera examination of the requested material.
35. *Harper's* magazine, January 1985, p. 37.

CHAPTER VII

1. *New York Times,* November 29, 1985, p. A19.
2. Sims v. C.I.A., 467 U.S. 1240 (1984).
3. Houchins v. KQED, 438 U.S. 1 (1978).
4. See Pell v. Procunier, 417 U.S. 817 (1974).
5. Dombrowski v. Pfister, 380 U.S. 479 (1965).
6. *New York Times,* December 1, 1985, p. 37. Although members of the media rarely make public statistics with respect to lawsuits filed against them, this forty-six-day period coincided with a strike during which the paper suspended publication.
7. Jacobellis v. Ohio, 378 U.S. 184 (1964).
8. *New York Times,* September 12, 1985, p. B1.
9. Time, Inc. v. Firestone, 424 U.S. 448 (1976).
10. See Liberty Lobby, Inc. v. Jack Anderson, 746 F2d 1563 (CA D.C., 1984), in which the Court admittedly sought to "avoid the difficult inquiry into the issues of falsity and malice."
11. The Lorain Journal Co. v. Milkovich, 106 S.Ct. 322 (1985).
12. Herbert v. Lando, 441 U.S. 153 (1979).
13. Time, Inc. v. Firestone, 424 U.S. 448, 476 (1976).
14. Rosenbloom v. Metromedia Inc., 403 U.S. 29 (1971).
15. Gertz v. Robert Welch, Inc., 418 U.S. 323 (1974).
16. Ocala Star-Banner Co. v. Damron, 401 U.S. 295 (1971).
17. Monitor Patriot Co. v. Roy, 401 U.S. 265 (1971). Cf. Time, Inc. v. Pape, 401 U.S. 279 (1971), in which a policeman sued for libel on the basis of an article discussing police brutality. Liability turned on whether omission of the word "alleged" from a summary of a report of the U.S. Civil Rights Commission was sufficient to find "actual malice." The plaintiff had already been found liable to a civilian who sued him for police brutality. The libel case was twice heard by the district court and twice by the court of appeals. The Supreme Court remanded the case to the district court which was required to hear the matter a third time.
18. St. Amant v. Thompson, 390 U.S. 727 (1968).
19. Dun & Bradstreet, Inc. v. Greenmoss Builders, Inc., 105 S. Ct. 2939 (1985).
20. Cox Broadcasting Corp. v. Cohn, 420 U.S. 469 (1975).
21. Street v. National Broadcasting Co., 465 F.2d 1227 (6th Cir., 1981), cert. den. 454 U.S. 1095 (1981).
22. Miranda v. Arizona, 384 U.S. 436 (1966).
23. Hutchinson v. Proxmire, 443 U.S. 111 (1979).
24. *Philadelphia Inquirer,* August 7, 1985, p. 8A. Senator Proxmire no longer gives the Golden Fleece awards. One must wonder whether he was discouraged by the libel suit. Again the public loses by being deprived of the information as to how tax dollars are spent and also deprived of some rueful chuckles.
25. Zauderer v. Office of Disciplinary Counsel of the Supreme Court of Ohio, 105 S. Ct. 2265 (1985).
26. Buckley v. Valeo, 424 U.S. 1 (1976).

27. *Philadelphia Inquirer,* October 26, 1985, p. 10A.
28. *New York Times,* December 30, 1984, p. E12.
29. Edwards v. National Audubon Society, Inc., 556 F.2d 113 (2nd Cir. 1977); cert. den. Edwards v. New York Times Co., 434 U.S. 1002 (1977).
30. Moscow World Service Commentary by Biltor Shragin, January 30, 1979.
31. *New York Times,* October 27, 1985, p. 52. See the move by the Rhode Island bar association to seek disciplinary action against Harvard Law Professor Alan Dershowitz, who represented Claus von Bulow in his successful appeal from conviction for attempting to murder his heiress wife, based on Dershowitz's book *Reversal of Fortune* (New York: Random House, 1986) that allegedly cast a cloud on the state courts and judges (*Philadelphia Inquirer,* May 11, 1986, p. 3A).
32. But see proposals by a Reagan administrator to make it a crime to release "classified information." *New York Times,* March 24, 1985, p. E5.
33. *New York Times,* January 14, 1986, p. A25.
34. *New York Times,* April 20, 1986, Section 2, p. 1.

CHAPTER VIII

1. Whether the use of actual crimes is a "failure of imagination" on the part of the author, as Norman Mailer charged Capote, is irrelevant to this discussion. Significantly, Mailer used the same technique in *The Executioner's Song.* Whether, as Capote charged, Mailer never saw Gilmore and was just a "rewrite man" is also immaterial. See Grobel, *Conversations with Capote* (New York: New American Library, 1985).
2. Gaylin, *The Killing of Bonnie Garland, A Question of Justice* (New York: Simon and Schuster, 1982).
3. *Philadelphia Inquirer,* December 3, 1982, p. 19A. Note that the ads for *Son,* a faction book about Fred Coe, the Spokane rapist, is touted as a classic, and *Kathy Boudin and the Dance of Death* by Ellen Frankfort is billed as "newsmaking." These books present the criminal as larger than life.
4. *New York Times,* July 26, 1984.
5. *Philadelphia Inquirer,* March 14, 1985, p. 9D.
6. *International Herald Tribune,* May 17, 1985, p. 18.
7. *Philadelphia Inquirer,* October 20, 1980, p. 9A.
8. Sirica, *To Set the Record Straight: The Break-in, the Tapes, the Conspirators, the Pardon* (New York: W. W. Norton, 1979).
9. *Wall Street Journal,* August 7, 1985, p. 2.
10. *New York Times,* September 14, 1984, p. E9.
11. *New York Times,* September 16, 1986, p. E9.
12. Lukas, *Murder for the Millions, New York Times Book Review,* June 16, 1985, p. 3.
13. *Philadelphia Inquirer,* October 7, 1984, p. 2H.
14. *Philadelphia Inquirer,* July 14, 1985, p. 3A.
15. Among the many criminals who have been the subjects of books, plays, and docudramas are Craig S. Crimmons, who murdered violinist Helen Hagnes Mintiks in the New York Metropolitan Opera House; Bernard H. Goetz, who shot several young men who hassled him in the New York subway; and Jack Henry Abbott whose book *In the Belly of the Beast* (New York: Random House, 1981) was widely touted by Norman Mailer. After Abbott's release from prison he committed a murder for which he was convicted.
16. *Philadelphia Inquirer,* April 16, 1983, p. D1.

17. Capote, *In Cold Blood* (New York: Random House, 1966), p. 11. An interesting sidelight on the crime that was the subject of *In Cold Blood* is the fact that the Kansas Bureau of Investigation agent who headed the investigation sold his memoirs. *New York Times,* November 18, 1984.

18. Bureau of Justice Statistics, U.S. Dept. of Justice, *Report to the Nation on Crime and Justice* 7 (1983).

19. Note, 94 *Yale Law Journal* 1787 (1985).

20. *Philadelphia Inquirer,* September 7, 1984, p. 4C.

21. For a discussion of the history of crime victims' compensation laws, see Forer, *Criminals and Victims: A Trial Judge Reflects on Crime and Punishment* (New York: W. W. Norton 1980).

22. 42 U.S.C. §§10601 et seq. (Victim Compensation and Assistance).

23. N.Y. Executive Law §622a providing in pertinent part that an offender is prohibited from receiving money for reenacting his crimes "by way of a movie, book, magazine article, radio or television presentation . . ." See Matter of Johnsen, 430 N.Y. S.2d 904, 906 (1979), in which the court characterizes royalties for the criminal as a "monetary windfall from the public's base delight in the ghoulish recounting . . . (of the crime)."

24. *National Law Journal,* August 19, 1985, p. 5.

25. *Philadelphia Inquirer,* June 4, 1986, p. 2E.

26. Pileggi, *Wiseguy: The Rise and Fall of a Mobster* (New York: Simon and Schuster, 1985).

27. See Eisman, "Shattered Vision: Was Dr. Jeffrey MacDonald Framed?" *The Shingle,* Spring 1985, p. 22.

28. Cf. Sheppard v. Maxwell, 384 U.S. 333 (1966), in which the conviction of Dr. Sheppard, who was accused of murdering his wife, was set aside because of excessive publicity. See also Estes v. Texas, 381 U.S. 532 (1965).

CHAPTER IX

1. See e.g., Lazar, "Toward a Right of Biography: Controlling Commercial Exploitation," 2 *Comment* 480 (1980).

2. Lasch, *The Culture of Narcissism* (New York: W. W. Norton, 1978).

3. See e.g. *The Vickers Papers,* Edited by the Open System Group (London: Harper & Row, 1984), pp. 102 et seq.

4. Levi, "Lorenzo's Return," *New York Times Book Review,* November 7, 1985, p. 3.

5. *Philadelphia Inquirer,* December 2, 1982, p. 29A.

6. *New York Times,* June 30, 1985, p. 10.

7. Grand Jury Matter, In re: Gronowicz No. 84-1721 (CA3 1985). See also *National Law Journal,* July 15, 1985, p. 16.

8. *Philadelphia Inquirer,* December 2, 1982, p. 29A.

9. *New York Times Magazine,* September 8, 1985, p. 45. See also the description of how Gerald Ford "produced" *A Time to Heal* in the Supreme Court opinion in Harper & Row v. Nation, discussed in Chapter II.

10. *Philadelphia Inquirer,* October 23, 1986, p. 7C.

11. Com. v. Barnes Foundation, 159 A.2d 500 (Pa. 1960).

12. *New York Times,* September 3, 1985, p. C17.

13. *Philadelphia Inquirer,* March 24, 1985, p. 3A.

14. Tunan, "Three on the Road," *New West,* November 20, 1978, p. 49.

15. DeSalvo v. Twentieth Century-Fox Film Corp., 300 F. Supp. 742 (D Mass. 1969). This case was decided before the enactment of the Son of Sam Law and similar statutes.

16. Bateson, *With a Daughter's Eye* (New York: William Morrow, 1984), p. 222 et seq.
17. *New York Times,* February 6, 1985, p. C22.
18. *Wall Street Journal,* September 26, 1985, p. 1.
19. Nixon v. Administrator of General Services, 433 U.S. 425 (1977).
20. Deedes, Diary, The *Spectator,* London, March 30, 1985, p. 7, cf. Pope v. Curl, 26 E.R. 1741, in which Alexander Pope obtained an injunction against the publication of his correspondence.
21. Sony Corp. of America v. Universal City Studios, 464 U.S. 417 (1984).
22. Meeropol v. Nizer, 560 F.2d 1061 (2nd Cir. 1977); cert. den. 434 U.S. 1013 (1978).
23. *Newsweek,* September 29, 1986, p. 66.
24. Hicks v. Casablanca Records, 464 F. Supp. 426 (S.D. N.Y. 1978).
25. Gurglielmi v. Spelling Goldberg Productions, 160 Cal. Rpt. 352 (1979).
26. See e.g. Oak Beach Inn Corp. v. Babylon Beacon Inc., 476 N.Y. S.2d 269, 464 N.E. 2d 967 (1984).
27. *Philadelphia Inquirer,* December 2, 1984, p. 1B.
28. Ibid., p. 14B.
29. See e.g. Murphy, *The Vicar of Christ* (New York: Macmillan, 1979).
30. Cummings, *The Pied Piper: Allard K. Lowenstein and the Liberal Dream* (New York: Grove Press, 1985).
31. Bellow, Robbins, and Tabak, *Documentation Concerning Serious Errors in Forthcoming Book by Richard Cummings purportedly about Allard Lowenstein,* privately distributed. Reviewed in *New York Times Book Review,* September 29, 1985.
32. Shevchenko, *Breaking with Moscow* (New York: Knopf, 1985).
33. Epstein, "The Spy Who Came In to be Sold," *New Republic,* July 15, 1985, p. 35.
34. *New York Times,* November 29, 1984, p. A31.
35. Freeman, *Margaret Mead and Samoa: The Making and Unmaking of an Anthropological Myth* (Cambridge, Mass.: Harvard University Press, 1983).
36. *Philadelphia Inquirer,* June 30, 1985, p. 36.

CHAPTER X

1. This subject has engaged the attention of legal academics. See Note "Clear and Convincing Libel: Fiction and the Law of Defamation," 92 *Yale Law Journal,* 520 (1983). The winter 1985 issue of *Brooklyn Law Review,* Vol. 5, No. 2, is devoted to a symposium on "Defamation in Fiction" exhaustively reviewing the recent cases. The 200-page learned discussion presents a variety of opinions. Professor Frederick M. Schauer would grant fiction less protection than political comment. Professor Marc A. Franklin considers it a problem of less importance. Professor Paul A. LeBel's suggestions would compound the difficulties faced by authors and courts by establishing five new criteria: "(1) the nature and purpose of the work, (2) the risk-bearing capacity of the defendant, (3) the work's artistic merit, (4) the degree to which the plaintiff is a target of the work, and (5) the extent to which statements made about a fictional character would subject the publisher to liability for defamation if they were made explicitly about the plaintiff in a nonfictional context." 51 *Brooklyn Law Review,* p. 319. Attorneys Martin Garbus and Richard Kunit urge protection of fiction "not only from liability but from the equally destructive engine of litigation." 51 *Brooklyn Law Review,* p. 423. This chapter urges that fiction be given very broad protections, not because of the literary merits and social value of fiction, but because it is a significant aspect of free expression.

2. *Salmagundi,* Fall 1984, p. 97.

3. This is a claim made by many academic commentators on defamation in fiction. See Stam, "Defamation in Fiction," 29 *American University Law Review* 571 (1980). Whether a novel is pure "sleaze" or purports to present higher truths should, I believe, be irrelevant to the legal question of defamation. Courts are no better equipped than literary critics to decide literary merit, higher truths, or other qualities of fiction. Unless some superior right is violated, the First Amendment should protect the author.

4. Bindrim v. Mitchell, 155 Cal. 29 (1979); cert. den., 444 U.S. 984 (1979), rehearing den. Doubleday & Company, Inc. v. Bindrim, 444 U.S. 1040 (1980).

5. But see Middlebrooks v. Curtis Pub. Co., 413 F.2d 141 (4th Cir. 1969), in which the court sensibly placed considerable weight on the fact that the allegedly defamatory piece was published in the fiction section of the magazine.

6. Note that Professor Franklin stresses the importance of predictability in the law of defamation in fiction. 51 *Brooklyn Law Review* 269 (1985).

7. *New York Times,* January 14, 1987, pp. 1, c14; *New York Times,* January 15, 1987, p. c22.

8. Davis, with Margaret Stranger Foster, *Home Front* (New York: Crown, 1986).

9. *Philadelphia Inquirer Book Review,* March 16, 1986, p. 5.

10. *Wall Street Journal,* December 3, 1984, p. 12.

11. Spahn v. Julian Messner, Inc., 253 N.E. 2d 840 (N.Y., 1967); app. dismissed, 393 U.S. 1046 (1969).

12. Koussevitzy v. Allen Town & Heath, Inc., 188 Misc. (NY) 479 aff., 272 App. Div. 759 (1947).

13. Leopold v. Levin, 45 Ill. 2d 434, 259 N.E. 2d 250 (1970).

14. Wheeler v. Dell Publishing Co., 300 F.2d 372 (7th Cir., 1962).

15. Springer v. Tine, *Washington Post,* November 28, 1983, p. C1.

16. *New York Times,* August 25, 1985, p. 59. See also Lyons v. New American Library, Inc., 432 N.Y. S.2d 536 (1980), based on the Son of Sam case in which the unidentified sheriff sued for defamation. The claim was dismissed on the sensible grounds that the author clearly stated that it was a work of fiction. But see Corrigan v. Bobbs Merrill Co., 228 N.Y. 58, 126 N.E. 260 (1920). This case was decided under the law of libel prior to New York Times v. Sullivan when libel was deemed to be outside the ambit of the First Amendment.

17. Binns v. Vitagraph, 210 NY 51, 103 N.E. 1108 (N.Y. 1913). When a real person's name is given to a fictional character that in no way resembles the individual, recovery has been denied. Wheeler v. Dell Publishing Co., 300 F.2d 372 (7th Cir. 1962).

18. *American University Law Review* 571 (1980). See also Stam, "Defamation in Fiction" 92 *Yale Law Journal* 529, 534 (1983). Smirlock, "Clear and Convincing Libel": Fiction and the Law of Defamation, 92 *Yale Law Journal* 520 (1983).

19. Vargas Llosa, "Is Fiction the Art of Lying?" *New York Times Book Review,* October 7, 1984, p. 114.

20. See *Newsweek,* the "New Journalism," March 31, 1975.

21. *Time,* February 11, 1985, p. 99.

22. *Harvard Law Record,* February 15, 1985, p. 11.

23. *New York Times,* February 10, 1985, p. 20E.

24. Falwell v. Penthouse International Ltd., 521 F. Supp. 1204 (WD Va 1981). Court of Appeals decision August 5, 1986 (not reported as of this writing).

25. University of Notre Dame DuLac v. Twentieth Century Fox Film Corp., 15 N.Y. 2d 940, 207 N.E. 2d 508 (1965).

26. *New York Times,* October 6, 1985, p. 65.

27. *National Law Journal,* August 12, 1985, p. 1.

28. *Wall Street Journal,* August 2, 1985, p. 1.
29. Girl Scouts of the U.S.A. v. Personality Posters Mfg. Co., 304 F. Supp. 1228 (SDNY, 1969).
30. Lodge, *Small World* (London: Secker & Warburg, 1984), p. 24.

CHAPTER XI

1. *New York Times,* September 24, 1985, p. A26.
2. Federal Election Commission v. National Conservative PAC, 470 U.S. 480 (1985).
3. Very few commentators take this position. A notable exception is the article by Robert Filson and Madelyn Leopold, "Restoring the 'Central Meaning of the First Amendment': Absolute Immunity for Political Libel," 90 *Dickinson Law Review* 559 (1986). See also Chapter XIV discussing the proposals of other critics.
4. See Harper & Row v. Nation, 471 US 539 (1985).
5. Virginia State Board of Pharmacy v. Virginia Citizens Consumer Council, 425 U.S. 748 (1976); Bolger v. Youngs Drug Products, 463 U.S. 60 (1983); Bates v. State Bar of Arizona, 433 U.S. 350 (1977).
6. Valentine v. Chrestensen, 316 U.S. 52 (1942). For a discussion of the law of commercial speech unrelated to libel see Rome and Roberts, *Corporate and Commercial Free Speech: First Amendment Protection of Expression in Business* (Westport, CT: Quorum Books, 1985).
7. Falwell v. Penthouse International, Ltd., 521 F. Supp. 1204, 1210 (WD Va. 1981).
8. Prosser and Keeton, *On Torts,* 5th ed., Ch. 4 §128.
9. Bose v. Consumers Union, 466 U.S. 485 (1984). But see F.T.C. v. Brown and Williamson Tobacco Corporation, 778 F.2d 35 (D.C. Cir. 1985), limiting restrictions on allegedly deceptive advertising.
10. Mr.Chow of New York v. Ste. Jour Azur, S.A. 750 F.2d 219 (2nd Cir. 1985).
11. Buck v. Bell, 274 U.S. 200 (1927).
12. McKillop v. Regents, 386 F. Supp. 1270 (ND Cal. 1975). See also Banas v. Matthews International Corp., 348 Pa. Super. 464 (1985), in which an award for wrongful termination of an at will employee was reversed but an award for defamation was reinstated. See discussion, *Pennsylvania Law Journal Reporter,* January 6, 1986, p. 1. Cf. Connick v. Myers, 461 U.S. 138 (1983), in which the Supreme Court held that discharge of an employee who complained about an assignment did not involve First Amendment rights.
13. Cal. Labor Code §1198.5.
14. Board of Trustees of Leland Stanford, Junior., University v. Superior Ct., 119 Cal. App. 3d 516, 174 Cal. Rptr. 160 (1981).
15. See Westin, *Whistle-Blowing: Loyalty and Dissent in the Corporation* (New York: McGraw-Hill, 1981). Westin, "Faculty Research and the Whistle Blowers, *New York Times Perspectives,* January 10, 1982, p. 61.
16. Rouse v. Judges of the Circuit Court of Cook County, U.S. D.C. N.D. Ill. (1985), *National Law Journal,* June 3, 1985, p. 9.
17. Quilici v. Second Amendment Foundation, 769 F.2d 414 (7th Cir. 1985).
18. Gordon v. Lancaster Osteopathic Hosp. Assn., 489 A.2d 1364 (Pa. Super., 1985).
19. Elbesheshy v. Franklin Institute, E.D. Pa. No. 85-0496. Note that the Supreme Court refused to review a decision dismissing a libel suit by a professor against columnists Evans and Novak who charged that he had "no status in the profession." Ollman v. Evans, 750 F.2d 970 (D.C. Cir. 1985); cert. den. 105 S. Ct. 2662 (1985).

20. See e.g. Lewis v. Equitable Life Assurance, Minn. See *New York Times,* June 9, 1985, p. 8F.
21. *New York Times,* October 5, 1985, p. A6.
22. *Lawyer's Digest,* October 1985, p. 12.
23. McDermott v. Biddle, 9 Pa. L.J. 320 (1985).
24. See Forer, "Recusation of Judges," 73 *Harvard Law Review,* 1325 (1960).
25. Bruck, "How Dan Burt Deserted Westmoreland," *American Lawyer,* April 1985, p. 117.
26. Sawabini v. Sensenberg, *National Law Journal,* June 24, 1985, p. 8.
27. *New York Times,* September 22, 1985, p. 59.
28. 5 U.S.C.S §2302.
29. Re R.M.J. 455 U.S. 191 (1982).
30. Valentine v. Chrestensen, 316 U.S. 52 (1942).
31. Virginia State Board of Pharmacy v. Virginia Citizens Consumer Counsel, 425 U.S. 748 (1976).
32. Bigelow v. Virginia, 421 U.S. 809 (1975).
33. Zauderer v. Office of Disciplinary Counsel of Ohio, 105 S.Ct. 2265 (1985).
34. Central Hudson Gas & Electric v. Public Service Commission, 447 U.S. 557 (1980). The decision of the Supreme Court in Posados de Puerto Rico v. Tourism Co., July 1, 1986, upholding a ban in Puerto Rican newspapers but not in mainland media on advertising of casino gambling, a licit activity in Puerto Rico, implicitly involves First Amendment rights of many commercial enterprises, particularly the tobacco and liquor industries. Again a federal statutory ban on restriction of commercial advertising might obviate these problems with respect to publications sold in interstate commerce.
35. See Lowe v. Securities and Exchange Commission, 472 U.S. 181 (1985).
36. Greer v. Spock, 424 U.S. 828 (1976).
37. Dun & Bradstreet, Inc. v. Greenmoss Builders, Inc. 105 S.Ct. 2939 (1985).
38. Poller v. CBS, 368 U.S. 464, 475 (1962).

CHAPTER XII

1. Held at the University of Pennsylvania Annenberg School of Communications, Philadelphia, Pa., October 25, 1985.
2. See Jucovy, "Illiteracy Today," *Philadelphia Inquirer,* January 23, 1983, reporting that one of every five adults lack the most basic reading skills. For blacks the rate is 44 percent. In addition 32 percent of the population read poorly. In Philadelphia more than 40 percent of the adults cannot read English. The U.S. Department of Education reported in April 1986, that 17 to 21 million adults are unable to handle written English texts (*Washington Post,* May 11, 1986, Book World, p. 15). The University of Texas study, *The Adult Performance Level Project,* 1975, found that 13 percent of American adults are illiterate in English, almost 20 percent of American adults were unable to perform everyday adult tasks and another 34 percent did poorly. The test evaluated such skills as the ability to read a help-wanted ad in a newspaper or write a grocery list (*New York Times,* April 21, 1986, p. 1). For a discussion of the various adult literacy tests and their conclusions—ranging from 17 million to 74 million functionally illiterate adults—see Insight, *Washington Times,* September 29, 1986, p. 13.
3. *National Law Journal,* January 27, 1986, p. 26.
4. 6 & 7 Vict. C. 96 §§1, 2. A subsequent statute, 8 & 9 Vict. C. 75 (1843), requiring repayment as well as retraction, proved to be unworkable. For a discussion of retraction and right of reply, see Chafee, "Possible New Remedies for Errors

in the Press," 60 *Kansas Law Review* 1 (1946). The author never contemplated that a retraction statute would run afoul of the First Amendment. Note that South Dakota by statute provides that punitive damages are avoided by a retraction. S.D. Laws §20-11-7. See also Cal. Civil Code §48a providing for retraction. The law of Israel recognizes good faith as a defense to libel unless the defendant refused to publish a correction "in a manner as similar as possible to the publication of the defamatory matter and within a reasonable time from the receipt of the demand (from the plaintiff). . ." Defamation Prohibition Law (No. 62) 5752-1965.

5. Gertz on Gertz, *Trial,* October 1985, p. 66.
6. Miami Herald v. Tornillo, 418 U.S. 241 (1974).
7. *New York Times,* January 27, 1985, p. E9.
8. See Middlebrooks v. Curtis Pub. Co., 413 F.2d 141 (4th Cir. 1969), in which the court held for the defendant in an action for libel and invasion of privacy based on a story published in the *Saturday Evening Post.* The court concluded that because the story was listed in the table of contents under the heading "fiction," the reader would not be misled into believing that the story was about the plaintiff. This is a much simpler test than the "of and concerning" standard employed since New York Times v. Sullivan.
9. See Justice Frankfurter's remark in his concurring opinion in Smith v. California, 361 U.S. 147, 162 (1959), drawing a distinction between the "power of a state to regulate what feeds the belly and what feeds the brain." However, he upheld the obscenity conviction. Regulation or prohibition of communications is vastly different from a requirement of truth in labeling.
10. Street v. NBC, 645 F.2d 1227 (6th Cir. 1981); cert. den. 454 U.S. 1095 (1981).
11. See Carter, "See You in Court," *Publisher's Weekly,* September 7, 1984, p. 39.
12. Harold Laski, *A Biographical Memoir* (New York: Viking Press, N.Y., 1953).

CHAPTER XIII

1. Erie Railroad Co. v. Tompkins, 304 U.S. 64 (1938).
2. Keeton v. Hustler, 465 U.S. 770 (1984).
3. *New York Times,* October 30, 1985, p. A13.
4. In Atlantic Coast Line R. Co. v. Georgia, 234 U.S. 280 (1914), the Supreme Court held that state regulatory laws were subordinate to federal law and could not apply to interstate railroads.
5. Erie Railroad Co. v. Tompkins, 304 U.S. 64 (1938).
6. Swift v. Tyson, 16 Pet. 1 (1842).
7. For a compilation of these statutes see Sanford, *Privacy and Libel* (Washington, D.C.: Law and Business, Inc., Harcourt Brace Jovanovich, 1985).
8. See International Shoe Co. v. Washington, 326 U.S. 310 (1945); Rush v. Savchuk, 444 U.S. 320 (1980).
9. World-Wide Volkswagon Corp. v. Woodson, 444 U.S. 286 (1980).
10. Ettore v. Philco Television Broadcasting Corp., 229 F.2d 481 (3rd Cir. 1956). These same questions of choice of law still plague the courts. See Baltimore Orioles, Inc. v. Major League Baseball Players, Association, decided by the Court of Appeals for the 7th Circuit October 29, 1986. At issue was whether the major league ball clubs own the exclusive rights to televised performances. The players claimed property rights in their own performances. The case was remanded to determine which state laws should govern.
11. Jones v. Calder, 138 Cal. App. 3d 128, 187 Cal. Rptr. 825 (1983); cert. den. 462 U.S. 1144 (1983).
12. Dun & Bradstreet, Inc. v. Greenmoss Builders, Inc., 105 S. Ct. 2939 (1985).

13. *New York Times,* October 26, 1985, p. 9.

14. See Malone v. White Motor Corp., 435 U.S. 497 (1978).

15. Cullom of the Select Committee on Interstate Commerce, Report, cited in Haar and Fessler, *The Wrong Side of the Tracks* (New York: Simon and Schuster, 1986), p. 40.

16. Beale and Wyman, *The Law of Railroad Rate Regulation* (Boston: William V. Nagle, 1906), pp. 753–54.

17. Lindsey v. Normet, 405 U.S. 56, 74 (1972).

18. Textile Workers v. Lincoln Mills, 353 U.S. 448 (1957); see also Allis-Chalmers Corp. v. Lueck, 471 U.S. 202 (1985).

19. In upholding the constitutionality of the Federal Speedy Trial Act, a federal court wisely observed, "In no way does the [Sixth Amendment] prevent Congress from according the accused more protection than the Constitution requires, nor does it preclude Congress from acting on the public's interest in speedy justice." U.S. v. Brainer 691 F.2d 469 (4th Cir. 1982). In like manner, the Congress can accord both subjects and authors more protection than the First Amendment requires and act in the public interest in resolving these conflicts.

20. *Philadelphia Inquirer,* August 25, 1985, p. 27.

CHAPTER XIV

1. The Institute for Civil Justice, *An Overview of the First Five-Year Program 1980–1985* (Santa Monica, CA: Rand Corporation, 1986).

2. McNabb v. U.S., 318 U.S. 332, 347 (1943).

3. Abrams, "The Supreme Court Turns a New Page in Libel," 70 *American Bar Association Journal* 80 (1984).

4. Gertz on Gertz, *Trial,* October 1985, p. 66.

5. *New York Times,* December 15, 1985, p. F7. See also the complaint of Lord Denning, a noted British jurist, who in describing a fifteen-day libel trial wrote, "Lawyers should be ashamed that they have allowed the law of defamation to become bogged down in such a mass of technicalities that this should be possible." Denning, *What Next in the Law* (London: Butterworth, 1982).

6. 54 L.W. 2057, July 23, 1985. See also letter from Peter H. Kaskell, Center for Public Resources, *American Lawyer,* October 1985, p. 8, advocating "private processes" rather than litigation.

7. See 66 *Judicature* 6 (1982).

8. *Philadelphia Retainer,* October 9, 1982, p. 12.

9. *New York Times,* September 21, 1985.

10. Franklin, "Good Names & Bad Law: A Critique of Libel Law and a Proposal," 18 *San Francisco Law Review* 1 (1983).

11. HR 2846 99th Congress, 1st Session, introduced by Charles E. Schumer of New York, June 24, 1985.

12. Lauter, "Libel Law," *National Law Journal,* January 6, 1986, p. S11.

13. *Time* magazine, February 4, 1985, p. 64.

14. Lauter, "Libel Law."

15. Abrams, "Is It Time to Change the Libel Doctrine for Public Figures?," 71 *American Bar Association Journal* 38 (1985).

16. Shields, "Rewriting the Law of Libel," *American Lawyer,* Special Supplement, July–August 1985, p. 14.

17. Abrams, "Why Should We Change the Libel Law," *New York Times Magazine,* September 29, 1985, p. 34.

18. *Philadelphia Inquirer,* November 10, 1985, p. 2C.

19. *Legal Intelligencer,* March 25, 1985, p. 3.

20. *National Law Journal,* March 31, 1986, p. 6. See the suggestion for a uniform state law on punitive damages. "A Uniform Statute for Punitive Damages in Insurance Cases?" For the Defense, March 1985, p. 3. "Tort Reform" bills have been introduced in forty-two state legislatures, many putting a cap on awards for pain and suffering. These bills are designed to limit recoveries in accident and malpractice cases. California's Proposition 51, which was approved by the voters, severely limits corporate liability for pain and suffering. Whether these laws will reduce insurance rates is problematic. See Lundy, " 'Tort reform' Gains Hold Nationwide," *Legal Intelligencer,* June 19, 1986, p. 1. Although these laws do not address damages in libel cases, they are indicative of a national trend in favor of limiting liability.

21. *Philadelphia Inquirer,* January 12, 1987, p. 7A.

22. Shields, "Rewriting the Law of Libel."

23. *New York Times,* July 20, 1985, p. 3.

24. Statement of Harold Evans, British journalist, in *American Lawyer,* special supplement, July-August 1985, p. 22.

25. *Ibid.*

26. The diminution of the size of the jury from twelve to six and the abrogation of a unanimous verdict in civil cases may presage further erosion of jury trials.

27. In re U.S. Financial Securities Litigation, 609 F. 2d 411 (C.A. 9th 1979). Although state courts do not hear antitrust cases, they do hear many long, complicated personal injury and commercial cases as well as difficult criminal cases. I find that juries can decide these cases fairly.

28. *National Law Journal,* July 8, 1985, p. 39.

29. Abrams, "The Supreme Court Turns a New Page in Libel Law," 70 *American Bar Association Journal* 80 (1984).

30. Bezanson, Cranberg, and Soloski, "Libel and the Press," Silha Center, *The Study of Media Ethics and the Law* (Minneapolis, MN: University of Minnesota Press, 1985), p. A10.

31. Institute for Civil Justice, *An Overview,* p. 27.

32. Schauer, *The Role of the People in First Amendment theory,* speech delivered at University of Pennsylvania Symposium, John Peter Zenger, October 25, 1985, p. 31.

33. *Philadelphia Inquirer,* August 25, 1985, p. 2F, 20B.

34. *Ibid.*

35. Attorney Steven H. Keene of Louisville, Kentucky, does advocate a federal law of libel. *American Lawyer,* October 1985, p. 7.

CHAPTER XV

1. Pennekamp v. Florida, 328 U.S. 331, 371 (1946).

2. See the recent decision of the Court of Appeals for the third circuit in Capital Cities Media, Inc. v. Chester holding that a newspaper had no First Amendment right to compel the Pennsylvania Department of Environmental Resources to release memoranda concerning an outbreak of intestinal illness caused by contaminated drinking water, 797 F.2d 1164 (1986).

3. See Bowers v. Hardwick, 106 S.Ct. 2841 (1986).

4. Smith v. Daily Mail Pub. Co., 443 U.S. 97 (1979).

5. ABC News Close Up, December 29, 1984, Show #124, transcript p. 10.

6. *Playboy,* August 1985, p. 57.

7. In California Federal Savings and Loan Association v. Guerra, 55 L.W. 4077 (1987), the Supreme Court upheld a California statute requiring employers to provide leave and reinstatement to pregnant employees. Justice Marshall writing for the Court explained, "It is well established that the PDA [Pregnancy Discrimination Act of 1978, 42 U.S.C. §2000e(k)] was passed in reaction to this Court's decision in General Electric Co. v. Gilbert, 429 U.S. 125 (1976)." That case held that discrimination on the basis of pregnancy was not sex discrimination. In the subsequent case, the Court clearly gave effect to the intent of Congress.

8. Wilkerson v. McCarthy, 336 U.S. 53, 68 (1949).

9. Marcone v. Penthouse International, 754 F.2d 1072 (3rd Cir. 1985); cert. den., 106 S.Ct. 182 (1985); rehearing den, 106 S.Ct. 548 (1985).

10. Franklin, "Why Plaintiffs Sue?," in Winfield, *Libel Litigation, Nineteen Eighty-One* (New York: Practising Law Institute, 1981), p. 500.

Table of Cases and Statutes

Cases

Statutes

Index

RENNER LEARNING RESOURCE CENTER
ELGIN COMMUNITY COLLEGE
ELGIN, ILLINOIS 60123